THE FIRE OX
AND OTHER YEARS

Nomad Boy from the Pamirs

Drawn by Alexandre Iacovleff

THE
FIRE OX
AND OTHER YEARS

By

SUYDAM CUTTING

New York

CHARLES SCRIBNER'S SONS

1940

Preface

~~~~~~

FROM the dawn of history men have left their homes to travel in distant lands. Diverse motives have inspired the desire to wander. Men have travelled in the interests of commerce, conquest, religion, science. Others with more sharply personalized motives have sought adventure, knowledge, even forgetfulness. But whatever their motives, most travellers have one thing in common: a virus in the blood that inflames the imagination and sets the feet straying from the comfort and security of home.

At the bottom of his soul the real traveller is a sceptic. He insists on verifying other men's evidence with his own eyes and ears. The Taj Mahal, the temple of Angkor Vat or the Pyramids become living entities only after they have received the affirmation of his senses. The strange folkways of primitive peoples are ponderable elements in the construction of the world only after he has seen them function. The geological marvels of the planet are dead facts when read in books. Tracked down by the traveller's restless feet, they become dynamic realities.

In days gone by, travel carried an auxiliary reward in the effort it took to get to one's destination. The traveller arriving at the end of a journey felt a glow of triumph at circumventing the odds against

PREFACE

him. But with the progress of modern science and technology, this reward has vanished. Trains, planes, and ships, as comfortable as one's own house, take one to remote places, where tradition has already indicated the proper response.

This writer has nothing to say against ordinary, routine travel. He has done plenty of it and he never sought out a stable where a Ritz hotel was at hand. Nevertheless, he has felt that standardized travel lacks a vital ingredient. It fails to awaken all the faculties.

There is such a thing as creative travel. This means going to distant and still inaccessible spots on the earth's surface where the approach is as important as the destination and where the destination requires all one's powers of observation for the simple reason that other men of one's own race have not had the opportunity to set up a tradition. To give one example: The Potala of Lhasa to the eyes of a man from the Western World is a completely fresh experience, and there are no ready-made standards for appraising its beauty. On the other hand, the same man might strive desperately to arrive at a fresh appraisal of Chartres only to realize in the end that it is impossible to disregard utterly what others have written about it.

This is a book about the less accessible places of the earth. Two of them—Tibet and Nepal—resolutely decline the pleasure of receiving white men. Getting into Lhasa, capital of Tibet, requires a bit of persistence and diplomacy. In such places as Chinese Turkestan and Chinese Tibet, nature conspires against the traveller. In Assam the obstacle is hostile natives. There are no transportation problems in connection with the Andaman Islands and the Galápagos Islands. But the reader who finishes the chapters dealing with these places will agree that they are not suitable objectives for conducted tours.

Fifteen years' travels are included in this book. The first major trip took place in 1925—the Roosevelt expedition to Chinese Turkestan.

PREFACE

In 1926 there was Ethiopia. In 1927 Assam. In 1928 Chinese Tibet. In 1930 the Galápagos. In 1934 Celebes. In 1937 Nepal. In 1939 Upper Burma. But most important of all, there were three trips to Tibet—in 1930, 1935, and 1937, or, to use the Tibetan chronology, the Iron Horse Year, the Wood Pig Year, and the Fire Ox Year.

Train journeys form a very insignificant part of this book. On the other hand there is a great deal about caravans, about pack animals, about *arabas, mappas, coracles*, coolies. The writer has covered 7200 miles by caravan alone.

He has written, but he hopes not too much, about hardship. The journeys that would be a hardship in the lands of mechanized transport are more than bearable, they are actually a pleasure, when they are the sole means of attaining an objective. A caravan trip from New York to Boston would be a painful and profitless affair. But a caravan trip through a comparable distance in Tibet is a rewarding experience.

Civilization and primitive life do not mix. In civilization the wise traveller demands everything it has to give. In primitive places he is satisfied with nature. He is mentally prepared for new conditions. He dresses appropriately. The real hardships of travel come in those regions where civilization and primitive life have mixed. The inns of western China, described in this book, are examples.

Travel in uncharted lands brings another compensation. It liberates the mind from the weight of routines, organized attitudes, conditioned responses. When every situation calls for fresh judgment, unrelated to anything in one's past experience, the mind arrives at a higher pitch of consciousness. On the plateaux, for instance, one ceases to be a creature protected or smothered by civilization. The phrase "Nature against man" is no longer a cliché. It takes on a new and abundant meaning. Then, up on the high plateaux of Tibet under the tall, luminous sky, away from human habitation, one seems millions of miles from pygmy human worries and frustrations. Man's relation to the firmament becomes a little clearer.

There is no cut-to-order adventure in this book. The writer has tried to bear this in mind: however difficult were the obstacles in arriving at a destination, it is the destination that counts with the reader. Across the pages file Tibetan lamas, Assamese head hunters, Andamanese pygmies, Mongolian porters. Jungles are followed by wide arid plains. The plains become rugged, unconquered mountains. If the reader sees these things as they are, not particularly in relation to one traveller who sought out their acquaintance, but as they stand in relation to their natural environment, he will, perhaps, gain a more vivid idea of the unity of human and inanimate life.

S. C.

Contents

~~~~~~

Illustrations

~~~~~~

The illuminated maps were drawn for the author in Hungary by a cartographer whose spelling of place-names followed the atlases in use in Central Europe. Though these spellings differ in some cases from those preferred by the author in his text, the reader will have no difficulty in identifying the places in question.

With a few exceptions, the photographs in this book were taken by the author.

IN COLOR

BLACK AND WHITE

ILLUSTRATIONS

[xiv]

ILLUSTRATIONS

[xv]

ILLUSTRATIONS

ILLUSTRATIONS

ILLUSTRATIONS

THE FIRE OX
AND OTHER YEARS

Green Paradise in Turkestan

THAT truant little phrase, "by the way," opens many a memorable conversation.

When Kermit Roosevelt sat down beside me while the train was pounding down from Boston to New York one February day in 1925 and started off, "By the way," I didn't brace myself for any stupendous revelation. His tone promised nothing more than a casual, pleasant talk—the kind we had been having ever since we became friends a good many years before.

But the little talk that day led eventually through the wilds of Chinese and Russian Turkestan, through towns and villages that had been ignored by white men despite the energetic blasts of publicity they had received from the great Marco Polo.

This journey led to another, and another, and all are leading into this book. The next fifteen years took me not only among the strange tribes of Turkestan but among Assamese headhunters, Tibetan lamas, Andamanese pygmies. Caravan journeys led into every kind of terrain, from sodden jungles to lofty mountain passes. There were hunts for rare animals: the water buffalo of Celebes, the golden monkey of Chinese Tibet, the ibex of the Tien Shan and Simien mountains. The Emperor of Ethiopia, the Maharajah of Nepal, and the Regent of Tibet came into view, to say nothing of many another minor prince and potentate.

Kermit got down to details. He proposed that I join him, his brother

Theodore, and George Cherrie, a naturalist, in an ambitious project for travelling in Turkestan, or Sinkiang as the Chinese call it. Its prime object was to collect specimens of animal life, and the Roosevelts had set their hearts on getting a specimen of the ovis poli, not represented at that time in any American museum. Some people believed, as a matter of fact, that it was extinct. The Field Museum of Chicago, due to arrangements made by the late James Simpson, was sponsoring the whole expedition.

I gave my answer and that night I got out an atlas. What wide, blank spaces! Turkestan seemed to have but few villages and towns. Much of it was either uninhabited or explorers had not yet caught up with the inhabitants. Only a few familiar names—Samarkand, Kashgar, Yarkand, Aksu—stood out on the wide stretch of map reaching from the Caspian Sea to the Gobi Desert. To the south lay Tibet and India.

I read more about the country. The word Turkestan comes, of course, from those peoples who once passed through the region on their western migrations and are now known as the Ottoman Turks. In the opinion of some authorities, the land was once inhabited by an Aryan population. At any rate, it was a battleground for warring races, the Chinese playing a preponderant part.

Although the Chinese finally imposed their undisputed authority on Eastern Turkestan, incorporating most of it in the province of Sinkiang, Chinese stocks form only a small percentage of the population. The bulk of the people are Turkis, liberally mixed up with three Mongol tribes, the Kirghiz, Kazaks, and Kalmuks.

The more I read, the more understandable became the gaps in Western man's knowledge of Turkestan. The more incredible, too, became the feat of Marco Polo, who passed through the Pamirs, Kashgar, and Yarkand in the latter part of the thirteenth century. Marco's book recounting his adventures and hardships inspired awe and admiration, but none of his readers cared to emulate him. Six centuries had rolled around before explorers retraced the historic route of "Marco Millioni."

The prospect of seeing this remote land was becoming more excit-

ing every day. It was clear now that we would meet not only a mixture of tribes but a wide variety of climates. There would be extremes
of cold and heat. Our trail would go through snow-swept mountains,
through jungles and deserts. To get from one region to another it
would be necessary to go over many passes, some at terrific altitudes.

Plans were going steadily ahead. Passports and visas were obtained,
and equipment purchased. All the luggage, including beds, saddles,
guns, cameras, compasses, thermometers, and binoculars, was handed
over to Cherrie, who sailed for Karachi in India.

On April 11, Kermit, Ted, and I sailed from New York. We spent
several days in London accumulating information that would be vastly
useful to us later. Russian visas were obtained in England, since the
United States at that time did not maintain diplomatic relations with
the U. S. S. R. These visas were purely a precautionary measure: the
complete details had not been worked out and none of us knew that
the projected expedition would become practically two expeditions;
that Cherrie and I would see not only Chinese but Russian Turkestan.

When we arrived in Bombay on May 11 the hot season was in full
swing, so there was no lingering to savor the delights of rooms that
felt like Turkish baths, and streets that seemed to be built on burning
volcanoes. That very night we took the train to Rawalpindi in the
Punjab of northern India. Rawalpindi was forty-eight hours from
Bombay, and is the northern railhead of the Bombay, Baroda, and
Central India Railway.

The first members of our personnel were two Punjabis, Ahmad
Shah and Feroze, service men, lent to us by the Indian army. Next
came two Kashmiris, the brothers Rahima and Khalil Loon, who were
employed as shikkaris (hunters). The fact that two were Punjabis
and two Kashmiris was to be a source of trouble later on.

To reach Srinagar, the capital of Kashmir, we had to take motor-
cars for a two-hundred-mile journey over narrow roads that twisted
up and down through towering mountains. No danger signs were
needed to warn the drivers, for one little slip anywhere would have
sent us spinning down into an abyss. The approach to the capital

brought out a lovely landscape. On the far horizon, black mountains lifted their snowy heads. The sky was deep blue, and under it the valley shimmered in the sun with a color scheme that rivalled a Kashmiri shawl. There were patches of green grass and green trees, patches of red, yellow, and blue, formed by flowers and fruit blossoms. Here and there were flashing streams running through the valley.

Cherrie was waiting in Srinagar with all the equipment intact. The personnel was enlarged by the addition of Jamal Shekh, the cook, who turned out to be an excellent choice, his assistant Roussala, and several other servants. All these were Kashmiris.

Finding ponies was a little more difficult. Sixty-six were needed for the caravan, and by the time the last one was checked off, Srinagar had been pretty well stripped of its floating supply of horses.

In Srinagar we settled on our route, or rather, it was settled for us. Two routes lay before us. The trail leading due north went through the Hunza Pass and by the Pamirs, traditional abode of the ovis poli, the great Asiatic wild sheep. The other turned east from Srinagar and then led northward in a great, undulating line. This was the Karakorum route, highest used caravan route in the world.

The Hunza route would have suited us perfectly, but the government of Kashmir had set strict limitations on its use. The pass was not for commercial uses, one stretch of it being so steep that goods had to be carried on the backs of porters instead of animals. Over other stretches the ponies had to be changed frequently. Travellers using porters and ponies were required to pay not only wages but often compensation for the crops abandoned when the caravan men were on trail. We would have been willing to pay a proper sum, but the government refused a permit on the ground that a Dutch mountain-climbing expedition had already used the pass, and a British official party from Kashgar was expected in the near future.

Our itinerary, therefore, was fixed as follows:

Leh—11,500 feet. An ancient mountain capital.

Khardong Pass—17,100 feet. An almost vertical, rocky climb to a knife-edged, snowy ridge.

A

shatta

RT PASS

AKSU

A KLA MAKLAN DESERT

orum

adak

NEPAL

TIBET

BUTHAM

Ganges

Brahmaputra

ASSAM

Calcutta

CHINA

Tatsientu

Yang-Tsze-Kiang

Ning-juan

Yung-Ning

Likiang

Talifu

Yunnan

Kohima

Nyitkyina

Bhamo

UPPER

BURMA

Mandalay

Hanoi

Irawadi

Rangoon

SIAM

Mekong

Bangkok

Saigon

Andaman
Islands

Pannamik—11,000 feet. In a valley; the last village before reaching the northern plains.

The Sasser Pass—17,500 feet. A dangerous glacier to cross.

The Karakorum Pass—18,600 feet. A sharp ridge, our highest pass.

The Suget Pass—18,000 feet. Slope more gentle, going better.

The Sanju Pass—16,600 feet. Very steep; the last pass, then down towards the plains.

Kargelik—about 5000 feet. A hot, dirty, Turki city of Central Asia.

Yarkand—the largest city of Turkestan; population about 60,000; unhealthy country; drinking water bad.

Marlbashi—about 3500 feet. Swampy country; pests of flies and mosquitos; malaria.

Aksu—northern city of Turkestan; cleaner and healthier.

The Muzart Pass—11,000 feet. A most dangerous glacier to cross.

The Tien Shan Mountains—camping at 5000 to 9000 feet. The promised land; I was to find it the most beautiful and pleasantest country I have ever known.

The best thing to say about Kashmir's capital is that it possesses a marvellous location. Built on both sides of the Jhelum River, it is surrounded by beautiful green valleys, while its horizon is a ring of soaring mountains. Its architectural variety deserves more than a passing glance, but the mind is distracted by the dirt, the slovenliness of the dwellings, the squalor of the people. Next to Phari in Tibet, it is the dirtiest city I have ever seen. Sociologists interested in slums would classify it as Exhibit No. 1.

Our expedition really began to take form in Gunderbal, ten miles beyond Srinagar, where the caravans were loaded and every man's work was laid out for him. The sixty-six ponies learned that it was not to be a lark, but they took it quietly as the packing cases were strapped to their backs and the long journey began.

Our next objective was Leh, capital of Ladak, the entrance to Chinese Turkestan. From Gunderbal to Leh is 228 miles, a mere nothing in the land of planes, trains, and motor-cars, but a staggering distance in this part of the world.

The thirteen days it took to reach Leh were a good prelude to the land that lay beyond, for we encountered endless variety in landscape, weather, temperature, and people. There was the valley of the Sind River, and then we climbed through gorges, through snow-covered passes. There were nights of bitter cold, days when the thermometer went streaking up to 60° Fahrenheit, the sun scattering a blinding glare on the snow. Such towns as Dras and Mulhbekh were impressive examples of human squalor. Up and down went the trail. The footing was often uncertain, and the danger of avalanches didn't add to our peace of mind.

Over the tree-line we climbed, and then down again to the state of Ladak, where by the banks of little streams lay fields of barley and wheat; even poplars and willows were persuaded to grow to a decent size. But growing things became rarer, and we passed into the bleakest, most inhospitable land I have ever seen.

Buddhists supplanted Mohammedans, and presently lamaseries began to appear on the remote hillsides. Often parties of lamas, attired in Burgundy-colored wool, would come down to the trail to peer at us. The laity, men and women, were dressed in robes of coarse wool trimmed with matted fur and many ornaments of silver and turquoise. Many of the women wore tall, pretty hats that resembled a certain kind of Tudor head-dress.

One of the tenets of Buddhism imposed a serious handicap on its followers: they were forbidden to take the life of any creature. In this part of Ladak their fields were devastated by flocks of voracious wild pigeons. Unwilling to use a gun themselves, they didn't hesitate to urge us to make war on their enemies. Some of the more energetic spirits even led us to fields well populated by pigeons.

Jamal Shekh, the cook, and Roussala, the assistant, rejoiced at the abundance of this game. Trained to do European dishes under the trying conditions of continuous marching, they turned out a succession of perfect meals. In addition to the pigeons, chickens and eggs were to be had in abundance. Our roadside purchases were supplemented by a good variety of stuff we had bought in Srinagar.

All along the trail, on good days and bad, Cherrie devoted himself to collecting. He had brought down more than sixty good specimens, including the Himalayan jungle crow, the chakkor partridge, the Indian rose-finch, the blue-headed rock-thrush, the fire-capped tit-warbler, the plumbeous redstart, the Kashmir skylark, the black-eared kite—all of which would be shipped home from Leh.

The routine of the thirteen strenuous days was pleasantly broken one evening when a group of villagers, led by their head lama, came to the grove where we had pitched camp and staged a show. The head lama's assistant made the villagers squat on the ground, women and children on one side, men and youths on the other.

The head lama wore an elaborate feather head-dress. Stripping to the waist, he and his assistant executed a grotesque dance with ritualistic steps and cadences. It was designed to amuse, and the audience laughed heartily, but the humor was too subtle for the white visitors. Also too subtle were the "serious" dances that followed. The whites were unable to see wherein they differed from the comedy, but the audience that had laughed heartily a few minutes before now looked awed, as if struck with fear.

Then the head lama took up his fakir acts, first thrusting a dagger through his cheeks. This is a well-known trick in India; it is possible that almost invisible slits already exist in the cheeks. He snatched up two other daggers that looked like Spanish cavalry swords, planted their handles in the ground, and rested his body on the upraised points. For the average man this might have meant the end. But the lama laughed merrily and commanded his followers to put a huge stone, weighing perhaps 150 pounds, on his belly. Another heavy stone was held above the lama's huge body and then released. After the crash we expected to find the lama flattened to the earth. The stone resting on his belly was split right across, but he leaped to his feet and took his bows. For us it was a pleasure to meet a man of God with so many useful accomplishments. It was my first trip to the East, and I was much impressed, remembering the many tales of its mysteries.

Approaching Leh, we saw many castles and chortens (shrines) rising from steep hillsides and suggesting from afar Italian hill country. Along the road were many attractive houses made of whitewashed mud bricks and stone. Their wooden balconies extending out from the second story were often made of exquisitely carved wood.

Leh first became known to Europeans with the visit of the Portuguese Jesuits, de Azevedo and de Oliveira, in 1631. Even at that time it was a famous trading center, and today, although it has but two or three thousand permanent residents, it plays the rôle of a metropolis because it has one of the highest meteorological stations in Asia, erected in 1882, and because caravans reach it from all directions—from India, Tibet, and Turkestan. We saw it in its quieter season when many of the shops in the bazaar were closed, but nevertheless it was a confused, bustling place, swarming with Ladakis, Hindus, Kirghiz, and Nepalese, many of them traders and caravan men. There were many varieties of merchandise for sale, and the most energetic traders seemed to be peddling emeralds and rugs.

The city, at 11,500 feet, is situated on a gaunt hill surrounded by high mountains. Some of the peaks stood out so clearly that at nightfall it often seemed as if they were chimneys of neighboring villages. The desert hillsides of the immediate environs give it a woebegone aspect on rainy days, but when the sun shines on the royal palace crowning a hill—a large white building with multitudinous awnings and balconies of lovely carved wood—and on the lower dwellings also with white façades liberally decorated with fine wood carvings, Leh has its undeniable attractions.

The Ladaki capital is connected with Srinagar by telegraph and by a courier mail service using coolies who cover the 238 miles in eight days.

We were somewhat delayed in Leh by a functionary known as the aksekal (the word means 'white beard' and hence 'elder') who acted as a sort of justice-of-the-peace and go-between in obtaining animals for caravan parties. Application was made to him for the horses that were to carry us into Turkestan, but because we were the first caravan of the season and he wasn't yet prepared for the season's traffic, and again because he was by nature somewhat addicted to bickering and bargaining, it took a little while to reach satisfactory terms.

While we waited, Cherrie had time to pack up and dispatch the collection of birds he had already acquired and to add some new specimens, such as the red-fronted serin, the Tibetan snow-finch, Hume's rock-pigeon, the eastern gray wagtail, and the Kashmir graytit.

Within the city there was a modern hospital run by Moravian missionaries who pointed out to us some of the difficulties of foreigners. Ladak, like all other parts of Kashmir, does not permit foreigners to own land. Lessors must pay high rents, and then, since only land-owners are permitted to cut down trees, wood being scarce, the foreigners pay stiff prices for fuel. Fuel was, as a matter of fact, so dear that the common people used yak dung.

Leh furnished an introduction to that phase of Buddhism known as Lamaism. Reaching its highest development in Tibet, this creed lays emphasis on the possibility of reincarnation. Only very holy people ever attain to reincarnation as human beings. Ladak had six re-incarnates.

Polyandry is fairly common in Ladak, and a girl often has two to four husbands, or, if she happens to be rich, five. The husbands are usually brothers, and the wife lives with the eldest, who is known as "the big father." The junior husbands find other dwellings. Although property rights pass down through the male line, the polyandrous wife is indubitably ruler of the roost. Divorce is rare, but if a woman happens to be the sole survivor of a family and thus inherits the property, she acquires special privileges and may dismiss her husband or husbands at will. Nowhere, even in Tibet, is polyandry so intensively practised as in this country.

Until a century ago, Ladak was an independent state ruled by a king. A direct descendant of the royal family still occupies the royal palace and is called king by the common people, but the actual sovereign is the Maharajah of Kashmir. Ladaki taxes levied by the Maharajah are collected sometimes in money, sometimes in grain or wood. Agriculture is carried on where the land permits, but the crops are always light. Many natives support themselves by cutting down a sort of rare rosewood found in the mountains, which brings good prices.

Ladakis are either Buddhists or Mohammedans. The Buddhists blithely ignore the rules laid down by their religion against the eating of meat; the Mohammedans, on the other hand, remember what the prophet said about alcoholic drinks. Among the temptations they resist are chung and arrak, both distilled from grain. Chung is a mild, thickish liquid that might be mistaken for beer. Consumed in large quantities it may cause drunkenness. Arrak is headier stuff, and one gulp usually convinces a white man it is not for him.

One of the curiosities of Leh is the existence of polo. It was not imported by Europeans but is an indigenous game, played by the upper classes on ceremonial occasions.

The aksekal finally rounded up our horses and accompanied us for several marches beyond Leh. The Roosevelts now plunged ahead, taking the two shikkaries with them. Travelling light, they would cover as much territory as possible in search of the burrhel (blue sheep). Cherrie and I, keeping the rest of the staff and most of the ponies, would continue more slowly. Our work required time and patience. There was a possibility we would meet the Roosevelts three days later in Khalsar. If not, it would be months later in Aksu. By that time, we hoped, they would have the sheep and we would have a good collection of birds and small mammals. Besides this, I was making a film documentation of the trip.

The first three days out of Leh took us into violent changes of altitude and terrain. Leh, as we have seen, was 11,500 feet. Our camp the first night was at 15,000. The Khardong pass was to take us up to 17,100 feet, and thereafter we would descend to 13,500.

At this stage of the journey we first became acquainted with yaks, the great pack animals of high central Asia. For the Khardong pass, about sixteen of these animals were taken on to supplement our horses. These thick, lumbering creatures, cousins of the ox and bison, with heavy woolly hide and long horns, are ideally suited to high altitudes. They are slow, but indomitably persistent. Sure-footed, tireless, they can go over the most treacherous precipices, where one slip would mean death, without faltering for an instant. At the same time they are stupid and cantankerous, and nothing can speed them up or slow them down. When they take it into their heads to stop dead in their tracks, they are immune to all persuasion.

From afar the trail leading up to the Khardong looked completely vertical, and even on closer approach it was none too reassuring. In a bleak wilderness of rock and glacial snow, with jagged mountains rising above us, we found the trail too steep for riding and were obliged to dismount and climb slowly and painfully, stopping every hundred feet to catch our breath. The wind whipped the light snow into violent whirlpools that lashed across our faces.

That night, when we stopped to make camp, both Cherrie and I were touched by mountain sickness, an illness characterized by headache and nausea that claims as its victims those who are not acclimated to high altitudes. So, renouncing all thoughts of supper, we slid into our waterproof sleeping-bags and tried to sleep. But the altitude was oppressive, and merely lying still was an effort.

The next day the trail led gradually downward, till at 13,000 feet the valley became a dense jungle of spinny. Ted and Kermit were waiting for us in the little town of Khalsar. Despite their lighter caravan they had been unable to make much speed because of the altitude. For the time being, we would all travel together.

From the snows of the Khardong we now got into the sandstorms of the valley of the Nubra River. These were recurrent high gusts of wind carrying blinding, penetrating sheets of sand. It was alternately hot and cold, wilderness one hour, marginal land the next. One vivid contrast lingers in my mind: from a bleak, barren mountainside we descended to the town of Pannamik, where the air was warm and still and the land was covered with small, wild, blue roses. A hip of this plant was brought back to Doctor Gerald Webb, who planted it on Pike's Peak, where it sprouted and took root but refused to bloom. In its native state it was a lovely flower, with petals of true sky-blue.

Pannamik was a pleasant village of white cottages set down in lanes of poplars, willows, rose bushes, and thorny hedges. Ladaki wood carvings were set against the white façades. One of the town's attractions was a hot spring where the natives had erected a bath house. Water had been brought by trough from the springs, and the bathers sat under a small trickle. One side of the house was used by men, the other by women, but there was no partition, not even a curtain between. It did not appeal to us, so we found an even better place, a tiny pool just big enough for one person at a time. It was fed both by the hot spring and by a cold brook, and by damming the stream with rocks we were able to regulate the temperature. The water, saturated with sulphur, was a rusty red color.

Pannamik is the jumping-off place for one of the toughest journeys in the world. The trail would lead into the high Karakorum mountains —a desolate land showing no human habitation, no sprig of bush or blade of grass. It is the land of glaciers, snow, hurricanes, and steep passes.

Our first problem was to clear the Sasser pass at 17,500 feet. The natives said it was impossible at this season, but not without some migivings we decided to try it.

In Pannamik our ponies and yaks were supplemented by dzos, a cross between the yak and native cattle. I also acquired a miniscular donkey, an amusing and ingratiating little beast, who was promptly named "Humming Bird."

The animals were a serious problem. Some, we knew, would die. All along the road we had seen piles of bones—animals lost by other caravans. Our animals had already suffered, but the worst was before them. We could afford to lose only a very few. There would be no other way of acquiring others before we reached the plains beyond. Nothing could be sacrificed of our food, fuel, or equipment. Although

A desert, mountainous country, with a narrow, difficult trail winding along
the steep edges of the slopes

Leh, an ancient Tibetan capital, at 11,500 feet, is a great trade mart
between India and Central Asia

Cairn at the summit of Karakorum Pass, 18,600 feet—highest
used caravan pass in the world

Campsite in a wilderness of big boulders at over 15,000 feet. A regular site
for trans-Himalayan caravans

Campsite at 16,300 feet. In the near background, the Remo glacier has stretched a tongue that has closed the valley

Ferry on the Yarkand River. The old contraption got us over in six trips

the packs would become steadily lighter as food and fuel were consumed, this advantage would be balanced by the growing weakness of the animals.

Meanwhile the beasts were having a rest from Saturday to Monday. The towering peaks around us were an imposing spectacle, too imposing, in fact, and I wasn't quite sure if it was comfortable to be in the midst of such rugged grandeur.

Early Monday we left Pannamik to rejoin the Roosevelts, who had again gone ahead. The trail led along the Talambuti River, just then a raging torrent. We passed through a series of desolate, narrow gorges, and whenever we got in the sun's rays, beating down on stretches of sand, it was blistering hot. The shaded areas were rather chilly.

At the end of the march we found ourselves in a wilderness of big boulders, and it was with difficulty that space was cleared for our tents. Clearing a place for the animals would have taken all night; so they were condemned to remain standing.

The Roosevelts appeared and said they had had a strenuous time of it with their burrhel hunt. Scrambling up and down the steep hillsides had worn them out, but they had got one specimen. They declined food and fell asleep. One of their shikkaries complained of being ill, maintaining it was a heart attack.

Another day we pitched camp in a little pocket of land within a stone's throw of the glacier, which gave off blasts of freezing air quite as if an icebox had been flung open in our faces. All around us were the black-gray mountains, rising up so steeply that we had to tilt our heads far back to see the color of the sky. The sun disappeared behind a peak in the early afternoon but the upper levels of the mountain were still shimmering in golden light.

We didn't bother with tents, but got into our sleeping-bags and lay on the ground, hoping that a few winks of sleep would brace us for the coming day. But there was no sleep. Up here at 17,000 feet breathing was an effort, and even when lying still one could never seem to capture enough oxygen from the thin air. During the night the temperature fell to 24° F. The caravan men and animals seemed in constant agitation all night long. Even if other conditions had been favorable it is doubtful if any one could have slept in such a hubbub.

Without reluctance we rose at four o'clock. There was barely light enough to trace the outlines of the peaks. The thick shadows about us were broken here and there by tiny yellow fires of yak dung over which were huddled the dark figures of the men boiling water for tea. We were thankful that the night had been so cold, for this meant that the snow covering Sasser's formidable glacier would probably be firm enough to support the weight of the pack-laden animals.

At five o'clock the ascent began. Soft gray light was filtering into the valley. The first breathless hour passed without mishap. The "trail" sloped steeply into a tremendous world of snow, ice, and scrambled rocks, and with every step, it seemed, the supply of oxygen grew scarcer. The temples throbbed, the heart pounded so loudly it seemed to awaken echoes in the rocky wall.

The animals floundered and slipped as they trudged through the snow and rocks. Near the top, one pony toppled over in a heap. It was not excessively loaded, and it had been well the night before. Exertion and altitude had finished it off. We looked apprehensively at the other animals, but though they were puffing and steaming, they showed no signs of collapse.

As the morning advanced, Sasser was a stupendous sight—the violet-hued limestone cliffs and fields of sn w, ineffably brilliant in the sunshine, and above us the snowy peaks sharply outlined against the blue sky. When we eventually got to the glacier, we found it flattened out to a smooth, hard surface. To traverse this area was easy compared with the ascent. Crossing the ice sheet took only an hour.

On the far side snowflakes danced in the air. Soon they thickened into a blizzard. What luck! We were over the worst of it now, breathing easier, literally and figuratively. Had the blizzard started earlier, lack of visibility would have kept us trapped in camp.

Moving downward to a level of 15,300 feet before stopping to make camp, we sat down at 8:45 to a breakfast that took on a festal air.

Sasser behind us, a more tolerable altitude, appetizing food in front of us—we asked for nothing more.

The ponies deserved a good rest, but this was out of the question. They were carrying their feed on their backs, and since the country had no grass, they were consuming it, despite careful rationing, at the rate of 150 pounds a day.

The march took us along the Shayok River. Confronted with a choice of routes, our men selected the shorter, which was also the more difficult because the stream had to be forded several times. The first time was easy, but at the second ford the men broke into complaints and lamentations. The water was so deep that they were obliged to pull their clothes up to the waist and lead the beasts through the icy flood. There was no turning back, and so, once reconciled to it, they carried it off with laughter and gay chatter. The performance was repeated four times.

Then, another day, we came suddenly to an impasse in the valley, where the end of the Remo glacier had come down and stopped the passage. Before us lay a glittering, mountainous wall of ice. After four hours of reconnoitering, we reached the sad conclusion that the ponies could never cross this icy rampart.

There was nothing to do but retreat, losing two days of the horses' energy and 300 pounds of their fodder. But even retreat was not easy, for the water in the Shayok had risen behind us, and it was not until the next morning that we could undertake the weary march back to the fork in the trail whence we could start on the alternative route.

Later on we met a caravan coming from Yarkand to Leh, the first one of the year to make the southern journey, just as we were the first to make the northern. This caravan, too, had attempted the shorter route and had met the Remo. In the attempt to cross, one man and six ponies perished.

The animals were constantly on our minds as we marched along the banks of the Shayok and its tributaries, the Dufson and the Mugu, climbing by easy stages to the wide, bleak Dapsang plains. This area, 18,000 feet high, surrounded by snowy mountains, is, I believe, the most benighted land I have ever gazed on. The rolling stretches of gray earth and gravel were hostile to human habitation and all vegetation except moss. Colors and contours suggested that the land had died years ago. The only sign of life in the whole region was a herd of Tibetan antelope. Two were shot, and then came the sad discovery that they were moulting and that the skins were of no value.

On the Dapsang plains two of our ponies died, and the rest were becoming exhausted. And now the Karakorum was before us. Highest caravan pass in the world, the Karakorum has ever been considered one of the formidable barriers of the world. The first European to cross it was a Doctor Thomson, who performed his feat in 1848. Not a few white men have crossed since that time, but one would hardly call it a populous highway.

At an altitude of 18,000 feet our ponies began to bleed through the nose. This was a healthy symptom, and, as a matter of fact, when an animal became exhausted and failed to bleed, the caravan men would thrust a long, sharp bodkin up its nostrils.

Mounting steeply, the trail took us into a region of stupendous, fire-colored cliffs that had been tossed into fantastic shapes by the earth's heavings and rumblings. This awe-inspiring grandeur reached another phase of black rock and white snow, touched off here and there with patches of delicate alpine flowers. The Karakorum was living up to its name: black rock. Snow was sifting over the mountain's monstrous shoulders as we came to the summit of the pass at 18,600 feet. I rushed ahead and took a film of the advancing caravan. When the others reached the top we planted the flags of the United States and of the New York Explorers' Club.

All in all, the Karakorum was less severe than we had feared. We made it in good time and without damage to the ponies. There was plenty of evidence, however, that it deserved its bad reputation. Piles of animal skeletons, whitened by the sun of many a long summer, lined the trail, and another sinister sign was the vultures wheeling over us, watching our animals with greedy eyes.

Packs of goods were seen here and there along the way, abandoned by caravans of the preceding season. These would be left in peace till their owners returned under more favorable conditions to claim them. The code of honor among caravan men was well observed.

The descent was fairly gradual. Sharp peaks rose magnificently above us, and all about us was a stony wilderness of mammoth gorges. Glaciers took on violet tints from the sun's rays, and the snow turned pinkish in the late afternoon. Caravan men of the past had erected a holy cairn topped by a big Tibetan prayer-flag to invoke the blessing of the gods on their crossings.

When we pitched camp that night at 16,400 feet, men and animals were glad to have a good night's rest. The worst of the journey to Yarkand was now behind us, but the pony situation looked bad. One animal, failing to bleed after the bodkin treatment, died during the night from exhaustion. Seven ponies had now died, and it was necessary for the four of us to give up the luxury of a mount apiece. From now on to the town of Sanju, the Roosevelts would share one pony, Cherrie and I another.

Leaving the Karakorum, we passed out of Ladak into Chinese Turkestan, situated in the heart of Central Asia.

Our obstacles were now two passes, the Suget and the Sanju. The Suget was the higher (17,400 feet), but our men, for two reasons, considered the Sanju more of an ordeal. Its trail was steeper, and by that time the animals would be in a still weaker condition.

From the Karakorum to the Suget was comparatively easy going as the land was fairly smooth. But continuous travel in high altitudes was telling on men and beasts. Supplies of aspirin, soda-mint tablets, bicarbonate of soda, and laxatives were doled out to the caravan men.

This country gave us an opportunity for shooting, and another male antelope was responsible for a change of plan. This one, losing its hair, made a sorry spectacle when the skinning was completed, and we could see the likelihood of a similar misadventure if we were to capture the ovis poli. It would be nothing short of tragedy to get one of the rarest animals in the world and then have it turn later to a mess of leather in the taxidermist's hands. The Roosevelts therefore put off their trip to the Pamirs till autumn. In the meanwhile they would remain with us as we continued northward to the Tien Shan or Mountains of Heaven.

The Suget was negotiated without serious difficulty, but the animals were near collapse by the time they had cleared the crest. We saw many clumps of dwarf willows—from which the pass gets its name— and far, far below us was a tiny, grassy meadow. In a few hours we were actually feeling the grass beneath our feet. The ponies, without waiting to be divested of their packs, rushed into it and devoured as much as they could hold.

With the return of vegetation came the first habitations we had seen since Pannamik. Groups of nomadic Kirghiz had set up their round, felt tents, called *yurts*, while their livestock grazed on the plains. The Kirghiz settlements, organized into family groups called *kosh* and ruled by a *beg*, became more numerous as we came down to lower land.

The Kirghiz are a Mongol race scattered over huge areas from the Ural mountains and the mouths of the Volga to China proper on the east. They are Mohammedans and famous nomads, driving their herds hither and yon wherever grazing is good. During the growing season they sow a little wheat, barley, and maize, but their principal wealth comes from their herds. Health and vitality were written on their weather-beaten brown faces and in their lively, almond eyes. They looked a gay and independent people. We saw a great many bearded men wearing skull-caps or vivid-colored turbans edged with fur. Their long, flowing robes, usually made of sheep or yak wool, were secured with a girdle of bright-colored cloth, elaborately twisted and coiled.

The women also wore these flowing garments, but theirs were often made of brilliant, striped Bokhara silk. Head-dresses were extremely beautiful, with a foot-high turban called a *kalak*, culminating in two lappets over the ears. There was also a muslin veil that fell from the top of the kalak to the shoulders, partly covering the face. The women made lavish use of a beautiful, intricate embroidery. Altogether they made a stunning effect.

All the people we met were addicted to that extremely healthful drink known as kumiss—fermented mare's milk. We were often offered drinks of it in silver vessels.

The sight of camels in the meadows gave us an idea: if we could hire camels to carry our packs through the streams, and more yaks to help us across the Sanju, it might save grief later on. A Khirghiz headman promised to provide both camels and yaks, but we were sceptical about his good faith.

Just beyond the Suget we came to an ancient Chinese fort, once used as a customs house. It was surrounded by a wall ten feet high with battlements at the four corners. Within the fort, now abandoned, were enclosures for men and animals. In the open space, covered with clean gravel, we pitched our tents.

At this point my little "Humming Bird," the one bright spot in the difficult marches, met his end. His body was found mangled one morning, and the tracks around him indicated that he had fallen victim to wolves. His antics had contributed a lot of amusement to otherwise unamusing situations, and it was a saddening prospect to go on without him.

The camels had failed to appear and it seemed unlikely the Kirghiz would ever produce the yaks.

We came to a place where the trail was completely blocked by a chuck of mountain extending out into the Karakash River and where the water around the base of the cliffs was manifestly too deep. Cherrie undertook to lead the caravan over a trail that surmounted the escarpment while the other three of us climbed the cliff.

The ascent was treacherous and steep, and we had to climb from one perilous foothold to another, excessively difficult because we lacked mountain-climbing technique. In some places the face of the cliff was so steep that we had to pull ourselves up inch by inch, clinging to uncertain pieces of rock. Before making any move we attempted to see if the foothold or handhold was secure, but often it deceived us, giving way and crashing downward to the measureless depths below. To retreat would have been impossible, for to clamber down would have been extremely dangerous. Once the top was reached, we descended on our seats, sliding, slipping, maneuvering for position. At the bottom most of our clothes were torn.

Cherrie appeared shortly afterwards and reported that his task had not been all beer and skittles, either.

It began to rain, and looking for shelter, we saw a Kirghiz family beckoning to us from the mouth of a cave. Smiling and hospitable, they bade us make ourselves comfortable. Woollen blankets were placed on the floor, and the inevitable kumiss appeared. That night our clothes received a thorough treatment with Keating's insect powder.

We were now at an altitude of 11,300 feet, the lowest since leaving Pannamik, but from here the trail got steeper till we reached the Sanju, the last of the five great passes. At the very moment when we had concluded that the Sanju, just opened after the heavy snows of winter, was going to be a disastrous ordeal for the weakened animals, the Kirghiz headman fulfilled one of his promises and turned up with the yaks.

The zigzagging, steep Sanju trail took us through fields of delicate blue snow, past iridescent violet peaks, but the top, 16,500 feet, a narrow trough of rock, was covered with swirling mist, shutting off our vision of what was doubtless a formidable landscape. As we started the descent, a snowstorm blew up and the road behind us was blocked.

Even without packs, our ponies grew perceptibly weaker, and before we had got down the far side four had perished. This brought our total animal losses to thirteen horses and one donkey. If it had not been for the yaks, the casualties might have been more severe and we might have had to abandon some of our loads.

Below us was a great, rolling, treeless prairie covered with grass. The ponies had a celebration and after a few days were revived.

There were many yurts and great herds of yaks belonging to the Kirghiz, who practised a crude agriculture by means of an intricate irrigation system that supplemented the scanty water supply. Their attractive, colorful clothes and the variety of jewelry indicated that it was a prosperous tribe. The prevailing colors for the men's robes were maroon and orange, harmonizing beautifully with gray gilets. The women wore quilted silk dresses and elaborate headgear. One type of hat was made of red, white, and blue silk with a visor dropping over the eyes and lappets coming down well below the ears. The visor had a fringe of beads, while the lappets were covered with hundreds of small buttons sewn into intricate patterns. These chic hats were finished off with beautifully embroidered veils of vari-colored silk. There was another popular form of hat that defied description: it looked like a great blob of taffy that hadn't had time to take a definite shape.

Our men told us at this point that it was the eve of the Hegira Feast, and they begged to have the next day off. Permission was granted, and they started the celebration by declaring their various ailments and asking for medicines. Their shindy went off in seemly fashion, and they were on the job early the next morning.

Marching down the Sanju River, we lost 4300 feet of altitude in only eighteen miles. Nightfall brought us to the village of Akas-Aghzi, where the elevation was 8700 feet.

The next day set a record for fords, since the Sanju River at this point swayed along a narrow ravine, leaving a slight strip of dry land on one side or the other—never both sides at once. This meant shifting every little while. As a matter of fact, we forded the Sanju ten times, and were fortunate in being able to hire camels, excellent animals in deep water, to relieve the horses and yaks.

Night brought us to the village of Kives, an oasis in a barren desert. Irrigation had made the land arable, and there were groves of willows and narrow fields of grain waving in the mild breeze. This march of the ten fords took place on the Fourth of July, and we held a celebration outdoors with the temperature touching 80° F. at 5 P.M.

Before dinner we managed some successful cocktails of Scotch whisky, sloe gin, juice of preserved pears, and a dash of cherry brandy.

The cook scoured the bazaar of Kives and did himself proud with a mutton curry. After dinner there was a supply of cherry brandy, cigars, and cigarettes, topped off in due course with a long drink of hot water, brandy, and sugar. Thus mellowed, we burst into song. One of the men came over to ask a question: "I am sorry to interrupt your religious observance, but . . ." We looked at him sharply but he wasn't laughing.

The next day's march led to an aggregation of oasis villages known collectively as Sanju Bazaar, where, for miles along both sides of the Sanju, fields extended a half to a mile wide. Beyond this was a belt of low mountains.

At the outskirts of Sanju Bazaar we were met by a reception committee sent by the *amban* or local governor, who had been informed of our approach by a message dispatched long before from Nanking to Kashgar.

On an enclosed, grassy meadow, brightened up with vivid Kirghiz carpets, an elaborate feast had been laid out. There were chicken, lamb, hard-boiled eggs, kumiss, fresh apricots, nuts, and tea. If the chicken was the toughest I had ever tasted and if the tea resembled dishwater, the lamb and apricots were excellent indeed. The fruit was particularly welcome, since we had been deprived of it for so long. I thought this ceremony arranged by the amban a very pleasant affair. As a matter of fact, I was guileless enough to hope there would be more of them later. The truth about amban hospitality was to come out soon enough!

All through the afternoon we passed rich-looking fields of peas, wheat, barley, Indian corn, and good hay. The prosperous inhabitants of this region were Turkis. It was our introduction to a famous people. Numerically the strongest race in Sinkiang, the Turkis are, of course, members of the great Turkic race and thus are related to the Ottomans living farther west. A superficial glance might have indicated that these desert Turkis, with their slanting eyes, their straight, aquiline noses and faces blackened by exposure, were a fierce, aggressive tribe. But history indicates the contrary, and so did our subsequent observations. The Chinese conquerors found the Turkis a docile people to rule.

The men wore loose trousers and a long white coat, often lined with fur, secured at the waist by an ample, wide cotton sash, wound around again and again to form a thick girdle. Some wore turbans, other skull-caps and fur-lined caps. The women were a little gayer, with long, flowing dresses of bright cotton cloth. White veils partly concealed their black braids but not their faces.

Fair eyes and blond or reddish hair were to be seen frequently in this area, showing that the Iranian of ancient times prevailed as far as Khotan and even farther east. At the dawn of history, it seems probable that eastern Turkestan was inhabited by an Aryan people, the ancestors of the present Teutons and Slavs of Europe.

In Sanju Bazaar, we were taken to our abode for the night—a garden intersected here and there by small canals, the whole surrounded by high walls. Beyond the garden were many houses, and groves of planted trees whose fresh, vivid green was a joy after so many days in the wilderness of snow, moss, and gravel.

Evening brought a visit from the local aksekal, who wanted to see our papers. He spoke only Chinese, not even the regional Turki dialect, and we had to speak Hindustani to one of our shikkaries, who translated it into Turki. Another man translated the Turki into Chinese. It was a polyglot stew, not altogether effective.

Leaving the Sanju River the next day, we turned northeast and travelled twenty miles to the village of Roztagh, somewhat smaller than Sanju Bazaar. The road took us through desert country, slightly rolling, parched by the sun, devoid of all animal life. In Roztagh we were installed in a small, airless, evil-smelling room where visitations of fleas caused a miserable night. Even the usually efficacious Keating's powder failed to dislodge the insects.

We were now only fifty-four miles from the thriving city of Kargelik, but to reach it we had to march two days over the torrid desert. At the end of the first day we stopped at Bora and, declining another flea-cage, insisted on pitching our tent in the best place we could find, which happened to be a dusty courtyard. Twice when passing through oases we were invited to eat—kumiss, apricots, and delicious native bread, spread out on carpets under the trees. These were good meals.

A guide met us at the outskirts of Kargelik, an attractive region with many groves of willows, plane trees, and jujubes, with orchards of peach, apple, apricot, plum, nut, and mulberry trees, and many vineyards and gardens of Indian corn, cucumbers, and melons. And then we were conducted through a tremendously long bazaar, part of it covered to make it cool and shady, and through tortuous streets of slack, shabby houses, to the residence of the amban.

Four white travellers, covered with dust and grime, sweating, impatient for a bath, were led into a garden and given to understand that festivities in their honor were about to begin. It was a foretaste of what was to come, for we were to have our fill of ambans before leaving Sinkiang. Many were Chinese aristocrats with good manners and pleasing personalities, but their hospitality was overpowering, merciless, unrelenting. Meals and visits were rituals, and we were obliged to conform to the rules.

Swarms of guests formed a welcoming committee. One official after another took charge of us and each seemed of higher rank than the last. Finally, escorted to a high dais, we came face to face with an elderly, fat, bald little man, clad in black Chinese silk. His eyes were brimming with laughter as people bowed to him right and left. This was the great lord himself, the ruler of Kargelik. There was a great babble of conversation, carried on by scores of officials who got in each other's way. We were enveloped in the confusion, and it was several minutes before we could get the English-Hindustani-Turki-Chinese translation system into operation. The amban regarded all this with smiling eyes.

Bowls of hot tea were brought in and we drank eagerly. But they continued to press it on us long after our thirst was slaked and the sweat was standing out on our foreheads in great beads. We yearned to escape the noise and confusion, to change our clothes, to rest. Observing our discomfiture, one of the officials ordered servants to bring bowls of water so we could wash our faces right at the table. We complied.

At this point came bad news: this tea was only a prelude to the entertainment, for the amban had scheduled two more dinners in our honor. Plans for leaving Kargelik early the next morning were hastily amended. While we knew the dinners would be a bore and a penance, there was no way out, for we couldn't antagonize the rulers of Turkestan.

The tea party ended an hour later, and we presented the amban with a bottle of brandy and agreed to be ready in two hours for the first of the big dinners. In the meanwhile our caravan had arrived and our tents were put up in the amban's garden. We went off and bathed in the turgid, muddy river, with a big crowd of men and women peering at us unabashedly. If they could stand it, so could we.

Next came the ticklish problem of what to wear. Back in Leh, our servants had been scandalized because we wore trail clothes at receptions. These would certainly never do at an amban's dinner. Nothing less than dinner jackets, soft white shirts, and opera hats—brought along for a lark—would do. They looked grotesque with our black beards but our hosts seemed satisfied with our appearance.

All the guests were Chinese; no Turkis had been invited. For two hours, course followed course till I lost count. The conversation gained in pace, led by the amban and his two sons who seemed to be enjoying themselves hugely. At the liqueur stage we discovered that the amban was drunk. Obviously he had polished off a lot of our brandy before dinner. His fat little stomach shook and his smile became more radiant by the minute. But suddenly His Excellency lurched to his feet, while every one looked at him with concern. He hesitated only a second and then made for the door. From my seat I had a perfect view of his zigzag course down to the canal.

On his return he seemed a little subdued. His smile was wan. He made no move to break up the party, but when we, worn out from the day's march and the heavy banquet, asked permission to leave, he seemed content to call it a day.

We went to sleep, with three soldiers armed with old single-charge rifles of an 1876 Russian model standing as sentries around our tents. It seemed unlikely we needed protection, but the amban's word was law.

The next morning we wandered through the bazaar shaded with pleasant willows and saw the famous but utterly undistinguished mosque. The city itself was a labyrinth of one-story houses made of mud-baked bricks. No building had anything of architectural interest, and the only sign of decoration appeared in boxes of flowers placed along the flat parapets. Kargelik is, however, a venerable city, an important stage on the famous Silk Road built in the second century B.C. by the Chinese emperor, Han, in order that Chinese silk and other produce might be transported to Persia and thence sold to the Greeks and Romans. Kargelik had its past; it was, I hoped, more interesting than its present.

The amban's second dinner was bigger and better than the first. Our seats were indicated by elaborate place-cards, with our names written in Chinese characters. The laughing amban was gay but quite sober. We had taken care not to give him more brandy. There was a succession of such things as mollusk soup, shark's fins, marine fish, chicken. Boredom and acute discomfort increased, but we were obliged to eat some of each course.

Drinks followed dinner, and it didn't take the amban long to work himself into a high glow. Toasts were proposed, and when our turns came we rose and, speaking English, of which no one knew a word, made speeches that would have aroused admiration in a fish market. "Listen, you old bald-headed drunk," was the opening of one, and from that it was but a step to making comments on His Excellency's taste, habits, and ancestry. Our host must have thought, judging from his expression, that we were dripping celestial compliments on his bald head.

It was getting late now and we had to take to the road. Much as we disliked night marches this one had a compensation: it was marvellous to be free of the amban and his Lucullan dinners. The fervor of relief pervaded our farewells.

From now on, our transport would be *arabas* and *mappas*, which are carts built without springs, equipped with iron-studded wheels. The larger arabas were for luggage; we rode in the mappas.

We had been going about twenty minutes when we saw, off in the distance, a number of flickering lights that looked like fireflies. Drawing nearer, we saw they were Chinese lanterns, and behind the wavering light stood a crowd of people. A soldier came out and saluted. Then it was that we saw the amban standing at the roadside calling out greetings, as if we were ancient friends meeting after years of separation. The explanation was simple: the amban, it seemed, had an inexhaustible appetite for saying good-bye; so, while we were changing our clothes and preparing for the road, he had simply ridden ahead with his retinue. This supplementary farewell took half an hour. We were escorted to a small house and plied with tea, liqueurs, and some cigars that were worse than anything ever produced in the State of Connecticut.

Once again on the road, I felt that even the trees were infested with ambans. After that staggering dinner, the mappa, jolting up and down the rough road like a tin can in a gale, was a torture. There was just room to curl up. When this posture got tiring one could lie on one's back and stretch one's legs over the horse's tail. When the road became unusually bumpy, it was necessary to sit upright and grasp the sides of the cart firmly. Then, to add to the misery, we came into the mosquito country.

The night's jolting took us thirty miles to Posgam, where we warded off an amban dinner by asking the officials to dine with us.

And then we were off again at dusk for Yarkand, biggest city in the country. In the fading light we could see prosperous-looking fields on both sides of the trail and an extensive irrigation system wherewith the natives bled the Yarkand River to provide garden spots in the desert. Dawn brought us to a ferry on the Yarkand River. The old contraption got us over—men, beasts, baggage, and carts—in six trips.

About ten o'clock, when Yarkand's battlemented walls and towers were rising in the distance, we saw a brass band coming down the road. This looked to me like a piece of ambanishness, and I was not wrong. Yarkand had not only a ruling amban but an auxiliary amban and an amban emeritus. No matter how you parsed them, I felt, they were still ambans. We would naturally have to visit the three of them and, in addition, the Chinese general in command of the district. It looked like heavy times ahead. While the band blared away, we were escorted to an elaborate house set down in a handsome garden where a *beg* entertained us at tea. After this, progress was resumed to the center of the city, the band still playing.

Yarkand is supposed to have a population of 60,000, and since the buildings of mud brick are only one story high, the city bulges out into straggling suburbs. We saw the massive walls of the Yangi Shahr (new town) with their heavy towers and parapets, but no noteworthy buildings or monuments. The bazaar showed nothing but junk, and the people were ill-clad. The city's sole attractions came from the lovely groves of fruit trees and the many gardens, for Yarkand, unlike most towns of the Sinkiang plains, is plentifully supplied with water.

We were installed in a pleasant little house where each had a clean and comfortable room spread with beautiful rugs. The ambans were waiting to receive us; so we were taken to a large house, and there, in the noise and confusion we had come to associate with amban hospitality, we were given tea, fruits, spices, and raisins. The amban smiled benignly and, through the cumbersome interpreter-service, told me he was a brother of the Kargelik amban. He offered liqueur, of which he had obviously drunk more than enough. Knowing he knew no English, I found myself speaking my thoughts aloud: "Drinking certainly runs in your family, doesn't it?" His Excellency smiled brightly.

The rest of the day was spent in travelling from one house to another, drinking, eating, and carrying on the fantastic four-dimensional conversation. The next day the ambans were dining with us, and the day after that we were to be their guests.

The following morning we visited the Swedish Moravian mission, which had been a Yarkand institution for thirty years. Formerly the missionaries had come overland from Russia, but now the Soviet was refusing passes of safe-conduct, and the men travelled up by way of India. It was a lonely post. Ministering to the needs of Turkis, Kirghiz, and others, they sometimes went for long periods without ever seeing a white face. Their medical supplies came by way of China and were sometimes a year late.

During the afternoon we visited the fair grounds to see a special show wherein a twelve-year-old boy did some remarkable tight-rope walking about a hundred feet above the ground.

Our dinner for the ambans started off with cocktails. The guests were a little sceptical, but when told it was only a mild American brew, they consented to try it. It was as hard to stop them as start them. They pronounced our dinner excellent, but that was not surprising: after five of our cocktails not even an amban could tell the difference between a shark's fin and a shredded-wheat biscuit.

Next day, after a twenty-course dinner that set an all-time high for amban hospitality, our party split up. The Roosevelts were to continue to Marlbashi and Aksu, then through the Muzart pass into the Tien Shan mountains, to spend two months hunting. Cherrie was to follow behind to Marlbashi, stopping off here and there whenever he saw good collecting opportunities. As for me, I started off northwest for Kashgar to transact business and post letters.

This plan made it necessary to divide up the staff, ponies, and carts. The Roosevelts took two arabas and the two shikkaris, while I took one araba and Feroze. The rest of the men and transport stayed with Cherrie.

My route from Yarkand to Kashgar provided bad weather, bad roads, and sundry other discomforts. We were hardly out of Yarkand into the brown, dreary desert when a storm blew up. Hour after hour the araba jolted over rough roads and rain poured from a gun-metal sky. Late in the day the rain ceased and a glaring, broiling sun appeared in a sky of greenish-blue. Clouds of moisture quivered over the sodden earth. Nature in Turkestan surrounded her caprices with plenty of atmospheric effects.

It was a hot, desolate land, stretching flat and barren to a far horizon, and after each rain the earth became a morass. At longish intervals came oases, surrounded by houses, gardens, and clumps of planted trees. All had congested, dirty, foul-smelling inns patronized by the caravan trade. Once or twice I slept in a courtyard, surrounded by animals and sacks of grain.

Beg hospitality, proffered here and there along the road, made a pleasant break in the journey. The refreshments were tea, melons, and apricots. These delicious melons, certainly the best in the world, were the only kind of food one could rely on in this region.

So passed the five days of the 110-mile trip from Yarkand to Kashgar. All day the eye fell on the monotonous stretch of desert land. The sun was broiling, and the araba jolted over the ruts so abominably that every position one could devise was uncomfortable. Sitting, squatting, lying on the back, it was all the same. Above me, the driver's voice rose and fell in wearisome refrain. If he said "oowah" the horses shifted to the right. "Oochaie" meant giddap, and "tuh," slow up. For centuries caravans had been using this famous Silk Road, but no one had ever turned a finger to improve it. The road and the inns along it were probably little changed from the day Marco Polo took this route from west to east.

During the latter part of this trip I picked up a fever and it dulled my senses to a lot of discomfort.

As we approached Kashgar, Feroze, fearful lest I enter the city looking like a vagabond, got out a fresh khaki suit and placed it before me hopefully. I put it on indifferently, for I was restless with the fever and unable to concentrate on anything except cool, shady spots where one might rest.

The welcome given to me by Colonel Lyall, British consul-general in Kashgar, stands out as one of the pleasantest incidents of all my travels. He led me into the house, clean, cool, spacious. The bedroom had a real bed with springs and clean white sheets. The bathroom had a concrete tub and a gadget for heating water. There were soft chairs, rugs, books, a floor of wood instead of mud. And beyond the house were pleasant terraced gardens filled with bright flowers, and a tennis court.

Kashgar is not the Cascar or Casigar of Marco Polo, for that city was destroyed at the beginning of the sixteenth century by Mirza Aba Bakr. The ruins, called Eski Shahr, may be seen fifteen miles east of the present city. Today's 40,000 people live in a congeries of one-story, baked-mud houses lining the narrow, higgledy-piggledy streets, interspersed here and there with minareted mosques. If some of the quiet streets made it look like a small town, the bazaar with its wider streets and arcades of booths holding many varieties of merchandise and its swarms of buyers and sellers gave it the air of a metropolis.

The city has played a big rôle in the history of Chinese Turkestan, but today the administrative center of the region is Arumchi. The governor, though appointed by the central Chinese government, is practically a dictator. At the time of my visit the whole province of Sinkiang was tranquil, politically speaking, but since that time it has become a boiling cauldron of intrigue and fighting.

There are few Chinese in Sinkiang, with the exception of the ruling classes and a sprinkling of coolies. Turkis form the bulk of the population, and the alien residents, few in number, include Hindus, Persians, and White Russians.

Wave after wave of migration has passed over this land—"White Huns," Chinese, Turks, Tibetans. Many religions have left their imprint—Buddhism, Zoroastrianism, Nestorian Christianity, and finally Mohammedanism. Among the great personalities who emerge from the long scroll of Turkestan's history are Genghis Khan, the Mongol conqueror who overran the country in the twelfth century; Tughlak Timur, who became a power in the fourteenth century and transferred his capital from Kashgar to Aksu; and Timur, the great Tamerlane, whose glory stemmed from Samarkand. The Chinese invaded Dzungaria in 1758 and perpetrated one of the most shocking massacres of history; possibly one million persons lost their lives. But China went on consolidating its power in Sinkiang (the word means 'New Dominion') undeterred even by three serious revolts of the natives that took place in the nineteenth century.

At the time of my visit one could fairly say that the Turkis were wholly indifferent as to who ruled them. Had Russia seized the whole country they would have treated the news with less interest than some minor event in their own communities. Within the last decade, reliable observers have reported that Russia's secret maneuvers in Sinkiang have turned into open attempts at domination. China, engaged in a life-struggle with Japan, is in no position to control the situation, and Sinkiang's destiny is a vital matter in world politics whose solution reaches into the future.

When I was in Kashgar, Russian activity, interrupted by the great war, had not yet been resumed. It was a simpler world, and instead of intricate conspiracies, we were concerned with such matters as the folkways of the people.

While the prevailing religion was Mohammedan, few of the Turkis availed themselves of the privilege granted by their religion to practise polygamy. While monogamy was the general rule, divorce was exceedingly common. To get married a man had to have but one possession—a large brass urn for boiling water. This combination hearth and bankbook usually stood two or two and a half feet high and constituted a fairly valuable property. Nevertheless, the average man could acquire his urn without too much effort, and marriages were frequent.

To get a divorce a man had to provide his partner with a new outfit of clothing. Men tired of their wives did not demur at this penalty, and as for the women, the prospect of getting a new wardrobe made them more than acquiescent. But so strong was the monogamous instinct that divorced couples were constantly remarrying, for by the time a man had tired of his freedom, the woman had found that her clothes no longer made her the belle of the colony.

Ayesha, the consulate's washerwoman, was pointed out by Colonel

Lyall as an example. Thrice divorced from the same man, she was still fairly attractive, but the Colonel believed that her marrying days were over. At thirty her chances were no longer so bright, and her next remarriage would probably be her last.

Long talks and tennis with Colonel Lyall made Kashgar a pleasant interlude. One afternoon we went to the theatre, occupied by a strolling company of Chinese players from eastern China, who were making a two years' tour of the provinces. There was such a swarm of actors, so many plays in the repertoire, such a profusion of sets, that the company was able to maintain a continuous performance.

The plays were in Chinese, of course—the ancient, allegorical dramas that educated Chinese in the East knew by heart. The Turkis who came in droves to the open-air theatre in the center of Kashgar couldn't understand a word but this did not interfere with the fun. They marvelled aloud at the gorgeous sets, the show of silk and satin, and the flash of swords and hatchets. There were no seats, and so they shuffled around, stirring up clouds of dust.

By this time all my business had been dispatched and there was nothing to detain me further. Yet I was loath to leave the house that had been such a pleasant haven, and besides, the hot, dreary road between Kashgar and Marlbashi, where I had agreed to meet Cherrie, was not an agreeable prospect. It would take seven days to cover these 157 miles.

The July sun beat down mercilessly on the stretches of dry, alluvial soil and tamarisk jungle. I was no longer travelling in an araba because I had decided that, whatever the custom of the country (riding on an animal's back was infra dig.), and whatever the arguments for exertionless travel, the jolting of the cart was intolerable. Riding horseback was strenuous on these roads, but much faster.

Much of our travelling was now done in the cooler hours. Sometimes we rose at dawn and rode till eleven o'clock, an hour when the heat, coiling up from the brown, parched earth, was like a breath from a furnace door. The dust swirled in yellowish clouds, forming layers on my face, already running with sweat. There were swarms of flies and mosquitoes. Sometimes we passed a *beg* or some other member of the Chinese gentry jolting up and down the road in a cushion-filled mappa, while over him a servant brandished a switch to drive off the flies.

Occasionally we varied the routine by setting out at dusk and travelling through the night, and spending the days in one of the filthy inns. Night travel was favored by the Chinese, not only to escape the heat but to avoid bandits, who couldn't spot victims so easily in the darkness.

When my appetite began to fail, the melons were a life-saver. The evil deities who manage the climate of the Sinkiang plains forgot to put their blight on the melon, a refreshing and luscious food. Still, not being able to subsist on them entirely, I forced myself to eat heavier food—tough native chicken, and Indian chappati (a flat cake of un-leavened bread). Drinking the heavy, alkaline, silt-saturated water was another chore. The natives of this region had never seen clear water in their lives.

For some odd reason, the natives never suffered from cholera or similar plagues, though they had plenty of other troubles. A great proportion of the population had venereal diseases. These rarely reached a virulent form, however, and the victims managed to carry on their lives to a normal old age.

The natives were also afflicted with goiter, which was considered a normal human development. Colonel Lyall said he had asked a group of Turkis if a girl with a normal neck had any special attraction for them. On the contrary, they liked a mild goiter.

The prevalence of goiter in this district—much worse than in other parts of Asia—provides a problem for medical men. It seems to occur abundantly in certain regions and then, without rhyme or reason, to be absent from regions that present the same conditions. It is worst in the Khotan district, where about fifty per cent of the populace is afflicted. Next worst is the Yarkand district. It does not seem to exist south of Kargelik or north of Aksu. In some regions mainly women have it, in others mainly men.

On the seventh day out of Kashgar we came to the swampland district of Marlbashi, and out of the bogs came clouds of flies and mosquitoes. No matter where one turned the air sang with insects. By the time we had got within a mile of the town, our clothes were completely covered.

In Marlbashi I found Cherrie installed in a garden, and his tents and working equipment, to say nothing of the bright Kirghiz carpets strewn about, made a cozy picture. One of the tents had been lined with netting, and here was kept the rapidly growing collection. It was filled with purple-backed starlings, Hume's lesser whitethroat, Turkestan hill pigeon, Staliczka's kite, Severtzow's rose-finch, the Suget horned-lark, the Eastern yellow-billed chough, and dozens of others.

Cherrie was eager to get on. His collection was good and the damp, malarial climate had affected his health. At five the next morning we took the road for Aksu, Cherrie abandoning his araba to ride with me. It was now August, and the burning heat of the Turkestan plains was at its height. We went through town after town, many thickly populated, according to Turkestan standards, all providing squalid inns infested with flies, mosquitoes, and fleas, incubated by the swamps.

Yet we were forced to stay in the inns, when our tents would have been more comfortable and cooler. There was no room for tents. Wherever there was water, there was unutterable congestion. Dwellings and irrigated fields took up every square inch of space. Like the natives, we gravitated towards the water and, once there, took whatever accommodations we could find.

Our route took us through an outer part of the Takla Makan desert, where there were fewer oases and hence fewer inhabitants. We exchanged the insect pests for sandstorms that kept burning sand blowing into our faces hour after hour.

This desert land seemed to pass through recurrent cycles in its relation to man. The natives bled the rivers systematically to irrigate their fields. As the stream shrank in size, so did the jungle along its banks. As the jungle disappeared, the desert encroached on the fields. And finally the population was obliged to move away. Then the pendulum swung the other way. The irrigation canals filled with sand, the water, no longer diverted, rose higher in its proper channel; the jungle sprang up again, and presently conditions were tempting the natives back. These cycles had evidently been going on for ages.

We saw many examples of this process, the most conspicuous being small villages completely abandoned to the encroaching desert. The shapes of former dwellings were barely perceptible under their coating of sand.

The natives of this region got the idea that we were medical men. They came to us in droves, imploring us to cure their ailments. Eczema was the outward sign of more serious diseases. There were many cases of tumors and scrofula. At first we passed out medicines from our kit to any one who came to us. But soon it became apparent that we could strip ourselves of our last aspirin tablet, our last drop of iodine, without helping more than a tiny fraction of the ailing. In the end we were obliged to curtail the practice, handing out medicines only where we knew they would produce results.

It was a heart-breaking experience to have to reject scores of petitions every day, particularly when the unfortunates were certain that we possessed the power to cure them. But the truth of it was that for every case of eczema that required a simple prescription such as tallow and sulphur, there were dozens that defied the diagnostic skill of two men who were doctors only by virtue of Turkestan superstition.

We were still travelling along the Silk Road, even now a great commercial highway thronged with couriers and caravans. Many riders had gourds suspended from their shoulders—large ones for water, small ones for snuff and tobacco.

August 4 brought us to Aksu, a typical desert village of yellow mud houses, redeemed by many large, beautiful gardens where fruit trees and rose bushes grew around lotus ponds. The bazaar, too, was an amusing spot, with its great variety of merchandise such as bales of gaily-colored cotton cloth, exquisite saddle-bags, red leather boots, porcelain, embroidered headgear, silks, and rows of gleaming copper pots. The food sections, too, were lavish for this part of the world with their potatoes, cabbages, and ears of corn. To our eyes, the most attractive stalls were laden with golden melons and apricots.

We found ourselves in a large garden of fruit trees and rose bushes. The ground was covered with thick Kazak carpets, and here and there were cushions and tables covered with white cloths. While we were getting installed, a messenger arrived with gifts from the amban: tea, sweetmeats, and three chickens. In a few hours the amban himself came to invite us to dinner. The Roosevelts, it appeared, had rushed through the town without stopping for the usual formalities, but to placate the officials had said we could dine with the amban directly we arrived.

So it was that we met the best of the ambans—a charming, gracious Chinese of the old aristocratic mandarin type. He was tall, and beautifully dressed in black and yellow silk. His greeting showed dignity and affability mixed in the proper proportions.

The dinner, consisting of many Chinese delicacies brought from the East, was not too taxing, for this amban had had some experience with Occidentals. Host to a great many travellers and explorers, he had picked up much information of the outside world, and this had sharpened his perspective on Sinkiang. The result was several hours of informative and amusing conversation.

Beyond Aksu there were only fifteen more miles of road and then we would have to shift from arabas to pack trains as the trail turned up to the Tien Shan or Mountains of Heaven. The spur of road ended at Aksu-Koneh Shah, where there was a delay of three days while the necessary pack animals were rounded up.

For two days of our stay here we were perpetually serenaded by a four-piece orchestra that established itself in the garden next to our house. Crowds collected; their idea of entertainment seemed to be walking up and down the garden in the broiling sun. The hedge protected us from the mob but not from the music. All the livelong day the orchestra kept up its infernal noise—not only the same tune but the same three chords. Every time we left the enclosure the natives would stand and stare at us in awe. And when the performance was over, we had to pay for the unwelcome attention by handing out tips to the band.

On the third day our horses arrived, fresh, well-fed, in thoroughly good condition. At the same time a courier appeared with a message from the Roosevelts saying that they were remaining in the Tien Shan until September 20.

The trail led upward, and one march took us through a desert, through grasslands, and through cultivated land along the banks of streams. Then, on the second day, we entered a new, radiant world, the world of the lower Tien Shan mountains. Instead of hot, yellow sands, we could see plains of green grass and forests of spruce above us. Instead of filthy oases, there were swift, clean rivers, and brooks streaming down the hillsides and rushing across the plains. It was a clean, shining land, undespoiled by human beings.

In the quiet, cool evening we climbed a gentle slope, and within view of the mountain ridges, dark and aloof now in the gathering dusk, we breathed a sigh of relief at being restored to a world where nature was permitted to operate in a sane, orderly way. Our tents were put up on a stretch of green grass. The air was fresh and invigorating. Not a sound broke the silence. This was the beginning of the Promised Land!

Moving on the next day, we came to a steeper terrain that showed abundant signs of animal life. We saw gazelles from a remote distance, and footprints of mountain sheep, probably a new species. Among the birds were the white-bellied dipper, the Tien Shan nutcracker, the Isabelline chat, the Eastern wheatear, the Tien Shan bluetit, the Eastern linnet, and the greenish willow-warbler.

The principal range of the Tien Shan was now directly ahead of us, but there was no straight approach to the mountains. We had to follow the Muzart River along a tortuous eighteen-mile course leading through grasslands and groves of willow and cottonwood.

This particular region had a drawback, however, and a serious one.

Great green horseflies, at least three-quarters of an inch long, buzzed around in swarms. While riding we were not molested, but the minute we left the horses, the flies were a serious pest. The Kirghiz ignored them, but Cherrie and I spent a lot of energy swishing.

At one point where the broad valley narrowed down to a mere gap, a half mile broad, there stood an old Chinese rampart that in days of old must have been an impregnable defense against invasion from the north. Its solid walls were surmounted by loopholes.

At another point we had to cross the rushing stream by means of an ancient bridge with a floor of rough-hewn poplar logs and fragile railings. We dismounted and led the horses over one by one, a rather amusing experience; it was like dancing on air. Bridges of this type in Asia usually shake like old-fashioned rope hammocks.

When we first saw the Muzart River it was a broad, rushing torrent, enlarged by numerous tributaries, but farther north, above these tributaries, it was much diminished in size. High above us were the mountains. They were a curious sight. At many points their steep sides were as barren as the high Himalayas, but the summits were tufted with giant spruce, and at nightfall and other times of poor visibility, the trees created an eerie optical illusion: while the mountains faded away in the dim light, the trees seemed to be growing in the sky, quite without support.

The caravan men gathered wood and grass, packing them on the horses' backs. For the next three days we would be passing through a treeless, grassless area. The green horseflies had now vanished.

The next day brought us into a freak district evidently never touched by rain. The sky above us was ringed with swarming black clouds pouring water on all the surrounding land, but in our valley the slopes glittered in a hot, brilliant sunlight. There was not a tree, not a blade of grass to be seen. From the beginning of time, it seemed, the rain clouds had spurned this valley.

Emerging from this pocket of land we ran into a driving rain that continued all afternoon. Arrived at the foot of the Muzart glacier, we sat huddled in a cave for two hours waiting for the storm to blow over so the men could set up camp. A smoky fire enabled us to dry our clothes, but it was a cold and dismal evening. Here, at the foot of the glacier, the river was a narrow stream that seemed to run with milk instead of water. It was a picturesque sight, the foaming, white stream rushing through the rocky channel. The color of the water was due to the marble river bed.

Near the glacier I saw several ibex on a sheer mountain wall. The distance being too great for shooting, I tried to photograph them with a telescopic lens but they eluded me. Serious as my intentions were, it was impossible not to feel joy at their escape.

What a magnificent animal is this largest of the world's ibex! Dweller of the high and inaccessible places of the earth, from his rarefied abode he has acquired incredible speed, grace, agility, and hardihood. Seen from afar, scampering from crag to crag, he presents one of the most beautiful sights in the animal kingdom. No less appealing is a close-up picture showing the lovely sweep of horns, the sleek, clean body, and the air of preternatural alertness.

There are four species of ibex, a sub-genus of the goat family. They grow as high as forty inches, and show a nearly uniform coloration in gray, yellowish brown, and darker brown, shading to lighter hues on throat, belly, and inside the legs. Their beards are usually heavy, and their roughly knobbed horns often measure more than fifty inches along the inside curve and eleven to twelve inches in greatest girth. All species inhabit mountain tops, descending in winter just far enough to find uncovered pasturage. They are extremely prolific, and survive because of their fleetness and great resistance to cold. The particular species we sought in the Tien Shan is known as the *capra sibirica*, incomparably the finest type, I think, after seeing the others and hunting the famous Wallia ibex in the Simien mountains.

A more important matter than the ibex now engaged us, for the route lay across a slanting field of ice ranging from half a mile to a mile wide—a fantastic, glacial region of ice and boulders, scattered about in masses as high as houses. Fissures and holes in the ice and gravel surface were as deep as thirty and forty feet. And all around this was a creamy glacier—sheer walls of blue-green ice rising to prodigious heights. This was the Muzart glacier.

For hours we followed local guides who seemed to know this waste like the palms of their hands, though it was an intricate maze, through gigantic piles of ice and boulders. We turned and twisted, moved up and down, walking our horses all the while. Sometimes it was necessary to hack our steps with axes over the ice hillocks. In crossing glaciers the great hazard is a storm, for then visibility is lost and the shifting snow on the surface makes it easy to lose a trail. Camping in the ice till the disturbance is over is the only solution, but offers no pleasant prospect for man or beast. Against this contingency our caravan carried plenty of firewood, which fortunately was not required.

At various points we encountered subsidiary glaciers covering narrow valleys, and we also saw skeletons of horses, now whitened bones. Finally, two-thirds of the way to the top of the glacier, there was an opening leading to a narrow valley, free from ice and snow. Here we said good-bye to the glacier guides.

Through the valley ran the North Muzart River, glacier-fed and having no connection with the Muzart we had followed below the glacier. Its banks were lined with trees.

A bend in the North Muzart, a two-hour march from the glacier, brought us into a beautiful, fertile valley, covered with green grass, dotted here and there with groves of willows. Contrasting with the bland green of the willow groves was the darker hue of spruce on the hillsides. We were at last in the central Tien Shan, this particular region being called the Hun Sala.

The more I looked at it, the more I was inclined to call it the most beautiful land I had ever seen. Time has not effaced that impression. Nature has, perhaps, created more spectacular effects elsewhere, and other lands may show more decorative aspects. But here all of Nature's subtlety seemed to have been expended on creating a harmonious whole. The rippling valley merged with the soaring mountains, and the spruce-scented air at this elevation of 9000 feet was fresh and luminous under the bright summer sky. The land deserved its name: Tien Shan, the Mountains of Heaven.

About the same latitude as New York City, this country is so fertile, so eminently suited to human habitation, that one might have expected to see a teeming population. But all we saw was a few auls of Kirghiz yurts off in the distance. The nomadic Kirghiz are by nature well disposed towards other wanderers; so we found a cheerful reception, with refreshments of kumiss and fragrant, fresh-baked bread. This was a good spot to pitch camp and rest, for Cherrie was still feeling seedy from the bad water of the Turkestan plains, aggravated, perhaps, by the tremendous exertion of crossing the glacier.

While Cherrie rested for three days in this garden spot, I hunted the ibex. One morning a group appeared on a crag two or three hundred yards away and then vanished in the twinkling of an eye. Up and down we went, across one rocky shelf after another—back-breaking labor! My admiration went out to the Kirghiz guide, whose heavy felt boots moved with sure ease from one rocky perch to another. Some sixth sense seemed to tell him whether a rock was firm. He never slipped, but I often picked the wrong footing and fell. Here and there my feet sent showers of loose rock clattering down the mountainside with a prodigious echo that must have warned every ibex for miles around. The Kirghiz moved smoothly and silently, sometimes indicating the rocks I was to use as stepping stones. The net result of three days' work was two brief glimpses of ibex, certainly one of the most elusive animals in the world.

Ten miles of marching through a narrow, well-wooded valley brought us into an open, grass-covered region watered by the North Muzart. Here, lured by good grazing, numbers of Kazak nomads had set up their yurts. We were received warmly in true nomad fashion; the women went to work over their samovars and produced a delicious meal of tea, kumiss, freshly baked bread, and boiled eggs. Our hosts were such a friendly, vital lot that I couldn't restrain my picture-taking. They were not camera-shy, particularly one six-year-old who paraded around naked while his elders were all bundled up in warm clothes.

The men wore their typical caftans, long flowing robes, held in at the waist with rolled girdles. Many of these were heavily padded and trimmed with fur. Hats were also lined with fur, the linings dipping down over the ears. Their flat, brown, Mongol faces and little oblique eyes lighted up instantly with friendly smiles. The women were friendly, too, if a little distant. A typical costume was a flowing black skirt of brilliant coloring, a black bodice, and an elaborately embroidered bonnet from which fell a long veil. Nearly all the women wore beautiful silver rings.

The yurts were plentifully supplied with the famous Kazak rugs, but one glance indicated their varying quality. Later it was explained to us that the deterioration of their rugs comes from the fact that Turki traders appear among them from time to time and undertake the coloration with commercial dyes. The process is quick and cheap, and the Kazaks are unable to resist.

The Kazaks are, of course, a Mongol tribe, and, like the Kirghiz, have a wide circuit. The word "Kazak" means "vagabond."

The valley around this settlement had no game, but Cherrie had fairish luck with his collecting. New additions included the Pamir horned lark and Mongolian desert finch. Another march of twelve miles took us into the valley of the Tekkes River, where, in beautifully wooded country at an altitude of about 5000 feet, we reached Shatta, a settlement of Kirghiz yurts huddled around a wooden fort. Shatta is 149 miles from Aksu, and only fifteen miles from the border of Russian Turkestan.

The Shatta fort was headed by a Chinese officer with the powers of an amban. He invited us to tea, and a number of his Kirghiz retainers, with whom he seemed on friendly terms, trooped in and sat at his feet. Like greedy dogs they watched us drink the tea and eat various sweetmeats. When we had finished they snapped up the leftovers.

The officer showed great interest in our maps; so I brought out one of his own district. He studied it with a knowing air and said, "Please point out where America is." His dainty little Chinese wife now appeared and greeted us smilingly, with so much poise that one might have imagined meeting white men was a routine part of her day. Arrangements were made to set us up in a yurt, nicely supplied with good felt carpets.

Our friend, the officer, ran the most slovenly military post I had ever seen. The soldiers wore loose fatigue clothes, and only their caps and rifles indicated their profession. Except for a desultory bugler blowing taps twice a day, I never saw a sign of military activity.

Late in the afternoon a party of soldiers rushed into our yurt and from their confused shouting one might have thought an enemy was swooping down on the country. It turned out that a flock of sparrows had settled down outside, and Cherrie was being informed his big chance had come. The soldiers were rewarded, for Cherrie used a 41-gauge shell in a 16-gauge shotgun, and the resulting explosion not only killed a dozen birds but gave the town the thrill of its life.

The chief returned after dinner. It was clear we were going to see a great deal of him; an inordinate craving for coffee, I suspected, was the motive for his visits. That night, unfortunately, we happened to be drinking chocolate. He accepted it, but his face sagged with disappointment. He looked longingly at the water bottle, believing, no doubt, that it was arrak, but one gulp from it made him cough and choke. His expression indicated it was his first and last drink of water.

During the next few days we were the center of attraction for the villagers. They all managed to include our yurt in their evening strolls, while the officer popped in at all hours to get coffee, to use our field-glasses, and to look at pictures. A few old copies of the *National Geographic Magazine* seemed to give him a lot of pleasure, and his favorite picture was one of New York by night. Killing time was evidently his chief concern. He was always willing to pose for photographs, but first his loose Chinese gown had to be exchanged for full military regalia, an olive-drab uniform, high boots, sword, and two medals. Every afternoon he took a ride in a victoria. Why and where he bought it was a mystery we never cleared up. It must have been

Street scene typical of the villages passed on our route

One of our arabas waiting to be loaded up for the day's journey

A group of Turkis we passed on the road as we neared Marlbashi

Theodore Roosevelt, George Cherrie, and the author, breakfasting in the
Turkestan plains on the return journey

Part of our caravan weaving its intricate way over the black gravel and ice of the Muzart Glacier

A Kirghiz yurt in the beautiful valley of the Tekkes River, in the central
Tien Shan Mountains

In the Tien Shan, native trails led along the valley, by open grassy parks
and through virgin forests of spruce

carried into the valley by pack train, each piece tied to a horse's back. It was a perfectly useless possession, since there were few roads, and a ride in the fields would have broken the springs in no time. But every afternoon, barring rain, the chief made a triumphal tour of the village streets, a circuit of three or four hundred yards.

His wife was also a frequent visitor. Attired in blue and white striped trousers and a blue jumper, she would stroll into our yurt, examine all our belongings, watch Cherrie skinning birds, and then take up our field-glasses, which seemed to be her particular pet. As she turned round and round, examining every segment of the horizon, she would murmur in a dreamy, ecstatic voice. She had never seen anything so wonderful.

This was a good station for Cherrie. The birds were already migrating southward, and he caught several interesting specimens, among them an Eastern rook, Eastern skylark, Sharpe's hooded crow, and a Tarim thick-billed reed bunting. We also got an eagle for the collection, but not through our own efforts. One of the villagers had trapped the bird and had tied it to the roof of a yurt as a proud possession, for the Kirghiz for centuries have used eagles as auxiliaries in hunting, just as other peoples use the falcon. A Chinese soldier, possessed of the devil, killed the bird, to the grief of the owner. We succeeded in getting it, an excellent specimen.

Every day I took rides in the surrounding country. It was a glorious land, the air fresh and cool, the rolling green prairies stretching off to mountainous horizons. The mountains were well-covered with timber, and even the prairie was dotted with spruce, some growing as high as eighty feet. There were a few Kirghiz settlements in the district, and they were a joy to visit, with their friendly, brown-skinned inhabitants always arrayed in brilliant costumes.

Our last day in Shatta was memorable for a great Kirghiz sheep feast. Several iron cauldrons whose top circumference must have been ten feet were set up on tripods over fires of spruce logs. The sheep, slaughtered the night before and cut up into pieces, were tossed into boiling water, and it was not long before the air took on a fragrant aroma for the twenty-five hosts and their two white guests. Old women were in charge of the cooking, but the men co-operated by sniffing and asking for samples—"just to see if it's cooked enough." The cooks willingly handed out the samples in cups, but they had their own ideas about the time necessary to do a good job on the stew.

When it was ready, in the late afternoon, the men sat down in a ring to be served by the women. Low tables had been set up for us, supplied with bowls and plates of salt. The feast was well worth waiting for, and the Kirghiz lunged in with enthusiasm and joy, chewing vigorously, sprinkling salt on their pieces, licking the bones, and sucking the marrow. It was the noisiest feast I had ever attended and also one of the best, for the crones had turned out a marvellous, succulent stew. The heads of the animals, kept intact, were saved to the last, when even the most abstemious eater knew he had overdone it. Nevertheless, there was no lessening of enthusiasm. When at last it was over and every man, woman and child had succumbed to torpor, I saw that it was the most thorough job of demolition one could imagine. Bones had been broken and stripped of the last fiber of edible substance, so that even a vulture would have gone hungry.

Our travels during the latter part of August and the first part of September took us into one of the loveliest parts of the Tien Shan, or for that matter, of the globe. It was a tranquil world of rolling grassy plains, of meadows carpeted with buttercups or more vivid alpina of red, blue, and mauve, of swift, clean streams and forests of black spruce, all rimmed by the snow-clad mountains. The air was heavily scented with spruce.

The auls of the nomads always made a thrilling sight in this upland paradise. We could see them from afar, the round-domed tents, usually decorated with brilliant embroideries or appliqué work. There were herds on the hillsides. Closer approach showed us the children playing near the tents, the fat, shaggy dogs, the ponies with silver-decorated saddles and bridles. The nomads were invariably hospitable, offering a meal of mutton and rice or at least some kumiss, served in a pewter or silver bowl.

In this region we met another tribe of nomads, the famous Kalmuks. Like the Kirghiz and Kazaks, they have brown skins, Mongol eyes, and high cheekbones. But the Kalmuks were easy to distinguish, for they were shorter and squatter, and wore pigtails. The first colony of Buddhist Kalmuks we saw had a way with fur that turned into handsome costumes. The caftans of men and women were trimmed with red fox, snow leopard, lynx, and lamb, arranged in beautiful combinations of color and texture. Their smart-looking hats represented a fortune to the outsider, for they made prodigal use of mink, sable, and other valuable furs.

The Kalmuks were no less generous than their neighbors, and many a good meal we had of fresh bread and kumiss.

Although the Kalmuks are Buddhists, they live in the Tien Shan on peaceful terms with the Mohammedan Kirghiz and Kazaks. All three tribes have been roving, pastoral peoples since the beginning of time. They are constantly on the move in search of grazing. The Kalmuks, however, have a tragic history. During their greatest migration, several hundred thousand of them moved westward and settled in Russia. In the middle of the seventeenth century they became discontented with their lot—other tribes were persecuting them and efforts were being made to snuff out their Buddhist faith—so they resolved on a secret flight to China. When this actually got under way, Kirghiz tribesmen harassed them from the rear and other tribes attacked them as they moved eastward. One of the most considerable attempts in history to transplant a whole nation ended in a débâcle: only one third survived.

While livestock is the principal concern of these nomad tribes, we saw along the Tekkes River many fields of wheat, oats, mustard, and hay, now golden yellow as summer deepened. All three tribes were well fed, and their physiques showed it. Life-sustaining food came to them without effort. Meat, grains, and vegetables were to be had in abundance, and even fruit trickled in from the south. Their large consumption of milk, cheese, and kumiss contributed to their health and vitality.

All the tribesmen were more at home in the saddle than on their feet. Used to horses from infancy, they found it more natural to ride than to walk, and a man who had to cover three hundred feet between his yurt and another man's would, without giving it a second's thought, throw his foot over the back of the nearest horse. The horses, a healthy strapping breed, were as good as their riders. They could take the steepest mountain trails without faltering, and places that would have sent the average horse spinning down to destruction merely inspired the Tien Shan horses to a little extra caution. They understood the technique of sliding and slipping down hillsides of slippery earth or rocks.

The bull is a more domesticated animal in this region than it is with us. Never penned up, it is taught to become docile and obedient, and is used for many domestic purposes. Everywhere boys and women were seen riding bulls; they used saddles and stirrups and guided the animal by a rope tied to his nose. Tien Shan bulls could climb steep mountain paths, heavily laden, with sure-footed ease.

The Kirghiz, Kazaks and Kalmuks inhabit a tight little world of their own, and never realize how lucky they are compared with the Turkis who inhabit the sweltering, dusty plains to the south. The Tien Shan region with its fertility, beneficent climate, and great unoccupied areas has escaped the attention of the outside world, a curious fact in a world clamoring for expansion room, for this land in all likelihood could support masses of people. The grassy plains could hold endless herds, and the fertile valleys could become vast granaries. Of course it is possible that this region once nourished a richer, more integrated civilization long before the time of the present nomads. We have an inadequate knowledge of Turkestan and particularly the Tien Shan region before the Christian era.

The country may provide good opportunities for archeological research. One could start in, for instance, in the Shatta region with a series of monoliths inscribed with Chinese characters, or a series of old stone images about four feet high, some broken, the fragments lying in the grass. The natives had no idea of their origin, and the features of the images certainly did not delineate the present dwellers in the Mountains of Heaven. Again, there are great mounds, probably ancient burial grounds.

One trait the Kirghiz, Kazaks, and Kalmuks possessed in common was an astounding ignorance of geography. It was impossible to get accurate directions, and very often we were unable to find out the name of a locality from its inhabitants. Some of our men spoke the local dialects, so there could have been no difficulty on the score of language. Once when we asked, "What is the name of this place?" we received the reply, "Agias." No sooner was the word spoken than a squabble broke out among the villagers. Our astonished men explained to us, "Some say this is Agias and others say Agias is five potai up the valley." A potai, incidentally, was about one and a half miles on level ground, but could be less when the terrain was hard to cover.

Agias or no, the place looked auspicious for hunting; so before dawn the next morning I set off in the mountains with three Kazak guides. It was pretty steep going, but I was dissuaded from dismounting by the guides, who put no limit on a horse's climbing ability.

On a jagged stretch of open ground we stopped and made a plan. One Kazak had a Russian rifle, an antique affair with a folding pair of wooden prongs attached to the barrel that was used as a support when the hunter was shooting. Two of us, then, would take up separate stations and prepare to knock off game while the others beat the spruce forest. I was posted on a height whence I could see two long tree-lined vistas. In a few minutes lusty shouts came from below, and quite clearly animals could be heard rushing through the woods. But not one came within my vision. The Kazaks pretended to know the direction the deer had taken, but a two-hour search ended in failure.

The next morning we again started in the dawn. The first hour I collected a Siberian roe deer, largest of its species in the world. Later I saw four bears—an adult and three cubs. One shot wounded the adult, who fell down a slope and rolled into a stream, while the cubs, which would have completed a marvellous museum group, disappeared into the bush. Scrambling down to the stream, I found the bolt of my gun had jammed but I had time to work it loose and finish off the wounded animal, a fine specimen of the Asiatic gray bear, hitherto undescribed.

During the afternoon I caught a glimpse of a wild boar almost hidden in bushes, but my shot evidently missed. Then, when the Kazak and I were about to plunge into the thicket, fully conscious that it was a risky thing to do, the boar obligingly came out and stood thirty feet away, enabling us to dispatch him without effort.

The Kazaks were in a mutinous mood when the time came to take the kills back to camp. Being Moslems and hence opposed to touching swine, they would have nothing to do with the boar and I had to get the assistance of some Kalmuks, who were aided in turn by the Chinese soldiers who had escorted us ever since we left Shatta. It took a great effort to get the 300-pound boar back to camp.

The next morning, rejoicing over my bear, boar, and roe, we went off to join the Roosevelts, who were camping at Mointa, twenty-eight miles up the valley. We found them camped by a brook in a cool, lovely spot at the edge of a grassy meadow gently rising to a horizon of green woods. Here, at an altitude of 7000 feet, there were no inhabitants.

Over two bottles of champagne, given to the Roosevelts by some amban who had received them from Russia, we exchanged notes on our experiences. After many reverses, many tiresome climbs in regions where the animals seemed gifted not only with agility but a sixth sense to tell them that man had invaded their domain, the Roosevelts had bagged specimens of the ovis Karelini, the wapiti, the ibex, and the brown bear. These, combined with my bear, boar, and roe, and Cherrie's magnificent set of birds, constituted a good haul. In certain instances female specimens of the animals were missing, but we hoped that these might be captured before we left the Mountains of Heaven.

Our plan was now to move in a southeasterly direction through the Muzart pass, through Aksu and Marlbashi and on to Kashgar. Here we would part again, and while the Roosevelts turned southward to the Pamirs and India, Cherrie and I would add another chapter to the trip by returning through Russia—Andijan, Samarkand, over the Caspian Sea, overland from Baku to Batum, and over the Black Sea to Istanbul.

In the quiet evening while we sipped the amban's precious champagne, chilled in the near-by stream, cries and shrieks tore the air. Simultaneously we all jumped to our feet. Fifty feet away our men were having a free-for-all. We could see flying fists and hear the shouts of the fighters. A Punjabi was lying on the ground, and two Kashmiri were bent over him defying him to rise.

We ordered them to stop but when no one heeded we used fists ourselves. When the fight stopped, the brawlers stood before us with dishevelled hair, and torn, dirt-covered garments. A few were bleeding.

The Roosevelts were mystified but Cherrie and I knew what had happened. Between the Punjabi and Kashmiri there was an undying enmity, going back to racial antipathies. Out on the trail, in a life of utterly new conditions, they had managed to control their malevolence, but it was only a truce, which we knew would eventually end. The Kashmiris murmured now that the Punjabis always seemed to get the pick of everything. In any equal struggle I would have bet on the Punjabis, who were better men. But in our outfit Ahmad Shah and Feroze were confronted with eight enemies.

Before the evening was over, the fight broke out again and we were again obliged to quell it with our fists. It was obvious now that the feud would never be patched up, and we kept the guns under our eyes. The next morning Feroze and Ahmad Shah were told to return to Shatta and wait for us there.

Before leaving Mointa we had one more hunt for roe deer in a forest of lofty, black spruce trees. It was an enchanted spot, this primeval wood that had remained through the centuries untouched by the hand of man. The trees, beautifully spaced, rose straight and tall to the sky, with the soaring perspective of Gothic columns. Flashes of blue from the sky filtered down through the dark green boughs, and the air was saturated with the scent of spruce. Wild pigeons flitted from bough to bough.

Wolf and snow leopard tracks appeared, but we had never a sight of these animals. A drive by the Kazak guides resulted in one good specimen, the female counterpart of the male Siberian roe we already possessed.

Heading now for Shatta, we stopped off the second day in search of female specimens to complete the groups. Neither the Roosevelts nor I got anything after two days' hunting in strenuous country, but our head shikkari balanced accounts by bringing in a female wapiti.

On the way to Shatta we saw a picturesque Kalmuk wedding-party crossing the plain. All were mounted, the men in one group, the women in another. The bride, wearing a high, pointed hat, a brilliantly embroidered cloak trimmed with fur, and a great deal of silver jewelry, looked like pictures of Isabella the Catholic making her triumphal entry into Granada. Her two attendants carried banners suspended from long poles. The men of the party were no less brilliant and dashing in their long, quilted caftans of brown and red, trimmed with fur, and their peaked caps of rich sable. Saddles added another festive touch, red leather and embroidered blankets gleaming with silver and pewter ornaments.

As a preliminary to the actual ceremony, the women formed a sort of guard around the bride. The groom galloped across the field, carrying out the traditional feint of capture. All this made a good film.

Rain blew up, and we got soaked riding into Shatta. Our old friend the officer was a long time in receiving us, however, and the reason for the delay became apparent when he appeared in his best uniform, sword in hand and decorations shimmering on his breast.

He provided us with fine fur coats and a good meal of fresh bread, kumiss, tea and baskets of luscious fruit that had just come up from the plains—melons, grapes, apples, and apricots. He also invited us for breakfast the next day.

From Shatta the Punjabis were sent back to India alone. It turned out that in taking employment with us they were secretly committed to provide the British with information about Soviet propaganda methods in Sinkiang. We had no reason to feel that the Chinese would have resented this, but after all we expected to travel through Russian Turkestan, and it didn't seem likely that the presence of two informers in our entourage would help us to obtain Russian privileges.

Many caravans appeared on the trail as we got nearer the Muzart pass, for this was the busiest season of the year, when southbound groups took their horses and sheep down to markets in the plains and the returning groups carried back the results of their barter: blankets, rugs, riding boots, and baskets of the marvellous fruit.

A two days' march from Shatta brought us to the site Cherrie and I had used for a camp after crossing the Muzart. It was the last day of September; the air was cool and the surrounding mountains were blanketed in snow.

One more day's hunt was decided on before crossing the pass. After several hours spent in climbing sharp ridges and descending steep gullies, a herd of tawny ibex appeared in a valley below. Settling down on the rocks, well hidden from the herd, we counted fifteen animals. It was agreed that Kermit would shoot first as a signal. His shot was followed by a terrific barrage that sent the animals rushing to the opposite side of the mountain. We brought down five. Our collection was complete and we could now start the pass. Good fortune awaited us at the Muzart, for the weather was exceptionally good. Men and beasts got over that towering wilderness of rock and ice without trouble.

It was sad leaving the Tien Shan, a lovely, unspoiled land. We had our last view of it under the best conditions—bright autumnal sunshine flooding the mountains, the spruce forests, and the wide, grassy plains.

The road to Marlbashi was not a succession of well-loved houses and inns. The most that could be said for it was that the weather was more bearable than when we first saw the country under the July sun. The day temperatures were cooler, and the nights permitted a decent rest. Moreover, the flies and mosquitoes had abated. The knowledge gained from our first trip told us which inns (serais) to avoid. The substitutes were not always successful, but we did succeed in avoiding the worst.

It was a fast trip, for the Roosevelts were returning to Kashmir by way of the Hunza pass, a difficult business at that season of the year. With the days growing shorter and the late autumn winds lashing down from the mountains, they were certain to suffer greatly from the cold. But before reaching the Hunza they would pass through the Pamirs to seek out the ovis poli, chief objective of the whole expedition.

Aksu-Koneh Shah detained us briefly because the amban insisted on giving a lavish, boisterous party at which the guests temporarily forgot the ovis poli and the merry host dallied with the idea of chucking Turkestan for New York.

At this point we came to the spur of road, and pack trains were exchanged for arabas. No more mappas, however. We were all of us sick of the miserable, jolting little carts and preferred horseback.

Down from the mountains we came into the spinney-covered plain, and on through Aksu and out of the plains into real desert. As we neared Marlbashi, the land sloped downward and the thermometer moved upward. This brought us back on the ancient Asiatic highway between Pekin and Bagdad. One pest had definitely disappeared from the zone of infamous serais, dirt, and bad water: the flies and mosquitoes had called it a season.

At the hamlet of Oku Msar, one march short of Marlbashi, the Roosevelts left us. They would have to make speed, whereas Cherrie and I could take our time through this region in order to have a last fling at the birds. Cherrie's collection now numbered hundreds of specimens, but it would be still better by the time he finished.

We got through Marlbashi without dining with the amban and took the road to Kashgar, something I had been dreading for a long time. I hadn't forgotten how the fierce sun of July had scorched the desert, how the dust rolled in clouds and the air seemed made of invisible flame. But now at the beginning of autumn, the days were cooler and the nights afforded rest.

One new annoyance, however, was the swarms of mongrel dogs that beset us in the villages. There was evidently something offensive in the smell of white men, for they never failed to pursue us, snarling and yapping. We could never take a walk without bringing a whip for protection. While most were cowardly brutes, easily driven off, one pursued us till Cherrie, exasperated, took out his gun and laid the beast low with a blast of small shot.

A village called Junge Abad provided a little excitement when our caravan men elected to set up camp in a small square in front of the mosque. A delegation of bearded elders came down to complain. It was sacrilegious, they thought, to set up tents near Allah's dwelling. The elders recited their beads, but the Kashmiris went right on setting up the tents.

Something that should have offended Allah far more was a filthy pond covered with beetles and scum. This was the town's main water supply, and how the natives escaped destruction from drinking the water was a poser for bacteriologists. I saw one woman bring down a heap of dirty bowls, wash them in the pond, and then fill up her bucket for drinking purposes. The natives never bothered to boil water unless it was used for tea.

All along the road I thought fondly of the British consulate in Kashgar, for the memory of its cool, white-washed walls was a consolation out in the heat and dust of the plains. I knew, however, that Colonel Lyall was there no longer, and his successor might not be so eager to welcome a pair of begrimed travellers. But Major Gillan, the new consul-general, accompanied by Mrs. Gillan, gave us a warm welcome. A cool, clean room, a bath, a change of clothes, and a visit to the barber impressed us forcefully with the joys of civilization.

And now there was a most important piece of business confronting us. A Russian consulate had been established, since my other visit to Kashgar, and the consul must be asked to approve our journey through Russian Turkestan. The old, palatial building, once the Russian imperial consulate, was just being put into order for the first representative sent to Kashgar by the Soviet government. We asked to see the consul.

Mr. Doumpiss, a man of about forty, sat behind a huge desk, looking like a stage Bolshevik. He had a poker face with blank eyes, but his hands were highly expressive. They were thin, nervous hands, which were forever fingering his mustache, putting on or taking off his pince-nez. We were willing to trust him as far as we could throw him.

Because we did not speak Russian, Mr. Doumpiss summoned the vice-consul, Mr. Krisselhoff, whose main purpose in life seemed to be to maintain his dignity. He was still in his thirties, a man with a naturally open face, trying to look mysterious. He spoke excellent English. After our passports had been examined, he told us that the visas had expired. This was a tiresome and annoying piece of information. Six months before, the Russian consulate in London had heard all about our plans and had assured us that the visas were good for a year. But Mr. Krisselhoff was positive. He wanted to know how it happened that we were just finding this out.

Neither of us could read Russian, of course, and we had accepted the word of the people in London that the visa was in order. Still, none of this seemed serious till Mr. Doumpiss announced emphatically that he had no power to prolong visas. He must ask instructions from Moscow. He would send a wireless through the Chinese station in Kashgar. Asked how long this would take, he shrugged his shoulders.

This placed us in a bad spot. There had never seemed to be any question about the trip through Russian Turkestan, but now, if the visas were not extended, we should be obliged to turn southward to India through the Karakorum pass at a season when snowstorms were inevitable. With our immense luggage, it would be a dangerous journey.

The days passed, and as we returned again and again to the consulate, the answer was always the same: no word from Moscow. Our anxiety grew, for if we were doomed to retrace our steps through the Karakorum, every day's delay added to the danger. There we waited, twiddling our thumbs while Moscow made up its mind.

If it hadn't been for the uncertainty, it would have been a happy time. The weather was bright and sunshiny by day, cool by night. The insect pests were gone. And it was a pleasure to remember that the plains were behind us. The Gillans were thoughtful hosts and not the least of the diversions they provided was the daily tennis game.

We visited Kashgar's Chinese governor, the taotai, who returned our call by driving up to the consulate in a brougham. Our ramblings took us to the bazaar, to the Marconi station four miles out in the country and to the Moravian mission, a large, comfortable stone structure where four missionaries taught trades to the natives, trying at the same time to convert them to Christianity. Other idle hours were devoted to my series of photographs illustrating life in Kashgar and to a special movie reel for Major and Mrs. Gillan, who planned to send it home to their relatives in Scotland. There were plenty of things to do and under other circumstances we should have enjoyed doing them. But in this welter of uncertainty, minor pleasures began to pall. Only tennis was a steady consolation. To add to my discomfiture, I felt we were imposing on the Gillans' hospitality. When I say that this notion never had the slightest word or glance of confirmation from them, I express the full measure of my appreciation.

A week after our arrival, invitations came to attend the formal opening of the Soviet consulate, now somewhat restored to its old grandeur. If this had been the most boring party on earth, I would have accepted. What's more, I wrote a note asking if I might take a film of the reception and received an affirmative reply.

The palatial façade of the consulate—by far the biggest building in Kashgar—was decorated with three enormous red flags and a picture of Lenin. A big crowd had collected to gape, for, however proletarian his sympathies, Mr. Doumpiss had invited none but "the best people" to his shindig. We pushed our way through a crowd of Turkis and were taken to a large hall opposite the entrance where the consul, center of a large group, was wearing his best Cheshire-cat smile.

All the guests were assigned to tables for a snack of tea, cakes, and candy. We sat with two Hindus. There were other tables for Chinese and Mohammedans.

The next act took place on the front terrace, where a group of Turkis, residents of the region who had been Russian subjects under the old regime, presented the consul with a magnificent Turki coat of rich, dark brown wool embellished with valuable lynx and sable trimmings. The donors said their loyalties were still with Russia, and Mr. Doumpiss looked down at his hands and up at the speakers as if he couldn't tell which thrilled him more, the coat or the loyalties. More speeches were followed by the presentation of bread and salt, the traditional Russian ritual.

Incited to a speech of his own, the consul addressed hoi polloi, still streaming around by the hundreds. Since he spoke in Russian they could understand no more than could I. They listened with blank faces, but even when the speech was translated into Turki there was no perceptible rise in enthusiasm. The consul's theme song, I learned later, was "Russia, the friend of the poor in every land."

Enthusiasm picked up somewhat at the hoisting of a big Soviet flag, the hammer and sickle embroidered in gold, for this at least provided something to beguile the eye. The ceremony was accompanied by a strident native band, composed exclusively of cornets, playing regional music. A special place was provided for me and I obtained many feet of excellent film. The outdoor show was now completed; the consul had done his duty by the proletariat.

Inside, the women of the consulate, Mrs. Doumpiss, Mrs. Krisselhoff, the wife of the doctor, and a young woman of undefined position who had no husband in evidence, but was addressed as "madame," were busy disposing the guests around tables for luncheon. It was first-class food for Turkestan: chicken, tongue, and pastry. No alcoholic drinks were served. The reception started at eleven and was to continue till two, but about one-thirty Mrs. Gillan looked at me with a very marked, "Let's get going" look in her eye.

Outside the crowd was as thick as ever. What docile, uncomplaining people! They stood in the glaring sun for hours, gazing blankly at the doors. Whenever they edged in too closely to the house, ruthless guards slashed them with riding whips. They didn't rebel, merely stepped back; obviously they were used to it.

Back home, Major Gillan told me he had asked the vice-consul for news and was told something was expected shortly. Two weeks now passed, full of nagging, ceaseless worry. One day we heard that a caravan of Hindus was planning to return to India through the Karakorum, and in an oblique way this was good news. It was late in the season, indeed, for a caravan to make this attempt. With light baggage, we were told, travellers had got back to India in the depths of winter. But our baggage was not light. Ever in my mind's eye was the picture of that towering mountain broken by the narrow pass wherein howling gales would stir up the snow, covering with a whiter blanket the whitened bones of the fallen animals, relics of past disasters.

This subject became such a sore point with us that we never mentioned it. Major and Mrs. Gillan also kept silent.

The monotony of the days was broken by the amban of Yarkand, who suddenly made an appearance at the Gillans', announcing that he had been appointed Chinese consul-general in Russia. Back in Yarkand he had been fat and jovial, but now he was fatter and positively irrepressible. Fate, in the person of his father-in-law, governor of the whole province of Sinkiang, had given him a good job with plenty of opportunity to issue trade-permits and thus dip into graft money. He seemed overcome with the glory that had descended on him.

The Gillans provided tea and cakes. The chubby little man received these gratefully, but it was brandy that aroused his real enthusiasm. Vodka, I could see, was shortly to have an ardent customer.

Later in the evening, Cherrie and I, inspired perhaps by the talk about Russia, collaborated on another letter to the consul asking for immediate action. A reply came that night saying that nothing had come from Moscow, but the consul would like to see us the next day.

Mr. Doumpiss relegated the business of seeing us to Mr. Krisselhoff, who was not encouraging. He still "hoped" something would develop. In three weeks obviously no progress had been made. Before the interview was over, Mr. Krisselhoff learned what we thought about Russian red-tape. It was intolerable, a dangerous situation, being held here in Kashgar while the weather was daily getting worse in the Karakorum. It was the fault of the Russians that our papers were not in order, and yet they were submitting us to unnecessary danger, while they carried on this outrageous joke of "taking it under advisement." More experienced men than we had perished in the Karakorum, and the delay had put our nerves on edge. If Moscow was going to refuse us permission, the least it could do was to say so—now!

After this came another delay: Mr. Doumpiss "had a headache." A few days later Mr. Krisselhoff advised us to fill out a series of elaborate forms giving data about ourselves and our servants. This had already been done weeks before. The forms were produced and filed away again, but somehow this insignificant episode made me optimistic enough to lay in a supply of Russian money and to hire a new servant who knew Hindustani, Persian, Russian, and Turki.

On October 23, almost three weeks from the day of our arrival, the Gillans left Kashgar on a duck-hunting trip, leaving us use of their house. Just before their departure, a note from the Roosevelts caused general rejoicing. The trip through the Pamirs had been a success, for three specimens of the ovis poli, two male and one female, had been added to the collection. By this time the Roosevelts were out of the mess.

Soon it would be November. Snow was already falling in the Karakorum, and here we were, penned up as effectively as prisoners, at the mercy of a petty, provincial autocrat. It seemed doubtful now if we could ever get the collection through the passes. On the other hand, if the skins were to remain in Kashgar all winter, protected by only salt and naphthalene, the rats might destroy them. A pretty dilemma!

With the Gillans gone, life was much duller. There were a few tennis games with the consulate's Indian clerical staff, epochally bad players, and a few photographing jaunts out into the country. For the rest, it was tension and unceasing worry. We were well into the autumn and every night brought a blustering wind. By day the sun's rays filtered down through layers of cool air. The chill of early winter seemed to have crept into the voice of the muezzin pronouncing his invocation to Allah. Faint and mournful, the words fluttered down on the wind: "I testify there is no God but God. I testify Mohammed is the apostle of God."

Khirgiz Nomad Woman

Drawn by Alexandre Iacovleff

The end came with exquisite abruptness, peculiar to Mr. Doumpiss. On his own authority he was granting us permission to cross Russia via Baku, the Caspian, and on to Istanbul.

Immediately there was a rush of activity. Twenty-two horses to take us from Kashgar to the railhead at Andijan were ordered. The price, $270, was a swindle, but this was no time for bickering.

Our visas directed that we were to enter Russia at Irkistan, no later than November 7, nine days from our date of departure. While we had planned on eight days from Kashgar to the Russian border and thus had a day of grace, we wondered at the speed forced upon us by the consul. After all the long wait, holding us up for no purpose, turning the entire trip into a hell, he was now offering every inducement to get us out of his sight on the moment. The secret of these tactics was locked up in the Doumpiss brain.

On October 29 we took the road to the frontier, feeling like joyous prisoners released at the end of long terms.

Summer had vanished from the plains. Drab, cheerless hues met the eye whether one looked at the sky or at the desert stretching to the horizon. The first march took us to Mingyul, where we stopped at a comfortable inn. Leaving the Kashgar River, we got into the eastern foothills of the Alai mountains, low and covered with silt. During the third march, however, the land rose and we gained elevation sharply. Kanjygan's altitude was 6100 feet.

The next march of eighteen miles took us to Shir Bulak, through a desert wilderness. The trail rose a thousand feet and then dipped sharply to another plain. Only two rooms were available at the serai; so the caravan men put up their felt tents as they had back in the Tien Shan.

Fortunately there were fireplaces in all the rooms along the march. They differed in size, cleanliness, and comfort, but there was always a supply of carpets for the floor, and firewood from pruned willows to heat up our rooms in the evening and again in the morning before we rose. We were profoundly grateful for this escape from the cold, and if it hadn't been for the fleas we would have pronounced the inns perfect. But it would have been asking too much of a Turkestan serai to expel its fleas.

Out from Shir Bulak appeared two other caravans, one composed of twelve donkeys, the other of five camels. We were to see them day after day on the road. Although we were invariably the latest to get going in the morning, we were first to reach the serai. The donkeys were a bad second, and the camels trailed far into the night.

Snow-capped mountains came into view as we approached Oksolar, on the river of the same name, twenty miles from Shir Bulak. The trail rose 1800 feet, and this time we held a great deal of our altitude.

An extraordinary geological formation had given this region an aspect of unreality like a seascape painted for the theatre. Wind and water coming down from the mountains had scarred the landscape, creating a tumultuous effect like a storm on the ocean. Farther on, the work of erosion had wrought strange shapes, such as flat shelves coming out from the hills, and narrow-legged, broad-topped tables rising from the plateaux. The mountainsides wore zebra-like color combinations of red, violet, purple, and green. It was one of the most flamboyant landscapes I have ever seen.

Ulugh Chat, twenty-five miles beyond Shir Bulak, brought the first snow, a light, powdery carpet which covered the ground. During the night the thermometer fell to five degrees above zero. This village had a main street, a bazaar, a yamen (amban's residence), and a mud fort housing a hundred soldiers.

Hardly had we arrived at the serai when the amban came in wearing an expensive-looking fur coat. After a second's hesitation, he told us in faltering but understandable English that we had met at a Kashgar reception. I couldn't remember the incident, but the amban went on to say in his spotty English, picked up in Pekin, that he couldn't fail to remember anything so rare as a white man. We offered him tea, hoping this would stave off an invitation for dinner, but it was useless. We had to dine with him that night.

The next day supplied a little comic relief. Ahead of us on trail was a fat Turki, weighing some 250 pounds, riding a tiny donkey. The man turned his round, cheerful face toward us and began to chatter. Although we indicated we couldn't understand a word, he went right on. A silly-looking figure on his tiny mount, he talked and laughed for an hour and then suddenly burst into song that reverberated grotesquely through the rocky defile. Evidently this was the last straw for the donkey, who reared suddenly and tossed his fat master into the air, whence he landed on a rock pile.

Only two marches now separated us from the Russian border. When the Yezi River turned southward we followed its tributary, the Zighin. Along the banks of both rivers were groves of willows, alternating with grass and cultivated land where the good Kirghiz were settling down for the bleak winter.

Snow and cold whipping winds were with us as we climbed steadily over the Zighin pass at 10,100 feet. Just before the Chinese town of Irkistan we overtook a donkey caravan and saw one of the men unconcernedly taking off his shoes to cross the icy banks, to walk through the glacial water whose bed was covered with sharp, mean stones. The man walked slowly, but his face was utterly impassive, showing either complete insensibility or superb self-control. On the far side of the stream his feet were fiery red, indicating an amazing power of reaction. A white man's feet would have remained white and bloodless for a long time.

Irkistan, only three miles from the frontier, must have been a bleak place even in summer, but now, caught in winter's grip, it was the last word in desolation. There were no trees, only stretches of desert, partly covered with a shifting carpet of snow. Snow-laden winds howled around the mean, shabby houses. Another amban whom we seemed to have met in one of those populous Kashgar receptions arrived to rescue us from the dirty serai, and we were grateful to have decent quarters for our last night in China. A large, clean room with plenty of space for our bed and luggage was assigned to us. It had windows of real glass, and a cast-iron stove that exuded waves of heat from a dung fire. To atone for the slight odor, a brass Buddha in the hall discharged incense. The floor was covered with exquisite rugs, and the walls were decorated with old swords and Mandarin clothes. The Chinese Republic had forbidden its officials to wear old raiment, and such beauty could survive only as wall hangings.

After getting installed we looked out the windows and saw that snow was falling with the falling night. The ground was now thickly covered, and while it was good to be in a warm, sheltered spot, the snow seemed a bad omen for crossing the passes farther west.

The amban produced an excellent dinner of veal and lamb, rice and vegetables, topped off with glasses of Three Star Hennessey, luxury of luxuries for this part of the world.

I looked forward to crossing the frontier, now only three miles away, with a certain amount of trepidation, for Russian red tape was a mysterious thing, and it would cause me no surprise if the officials should decide our papers were not in order. Russian Irkistan proved to be a dreary village, set down in a snowy mountain waste. There was a military post with one officer and twenty soldiers, and a great number of uninhabited houses, at least three quarters of them in ruins.

The officer, a gloomy, malevolent cuss, took our passports into another room to examine them at his leisure. We sat in the barracks, where the walls were covered with huge, gaudy posters depicting the evils of the bourgeoisie and the Russian Orthodox Church. In contrast with the officer, the soldiers were a young, cheerful lot, and they fraternized immediately with the Chinese soldiers who had escorted us to the border. At length the officer emerged and announced gloomily that we might proceed. Our Chinese guard was dismissed and a Russian soldier was assigned to accompany us.

Crossing the Yezi River, we came into grass country and then crossed a pass to reach Ishke Kizak, a name but no settlement. I had been hoping to see some Kirghiz, which might mean refuge in a yurt, kumiss, and a bit of new bread. Instead we put up our tents in the abandoned settlement. Our men found a small amount of dung left by the nomads, which kept up our fire throughout the evening.

The next morning we marched along the Kok-Su River, climbed upward, and went through a pass thickly crusted with snow on both sides. The trail dipped as abruptly as it went up, and beyond the pass we followed a tributary of the Kok-Su—the Kathukonosh. All that afternoon we rode above the tree line, through such rocky country that we wondered if we would find a spot flat enough to put up the tents.

By four o'clock the problem was getting acute, and I rode ahead with the Russian soldier to look for a camp site. Just when things began to look bad, we saw three yurts perched on a flat, grassy surface above the banks of the river, and below, the horses, cattle and yaks of the nomads grazing near the water's edge.

A gray-bearded patriarch accepted us for the night, although his yurt, only fifteen feet in diameter, already housed his two daughters, his son, the son's wife, and small child. The inhabitants sat around the fire, looking solemn and preoccupied, scarcely glancing up when Cherrie arrived forty minutes later. Our supper, prepared by our cook in another yurt, was brought in to us, and while we ate it the Kirghiz sat and stared, never moving. Later the two unmarried girls went down to the stream for water and then rushed back to warm their hands before the fire. Again there was silence. The yurt was cold, since dung fires at their best give off little heat, and this one was hampered by a heavy draft coming in through the ventilating hole in the roof and through casual vents in the sides.

Keeping on most of our clothes, we rolled up for the night. For a few minutes the silence persisted, and then suddenly the yurt became a cyclone of activity. The inhabitants came to life. There was laughter and loud talking, and through half-closed eyes I could see the women making a stew of some kind in a huge bowl. Other Kirghiz drifted in, and soon our caravan men joined the fun. More noise and laughter. Dogs slithered in through the vents in the felt walls. How long the merriment went on I had no idea, for after a few heaves and starts from flea bites I went to sleep, and the next thing was a servant standing over me with a cup of tea.

It was morning. The Kirghiz were lying on their felt rugs on the earthen floor. They rose before we left, however, only to resume their silent, staring business of the night before.

In a few days, this region, though plentifully supplied with grass, would become impossible because of the cold, and the nomads would take their flocks down to lower levels.

The great Terek Durwan, at 11,600 feet (the Turkish word "durwan," like the Tibetan "la," means "pass"), now lay before us—the climax of the mountain country. After this the land would slope down gradually into the plains of Russian Turkestan. We were glad to meet the pass and have done with it. The lower slopes were not too difficult, but suddenly the trail became very steep and the snow drifted badly. We passed small caravans of Kirghiz coming down the slopes as we went up, all on foot, their donkeys laden with food, blankets, and some firewood.

It was 9:30 A.M. when we cleared the crest of the Terek Durwan and congratulated ourselves, with good reason, for getting over it that early. For a terrific gale was gathering speed, and the snow was stinging our faces. There was practically no visibility. Caravans of nomads multiplied, and we marvelled at the astonishing hardihood of these people. All wore padded woollen garments, but many of the men had their coats open at the neck so the snow could penetrate their skins.

After descending 1500 feet or so, the trail became more regular. Soon we met the Sofi Kourgan River and followed it along a very long and deep canyon. Then through a narrow valley sloping downward through high mountains, where a cheerful sight met our eyes: cedars growing on the slopes. These were the first trees we had seen growing naturally, except on river bottoms, since leaving the Tien Shan. The main point of it was that we would soon have wood for fires.

The whole day's march including the pass amounted to twenty-five miles. It ended at Sofi Langar, where we had two large, clean rooms and fireplaces with roaring fires. The very thought that the Terek Durwan was behind us was a solid consolation. From our windows we could see the foothills of the Alai mountains, and soon we could be down in the plains where the cold would be much less severe.

Twenty miles more brought us to Kizil Kourgan, where the serai was full up with members of Kirghiz caravan parties. But the Russian soldier who had been with us since Irkistan proceeded in a masterly way to evict tenants. We were given a tiny room, but instead of sleep we had a set-to with fleas emerging from those perfect incubators, the sheep-lined clothes of the nomads. There was a hole in our roof to let smoke out, but even at that we had to squat on the floor under the smoke level to keep breathing. Conjunctivitis was a common affliction in this region, as it is, indeed, in many places where dung is used for fuel.

I was sorry to part with our soldier guide the next morning. I had liked him. He had nothing to look forward to now but the hardships of the passes and, at the end, the desolate frontier station. I gave him a present but wondered what on earth he would do with money out in this wilderness.

Fifteen miles farther on, we were welcomed by another military post of three soldiers, youths between nineteen and twenty-one, whose officer was absent. We were thankful to the lads for offering to put us up, for Goulcha was a mean, dirty little town, inhabited mainly by Kirghiz. In the bazaar, prices were quoted in roubles, whereas in the Russian territory we had just crossed, trade flowed towards Kashgar and the Chinese seer was the prevailing currency. This little village was the terminus of the Russian telegraph line coming from the west. The telegraph poles were iron rails, not very decorative but much more stable than the thin poplar poles used by the Chinese for this purpose.

The three youths generously asked us to share their meal, consisting of black bread and tea without sugar or milk. Occasionally they got a little pork, but this was an off night. We brought out some of our own supplies and were having a merry time when the officer returned. Whether he was displeased to see two strangers making a "feast" with his men, I didn't know. Obviously torn between a desire to be officious and a desire to share the meal, he compromised by drawing up a chair and lunging into a pot of jam. His manner remained stiff and awkward.

We slept in an unheated room, but it made little difference, for at this altitude the temperature was much milder.

Our friends, the young soldiers, seemed to be having a dreary time of it. With no military duties, they spent their time cleaning up the barracks, baking black bread, and sitting by the fire gabbling. The youth assigned to accompany us accepted the order as a piece of good luck. As a consolation to the others, we left part of our supplies, including pots of jam for which they had a particular fancy.

A march through the broad Goulcha valley, a climb of 700 feet to a pass, and we were able to look back thankfully at the Alai mountains, a picture of wintry desolation. The afternoon brought us to an excellent serai at Kaulan Ku that quickened our desire to regain civilization. Twenty-eight miles beyond was the thriving town of Madi.

The majority of Madi's population were Uzbeks, a Turki tribe, swathed in heavy padded coats and fur caps. Instead of going to a serai, we rented a shop in the bazaar, equipped with a fireplace and a screen to keep out the street crowds. But we attracted peeping Uzbeks, who pushed up to the screen and even into our room all through the evening. When Cherrie and I rolled up in our blankets and put out the light, a crowd of natives went into our kitchen and made merry the rest of the night. Just why our presence stimulated the party spirit, I couldn't make out.

The next day's march bought us to Osh, the most modern city we had seen since Kashmir and the largest since Yarkand. Osh had separate Turki and Russian sections. The Russian quarter, situated on a hillside at the north end of the town, had once been a thriving place, but now the houses were woefully out of repair.

Our papers were examined by eight Russian soldiers who questioned us at length about our travels. The interpreter was a native of Riga, named Braun, customs commissar for the district. The soldiers, all smiling and amiable, wanted to know what we thought of Communism, what Americans in general thought of it, and if we had expected to find a race of brigands and cutthroats. Cherrie and I had made up our minds never to discuss politics in Russia, so we replied that America was so far away we really received little news of Russia— nothing, at least, on which to base a solid opinion.

Braun now told us that our plan to send our goods through the rest of Russia under bond was quite feasible. He took us to a pleasant house made of sun-dried, whitewashed clay, of which one side served as the customhouse, the other side as living quarters. The office was placed at our disposal for the night, and Braun's friendly wife gave us glasses of vodka, a tureen of soup, and huge platters of good mutton.

We rose early the next morning to carry out an ambitious program. Here at Osh we would abandon pack animals and transfer our belongings to arabas. These had to be arranged for, and the collections had to be bonded. This would obviate rummaging through bales of hides at every customhouse.

We hoped to finish up the program by ten A.M. and then set out on the thirty-mile trip to Andijan, the railhead, whence we would continue by train. But our plans miscarried. The officials refused to hurry, and each piece of luggage had to be weighed, marked with ink, corded up, sealed with lead, and marked with the government stamp. This performance, carried on in utter confusion, took till three-thirty in the afternoon.

The arabas were waiting, so we had the stuff loaded up and decided to reach Andijan if it took all night. The carts jogged along painfully through the town and out into the plains. Instead of riding in the carts as did the natives of Sinkiang, the Uzbeks mounted the horses, which slowed them up. Canals cutting athwart the roads at frequent intervals were a serious nuisance.

At six-thirty we arrived at a small village, and the drivers clamored for a rest. Unharnessing the animals they went into the serai, a mere shed without front or side walls, and lay around a fire, drinking tea. Cherrie and I stood outside examining weather portents. It was cold and gusty, but we could reach Andijan by carrying lanterns to light the road. Just then a few drops fell. In a few minutes there was a downpour, an alarming emergency, for our pelts were not covered and if they got soaked and then froze, they later on would most certainly rot. Through all the journey back from the Tien Shan, rain had never been a problem. The carts were pushed under the eaves of the shed and flaps from one of our tents covered the hides.

In spite of the fleas, we fell asleep, but the cold, attacking our feet, roused us to intervals of rising, stamping around, and drinking tea. By four o'clock it was too cold to lie still; so we roused the men and were off in half an hour. One man rode ahead lighting the way with a candle-lantern. An icy wind was blowing in our faces. Cherrie and I alternately walked and rode.

Four or five miles before reaching Andijan we stopped in a tea-house, started a fire, and ate an excellent breakfast. Then on to Andijan, proceeding directly to the transport office of the railroad. It had taken us seventeen days to cross the 275 miles between Kashgar and Andijan, one of the most difficult, most unpleasant stretches I have ever encountered.

Andijan, half primitive, half civilized, was a bewildering sight for white men just emerging from the wilderness. Ancient and modern jostled each other with a fine, careless disregard for consistency. Everywhere was a scramble of camels and motor cars, caravans and locomotives, paved streets and muddy lanes, brick houses and mud huts, candles and kerosene lamps and electric lights. It looked like the raw material for something that had not been put together.

At the warehouse next to the railroad we dumped our goods, and then, with the payment of wages and a word of farewell, we acquitted ourselves of our obligations to all the servants save two. I had signed an agreement making me responsible for the return of Jamal Shekh, the cook, and his assistant, to their homes in Kashmir. These two would be constantly on my mind till they could be put on a boat at Istanbul and shipped back to Bombay.

At the warehouse office, language difficulties threatened to upset the applecart, but the chief's wife, speaking atrocious French, understood at last that we wanted our goods shipped to Marseilles via

Batum and we in turn understood that the boxes and bales would all have to be reweighed and registered, and would then follow us on a special freight train.

There would be ten hours now before the train left—ten hours in which to see how a new regime was impressing itself on an ancient city. It was Sunday, but all the shops were open. Not until evening, however, did the streets become thronged, and then they offered a colorful spectacle of many races and every imaginable sort of costume. Kirghiz, Kazaks, and other Mongol tribes mixed with Turkis and Uzbeks. Peoples from the Caucasus could be distinguished from northern Russians. White faces and brown faces. Clothes ran a gamut of quilted nomad coats, Moslem veils, colorful embroideries of Caucasian peasants, overall modes of the new proletariat, and conventional Western clothes of the surviving bourgeoisie.

In one place the crowd was converging on a cinema. In another, a political harangue in a hall seemed the center of attraction. The audience in the hall were listless and obviously relieved when it was over. Then the band struck up a tune and the men stood up, removing their caps. This reminded Cherrie and me that there was no longer any necsity for wearing fur hats. The haberdashery, however, had no headgear except the blue workingmen's caps, which went well with our clothes, now dreadfully ragged, and with our faces, weatherbeaten and unshaven for many a day. Thereafter I was often addressed as "Tovarich,"—"Comrade."

A restaurant of dirty tables and sawdust-covered floor served chunks of beef floating in greasy cabbage soup, and pieces of corned beef flanked by potatoes and macaroni. The quality was pretty bad, and the price was one rouble apiece. The waiter refused a tip, and we discovered later that tipper and tipped were liable to arrest.

So much for Andijan under the Soviet. It was getting cold and we waited in the station to buy "Platzkarten" or third-class sleeping accommodations, the best the railroad had to offer. There was a great throng, but the ticket office didn't open till half an hour before train time, lest speculators buy up all the places and sell them at a profit. In the waiting room there were hordes of people sitting on the floor while a perfectly good wooden bench remained empty. We wondered if the comrades were forbidden to use it, and if so, why.

Cherrie and I undertook to find out, and the bench collapsed with a terrific bang. An uneasy silence descended on the crowd and all eyes were turned in our direction as if we had committed a felony. Two soldiers with drawn bayonets marched into the room and straight up to us, and indicated that we were to follow them. In a room that looked like an arsensal, a commissar attempted to grill us on our misdeeds, but finding we couldn't speak Russian he shrugged his shoulders and waved us free.

A modern locomotive puffing into the station gave me an entirely too optimistic idea of the train, whose coaches, it developed soon enough, looked like aboriginal cousins of European third-class. Our coach had three tiers of bunks built at right angles to one wall, while on the other side two tiers ran the length of the car. There was more space than in American or European cars, as Russian railroads are built at wide gauge. There was no running water, and the only light came from a lantern at one end of the car. Heat was supplied by a small stove, also at one end. Despite our sheepskin coats we were cold all night.

Our expectations of reaching Samarkand in twenty-three hours were dashed the next morning when it became clear that the train had no respect for schedules. With a maximum speed of twenty-five miles an hour, it usually jogged along between fifteen and twenty, stopping in all small towns and sometimes delaying an hour at the larger stations. The road was single track, and the poor roadbed contributed to the bumpy movement. At one point a hotbox held us up for four hours, and no effort was made to pick up time.

Food was obtainable at nearly all wayside stations. Old women with samovars did a thriving business in hot water for passengers' tea. Peasants were selling bread, beef, and cooked chicken. One medium-sized hen, roasted and ready to eat, could be had for one rouble.

During the afternoon I struck up an acquaintance with two Russian dancers. The wife spoke French. She had a long tale to tell, and she told it with Russian vivacity and no lack of detail. The Imperial School of the Ballet in Petrograd was her alma mater, she said, and her father had been a rich banker, slain by the Reds. After the revolution she and her husband fell on evil days, and began giving recitals in the provinces. At a maximum of one performance a town, since few people had money to buy seats, they were constantly on the move. Discussing the Soviet regime, the dancer grew bitter. "C'est affreux," she kept repeating. "C'est quelque chose de fantastique!"

The husband was indignant at the train service, pointing out that we were going to miss our connection at Samarkand. Then he proposed a way to beat the game. Later in the evening, a faster train, known amiably as "the express," would overtake ours. It would skip some of the local stations and arrive in Samarkand hours earlier. Knowing that it was risky to leave one train for another when trains were at such a premium, we hesitated, but being eager to have done with the trip, decided to take a chance.

At the transfer station, the dancers interviewed the chief, who made no promises but said he would do his best if we returned in one hour.

Men, women and children, their goods piled around them, were camped in the waiting room and on the platforms. Some had been there for two and three days, yet they seemed cheerful and hopeful. In this part of Russia, crowded trains were the rule. There was always a fight for place in the queue before the wicket because the service was woefully inadequate. To add to the confusion, the government encouraged travel by offering excursions at ridiculously low rates.

After returning to the station-master three times, we were given tickets late in the evening and had to jump on the train as it was pulling out, pushing the Kashmiris, now a constant source of worry, ahead of us. No lower bunks were available, but we were willing to stand the cramped quarters, knowing that at nine in the morning the train would reach Samarkand.

Samarkand, the ancient capital of Timur! Samarkand, the magic name that evokes rhapsodic pages from travel writers! Reading those pages in my youth, I had dreamed of the day when I should see the fabulous city with my own eyes. Now a train was setting me down in the middle of it—and I must confess my thoughts were less on ruined temples than on food and soap and water.

The station buffet supplied meat, pastry, tea, and chocolate, and few meals have ever tasted so good. But finding a place in which to wash was a more difficult problem. Our friends said we must apply to a commissar. One government bureau passed us on to another till we reached the old Imperial Opera House. Only one particular official could handle our case, it seemed, and a permit was required merely to get into his presence. This was granted with no more than the usual red tape, and passing through a guard of soldiers holding bayonets, we were ushered into the presence. The preliminaries had rather indicated a grim dragon snorting fire, but the reality was a mild and amiable man sitting behind a desk, who asked the nature of our errand and then, with an indulgent smile, wrote out the ticket of admittance to the pitcher and washbowl zone. Out in the streets again, we were directed to a large, white mud building with an unkempt courtyard behind it. Across the courtyard was a vast room holding some forty beds, washbowls, and jugs of water. Our passports were taken away temporarily and we were free to wash.

For lunch we rejoined our dancers. Four and a half roubles ($2.50) bought fresh-boiled eggs, rolls, cheese, cakes, and excellent café au lait with sugar. As we ate, the wife gave another of her interesting discourses on Russia then and now, while the husband looked on, interested but silent.

After lunch Cherrie and I were denuded of our beards, a painful operation since clippers and razors were dull, and then the wife offered to accompany us on a sight-seeing tour while her husband visited friends. A steam tram took us from the European quarter, which looked sadly down at the heel, through a congeries of narrow, labyrinthine streets to the Moslem town of mosques and tawny old houses. Pale winter sunshine fell through clouds of dust, stirred up by a cold wind.

Timur's glory, now in sad decay, came into view with the Registan, a little world of domed and minareted buildings, connected by cloisters and cobblestone courts. The original material was brick, made of loess from the Zarafshan valley, and this was faced with clay and glazed in exquisite turquoise and cobalt blues. In the sunlight it still retained enough of its jewel-like quality to convey an idea of its original beauty, but many of the tiles had fallen away, breaking the intricate geometric patterns and leaving stretches of ugly brown.

Out in the main thoroughfare again, we saw that faces and costumes fitted the setting. There were brown Mongol types, and scarcely fewer of Turkic origin. Some women wore veils to cover their faces, but others pushed them back, and still others had abandoned the custom. But all were attired in brilliant clothes, usually of flowered silk or cotton. Jewels were by no means absent. Turbans and quilted coats were the rule for the men.

The mosque of Bibi Khanum is a mere relic of past grandeur, so heavily has time taken toll of the famous cupola, but its octagonal minarets faced with blue tiles and faience are still beautiful and touching. Also in a sad state is the Gur-Emir, Timur's tomb, which looks best from a distance, with its huge dome rising over lines of acacia trees.

Many have called the mosque of Shakh-Zinda the crowning glory of Samarkand, and enough remains of the noble marble staircase leading up to the paved street of tombs, surmounted by graceful domes, to give an idea of its former beauty. Here again the designs in blue tiles and faience, occasionally finished with bas-reliefs in gold, glittered like jewels in the sunlight.

Timur, the lame and one-eyed, has been shorn of much of his glory by time and earthquakes, but the intrinsic evidence shows that he was guilty of hasty and slipshod building. His work must have been ravishing in its heyday, but the builders must have known that that heyday was to be all too brief. And yet, all in all, the traveller who looks at Samarkand today readily accepts the fact that it was once the town of Alexander, of Genghis Khan, and of Timur himself. It bears the imprint of the Arabs who made it a great seat of culture and supplied it with an irrigation system, and also the imprint of the Turks,

Mongols, Chinese, and Russians who came after them. It probably has a future as well as a past, for the Soviet made it the capital of the Uzbek Republic in 1924.

At the time of our visit there was not much to be said for the modern city, and the greatest curiosity, it seemed to me, was the packs of the famous "wolf children," abandoned little outlaws who had presented the government with a thorny problem. They were the offspring of upheaval, and many of them doubtless were the children of wealthy families, dispersed or even killed by the revolutionists. They roamed the streets, even from village to village, picking up food where they found it. Murders and robberies galore were ascribed to them, and though they were brought into the courts now and then, the judges invariably treated them indulgently. Many of those we saw in the streets of Samarkand were as young as eight and nine, and yet bore the countenances of hardened adults.

Although our train did not come in till midnight, four hours late, our friends, who were remaining in Samarkand, stayed on to the end, helping us again to procure tickets and find places.

Dawn took us through Bokhara. Beyond it we came into a desert plain, looking wan and brown in the morning light. There was no grass, only clumps of tamarisk here and there to relieve the monotony. Twenty hours out of Samarkand the railroad dipped southwest and ran along the Persian border. Then it turned north along the eastern shore of the Caspian Sea, where the land rose into green, undulating hills. At eight-thirty the next morning the train reached Krasnovodsk, whence we could take a boat across the Caspian to Baku.

Krasnovodsk was a dreary city with no reason to exist except as a port where cotton, timber, sugar, dried fruits and oil from the Caucasus were received and shipped to eastern and northern destinations. The hinterland was a region of raw-looking, barren mountains, supporting neither agriculture nor forestry. In consequence, all food and fuel had to be brought from distant ports, and poor Krasnovodsk seemed to be leading a hand-to-mouth existence.

While a visit to the police was mandatory, we believed—a trifle

Turkis, near Kashgar, en route to the bazaar. The young bride on the donkey is crying in fear of the camera, to the amusement of her companions

Kirghiz yurts on the Kathukonosh, where we found shelter overnight. They would soon move down to lower levels for the winter

optimistically—that we could put off this chore long enough to get a cup of coffee in the station buffet. Before the coffee was finished, a group of soldiers filed in, accompanied by a member of the Ogpu in civilian clothes. Confusion, due to the fact we knew no Russian, was ironed out when one of the soldiers spoke up in German. Permission to finish breakfast was accorded by the Ogpu man.

The German-speaking soldier proved an affable cicerone, for our ragged clothes evidently stimulated his desire to be helpful. Shocked at our intention to travel first-class on the boat from Krasnovodsk to Baku, and persuaded, obviously enough, that we were foolish peasants resolved to spend our last poor coins on a big bust, he determined that we must travel second. To ease his conscience, I explained that a museum was paying our expenses.

Conditions were pretty bad in Krasnovodsk. Although the boat and railway service provided the only chance for employment, every boat brought flocks of unemployed from the Caucasus to join the already large ranks of the jobless.

Our boat, an ancient model with side wheels, pulled in at three in the afternoon, and since there was little freight to load and the peasants stormed up the gangplank like stampeding cattle, we were able to leave in half an hour. The boat grounded on the mud bottom, giving her a list, and in getting off, the churning paddles brought up a lot of vile-smelling mud. Two hours later the boat grounded again in the open sea! It appeared there were many shallow spots in the Caspian, but as the bottom was all soft clay, it didn't matter much. Backing out, the vessel continued on her way.

The crowds on deck looked like a costume ball. There were browns and whites, Turkis and Georgians, South Russians, North Russians, peasants, artisans, and soldiers. Uniforms, padded coats, fur cloaks accompanied every variety of headgear from turbans to ancient Paris hats. Most attractive of all the costumes were the brilliantly embroidered regional dresses, all unfortunately on the dirty, shabby side.

Center of attraction for the first-class passengers was a Chauve Souris troupe making a tour of the provinces. There were several women singers, but they went to their cabins, announcing they were seasick, though the sea that day was as smooth as a millpond. But the men of the party and particularly the old piano maestro managed to keep every one entertained.

Dinner, served at seven, consisted of bad soup, good chicken, middling vegetables, and atrocious coffee. Afterwards every one ordered drinks. Cherrie and I bought a bottle of native white wine, took one sip, and ordered beer. A long-robed Turki beside us took the wine, drank it to the last drop, and offered us arrak. We thought a sip or two would serve the cause of politeness, but the Turki considered a sip a mortal affront. So the sips multiplied, and put us into a mood to appreciate the fun to come.

The piano maestro had enlisted the services of two baritones in the company, and together they gave a superb, rollicking performance. Drinking arrak liberally from a goblet on the piano, the maestro played and talked, explaining that he was trained in the old rigorous tradition of the Petrograd Conservatoire. His round, baby face turned redder by the minute, and his wide, naïve eyes seemed to be looking out into another world. The arrak gave him a laughing jag that communicated itself to the audience. During a breathing spell the maestro plied me with questions about the White Russians in America. He hoped to make an American tour with his company, but it would take the Soviet government, he explained with a good-natured laugh, two years to issue the passports.

The party came to an end when a sinister little man who had been watching the proceedings with hostile eyes as he drank arrak, staggered to his feet and said he had a few accounts to settle with certain people in the room. I had suspected that he was a member of the Ogpu, but seeing this performance, I wondered. Out on the deck, he called for the captain, roared, bellowed, slammed his fists around, and made vague insinuations. The maestro seemed to take this seriously; so the jovial evening was finished. I slipped down to my cabin before it was over.

Next morning all was quiet. The brawler remained in his cabin and no one could explain the strange scene. The musicians looked seedy. The maestro had a forced smile, watery eyes, and a breath like a buzzard's.

Baku is a modern city with well-paved streets, trolleys, electric lights, stone buildings (the first we had seen in many a day), theatres, and shops. Business seemed to be thriving. Oil from the great Caucasus fields had brought the city prosperity and also a lot of ugliness, for vast storage tanks lined the water's edge.

Ogpu regulations in Baku were so severe that we were kept under guard all day, first in the waiting room of the steamship line and then in the railway station. The Kashmiris were permitted to go out and buy food, and we had nothing to do but stare at the posters glorifying freedom and brotherhood. Just before train time, an Ogpu official explained that the bad stories of his organization were untrue; it was like the police force of any other country. He smiled pleasantly and installed us in a comfortable second-class Wagons-Lits compartment.

The scenery flashing by the window was a pleasant sight after so many mountains and arid plains. Here the land rolled green and opulent to the far horizon. There were forests, meadows, prosperous fields, and trim farmhouses.

In Batum, which seemed larger than Baku but not, perhaps, so affluent, the Ogpu would doubtless have been happy to see us, but they were deprived of the pleasure. It was our last city on Russian soil and the worst they could have done was to put us on a boat for Turkey, which was precisely what we wanted. Although we roamed about the town at will, no one paid any attention to us except a few friendly spirits who glanced at our shabby clothes, smiled, and murmured, "Tovarich."

A representative of the Near East Relief took us to the Dobra Flotte offices, where there was bad news. Our request to have the collection sent to Batum by fast freight had been ignored, and it was on its way by slow freight, which would take a month or more. The Russians had lost some 500 to 600 roubles by this error, but it was no consolation to us. The only solution was to sign a power of attorney, so that the Dobra Flotte could receive the goods and reship them to New York.

That settled, we took passage on the French liner *La Phrygie*. Just before sailing time, guards searched us thoroughly to see if gold was concealed on our persons or in our luggage. Then, with hundreds of immigrants, we were herded into barbwire enclosures on the dock and kept there for over an hour under a soldier's rifle. It appeared that in other days immigrants often received packages of gold from friends who slipped up to them after the examination had been completed.

La Phrygie, which had stirred up anticipations of good French meals as we traversed the Black Sea, let us down badly. Although the courses were many and the service fastidious, the food was atrocious. Worse still, a two-day journey stretched out into six, as the boat stopped at one little port after another to take on shelled almonds, tobacco, and eggs destined for Paris and London.

In the port of Istanbul, the Turkish authorities, grumbling about the technical distinction between transit and tourist visas, refused to let us off the boat. A message to the American chargé d'affaires, however, got us off in short order.

Hastening to a shop that sold English clothes, we bought suits and accessories and then consulted the Near East Relief about our collections. Here again was bad news. The director's opinion was that one of us ought to stay till word came from Batum that the goods had been shipped or that our presence was required to unravel difficulties.

This meant Cherrie. My part of the expedition was over, but he, as a regular member of the museum's staff, was responsible for getting the collection back home. If anything went wrong, he could seek a new visa and return to Batum.

The Kashmiris were now shipped back to India, a great relief despite the fact we had grown attached to them, for they were attracting altogether too much attention. The Turkish government had banned not only the fez but the turbans once worn by the mullahs or priests. A large part of the people accepted these decrees with so much enthusiasm that only a short time before a mob had lynched three men for wearing fezes. The official punishment was only a short jail sentence. Our turbaned Kashmiris attracted·much attention but the mobs evidently decided to show forbearance towards foreigners.

After three days in Istanbul, I said good-bye to Cherrie and took the Orient Express for Paris. The Russian embassy in Paris promised to speed the collection, and a month later Cherrie received word that everything had reached Batum in good shape and had been reshipped to Marseilles. Even the films, usually censored in Russia, reached us intact.

This wrote period to a long and arduous journey. Back in civilization, all the difficulties and hardships of the trip began to pale, finally sinking into oblivion, and permitting me at last even to mention the name Doumpiss with composure. Nothing could ever efface the picture of that unsullied paradise, the Tien Shan.

The Head-Hunters of Assam

SHARP contrasts with the Tien Shan in the matter of terrain, inhabitants, and tradition were provided by another trip that took me to a little known part of Assam, a hill section of northeastern India. The jungle country covered in this expedition is occupied by the Nagas, a redoubtable, vigorous race of savages whose behavior and appearance indicate that they have had no contact with civilization. In fact, the Nagas are fond of hunting human heads. Before the advent of the British in India, petty warfare, murder, and rapine were their chief occupations. Lacking a common enemy, they fought among themselves, village against village.

The British eventually conquered a strip of territory lying in the hilly country along the left bank of the Brahmaputra in Assam, and the Nagas in this territory learned in short order that head-hunting was as dangerous for the hunter as for the hunted. British guns persuaded them to forgo their ancient art.

But not all the Nagas live in British-administered territory. Those beyond the pale of this buffer strip are free to hunt to their heart's content provided they do not seek their victims in the administered territory. Now and then, however, they swoop down into Britain's protectorate. The result is a punitive expedition. It was one of these missions that introduced me to the Nagas, their bamboo-fortified villages, and their sinister collections of human skulls.

Physically the Nagas are a fine racial type. Light brown in color, with clear-cut features, high cheekbones, a very marked slope of eye, broad-shouldered and sturdy, they classify as one of the handsomest of primitive peoples. Their exuberant vitality demanded an outlet, but all their brains could devise was head-hunting. Often in their quieter moods they stage ceremonials with finely developed dancing and with rites leaning toward nature worship.

These observations, I realize, do not fully answer the question: where did the Nagas come from and what racial strain accounts for their anti-social behavior?

The question is not easy to answer, for the Nagas have no written language and no folklore. They seem completely devoid of time sense. Nothing definite can be learned about their origin. They must have reached their present home from the north or the east, since the plains to the south have always been held by the Shans, and the lands to the southwest have been the kingdom of Assam since the dawn of history. A logical route for the Nagas would have been from east to west by way of North Burma. In this way they could have avoided crossing any part of the high Tibetan pleateau. Coming down to the plains of Assam in the Brahmaputra valley, they must have found the country occupied and strongly fortified by the kings of Assam, and they were probably forced to settle in the hills where they now live.

Like most hill tribes, they are fiercely hostile to strangers. Next to self-preservation and reproduction, their strongest urge is head-hunting. Felling a stranger and cutting off his head to carry it home in triumph is the Naga idea of grandeur and glory. The hills rising from the Brahmaputra valley provide a perfect setting for their guerilla tactics. The tangled jungle makes them fairly safe from pursuit. The invigorating air of their hill country makes them strong and vigorous. The Nagas living beyond the British zone are untouched by civilizing influence.

Before the coming of the British, the raids into the valley were so frequent that we can only marvel that there are any Assamese alive today. It took the British quite some time to produce any impression on the Nagas. Threats to the chieftains produced no results; punitive raids were only temporarily effective. But the day came when Indian army troops had to be sent into their country. The border lands were conquered and administered by the government. This particular area now acts as a buffer state between the Brahmaputra valley and the unadministered country out in the blue.

For the Nagas, the creation of the buffer state was a setback but not a complete defeat. Those in the British zone, as has been pointed out, had to forswear their ancient practices. But the others beyond the border were still free to fight among themselves. Every so often, despite British vigilance, the hill warriors slipped through the dark jungles, descended into the Brahmaputra valley, and took a few heads.

Whenever such raids became bad, a punitive expedition was formed. Out from Kohima, capital of the administered territory, went a detachment of troops. Nagas learned what happens when the white man's finger touches the little piece of steel on the long steel barrel. They saw their villages go up in smoke. They saw some of their boldest warriors being led off as hostages. Head-hunting began to lose some of its lure, until they learned the white man didn't care what they did so long as they stayed out of the administered territory.

For a time they practised their game among themselves. Then the urge for travel got the better of them again and they began their sinister journeys down the jungle hillsides. A few decapitated heads were found in the British zone. A new punitive expedition was decreed.

I was invited to be a member of the expedition by Doctor J. H. Hutton, the district commissioner, who was also an ethnologist. The trip was to cover first administered areas inhabited by the Angami and Ao tribes. Later I would have a long-wanted opportunity to see the untamed Koniaks, and I knew that civilians were forbidden to set foot in their territory. Any man who disobeyed the order and returned from the Naga country with his head on his shoulders knew that he would be fined and jailed.

This was a hard-boiled attitude, but if any adventurer felt like saying to the British, "My head is my own and I'll give it to the Nagas if I like," the answer would have been, "Your head is your own but if you give it to the Nagas it damages British prestige."

Doctor Hutton, as was his custom, led the expedition. It included only three other white men: his subdivisional officer, an infantry officer, and myself. We were to be accompanied by fifty native troops, a native army doctor, and our personal servants. I had brought with me to Kohima a Kashmiri servant named Lussoo who had been a great success when I took him to Turkestan. But Lussoo had to be left behind; it would not do to take an alien into the land of the Nagas. Doctor Hutton got me a Naga called Nymsao who turned out to be a perfect servant.

We required fifty porters to carry our supplies. The native troops who were to march through the jungle with levelled bayonets could not be expected to assume any extra burden. The commissioner thereupon conscripted fifty Nagas from the administered area. They would be paid in rupees; later they would be sent home, and wild Nagas would be conscripted. *Their* pay would be red cloth. They had little use for money, whereas the red cloth would serve them admirably for breechclouts.

In the oppressive heat of early March we set off into the jungle. It was a strictly military procession. Every detail of it had been organized in advance with the thought in mind that we were constantly open to attack. Gleaming tips of bayonets stood out against the dark masses of foliage. First went the advance guard. In the center, interlaced with more troops, came the laden native porters. We whites followed with our servants. And then came the rear guard, all guns levelled, ready against any surprise attack. Because of the narrow trails, the little army marched usually two by two.

Doctor Hutton explained the expedition's modus operandi. We were to stop in as many villages as possible and put the fear of God into the head-hunters. He had laid out a routine in advance. Part of it was to lecture the chief in every village where we paused, to impose fines on warring villages, and perhaps to take a few prisoners.

Starting at eight, we marched four and a half hours, covering twelve miles. The trail now showed that we were approaching a Naga village. To the right and left we saw small pot-holes, each with pieces of sharpened bamboo sticking up from the bottom. These were defenses against a night attack. Since all Nagas go barefoot, a wound from one of these sticks would be crippling; in daylight, of course, they could be easily avoided.

We stopped. Doctor Hutton shouted out a brief command: "Lay down your packs and march back to your homes." The porters obeyed with alacrity. When the last of them had disappeared down the trail, two soldiers were named to guard the packs.

A short distance farther brought us into full view of the village. It consisted of a score of circular, rattan-covered huts built around an open square, and surrounded by a palisade of sharpened bamboo sticks. Doctor Hutton eyed the landscape attentively. "We'll set up camp over there," he said finally. He had selected a high, dry spot near a giant bamboo grove, about a hundred yards from the village.

After a lunch that had been brought along already prepared, the soldiers set to work to make camp. First they fetched our supplies from where we had left them down on the trail. They brought back tools, tents, clean clothing, food, a canvas bathtub. With dexterity and precision they cut down bamboo sticks and sharpened them at both ends. These were thrust into the ground, not perpendicularly but slanting outward, and then braced from the outside.

The finished product, completed in three hours, was an oval palisade about 300 feet in circumference, large enough to surround the tents for the leaders, their servants, and the troops. Wicker sentry boxes, three of them, were placed at strategic intervals. It looked flimsy, the whole construction, but it was too high to jump, and the sharpened bamboo sticks pointing outward were an effective barrier against surprise attack. Our lives depended on a pretty simple mechanism; yet against the Nagas it was as effective as a Maginot line.

Directly the tents were up, the servants laid out our fresh clothes with as much care as if we were back in the government house. They heated water and we took turns at the folding tub. Then we changed our clothes and watched the soldiers erecting their own tents and putting the finishing touches on the palisade.

When we first arrived the village had looked deserted. "It probably is," observed Doctor Hutton. "They take to the hills long before we arrive. Remarkable how news spreads in the jungle."

But as the afternoon wore on, I noticed a few signs of life in the village. Doctor Hutton explained that one of the great Naga terrors is fire, punitive expeditions of the past often having put the torch to their villages. Since we had been there several hours without showing any incendiary inclinations, a few of the bolder spirits had crept back from their jungle hideouts. More would drift back later. Meanwhile we would follow our plan of maintaining a mysterious silence; in due time the head man of the village would come to us.

At four-thirty we had tea. When it was over, Doctor Hutton set up a folding table and started writing his reports. He had business to transact in the village, but he showed no signs of hurry. Manifestly he had no intention of summoning the head man. He knew what I did not—that the head man, drawn by fear and curiosity, would usually come of his own accord.

It was getting on toward five-thirty. A faint chill invaded the air, and the sun, the color of an over-ripe blood orange, sagged toward the jungle.

One of the servants came up to the table and whispered that the chief with two attendants was waiting at the gate of the compound. There was a silence while the pen scratched across the paper. Then, without looking up, Doctor Hutton murmured a few words in Assamese. "Bring them in."

Three stalwart, half-clothed savages were led in. Two were in their early forties; the third, around fifty, was the chief. Not only his greater age but his more confident bearing and the crafty look in his eye established his identity immediately. He wore a loose mantle hanging from his shoulders and a brown shirt reaching to his knees. It exposed his chest, scarred in a criss-cross effect as if a waffle iron had been pressed against his skin. This scarification, self-imposed, was a very fine decoration among the Nagas.

I photographed them. They never wavered from their solemn self-possession, but I knew they were concealing fear. Although the Nagas, like all savages, had short memories, the shortest of memories would never have forgotten the punitive expeditions of the past. Burned villages, fines, and prisoners had given the head-hunters plenty of material for conversation.

The Nagas squatted down before the table. Only a few sentences were exchanged, with the aid of an interpreter; to my ears it sounded like vocal shorthand. Doctor Hutton said he must have fifty porters for duty early in the morning. He proposed to visit the village before setting out. Then the savages took their departure.

Now came the soldiers' drill. All our fifty men took their allotted positions crouching behind the barricade. Then the whistle blew, and all but the night guard returned to their tents.

All the ammunition was taken away from the soldiers for the night. We, of course, retained our weapons. It would not have been safe to leave ammunition with the troops. Should an attack have occurred during the night, shots would doubtless have gone wild and casualties would have been as likely inside as outside the enclosure. After all, the Nagas possessed no guns, and we were perfectly ready to trust the barricade and the bayonets of the men.

At seven there was a supper consisting of ham, tongue, and plenty of rice. For reasons that will appear later, we had brought food for the entire trip.

It was getting cooler now. The March night was a reminder that we were perched on a hillside 5000 feet above sea level. The troops were resting. They had not only marched but made camp. Some had stretched themselves out on their beds. Others sat around in groups. Only a faint, desultory murmur of conversation reached us. Our servants were making up their beds.

A cold silence lay over the Naga jungle. There was something eerie in the quality of this stillness. Had we been lower in the valley there would have been a shrill chorus of cicadas. Up here, at 5000 feet, there were few insects, and none was audible at this hour. There were no wild animals on nocturnal prowls. Not a leaf stirred, not a twig crackled. Knots of clouds dangled from the ceiling of the lofty sky; there was not a beam of starlight. The silence was something more than the mere absence of sound; I realized I had never known the meaning of the word before.

I recalled that I had often heard it said that the Nagas managed their raids in efficient fashion. They gave no advance signal of what was to come. There were no war whoops. Their naked feet made no sound in the jungle. You realized you were in a raid when you saw a dhow—a long metal jungle knife—or a spear above your head. With this heartening thought I fell asleep.

When morning came the jungle wore a more cheerful aspect. After breakfast Doctor Hutton indicated it was time to go over to the village. Twelve armed soldiers accompanied us. As soon as we approached the village we could see signs of life. A dozen men were lounging around the barricade. A woman's face appeared briefly from behind a wall. From somewhere in the remote distance came the grunt of a pig. "Whenever they flee to the woods at our approach," remarked Doctor Hutton, "they take their pigs with them. Pigs are valuable property. Sometimes they hide them in trenches covered with bamboo and sod."

We walked through a street lined with bamboo-and-thatch houses and took our places on a bamboo platform that jutted out from the chief's house.

If the villagers were experiencing any consternation they failed to show it. With blank faces and an air of indifference, they straggled up to the platform, a score of men, a dozen women, a few children. They behaved as if they had been expecting us for weeks and our appearance interested them no more than a passing shower. I looked for signs of levity, for the Nagas of the administered territory always seemed smiling and gay. Gaiety was certainly characteristic of the race, but this particular group was too overcast to show it.

The head man and his two attendants again squatted before us. By taking these positions voluntarily they assumed the role of suppliants. Yet they maintained perfect composure.

Doctor Hutton began the proceedings. He talked Assamese in a firm, low tone. An interpreter put it into Naga. The chief looked straight ahead as if oblivious of his surroundings. Yet the flicker of light in the corner of his eye showed that he was absorbing every word.

"Are the porters ready?" asked Doctor Hutton.

Yes, the porters were ready. Fifty of them.

Doctor Hutton called attention to the fact that we had dismissed the porters from the administered area because we were approaching this village. Did his listeners know why? It was because he intended to show no discrimination. He did not plan to introduce fifty strangers into a village lest they get into a fight or observe the defenses for later use. So, today's porters would be dismissed before we reached the next village.

Then to a grimmer subject. The village must hand over two hostages. When the village showed a mind toward better behavior they would be released.

I looked carefully at the natives, now squatting in irregular rows before us. Not a quiver of expression had appeared on their faces; they were droopy and listless.

Doctor Hutton's voice took on a harsher note as he told them that the government of India would not permit head-hunting in British territory. No more raids! At the first sign of mischief, terrible punishments would be visited on the Nagas—not only on the criminals (Doctor Hutton was fully aware that the Naga killers could never be identified) but on the village.

The chief made his reply. He promised to carry out all orders. The people of his village did not carry on raids, did not hunt heads, in British territory. This tacit admission was no slip of the tongue. The chief never intended to deny that his men were head-hunters in their own territory.

As soon as the porters were ready, the two hostages were named. The chief hoped they would be released soon because he wished to repeat that his men were guiltless of raids.

Doctor Hutton seemed unimpressed. He had heard the same story from every chief he had ever interviewed. At the end he remarked in a casual tone that was not lost on his hearers, "You understand then that if my orders are not carried out, this village will be burned to the ground."

The chief nodded gravely.

"For pay," Doctor Hutton continued, "the porters may have rupees or red cloth."

The chief hesitated, then said he wanted red cloth. For the first time he smiled, showing strong white teeth. We rose. While the three leaders accompanied us to their barricade the others drifted away without giving us a second glance.

When we returned to our camp, everything was in readiness to resume the march. The porters appeared immediately and took up their burdens without complaint.

The hostages seemed indifferent to their fate. Unarmed, under constant surveillance, they were not under a very strong temptation to attempt an escape. They probably realized that in enemy territory their only safety zone was the white man's camp. Only one more hostage was taken during the rest of the expedition. The three men were put into the Kohima jail for a short time, and were then sent back to their villages to serve as warnings to ambitious head-hunters. Several villages visited by the expedition were "fined," which meant that their meager store of rupees were taken away from them.

We were now getting deeper into enemy territory, and Doctor Hutton reiterated certain rules. A native attack is always sudden, without warning. It begins with the throwing of spears from ambush. The attackers try to disorganize the marching men. If they succeed, they close in with dhows. When attacking by day, the Nagas often conceal themselves in a spot at the crest of a hill and wait to pounce on the advance guard.

Natives reaching the top of a hill after a long climb have a tendency to halt for a moment to catch their breath. At such times their vigilance is relaxed. This is such a well known fact that Doctor Hutton forbade any such halts; on the contrary, precautions were to be redoubled near hilltops.

It can be readily understood that advance guards are not popular details. In fairness to all, the commander changed details every day. Incidentally, in jungle marches such as ours, there is no way to circumvent ambush attacks. The jungle along the trail is so dense that flank guards cannot be sent out.

Seven times we got up early in the morning, organized fresh squads of porters, marched through the jungle, and built fortified camps. Only the records of the district commissioner would show how many villages we traversed, how many lectures were delivered on the wickedness of head-hunting in British territory and on the penalties thereof. I confined myself to making a non-official record of the Nagas and their country.

At first glance all Naga tribes look alike. At fifty-seventh glance they still look alike. There may be subtle anthropological differences between the tribes, but it would take an eye more expert than mine to detect them. It would likewise take an ear more acute than mine to perceive the variations in their dialects. To distinguish one breed from another I was obliged to examine their dress and headgear.

This was not easy, as the Nagas in the unadministered territory usually wore no more than breech-clouts. But sometimes, in deference to the white men's presence, they put on clothes, while at their ceremonials they outdid themselves. Everything they possessed in the way of cloth and jewelry was called into service. One tribe specialized in clothes made of cotton cloth printed in a black-and-white check pattern. Another had a supply of red and blue striped garments. Lengths of cloth were draped over their wide, athletic shoulders and around their waists, hanging down to the knees or lower.

Many earrings were in evidence, but the favorite decoration con-

An enemy Koniak impressed by us as porter, in the column with a Kookie soldier behind him

Young Koniak boys. Each of these future warriors carries his dhow
behind him on his belt

One of our fortified camps, showing the out-pointing sharpened bamboo sticks and in the center a sentry-box with a covering against rain

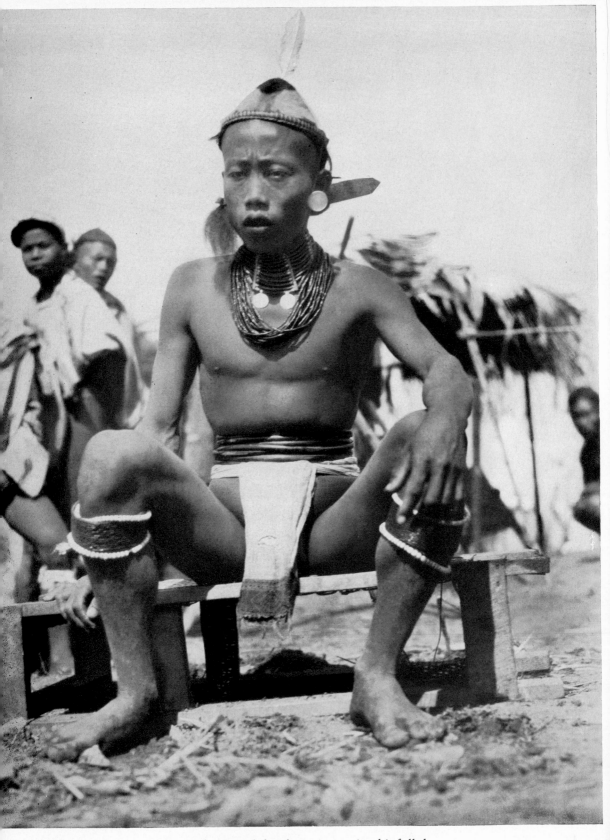

This son of a Koniak headman is wearing his full dress

Doctor Hutton interviewing the head men in an enemy Koniak village, relative to our taking hostages. Village observation post in rear

Our dining room in a fortified camp. Doctor Hutton is seated at the left

Ao men in ceremonial dress in the central square of a village. They are about to dance

Ao drums. Played for ceremonial dancing, they set the rhythm

sisted of three tight metal rattan rings fastened around their waists. The men, handsome, strapping specimens six feet tall, thin waisted, broad shouldered, cut dashing figures in these girdles.

All the Nagas had a flair for clothes, but their designing abilities were more apparent in the administered area, where they had easier access to bright-colored cloth. Here men and women went in for picturesque headgear, such as jaunty little straw hats decorated with feathers and worn on the sides of their heads. Some of these would have attracted favorable attention on Fifth Avenue.

For any tribe of Nagas, the world is bounded by its green, thorny horizon. Beyond this everything is foreign territory. What is foreign is, by the nature of things, hostile and hence an object of raids. In this isolated world it is Naga against Naga.

Because raiding is their favorite pursuit, the villages are constructed with an eye to defense. They are always set on ridges. I have already described the defenses against night attack at the approach to a village. Many times later I saw our porters furtively taking sideswipes at the sharpened bamboo sticks as they passed. They all showed an inborn instinct to harm a strange village.

The larger settlements were an intricate network of small streets. The houses, circular or rectangular, depending on the tribe, were made of giant bamboo, roofed with thatch or rattan, and completely water-proof during the heavy monsoon rains. These dwellings were jammed together along the narrow dusty streets. Each village usually had one open flat space, used as a sort of community center, where the natives gathered to hold their ceremonials. Nearly all the villages were tightly hemmed in by the jungle, tropical in its density.

Judged by our standards, the natives, as far as their persons were concerned, might have been fairly clean, but their houses and streets were dirty and flea-ridden.

During the rains the country is infested by land leeches, black devils about two inches long that lurk on the ground and in bushes, fastening themselves to human flesh with disconcerting persistence and causing tiny wounds. To this pest the Nagas show themselves almost indifferent. Having experienced land leeches in other places, I rejoiced that this was the dry season.

All the Nagas have the same food and drink. Rice is their main staple, and two types of terrain are used for growing it—the hillsides near their houses and the valleys below. Besides using rice for food, the Nagas distill a drink from it. The product, called *zu* and containing perhaps one or two per cent of alcohol, is drunk in enormous quantities from huge cups made of rattan leaves, the horns of cattle, or sections of large female bamboo. During ceremonial times they drink more or less all day, and succeed in becoming thoroughly drunk. Children, youths and adults all crowd around the liquor vats. Those who show the least moderation are the older and more important men of the village.

Meat is a great delicacy. The most common forms of it are the domesticated ox, called *mitten,* and of course the pig. The boar is kept in a pen, but the sows run everywhere in the village, where their scavengering activities keep the lanes from becoming unlivable.

Dog meat is a food de luxe. The Nagas have a distinct breed of dogs, large, with full brown coats and white socks. As they are very attractive and much prized as pets, dog meat is scarce, but every so often someone's pet wanders into the wrong precincts and some Naga family has an orgy.

I had plenty of opportunity to sample Naga food and I was thankful that I was in a position to refuse. Many a time I have eaten and drunk what I disliked because some primitive social code made it mandatory. But there I was a guest; in the land of the Nagas I was not. Their pork threw off a foul, disgusting odor to a radius of many feet. The rice was often mixed with grubs. The *zu* at its best was insipid and at its worst, nauseating.

The Nagas appear to eat almost everything. Near one village I was walking along a dry river bed with two of our porters. One stopped suddenly and turned over a large stone. In the damp earth there was a large, long-legged, wriggling insect. The porter put it, alive and very active, into his mouth, while his companion looked on with envy. Nagas also eat "stink bugs."

Each tribe has its own language. Even separate villages of the same tribe have distinct dialects. Without a common language or any written history, this people has never formulated any tradition. Each village is a self-contained unit, with only a few crafts and folkways passing down from father to son. Whatever a boy learns of village customs, he picks up quite casually in the community house, where he must live from the age of puberty till his marriage. The elders hold public meetings in the community house from time to time, and the youth are inducted into religious rites and the technique of jungle warfare.

The training of the young has developed, in certain regions, a curious method of promoting chastity, consisting of a metal ring fixed to the virile member and causing great pain till the victim becomes used to it. The origin of this device has been variously explained; one old man maintained, for instance, that the natural exuberance of young Nagas, leading to many an intra-tribal mixup, demanded some sort of deterrent. A more realistic explanation is economic: since a boy at marriage is entitled to two-thirds of the family property, the parents have plenty of incentive to encourage celibacy as long as possible.

The religion of the Nagas is simple nature worship. For them this is practically synonymous with devil worship. The evil spirits who harm man must be placated with prayer and sacrifices. The good spirits produce normal conditions and the Nagas, quite ungratefully, ignore them. They would never dream of asking special favors from the well disposed spirits.

Perhaps the greatest curse the Evil spirits can inflict is a drought season. Or it may happen that the streams become swollen from heavy rains and a bridge or ford is washed away. Occasionally a leopard or tiger attacks the cattle. Whenever a calamity of this sort descends on a tribe, the elders take counsel to see what the Evil spirits demand, prayer or sacrifice.

The ordinary method of warding off the evil spirits is the wearing of an amulet, suspended from the neck. If the evil spirits ignore the amulets a special propitiatory ceremony must be arranged. If it is something important, such as a drought, a human sacrifice may be required; for the Nagas, as for practically all other savage tribes, human blood is the ultimate sacrifice.

It is quite immaterial to the Nagas who is used for the sacrifice providing the victim is alive. A slave is usually chosen, an old worn-out female. If the village doesn't happen to possess such a creature, the headman will purchase one from a neighboring village. The negotiations are very informal—simply a message to the neighboring chief: "We must offer a sacrifice. Have you got anything you can spare?" In important matters of this sort villages are willing to co-operate.

The victim is always decapitated with the dhow. Human life is such a precarious thing in this jungle that the Nagas waste no pity on the victim. The old hag, her days of usefulness over, is led to the block and beheaded without a second thought. As a matter of fact, the victim who expected nothing of life and got nothing accepts her fate in a spirit of weary resignation.

Black despair over the caprices of the Evil spirits dictates the sacrifice of a human life, but exultation over a successful raid or a bumper crop calls for another kind of ceremony. Rich men turn these latter occasions into self-glorification programs. One popular diversion arranged by rich men is known as "pulling the big stone." Civilized whites, who have contrived many a dreary sport to kill their leisure hours, have never thought up anything so lunatic as stone-pulling.

These ceremonies start off with a gala feast for all the village, held in the village square. The rich master of ceremonies provides plenty of pork and vats of *zu*. For the celebrants it is an orgy of overeating and overdrinking. Everyone consumes several gallons of *zu*; even children toddle around with bamboo cups at their lips.

It is a period of festivity and joy. Everyone who owns a ceremonial dress puts it on. The celebrants pass the time between their bouts of eating and drinking in walking about or sitting in groups gabbling. For entertainment there are wrestling matches and highly organized ceremonial dances. The choreography is elaborate, but the tempo is excessively slow. The pork-stuffed dancers usually do not feel up to anything but the most leisurely steps.

After two days of this, the rich piper calls the tune. He wants his stone moved. A stone weighing a ton, left where nature put it, is just a stone. Moved a mile away, it is a monument to his glory. Offhand one would imagine that the Nagas would regard the stone-pulling performance as the inevitable and painful price of the fun, but in reality they seem to consider the pull a thrilling sport.

The stone has been selected well in advance. A wooden skid is run under it, and the men and boys harness themselves to it by rattan ropes. Once prepared for pulling, the Nagas are stretched out in a long, thin line, for the trail is usually narrow.

With a heavy stone the effort is great and the rate of progress slow. The stone is not dragged into the village itself: that place is already cluttered enough without a big boulder in the central square. So the stone usually rests somewhere near the trail after a mile of pulling. Here it remains, a testimonial to a futile day of glory. The heavier the stone and the bigger the feast, the greater the glory for the man who organized it.

One curious ultra-pagan custom of the Nagas is official organized cursing. I observed one magnificent example of a public cursing, and I regret that I was requested not to take photographs or motion pictures.

A little girl working in the fields within the administered area was slain, evidently for the beads she wore around her neck. The killer took nothing else, since head-hunting, as we have seen, is forbidden, and such a trophy lying in a skullery would have brought quick detection and punishment. No Naga would care to possess a skull he could not display to his neighbors. So the killer had to content himself with the beads.

Official investigations were fruitless. The inhabitants of the villages bordering the scene of the murder were devoted to the commissioner, Doctor Hutton, and were ready to help him out. They suggested a public cursing. The commissioner not only approved but agreed to take part in it.

He told the Nagas that his father and grandfather had been gifted cursers, and that he had inherited the gift. Three months before, when angered by a certain village, he had prophesied that the spirits would punish it by burning it to the ground. It did burn down. Villages are frequently destroyed by fire and are readily rebuilt, but in this case the Nagas decided that Doctor Hutton was an inspired curser.

Plans were laid for the cursing. Every man, woman and child was instructed to be on hand, and the commissioner pointed out that he had means of knowing if anyone was absent.

At eleven in the morning the Nagas turned up, the men all armed with spears. Doctor Hutton turned to the chiefs, asking if every man, woman and child was there. Each chief made the same reply. No one was absent. The killer, then, was present.

Doctor Hutton opened the ceremony himself, observing all the correct rites. First he built a tiny circular trench and filled it with water. This enclosed the Evil Spirits. Then he demanded the bamboo effigy the Nagas had designed to represent the killer. This was brought up.

For an incantation Doctor Hutton recited snatches from the Iliad and Odyssey—anything the natives could not understand would serve. Then he broke an egg on the ground and opened the trench to release the Evil Spirits. His curse was concluded, and it was now time for the Nagas to perform theirs.

Doctor Hutton scrutinized the audience one by one. The guilty man was there. Someone was exerting superb self-control.

Each village group in turn took up a chant. It was a ghastly performance, gathering force as it went along, and always its leitmotif was a bitter, ferocious hate expressing itself not only in tones of the voice but expressions of the face. As it ended in a chorus of wild, barbaric shrieks, the effect was more than awe-inspiring, it was blood-curdling. Worked up to a frantic pitch of excitement, the warriors sprang forward and hurled their spears at the effigy.

Doctor Hutton's glance strayed from face to face. Without exception every face was contorted with black rage. This meant that the killer must be cursing himself! A self-uttered curse is the worst of all afflictions among the Nagas, but the killer had no choice: he had to carry it through with conviction or betray himself.

The whole performance was now reaching a critical stage. The Commissioner handled it with a shrewd knowledge of Naga psychology. Before the natives had worn themselves out, he put up his hand and shouted, "Silence!"

The natives squatted on the ground. Doctor Hutton was silent for several minutes. Then he spoke in the voice of an oracle. "The cursing has had its effect. The guilty man will probably be dead in a week's time."

The throng remained still, awe written on every face. Then slowly the men arose, followed by the women and children. Darkly and sombrely they walked back to their villages. The cursing had been a terrible success. In a week's time the killer would be dead.

Nor was Doctor Hutton dissatisfied. Time and again, cursed criminals had perished among the Nagas—a kind of self-inflicted death brought on by their own gnawing terror. The sound of the curses shouted by their kinsmen and neighbors had undermined their morale. And a thousand times worse it was when they had been obliged to utter curses at themselves in order to conceal their guilt. Killing was nothing, but a curse was a scourge. The moral breakdown was followed by physical collapse, and then death.

In this particular case the outcome was never known. But when a villager died a few days later, the Nagas decided the guilty had been punished. Whether this man was actually the murderer, Doctor Hutton had no means of knowing, but he had a good idea the killer wouldn't live long with his dreadful secret.

Deprived of their old head-hunting thrills, the people of the administered territory sometimes seek compensation in staging mock head-hunts. I saw one in Kohima and it was an impressive spectacle, slightly on the realistic side. One saw the skulking hunter moving through the jungle, the unwary victim, the attack. The leading actors played their parts with desperate earnestness but directly it was over they changed and beamed like children. The performance turned into an impromptu festival with dances and beautifully executed calisthenics.

On such occasions the Nagas put more spirit into their dances than when they are only incidental to a stone-pulling celebration. Each tribe has its own exquisitely developed dances, and each requires an elaborate ceremonial costume. These dances are never orgiastic. When women take part in them they dance alone.

All Nagas are monogamous. Women, while admittedly lesser beings, are never enslaved. Most women marry, but should their husbands die they are not compelled to marry again. They inherit their husband's property and have full right to dispose of it as they wish; they also retain control of their children up to the age of adolescence.

Nearly all the villages have a clown and medicine-man. The clown occupies a position comparable to a jester's in the Middle Ages. As a common buffoon whose rôle is to amuse the crowd, he can say what he wants without fear of vengeance. Some of his observations might be indiscreet if uttered by anyone else in the village.

The medicine-man is an honored figure, consulted when important decisions are to be made by the village. Some medicine-men reach their verdicts by scrutinizing the yolks of eggs. Others decide by whittling. The way the chips fall determines the issue. The medicine-men have a hard time of it, from one point of view, since their prophecies are open to checking; but on the other hand their alibis are accepted as gospel truth.

Of implements the Nagas possess very few. They make bamboo containers, wooden bowls, spears, and the useful dhows. Pottery is made by only one tribe and that without the potter's wheel. All the tribes manufacture their own cloth. The raw cotton is crudely fabricated, and the dyers are rarely able to achieve more than a neutral tone. For this reason the gaudy cloths brought in from India are greatly prized.

Death the Nagas treat with much ceremony in their own grisly way.

A street in a large Angami village. Scavenger pigs and dogs help to keep the streets clean

Angami Men's Club. Here also the boys who have reached the age of puberty
live until they marry

Group of Angami men in ceremonial costume in front of a house

Angami men drinking rice beer from bamboo cups on a ceremonial occasion

Angami ceremonial diversion of pulling a big stone along the trail between villages

Close view of the stone, an unusually large one

Typical village of the Ao, who are not as prosperous as the Angami

Ao women making pottery; they do not know the potter's wheel

Ao women in front of a house

A Koniak grave, always situated near a village and never cared for after completion

A fine collection of human skulls. Passed down from father to eldest son, they are kept
in a room back of the house and greatly treasured

Among some tribes, a corpse is placed in a sort of oval coffin, open at the top. This is suspended from the rafters of the family house; a small fire is lighted and kept burning till heat has desiccated the body, the process usually taking more than a month. In the bottom of the coffin is a small hole through which the fatty liquids run out. The Nagas continue to live in the house and life goes on as usual.

After several months the body is taken down and broken up in a furious onslaught by the mourners, armed with heavy clubs. Thereafter an examination is made, and if any of the bones have remained intact, they are considered trophies and are kept in the house. The rest are tossed over a cliff.

The most common form of burial, however, is to place the body on a bamboo platform raised on poles about eight feet from the ground. Here, covered with leaves, it remains till nature disposes of both body and platform. The villagers never care for the "graveyards," though they are usually situated near the villages.

During the first few days with Doctor Hutton I saw my first skullery—row after row of grinning skulls set up on perches, each standing for a savage murder. The Nagas guard their skulleries with fanatic zeal. Heads are passed down from father to son, for a fine skullery adds to a man's prestige. Like family plate or a portrait gallery in civilized lands, it connotes past grandeur: one can point to ancestors who went out and did things.

Heads are distinctly classified in value. Offhand, one would think that the head of a strong warrior, able to defend himself, would have the greatest value. But this is not the case. A baby's head has the greatest value. Next comes a woman's, last—a man's. The reason, obscure at first, becomes logical as the Nagas explain it:

A warrior will, of course, never take the head of a fellow-villager. He must stalk his prey in foreign territory. This entails danger, but in the long run the man's head is the easiest to acquire because men are obliged to leave their villages in order to tend their paddies. A man may be trapped while he's walking on the trail alone. Caught in the ambush, he usually cannot put up a good defense.

A woman, however, usually remains in the village or its immediate surroundings. To get *her* head means danger indeed, since the hunter runs the risk of being trapped by others in the village. He knows if he is caught his own head will spend the night in a skullery.

For a baby, the hunter must enter not only a village but usually a house. It is the last word in daring, and it is no wonder that a baby's head is the most highly prized of trophies. Even in well-stocked skulleries, women's and babies' heads are extremely rare. Those who aspire to capture a woman's or baby's head must lay their plans carefully. They enter a village only after they have watched it for a long time and know that the able-bodied men are absent in the paddy fields. Even then there is danger, for the stranger has to cope with the unfamiliar design of intricate, twisting streets. Trying to escape at a dead run, he must be careful lest a wrong turning lead him into a cul-de-sac. Doctor Hutton knew of one case where a hunter bent on escape was trapped in a village. Caught red-handed with a baby's head, he was slashed to death and that night his head went into someone's skullery.

During our trip one of the members wished to collect a few skulls as anthropological specimens for a museum. He tried to buy them from the skulleries, but the owners refused to sell. He next sought to tempt a native boy to procure a few heads from the burial platforms. White-faced, trembling, the youth allowed himself to be persuaded by an offer of ten rupees a head, a fortune for him. In the dead of night he returned, shaking, with a package under his clothing. The head was hidden in one of the baskets containing our personal equipment, and the servants never saw it.

The next night the boy brought in a second skull and we saw that his nerve had given out. Neither persuasions nor money could induce him to steal another head.

China's Southwest Back Door

⊓⊔

THE geographies one used in school were primly explicit on the matter of China's southwest provinces. Yunnan and Szechuan hinged on to Burma and Tibet, and the dense Chinese population was liberally sprinkled with "border tribes." Frontiers were nicely set forth in contrasting colors.

Oversimplified, the school geographies provided no proper approach to one of the most confusing regions in the world. For Yunnan, Szechuan, and the vaguely defined area known as Chinese Tibet are, as a baffled traveler once said, "a veritable Noah's Ark of peoples." It would be difficult to chart out, anywhere on the earth's surface, a comparable area with so many diverse races, tribes, and clans. As early as the fourth century B.C., the Chinese started pushing into Szechuan, but the process of assimilation, accompanied by battles, rebellions, and massacres, is so far from complete that the region is still spotted with independent, feudal states, and the boundary between China and Tibet has never been accurately marked off.

Only a relief map on a broad scale can give any adequate idea of the difficulties encountered by the Chinese in subjugating the country. Although the distance from Shanghai to Chengtu, capital of Szechuan, is only 1800 miles, the two southwestern provinces provide some of the most rugged barriers on earth. A wilderness of mountain ranges, as low as 3000 feet at the Burmese border, rising to 24,000 feet where the ranges sweep to the west and join the eastern Himalayan spur, has halted the Chinese century after century. The flora ranges from subtropical to subarctic.

Entering China by the southwest back door provides a view of Chinese civilization that will never come to him who forms a composite picture made up of late Ming vases, decayed pagodas, and foreign concessions on the eastern seaboard. For the amorphous country of Szechuan and Yunnan shows the traveller, from the moment of his entrance, that Chinese civilization was a dynamic movement and that the Chinese have always been not only great fighters, but great administrators. "Living room," a phrase not peculiar to Hitler, was the motive for the historic *Drang nach Westen*. Ever westward pushed the Chinese as they extended their sway over alien peoples. Armies went out first, followed by governors and engineers who functioned in the manner of the Romans, building roads and bridges, re-routing commerce, solidifying political control by slow but not always merciful methods.

But as has been said, the process is not complete, though certainly hastened by China's growing nationalist consciousness, helped along in turn by Japanese aggression.

Few white men have travelled in the borderlands, but this is not surprising. As if the natural barriers were not sufficiently discouraging, Chinese red-tape becomes a positive thicket for those trying to enter the southwestern provinces. When Kermit Roosevelt, Theodore Roosevelt Jr., and I sought to penetrate the country in 1928, the attitude of the Chinese government was: we cannot be responsible for Chinese, let alone Occidentals.

But our expedition had a serious purpose—collecting animal life for the Field Museum of Chicago—and the State Department of the United States eventually intervened with the Chinese government and so brought about the necessary permission.

While the museum sought any animals the expedition could procure, the Roosevelts had set their hearts on a giant panda, one of the world's rare beasts. In 1928 no museum possessed a single authentic specimen, and the only clue to his identity came from mounted specimens put together from skins picked up haphazard in the panda country, a remote and inaccessible region of bamboo fastnesses. To get the giant panda would be a triumph for the expedition, but the very act of crossing this little known part of Asia would be a special event for the individual members.

As soon as the Chinese government had issued the permits, the Roosevelts and I sailed for Rangoon by way of London and Calcutta. This was in November, 1928. If it hadn't been for the episode of the "Red Sea fish"—surely one of the strangest catches ever dragged out of that legendary sea—the whole passage would have vanished from memory in a fog of heat, dreariness, and tedium.

Our boat was filled with British army men and their wives returning to India after spending their leaves in England. They were bored and restless all the way, and when we reached Aden and heard the bad news that shore visits were forbidden because some sort of epidemic was raging in the city their exasperation ran away with them. Late one afternoon a group on the deck discovered a good time-killer: the water around the ship was supposed to be teeming with a certain kind of white, flabby fish, and members of the group obtained hooks and lines and then fixed wagers with each other on who would be the first to drag in a catch. Six lines were lowered.

A considerable time went by, and the fish showed themselves aloof and suspicious. When the gong sounded for tea, the decks cleared on the instant; even the fishermen tied up their lines and temporarily forgot the game. On their return, one of the women who had laid a wager looked over the railing.

"Oh, there's a fish! There's another! Oh, fish on all the lines!"

There was a rush to the railing. Commotion and excitement, shrill voices. Yes, there was something on each line, a blur of white, well below the surface of the water. The first fisherman to bring his catch on board would be the winner of the stakes. Excitement mounted.

Frantically the lines were drawn up and almost simultaneously six "fish" appeared above the water-line. There was a murmur of dismay;

somebody spoke the word "jerries." Six white chamber-pots were lifted to the deck.

The shock to genteel sensibilities was immense, expressed not in loud condemnation but in low, refined murmurs. Never did a crowd yield so completely to a seizure of refinement. The only words that escaped were "Ghastly, you know," and "Such bad taste." It was plain that a bounder was at large, undetected, in this nest of respectability.

There was discreet speculation on how it could have happened. The answer was forthcoming but not the culprit. The person who did it had slipped below during tea, and with no trouble at all had grasped the lines through port-holes and had tied on the domestic crockery, which was within easy reach.

That evening an indignation meeting was held, and the spokesman expressed himself in the best tradition of genteelism. "This may be for some, a practical joke, but it went too far. The vast majority of us consider it an insult to our ladies. This meeting is for the purpose of expressing the public sentiment on the matter, and I for one do not hesitate to pronounce it execrable taste."

To an English major I said, "I rather imagine the man who tied on the fish is the same one who called the indignation meeting." His only answer was a large, contented grin.

In Calcutta our itinerary was set for northeast Burma, into Yunnan, and northward into Szechuan, including the border country near Tibet. When the expedition was over we would turn southward to French Indo-China.*

In Rangoon we stayed with Sir Charles Innes, governor of Burma, and as our equipment, classed as scientific material, passed the customs without a hitch, we proceeded to assemble a caravan personnel. Four Kashmiris, two trained hunters, a cook and his helper, were selected because they were excellent hill people, accustomed to stiff altitudes and to doing their work under trying conditions. The party now consisted of nine men: the two Roosevelts, myself, Herbert Stevens, ornithologist, Jack Young, interpreter, and the four Kashmiris.

*The route of the expedition is shown on the map between pages 4 and 5.

Mr. Stevens, who had joined our party in London, knew the East well, having been a tea planter in Darjeeling and later a field ornithologist in India and South China for the Tring Museum of England. Bird life in all the regions we visited was to be his special province.

Jack Young, a young Cantonese recommended to us by the Chinese embassy in Washington, had been born in Honolulu, had lived for years in America, and naturally knew English as well as the rest of us. In addition, he was familiar with two dialects of Chinese, the Mandarin and Cantonese, and had spent six weeks in the Field Museum learning to be a skinner as a preliminary to this trip. All this indicated, and quite rightly as events showed, that he was to be a valuable member of the party.

The personnel taken care of, there remained but one other important matter: money. In Rangoon we drew on a letter from the Hong-Kong Shanghai Banking Corporation, receiving a credit in rupees for the first part of the trip. Then, properly introduced, we visited a Chinese banker, an elderly man, who lived in a small, unpretentious house in the native bazaar. He exchanged American rupees for Yunnanese dollars, coins of silver alloy, the same size as the Shanghai dollar, but worth only about sixteen cents American against fifty cents American for the Shanghai standard. We also got a Chinese letter of credit. This process would be repeated at various key cities in order to avoid a too heavy bulk of currency.

Our first objective was Bhamo, last British outpost of civilization. The train left Rangoon on a Monday at 3 P.M. and the following night we slept in Mandalay. Beyond Mandalay, extraordinary floods were devastating the country and large stretches of track in some of the lower plains were completely under water. We were obliged to get out of the train, load all our belongings into native boats, and paddle for an hour before reaching another train. Thursday morning brought us to the town of Katha.

This trip had taken us through typically Burmese country, low and flat with mysteriously receding horizons. The eye fell endlessly on a world of paddy fields, wearisome and monotonous here as in Siam,

India, China, and Japan. The laborers were mainly low-caste Indians, imported for just this purpose because the land owners, grown prosperous on these fertile fields, usually considered themselves above common labor.

The Burmese are an exceedingly handsome race. Small, well-built, light in coloring, with slightly Mongoloid features, they carry themselves proudly, both city and country dwellers.

At Katha we transferred from train to boat for a trip up the Irrawaddy, one of the five great "mystery rivers" coming down from Tibet. The steamer provided a splendid journey. There were only four first-class cabins and we had complete privacy. The rest of the space was taken up by third-class passengers, natives bound for Bhamo. Late in the day the land rose, and in the late evening we passed some large gorges, radiant and spectacular in the moonlight.

Arriving early Friday in Bhamo we were received on the dock by a representative of Mr. Vivian Clerk, the frontier commissioner, who took us to the government bungalow where we were to spend one night. Bhamo is the terminus of an ancient caravan route between China and Burma, and at the time of our visit its white population numbered ten, including wives.

As a preliminary to forming the caravan, all supplies and equipment were checked and found to be intact. This news seemed too good to the cook, Jamal Shekh, who promptly began tinkering with the pressure cooker that had served us so well on the Tien Shan trip. All Kashmiris, it seems to me, have a natural gift for destruction, like children, and our cook was no exception. No repairs could be made and the cooker had to be discarded.

Long before leaving Rangoon, we had written to Vivian Clerk asking him to buy us thirty Yunnanese mules and to hire a chief muleteer and assistants to accompany the pack. In China proper, it would always be possible to hire mules and give our own a rest, but there would be many places along the border country where no transport at all was available. Thus a pack of our own was indispensable.

Mr. Clerk had done a good job of it. The head muleteer, a Yunnanese named Chen So Ling, was small and quiet, but obviously efficient. The animals were in good condition, well fed, their coats glossy.

This examination of the animals took place in the afternoon, and as we returned to the club, festivities were just beginning for Christmas eve. Our luggage still held a regular wardrobe which would be sent back to Rangoon. So out of the boxes came dinner coats and black ties for the last time in many a day. The guests congregated at Vivian Clerk's house for dinner, a gala occasion of good time and some champagne, followed by dancing. For us it was particularly merry; the big adventure was starting on the morrow.

Early Christmas morning the caravan was loaded up and sent on to Little Bhamo, fifteen miles distant. There was a carriage road over this stretch, so we enjoyed the last luxury of riding in a hack.

For the time being, the five members of the expedition—the Roosevelts, Stevens, Jack Young and I—planned to travel together. Later Stevens would drop behind, progressing at a much slower pace, because the country was full of interesting bird-life and quite devoid of big game for us. For the rest of the journey in Burmese territory, government bungalows offered good accommodations, but in a few days it would be a different story.

We were now in the country of the Shans, a hill district of narrow valleys and dense jungle, very much like the Naga hills of Assam with one important exception: here there was a good caravan trail, used by countless generations as the connecting link between China and Burma.

The Shans, a people with an ancient history and a physiognomy that sets them apart instantly from the Chinese and Burmese, originated in southwest China, radiating out northwest and southwest, cultivating the land and developing their own crafts. The Shans dwelling within the borders of Burma were organized in 1922 into a semi-independent collection of states. Those living in China are at least nominally under direct Chinese authority.

Even before their massive Mongoloid features and betel-nut smiles were visible, the Shans could be identified by their robes of natural wool that seemed to have no more shape than a potato-sack.

While this region did not seem too promising for game, we were encouraged one afternoon to find a pair of antlers in the bazaar of a Shan village. This might indicate game in the neighborhood. Guides were secured, but a stiff day in dry, steep, crackly jungle led to nothing. No more successful was a try at still hunting—sitting down in the cover to see what might turn up. Every sportsman knows what the chances are in this sort of thing.

There were no soldier guards, no granite shafts to mark the dividing line between China and Burma. But the land told its story in dramatic fashion. The caravan trail suddenly emerged from the jungle and before us was a landscape of wide, rolling valleys, circled by gaunt mountain ranges. Swarms of people, land cultivated up to the last square inch—these are the typical signs of China. They lay before us now.

Over iron bridges, and past a stone temple, we entered a Chinese town whose sloping eaves were visible from afar in the thickening dusk. A great crowd collected and wherever we looked there were slanting eyes filled with curiosity, for white men were rarely seen in this part of the world.

The inn or caravansery was a teeming, dirty hive without even rudimentary sanitation. Animals were stabled in a stinking courtyard, while the rooms for "guests" were on the second floor. Glass windows were unknown in this part of China, and the panes were of waxed paper.

The whole caravan was enveloped in a scene of utter confusion. Townspeople and visitors to the inn, all inordinately curious, swirled about us while the servants unpacked food and vessels to prepare our evening meal. The packers, all Yunnanese, had fastened the loads to the saddles with an intricate lacing of rawhides, so that loads and saddles were lifted off together. Undoing them was such a complicated process that we always kept our immediate necessities in our beds.

From the inn and restaurant, the focal points of the village, there spread out a maze of dilapidated hovels, all exuding horrible odors that seemed to be a mixture of fertilizer and human excrement. The cobblestone paths were covered with muck, with refuse from the hovels, sometimes with rotting carcasses of animals.

The inn's "guest" rooms were bare except for wooden benches and dirty, lice-ridden mattresses. The servants were told to remove the mattresses, and carried out this chore with unnecessary gusto: out from the windows went clouds of straw, dust, and fleas.

Our gasoline lamp dispelled some of the gloom from the miserable little rabbit hutches. Soon after supper we turned in, but the night was not tranquil. Rats and mice ran riot, foul smells floated up from the courtyard, dogs barked and human voices yammered. The inn, like all the others we were to see, had its opium smokers, and the acrid fumes of the smoke penetrated our quarters. The central government had forbidden opium smoking, of course, but no one who had a fancy for the pipe dreamed of obeying the law.

This was the standard pattern of a small Yunnanese village and its inn. Spending the night in these places was not a matter of choice, for this, like many another region of China, is so overpopulated that there is no spare room for any such luxury as a camping site. The area consists of towns and paddy fields, all cultivated up to the last square inch of earth. This part of Yunnan left an abiding impression with me because it provided a kind of discomfort that usually does not enter into explorations.

The caravan roads of Yunnan, usually eight and ten feet wide, were manifestly built by great engineers who expected them to last forever. Like Roman roads, they were designed to serve armies and traders, to hold the empire together, and more than that, to extend the frontiers whenever the occasion offered. Looking at these highways today, one cannot withhold admiration for the genius of the early builders.

But after all, the greatest roads in the world need repairs from time to time, and the Yunnanese of the last few centuries have let them slide into ruin. The good stretches have been worn smooth and shiny by the hoofs of countless decades, while the bad stretches kept us constantly on the alert lest a horse's hoof get caught between the unevenly shaped cobblestones. In hilly country the down grades were particularly difficult. But at least the trails were open, and the surface, such as it was, prevented the country from becoming an impassable bog during the rainy season.

One afternoon on trail we encountered a young Shan nobleman (the equivalent of a rajah), who was out hunting snipe in the paddy fields. He opened up in broken English, explaining that he had gone to school in Rangoon, where he had added the name Philip to his patronymic of Tau.

Philip invited us to his "castle" for breakfast the next day. We demurred, but he insisted, and we ended not only by accepting the invitation, but by following his recommendation of a certain inn in the neighborhood. This inn provided us with the worst quarters we had had up to that time, and while the night revealed only the usual filth and smell of offal, morning disclosed that the inn's chickens had been sharing our quarters. They had been roosting over our heads all night!

Sending the caravan on towards our next destination, we went off to Philip's "castle" to get the promised breakfast. For this district, it was really a mansion—a large stone house with porticoes, surrounded by attempts at landscape gardening. The main living room on the ground floor affected the grand manner, with a beautiful teakwood table, a cracked mirror of the dime-story variety, and bad lithographs scattered over the walls.

Breakfast consisted of a big stew made of meat, vegetables, and some suspicious light objects swimming in the mixture, which were eventually identified as grubs. It took some watchfulness to consume the stew and avoid the grubs.

This little interlude forced us to march late in order to overtake the caravan. Having neglected to hold out extra clothing for the coldish hours after sundown, we were chilled to the bone before arriving, very late, at the night's shelter.

The trail was now leading into higher country, and the weather was perfect, with warm days and cool nights. The population grew less dense, and while every bit of arable land was used for paddy, there were occasionally small, grassy groves beside little streams, allowing us to have lunch in the open. The groves were never large enough for a camp site, however; so the weary routine of putting up at inns for the night continued.

Often we amused ourselves by going into the bazaars and mixing with the native populations, Chinese of the south China type, Shans, and Kachins. In their steady push to the west, the Chinese had appropriated all the land suitable for wheat, buckwheat, and barley, while the Shans and Kachins occupied the more difficult hill country, coming down to the valleys to trade. The bazaars provided all sorts of necessities in addition to luxuries from civilization, such as flashlights without batteries and bicycle pumps without bicycles.

Our first real objective was the city of Tengyueh. When we were still two marches away from it, we saw a tall figure striding down the road towards us. From afar he looked like a Chinese with his knickerbocker suit of conventional Chinese blue cotton cloth, but at closer range we saw he was a white man.

This was Lawrence Peel, senior officer of the Tengyueh Chinese customs post. In an accent that would have sounded more natural on the roads of Ayrshire than in Yunnan, he explained that he had heard of our approach and regretted he was going to be absent for several days. He asked us, however, to occupy his house in Tengyueh as long as we liked. Few invitations have ever sounded so alluring. He gave us a note to his head servant, chatted awhile, and then passed on. There are many Scotsmen, we discovered, in the Chinese customs service. Before coming out, they get a good grounding in Chinese at the school of Oriental languages in London.

There was still one night to spend on the road, and we put up at an abandoned Taoist temple, run down, but more comfortable than the inns. The walls of the temple were strewn with a multitude of images, vivid reminders that Taoism, as it is practised among the Chinese masses, is in no way representative of the philosophic doctrine given to the world by Lao-tse in the fifth century B.C. The great teacher, repelled by the confusion and bustling he saw about him, adumbrated an individualistic, aristocratic doctrine based on his notion that in-action was the secret of the highest human conduct. "He who can overcome other men," he wrote, "is strong, but he who overcomes himself is mighty." The austere philosophy of Lao-tse evolved through the centuries into a vague creed made up of ritual, alchemy, demonology, and hocus-pocus. Accepting the word of the priests as gospel truth, the Chinese peasants and coolies are, nevertheless, negligent in practice; so it was no surprise to find the temple abandoned.

Since it was now only a short march to Tengyueh, we put on our best clothes in the morning—tweed coats and jodhpurs—and about 10 A.M. arrived at the customs post outside the city, where two junior officers, also Scotsmen, gave us the kind of welcome one always gets on entering the outposts of civilization, where the residents, limited to each other's company for months on end, are always glad to see an outsider.

Our luggage was deposited in the compound just as a formality and we were free to spend two days in relaxation, a pleasant prospect, for we were somewhat tired.

Mr. Peel's house was an exciting change after the inns. A large stone structure, surrounded by a small park, it was situated well out of the city proper, but within the walls. The exterior was Chinese, but the inside had been fitted up in European style with such attractions as a bath, easy armchairs, and books. The number-one boy, following his instructions, took care of us beautifully.

A thriving commercial center of 18,000 people, mostly engaged in producing or exporting raw silk, carpets, and musk, Tengyueh had no particular charms to detain us. It came into being in the fourteenth century and time has dealt with it rather harshly.

The chief magistrate was a dignified mandarin of the old school who received us graciously, examined our Nanking passports, proffered much advice, assigned a military guard to accompany us to Tali Fu, the next main objective, and finally made provision to supply us with a new lot of pack animals. When these could be obtained, we always hired them to save our own for marches when animals were unprocurable. While all this was going on, the magistrate kept his friendly eyes on us, chatting amiably as if he never believed for an instant that we could not understand Chinese.

Beyond Tengyueh, the land still showed the tight little paddies, the swarming towns, the noxious inns and mean cobblestone roads. But there were encouraging signs: the land was slowly rising and the weather was getting colder. Still in Shan country, we went through some low passes, through a good-sized forest, and, moving higher, came into a region where the Kachins, their brown bodies swathed in shapeless clothes made of grayish or brownish serge, were the majority population.

And now came the great Salween, designated, like the Irrawaddy, the Brahmaputra, the Mekong, and the Yangtze, as a "mystery river" by uncertain geographers. A fine bridge made of great cast-iron chains and floor of wooden boards enabled us to cross without difficulty.

All through this region the pack drivers were making a nuisance of themselves by refusing to get organized on an efficient system. With great cunning some of the drivers would load the animals in their charge as light as possible and get away, leaving the last to depart with excessive loads. After the last beast had been loaded, there was always a mound of baggage left over, and finding a place for it slowed us up. We never ceased our efforts to get the men into line, but still the caravan never got away till around nine in the morning, a late departure for a short winter's day.

It was decided now that Stevens with his personal equipment would fall behind us and explore the country's rich bird-life. It was clear by now that the ornithological collection would be a success. The specimens at this point included the Yunnan yellow-billed bulbul, Oustalit's laughing thrush, the dark-crested yuhina, the Japanese water pipit, the Yunnan goldcrest, the elegant pheasant, the spotted dove, and the narrow-tailed snipe. Since there was no hunting for us in this area we would press on for Tali Fu.

Stories of the redoubtable bandits of Yunnan had reached us before setting out, and now they became more insistent. One placid afternoon a man came running along the trail, shouting that there was a party of bandits just ahead. Our soldier guard, four very young boys in uniform, brandished their old-fashioned rifles and prepared for trouble. No bandits turned up, however, and later on it became clear that bandit rumors were standard conversation in this part of the world.

We always carried our Springfield rifles in holsters fastened to the McClellan saddles. At the beginning, our automatics were suspended by a leather thong inside our jackets, but they were uncomfortable, and seemed of doubtful value against an attack in the open anyway. So these pearl-handled automatics were put away and eventually given away along with ammunition belts carrying fifty rounds, to the great delight of the recipients, who considered them royal gifts.

Four marches averaging seventeen miles each brought us before the high, battlemented walls of Yunchang, a large city with a sanguinary history of sieges and rebellions. The streets and the great bazaar were teeming with gentry, merchants, coolies and beggars. Laden pack animals added to the confusion. There were tea shops, restaurants, and opium dens.

The apothecary shops were a fascinating part of this ancient Chinese city. They were filled with the sort of medicines Europe used to know in the Middle Ages. Velvet-covered shelves were lined with jars, all filled with herbs and various mysterious specifics, such as lizard skins and powdered deer horns. Presiding over the counters were venerable, bespectacled Chinese. The spectacles, incidentally, added to their sage appearance, but couldn't have done much for their vision. I tried on many pairs in the bazaars and found them to be of plain glass.

Our inn was larger than most we had seen, but no less dirty and disorderly. As a matter of fact, living in it was worse than in a small-town caravansery because we felt so uncomfortably shut in. It was the dry season. Dust and dirt whirled about the streets with every passing current of wind. I reflected on how unhealthful these cities must be, particularly during the rains and warm weather, when the fly nuisance would be aggravated.

That evening my notion was painfully justified when Kermit Roosevelt fell ill. Some form of poison had given him colic, and as his condition grew worse, the rest of us were really alarmed. He eventually shook off the attack, but he was to have several relapses.

Beyond Yunchang was another area of concentrated population, and over the miserable cobblestones streamed caravans with donkeys, horses, mules, and bullocks. And pigs. The country seemed alive with them, all going to market—little pigs, middle-sized pigs, big pigs. Squealing and grunting, they made a terrific clutter on the roads.

It was probably an extremely profitable business, since the Chinese are fond of pork and the land here was well adapted to swine-raising. But the swineherds had their troubles. Pigs don't care for straight lines: they have the zigzag habit of mind. While the young ones could be tied together and persuaded with a good yank on the string to desist from their habit of darting off at right angles to the road, the big ones had to be trussed up and carried in baskets suspended from the men's shoulders. But this authentic version of piggy-back was no joke for the porters, who had to take good care their burdens were carefully muzzled. The bite of an adult pig is a serious matter.

More rumors of bandits cropped up from time to time. Our eyes were open and our guns handy, but no trouble developed. The rumors were not all fiction, however, for in passing through one village, we had visual evidence the bandits *were* active. Charred shells of houses lined the main street, and even the yamen, or residence of the local magistrate, was in ruins. The bandits, having finished their looting, had applied the torch to everything in sight.

Yunnan in that era was infested with these marauders. Many were deserters from the armies of important magistrates, and since desertion was a crime punishable by death, they were desperate men, fleeing from place to place, robbing, pilfering, burning, and taking refuge in forests and lonely, abandoned mountain temples. With only our own guns and a guard of adolescents calling themselves soldiers, we had no desire to meet the bandits.

This area would have provided an excellent basis for a sociological study of banditry and political warfare. Remember that we are speaking of the western China of 1929, still hopelessly disunited. While the magistrates were nominally under the central government, they were actually independent of Nanking and independent of each other. A magistrate who couldn't protect himself would not last long, and each, therefore, had his own soldiers, not only for the safety of his taxable territory, but for his own protection. There were constant feuds between the magistrates, and sometimes the feuds turned into local wars. The soldiers were, of course, hated by the peasants, who in the long run were the losers. Soldiering in this region was considered the lowest of professions. Only the officers were paid, while the common soldiers received only their food and were not discouraged from looting.

When the soldiers of a magistrate, friendly or hostile, swarmed into a city, the townspeople commonly not only stopped all business but boarded up their shops. When the troops passed through the countryside, the peasants were terrified, for not only was their food cleaned out, but their daughters were often ravished and their sons carried away for military duty. Thus impressed into service before their characters were formed, the boy soldiers became wild and natural marauders, losing all desire to resume a peaceful life.

Since the soldiers were not responsible to any one save their officers, they ran wild at the slightest provocation. Looting was second nature to them.

The magistrates, of course, had their troubles. When one had grown fat and rich on taxes and extortion, there was another who coveted his power and possessions. Menaces led to wars. And there was the perennial danger of attack from out-and-out bandits. A French missionary who had been watching these fantastic upheavals for years told me it was not uncommon for a magistrate, on hearing that organized bandits planned to raid his city, to negotiate with the bandit chief. Eventually the outlaws would enter the city without interference, free to loot the dwellings of the civilians. It was all a nice system of frameup. The bandits got what they wanted, the magistrate obtained a percentage of the booty, conserved his power and possessions, and the only losers were the helpless common people.

This state of affairs persisted because Nanking was not strong enough to exert its authority to such a great distance. But even in those days, before Japanese pressure made itself felt, there were signs that the country was moving towards greater unity. No matter how important a magistrate might be, he would be impressed by the central government. It was easy to see which way the wind was blowing.

From now on, the country grew higher and wilder. The valleys were narrow, with mountains rising steeply on both sides, thickly covered with spruce and hemlock. Here and there appeared beautiful stretches brilliant with rhododendron and azalea. There were also areas of blue gentian, very vivid against the somber cedar groves. In this region the population grew sparser, and we passed through many villages with no more than six or seven wretched houses. It was getting colder and the nights brought heavy frost. Bandit rumors kept recurring.

On our eighth march from Yunchang we passed a gorge and entered a great cultivated valley. At our feet lay Lake Tali Fu, a beautiful sight with its dark-blue water reflecting the fleecy clouds lounging over the blue sky. It was late afternoon, and in the pale sunshine the junks moving idly over the water cast long shadows. Marching northward along the banks of the lake, which is about twenty-five miles long and three miles wide, one of the two great Yunnanese lakes, we came to the gates of Tali Fu, rosy red in the sunset, and proceeded directly to the Chinese Inland Mission, directed by Doctor and Mrs. W. J. Hanna. Here we had two days of rest in marvellously clean and comfortable quarters.

Tali Fu is one of the most historic cities in the world, though little remains today to mark off its glories and disasters. As early as 125 B.C. it was a thriving center for trade between Yunnan and Annam. There are large gaps in our knowledge, but we know that the Chinese were throughly conversant with its politics and geography by the end of the seventh century A.D. In the eighth century a tribal chief named Pi-Lo-Ko formed the vast empire of Nan-Chao, which consolidated the peoples of the northern and southern Shan states, parts of Yunnan and Szechuan, and parts of Cambodia. His capital was Tali Fu. By the year 938 this empire seemed headed for dissolution, but the tuan Sze Ying welded it together again and it lasted during the reigns of thirteen more rulers. In 1115 the reigning tuan sent an embassy to China.

A new era began when Kublai, the great khan of the Mongols, conquered the Nan-Chao empire. Mongols were triumphant everywhere, and thus Yunnan, which means 'The Cloudy South,' became a part of China. It was a nominal sovereignty only, however, for the component peoples, such as the Shans, the Wa, the La, the Palung, the Lolos, the Miaos, the Kachins, resisted absorption by the ruling race. Rebellion followed rebellion. One of the most dramatic crises in the life of Tali Fu came in 1867, when the Panthays, an Arab Mongol tribe, Moslem, of course, declared their independence, and their leader Sultan Suliman made Tali Fu his capital.

Five years later the Chinese besieged the city and finally obtained its surrender by a promise of safety to all the inhabitants. Instead they butchered the rebels in the beleaguered city and throughout the region. Chinese chroniclers blandly estimated that five million people lost their lives during the struggle.

Since that day, China's theoretical sovereignty is indisputable, as we have seen, but the indigenous tribes have paid only a nominal tribute to the conquerors. With the fall of Tali Fu, its days of political eminence were over, and Yunnan became the capital of the province. Today Yunnan with its 146,718 square miles, bigger than Italy and Switzerland together, is the second in size of the regular Chinese provinces. It is also one of the richest, with great silver, copper, and iron mines and a heavy production of cotton. The mountain regions are also well supplied with marble, which used to be jade—native legend says—till a wicked Burmese prince cast a spell on it.

No less interesting than Tali Fu's past was its contemporary life as related by our hosts, the Hannas. Speaking excellent Chinese, by means of which they had acquired an encyclopedic knowledge of the territory, they were able to do much good with a minimum of wasted effort.

The natives, they said, distrusted doctors and would come to the mission only when all other hope had fled. They had their hands full of desperate cases. Childbirth and injuries inflicted by the bandits brought them an endless stream of patients.

The toughness of these peasants astonished the doctor, with his wide experience, and his wife, who had been a nurse in the World War. Time and again women were brought to the mission apparently dying in the last stages of childbirth. Working desperately, the doctor and nurse would inwardly observe that white women, reduced to such a state, would never have survived even the trip to the clinic. But the Chinese women with grim persistence would cling to life through dreadful agony and live to tell about it.

Then there was a succession of bandit victims, often brought in during the night so badly hacked with swords that their cases seemed hopeless. Again it was the same story. The doctor would sterilize and sew up the wounds feeling sure that nature would end the suffering before dawn. But the next day the victim would be not only alive, but showing signs of recovery.

Doctor Hanna pointed out the grim, horrible lives of the natives. They were poor, ground to the earth by taxes, drudgery, and hardship. Opium was a terrible curse; 80 per cent of the people, including women, were addicts. They could go on for years, but as they gradually increased their consumption of the drug their vitality waned, and at the end they were useless for any occupation. It was easy to get the drug, since the poppy was grown everywhere. Even the soldiers smoked it. There was nothing uncommon in the sight of soldier bands sitting openly by the roadside cooking their black pellets or puffing their pipes.

Doctor Hanna also mentioned the campaign of the central government against the Chinese practice of binding the feet of female babies. The women who came to the mission had made such a fetish of their feet, that while they would placidly expose any other part of their bodies, the removal of the foot wrappings was always the signal for a scene.

This absurd custom, legend has it, dates back to an empress of China who broke her foot accidentally and was obliged to limp. Her walk was so much admired that others about the court imitated it, and in the end thousands and then millions of babies were submitted to a process whereby their feet became almost useless. The mincing, doll-like gait is due to turning the front of the foot under and binding it to break the instep.

The government campaign, however, was taking effect. We ourselves had noticed that the feet of all the children we had seen were normal. Nothing could be done, of course, for the middle-aged and aged women who had already endured the binding. They were a pathetic sight as they pattered around with so much difficulty, their tiny feet tied to wooden mules.

During our stay in the mission, the Hannas gave Kermit Roosevelt a thorough examination and provided certain medicines, and he was able to leave in a far better condition than when he arrived. Just before our departure Stevens caught up with us; so it was necessary to make new arrangements about transport. The larger caravan caused trouble when the muleteers repeated their old tricks. To punish the men for starting late, we marched our full quota for the day, although the latter part of the journey had to be made by moonlight. It was a dreary trip, men and animals moving with cautious steps over the uneven road. We were no less thankful than the muleteers when the punishment was over.

Now came higher, more rugged country. The canyons and the

uplands were covered with pine, spruce, larch, and hemlock. There were many spots ideally suited for an ambush; we kept our eyes open for bandits. The guard of six soldiers in ragged uniforms didn't seem much of a protection to us, but it impressed the natives. Often small travelling parties attached themselves to our caravan for their own safety.

Five marches averaging twenty miles each brought us to the city of Likiang, a vast labyrinth of mud huts, where we spent two nights as the guests of Mr. Andrews, a British missionary, and his American wife. The Andrews made us extremely comfortable and fed us royally. Our experiences with missionaries throughout the journey were extremely satisfactory.

Likiang's population, consisting of Tibetans and Nashis with only a few Chinese, was in a ferment because of bandit rumors. We were no longer taking them seriously, but the magistrate refused us permission to proceed. Then after a day's deliberation he relented and assigned a small guard to accompany us.

From now on, we would be in a country of few Chinese and this would certainly present language difficulties. Jack Young was a marvellous interpreter, assimilating very quickly the different tone of the Yunnanese dialect, but for the future he would not find Chinese very useful. Mr. Andrews settled the matter by producing a Tibetan called Aswen, who knew English, picked up in the mission, in addition to the dialects of all the tribes we would meet henceforth.

Out of Likiang the trail rose steadily in a beautiful, uninhabited region of snowy ranges and vast evergreen forests, till we reached an elevation of 10,000 feet. The first day ended in a valley about half a mile broad which proved to be a veritable funnel for the wind that rose in the late afternoon and blew all night, a furious gale. Only when we were in bed did it dawn on us that this was a country requiring tents. The beds, made of eider down and encased in strong, water-proofed canvas, had been warm enough up to now, but the winds in this valley penetrated them thoroughly and gave us a wretched night.

The animals had been tethered, but in the darkness fully half of them broke loose and disappeared. They were found next morning, but the delay reduced that day's march to eight miles.

Night found us in a glade flanked by tall conifers where the tents were put up and protected by big boxes piled on the pegs. Camp fires, lighted before the rising of the wind, were on the lee side of the tents. Yet before we turned in, they were blown away in a shower of sparks. Sitting in the tents was more comfortable than huddling around these erratic, precarious fires.

The man who suffered most from the cold was Chen So Ling, the head muleteer, who had never been out of the low country around Bhamo. We gave him heavier clothing, and he abandoned his broad-brimmed, lacquered hat. As for the Tibetan muleteers, no weather could daunt them.

The night was filled with alternating gusts and calms. During the lulls it was dead-still, but then from afar one could hear the next gust gathering speed. It would come roaring through the trees like an incipient cyclone, and finally lash down on our tents in a fury.

It grew colder and colder, with frequent snow flurries. The trail, no longer the cobblestones of China proper but simply good earth, wound through valleys and up around the edges of ridges. The going was particularly bad in the early morning when the ground was covered with ice.

The country was full of open evergreen forests of the kind natural to upland tracts. As we moved northward, the wind died down at night, but blew hard during the day. This was better for us, for we could now get proper sleep.

This part of the journey took us through the country encoiled by the meandering Yangtze. The five great "mystery rivers" of Tibet tried to find their way southward through the Himalayas to the sea. The Irrawaddy, the Mekong, the Brahmaputra, and the Salween succeeded, but the frustrated Yangtze, flowing southward in orderly fashion like the others, found its path blocked. It could not cut through; so there was nothing for it to do but go back northwards in another channel. It formed a loop and tried again. Again it failed. Then it

Open-air tea-shop in a street of Yunchang—a scene typical of any large teeming western Chinese city

In the city of Muli. With well-built houses and clean streets, it was most pleasing

The palace of the Lama King of Muli

Dawn after a cold, windy night. The tents are about to be packed, and breakfast is making ready

High Lamas. Right and left hand councillors to the King of Muli

found a way northeast that eventually led to Shanghai. We were travelling in its loop. One day we saw it struggling and churning in its canyon 2000 feet below. A rough trail led down to the river, where a boat carried us and our luggage across.

Thirty-six miles beyond the river we came to an interesting town called Yungning, where we had two days of surprisingly clean and comfortable quarters in a lamasery. The abbot was the ruler of the entire district, populated by Tibetans and Nashis.

A friend of ours, Doctor Joseph Rock, the well-known botanist, was somewhere in this region, we knew, collecting botanic specimens and data. The abbot gave us precise information: Doctor Rock was living peacefully on an island in a near-by lake in order to be safe from bandits. The latest rumor had it that a thousand marauders from Tibet were loose in the country.

A note brought Doctor Rock to the lamasery the next day. He had set up a permanent establishment with a trained staff of Nashis, and was busily engaged in preparing a treatise on their language, which he spoke fluently. It was a pleasant and useful meeting, for the botanist had spent years in China and Chinese Tibet collecting for the Arnold Arboretum of Boston and knew the country thoroughly. He offered to accompany us for the next half march, and the abbot joined him after getting us substitutes for the Bhamo mules, worn out by the rigors of the long journey.

We had felt this was good game country, but there was no evidence to support the notion and the natives were hazy on the matter. But over a good goat stew served on a black oilcloth-covered table by the Kashmiris, Doctor Rock described a good spot on our route. After parting with our friend and the amiable abbot, we reached a tract of land at three in the afternoon that seemed to tally.

Each of us went out in a different direction. The snow in the forest was deep enough to impede our progress, and there was considerable underbrush, usually about fallen trees. It was steep, rugged country at an elevation of about 8000 feet. At dusk we met again at camp. Kermit brought in one immature serow, a sort of goat antelope, while

Ted and I were empty-handed—not having seen even tracks of anything. The cold and the fading light made skinning difficult; so we put it off to the next day.

Early in the morning Ted and I set out again, while Kermit began to thaw out the serow by the fire, preliminary to skinning it.

That day neither Ted nor I got a shot; so we decided to charge off the loss of time to bad luck and move on towards the giant panda country. There was no time to squander, for after hunting the panda we were to go on to Indo-China and make a collection of the bos family, which would have to be accomplished before the rains set in on the lower plains.

Despite the cold we found this one of the most satisfactory parts of the journey, for the land had a wild, isolated grandeur and our tents were a welcome relief from the inns. The Kashmiris, however, were having a pretty thin time of it. Typical, everlasting whiners, they complained of the cold, the loneliness, and whatever else occurred to them. Their monotonous, singsong whimpering became a bit trying, but one had to admit they were diligent workers. They kept everything in good order, and their meals were miracles, considering the conditions under which they were prepared.

We had now entered the kingdom of Muli and in two marches would reach its capital, also called Muli. Clinging to the heights of Mount Mitsuga in the extreme southwest of Szechuan, this Buddhist kingdom had preserved its independence under the leadership of a lama king, supposedly of Manchu origin, known as the gyalpo. Chinese attempts to absorb the kingdom had been repulsed time and again, and with such success that no Chinese in the year 1929 would have dared to enter the realm. Muli, with an area of 9000 square miles, as big as New Hampshire, had a population of about 22,000.

The approach to the capital, twenty-one miles beyond, was difficult, but provided one of the most beautiful landscapes we had seen. There were forests of evergreen oaks and hoary, gnarled pines. Glorious alpine meadows covered with primulas and anemones were framed by black firs and hemlocks, sometimes a hundred feet tall, with trunks five feet in diameter. And above these enchanting prospects were the mountain ranges, some of the peaks covered with eternal snows.

Along the trail were many Tibetan shrines, prayer wheels, and prayer flags, all inscribed with the ancient Sanskrit legend: "Om Mani Padme Hum," or "Hail, Thou Jewel in the Lotus." The wind flapped the flags and the passers-by turned the wheels: prayers rose to the heaven of the Tibetans.

From a great distance the capital looked like a sketch of one of the Roman encampments in Gaul. Coming nearer, one could see a colony of some 150 buildings arranged somewhat in the shape of a horseshoe on a steep hillside. At the top there was one large, white building, several stories high, and at the bottom, clinging to the horseshoe like a magnet, was a building of equal size. Between them were the smaller houses, spaced irregularly along fairly wide streets. All the houses were built of solid stone, whitewashed, the wooden window frames painted in bright colors. The windows were unglazed, of course, and were built in the Tibetan style, wider at the bottom than at the top. At this altitude the air was clear and sparkling, and the sun shone with bright persistence from a deep-blue sky. Altogether, Muli was an attractive sight.

Lamas constituted a large part of the population, and a great throng of them with cropped, matted hair, dressed in shapeless robes of rust-colored wool held together by wide girdles, were on hand to watch our entrance.

The King, unfortunately, was absent from his capital, but he had received a message from Doctor Rock, who was high in favor at the Muli court, and two chief aides had been delegated to welcome us. We were established in a clean and comfortable house and told that on the next day we would start off to visit the ruler, four marches away. It took considerable explaining to make it clear that we were headed for Tatsienlu, in quite another direction, and time did not permit the visit to His Majesty of Muli.

The two head lamas took us through a succession of temples and shrines, many of them beautiful in design and furnishings. Both architecture and decoration were Tibetan in character. A small bazaar provided an index to the primitive daily life. Most of the commodities were simple food, tea, crude cloth, and hand-made shoes.

Our guides did not hesitate to show us the grimmer sides of their communal life. As a matter of fact, it probably did not occur to them that their manner of treating prisoners was likely to shock outsiders.

The King evidently did not tolerate much in the way of disobedience. Most of the prisoners then in custody had committed offenses of a political nature. In the great temple of the town, three men were locked up in an underground dungeon and chained to the walls. They wore kangs—heavy square pieces of wood—around their necks. These were never removed, and since the prisoners could not reach around them, they had to be fed by the lama jailers. The worst torture must have come in trying to sleep: the victims had to balance themselves on the kang, surely a painful form of acrobatics. Quite casually the jailers explained that these prisoners were doomed for life.

Leaving the temple I saw two heavy paddles on the walls and reflected that they must be perfectly useless ornaments, since there were no streams large enough for boats. But no! they had a practical purpose. Prisoners sentenced to capital punishment were tied to the floor, face down, and with these paddles it took just a few minutes to break their spinal columns. Tradition required the executioner to shatter the paddle in three blows. By the time one of these massive paddles was broken, the victim was usually out of his agony. This gruesome form of execution was carried out by the lama jailers.

We had been invited to spend the next night in the palace of the King's brother-in-law at Shikang. Muli's royal line descended through the son of the King's sister, a perfectly logical and even necessary system, since the King was a celibate lama.

A march of sixteen miles led to the town of Shikang, at an elevation of 9100 feet, where there was an elaborate palace, several stories high, built of stone and mortar. It was set in a large glade and surrounded by a high picket fence.

Standing in the door was a tall, heavy-set man, attired in loose trousers made of undyed wool, and a leather pullover. He greeted us amiably and directed the servants to take us to the quarters assigned to us. Orders were given that we were to be left alone for the rest of the evening.

Our rooms were approached by several flights of ladders. Except for the mission accommodations, these were the cleanest quarters we were to see on the entire trip. Low settees with tables made of local wood, carved in Tibetan style, were the only furniture. There was no light, but our lamps were put into service and presently, as the night grew cold, servants brought in braziers of burning charcoal. Thus snugly entrenched, we had our evening meal prepared by the Kashmiris and shortly afterwards turned in for the night.

Early in the morning servants arrived with buttered tea, the national dish of Tibet and also of Muli. This concoction is usually made of yak butter (yaks being common animals in Tibetan lands), and the butter is clarified by boiling and then stored in large quantities. When the brew is to be made, it is heated to a liquid in a metal pot.

In another pot is stewed a quantity of low-grade China black tea that comes from China in the form of compressed bricks and in most cases is the sweepings of low-grade teas. Then both tea and butter are poured into a wooden churn and properly mixed with salt and soda. It is a healthful mixture, the greens and fat tending to balance the diet. The butter, usually rancid, gives the mixture its characteristic taste, and the tea flavor is very subdued. It took me a long time to get used to this dish, but in the end I found it, when made of good tea and fresh butter, quite palatable.

The servant told us we were expected to join our host for breakfast. Downstairs the amiable royal brother-in-law presented us to his wife, the King's sister, and their son, the heir apparent. Our hostess was a tall, fine-looking woman of Tibetan strain. She had good features, constantly lighted up in a smile, and her Tibetan dress was meticulously neat and clean. The child who would one day become King of Muli, then six or seven years old, was elaborately robed in a lama's outfit of maroon wool.

The breakfast conversation, conducted through Aswen, the interpreter, was not, I am afraid, very enlightening to one side or the other. We said Muli was a beautiful country, and the heir apparent's mother and father repeated at frequent intervals that they regretted exceedingly we could not see the King. The hostess, like a Tibetan lady of high rank and of acknowledged equality with men, showed none of the Chinese woman's desire to mask her feelings or to retire into the background.

When the breakfast, consisting of buttered tea, fried chopped mutton, leeks and onions, was over, the host and hostess led us around the grounds. We lingered longest in the temple that formed part of the main building. The host's pride and joy was evidently a certain little shrine in the temple that held a large brass Buddha and a number of brass cups filled with water—offerings to the gods. The place was lighted with lamps, the wicks stuck into yak butter. Banners, mostly paintings done on silk or cotton cloth, lined the walls. I observed that there was no gold anywhere about the place, despite the fact that legend has this region rich in gold mines.

During our tour of the premises, lay servants stopped their chores to stare at us, but the lama servants gave us no more than an indifferent glance.

When lunch time came we were invited to take seats around a large table. No food appeared, but each of us was given a glass of arrak, a fiery distillation of vegetable juice bearing a resemblance to corn whisky. The guests at this "luncheon" drank only as much as politeness required and then announced they must be off. The caravan had started several hours before. Our hosts gave us presents of dried meat and grain, while we responded with turquoises—out of a little hoard we had brought for just such purposes.

For two days out of Shikang—we were now travelling in Szechuan—the country showed little change. Dense forests covered the mountain-sides until an elevation of 13,000 feet brought us above the tree line. After this the trail ran over a curious carpet of dark-green evergreen oak about two inches high. Climbing higher, we reached a terrain covered with coarse, drab-colored grass and moss.

We were all dressed for the climate, wearing plenty of woollen coats, mufflers, and windbreakers. But this midwinter travel at high altitudes, while healthful, was tiring for men and animals alike, particularly because the wind blew a gale against us. Our beards, grown quite long by now, were a good protection, but the upper parts of our faces were dark, chapped, and weather-beaten. Changing clothes for bed was no longer even considered: the penetrating cold would have gone through one like a knife even in the protection of the tent.

While the icy, lashing winds were a trial all day, evening always brought the comfort of the fire. Directly the tents were up the fire was built, and after supper all of us crowded around it with feet encased in many pairs of socks. At 14,000 feet, however, the joy of the campfire disappeared, and by poking in the snow the servants could find only enough brush to make a little fire over which to cook the evening meal. At such times one's annoyance at the whining habits of the Kashmiris would vanish, for they couldn't have been more clever and resourceful in collecting their little twigs, making their fire, and cooking an acceptable meal under conditions that would have floored the average cook.

One day when I happened to be riding with the Kashmiris far ahead of the caravan, my eye fell on a great mass of dry brush. It would be wonderful to have a fire again, I thought, my mind turning back to the nights of the roaring spruce logs. With some difficulty, a quantity of dry grass was gathered to help the sticks along. The high winds roared about us, scattering the snow-banks. In a lull the match was applied and the grass flared up, igniting the sticks. In a few moments the pile roared with grateful warmth. The lashing tongues of flame were a pretty sight against the snow's hard, metallic sheen.

By this time the Roosevelts had come up and promptly heeded my invitation to come over and get warm. But just then a ferocious gust swept down from a ridge and put out the fire as summarily as a giant would smash his hand down on a flickering candle. In one second the beautiful fire became a mass of black embers. I knew then why fire, for so many primitive peoples, is a divine being.

At times like these we did much walking, for although the metal stirrups had been replaced by wooden ones, the feet grew unbearably cold while riding. The cold winds and the snow were hard on the mules, particularly those in the lead. Often when breaking trail they fell into drifts and had to be helped up.

This high, snow-swept wasteland ended, much to our relief, with an escarpment and a descent into a forest of rhododendrons that grew as high as ten feet. Snow still covered the ground, but the sunshine, making a dazzling glitter, warmed the air. Dropping gently, the trail led through a forest of giant virgin spruce, and soon human habitations—small, lonely hamlets—came into view. Sometimes we went into the primitive houses of the Nashis to warm ourselves.

One afternoon we came to a great canyon and stood on the rim, 12,300 feet high, and looked down some 4000 feet to the Yalung River, a tributary of the Yangtze. It lay between us and the giant panda country.

The descent was postponed till the next day. The trail was steep, but not too difficult, and at the bottom of the canyon it was warm, almost hot. A brilliant sun beat down on a white sandy beach and on a colony of huge boulders. There was not a breath of wind.

A large party of Tibetans was lolling around near the beach, most of them stripped to the waist, the hair linings of their leather clothes exposed to the sun. This is the sort of thing fleas find intolerable. While their hosts revel in the warmth and light, they are obliged to seek shady retreats elsewhere. The Tibetans were also inconsiderate enough to take down their long hair, doubtless a nest of fleas, and give that a sunning too.

These Tibetans were not friendly and not at all interested in us. Our curiosity about them drew flinty stares, and when we took out cameras and photographed them right and left, they made it quite clear that we had approached the limit.

Our thoughts turned to bathing. There was a good place, but it was out in the current, about a foot deep. Before plunging in we soaped ourselves from basins, and then stepped into freezing, paralyzing water, that could be borne just long enough to rinse off the soap.

A ferry made of hollow logs lashed together looked none too stable, but it carried us over the river without a hitch. Men and packs made the crossing safely, while the mules were obliged to swim.

There was a pause on the other side long enough for a quick lunch, and then began the ascent out of the canyon. Night was spent in the lamasery of a small village. The people of this region were incredibly poor. One index of their condition was the absence of those ornaments that even low-class Tibetans use on their clothing.

The next day brought a steady climb through unmapped territory, culminating in a high and difficult pass. All about us were snowy uplands where the wind had obliterated all trace of a trail. Camp for the night was set up in a grove just over 10,000 feet.

Morning revealed a trail growing steeper. The narrow valleys were covered with magnificent evergreens, but soon they disappeared as we climbed into a region above the tree-line where the wind roared through rocky gorges. The wind and the altitude wore down the resistance of the loaded animals; they faltered, stopped, bled through the nose, and had to be pulled or beaten on. Finally, in one long effort, we gained the top of the pass at 17,300 feet and stopped in the lee of some tremendous rocks to drink tepid tea out of thermos bottles.

There was an immediate descent of 3000 feet, and as darkness was coming on we arrived at a small lamasery where the lamas, with traditional courtesy, offered us a room in the temple itself, provided we could wait till the evening service was over.

In the dim light of the temple one could see a row of elderly lamas sitting on stools beside beautiful brass braziers of glowing yak dung. All were intoning their prayers at a furious speed and even if it was mumbo-jumbo, one marvelled that human tongues would articulate words with such rapidity. There were other lamas in the background who blew long bronze horns and others who banged a sort of cymbal.

It seemed unlikely that we could sleep in this holy din, and yet it was to continue till midnight. The accommodating abbot found us another room, a filthy hole on the ground floor, half filled with grain bags and a favorite spot for hordes of fat rats that lived on the lamasery's plenty. But we were tired and fell asleep immediately.

The following day took us out of the Muli country, over a pass at 16,000 feet, and into a region peopled chiefly by the Nashis. All this was, of course, part of Szechuan, largest of the provinces of China proper. Szechuan, by the way, means "four rivers," referring to the important tributaries of the Yangtze.

The Nashis of this region were a wild-looking people, but not unattractive in their garments of natural color serge, usually decorated with vivid colored borders. A few of the men wore blue cotton slacks, revealing the Chinese influence, but pure Nashi were the jackets of goatskin. Men and women alike were decked out in massive earrings of silver and copper, many showing expert craftsmanship. Prosperous-looking villages of well-built, whitewashed stone houses appeared at frequent intervals.

One of the villages at 7000 feet was governed by a jovial Chinese magistrate who asked us to dine, examined our Nanking passports with interest, and then offered to organize a hunt for us. It yielded an adult doe sambhur, larger and darker than the sambhur of India's lower levels.

For several days we marched through broad cultivated valleys where a few Chinese faces appeared in Nashi villages. Our maps, which had been showing large uncharted blank spaces, now began to sprout names again. These maps were pretty to look at but for practical purposes were useless: villages invariably bore names that didn't appear on the maps; as for the names actually indicated in black and white, no one had ever heard of them.

Presently the trail left the valley and again climbed above the treeline into snowy regions where Tibetan nomads had erected enormous black yak-wool tents. There were many yaks in these settlements. Higher and higher we travelled till we were on a barren no man's land. The road to Tatsienlu, our next objective, took us over a 16,000-foot pass which afforded a magnificent view of Mount Minya Konka, 24,000 feet high and twelfth highest of the world's peaks. At that time it had never been scaled, but in October and November of 1932, two American youths, Richard Burdsall and Terris Moore, achieved the sensational feat of reaching the mountain's icy summit.

Beyond Minya Konka the trail led downward, and at nightfall we stopped in a massive gorge for a brief rest and some food. So eager were Ted, Kermit, and I to reach Tatsienlu that we packed up our beds, took one pack animal and a Tibetan caravan man, and plunged onward for a night march.

It was pitch black, snowing, bitterly cold, and the flashlights revealed a very rough road. By one o'clock we had descended to the shelter of a thick forest, and knowing there were but three hours to go, lay down on our beds till sunrise. The altitude here had got down to 6000 feet. Marching on again in the dawn, we saw no signs of cultivation or habitation until the very outskirts of Tatsienlu.

This city, 5400 feet high, a thriving center for Chinese-Tibetan trade, has one of the most spectacular settings in the world. A colony of low wooden houses with sloping roofs occupies a scoop in the mountains, and above the town rise the steep slopes of mud shale and granitic rock, completely denuded of trees. Bleak and isolated, the town seems to be occupying a precarious site, as indeed it is, for a little over a century ago it was destroyed by a landslide, and most of the Occidental visitors to the present town are unable to resist predicting that history will repeat itself.

Nominally under Chinese sovereignty, Tatsienlu is ruled by the King of Chiala, who has a palace here, a series of semi-Chinese buildings enclosed by high walls. There are also royal temples, filled with beautiful jades and porcelains. The rest of the houses are small and unattractive and even Tatsienlu's principal claim to glory—streets paved with beautiful marble—is invisible till a heavy rain washes away the filth.

The permanent residents comprise 700 Tibetan and 400 Chinese families, but there is a constant floating population of traders who bring in wool, musk, skins, and deer horns from Tibet, and receive tea and sundries from China. The comings and goings of caravans and the bickerings in the bazaars make Tatsienlu a lively city. It has no tourists, however, for the approach is difficult from all sides, and only motives of profit would induce Chinese and Tibetans to come here. The first white man to describe the place arrived in 1868, and he has not had many successors.

Tatsienlu is the first point of departure for a study of Chinese imperialism, because there the process is still in a dynamic stage. Farther to the northeast lies Chengtu, capital of Szechuan, and there Chinese domination is already a *fait accompli*. The "Red Basin" is a fertile country well adapted to Chinese methods of penetration. The land has been made extremely fertile by extensive irrigation, and both agriculture and forestry thrive. The Chinese have appropriated the land. But in the Tatsienlu region it is another story. The colossal mountain ranges make communication difficult, agriculture is often hopeless, and the mountain tribes behave as if they had never heard of the Chinese.

Before the Chinese came to Szechuan, the land was divided into the kingdom of Pa in the east and Shu in the west. Pa lost its independence as early as 315 B.C. There was a constant struggle till Kublai laid a heavier hand on the empire and created the basis of a control that continued under the Ming and Manchu dynasties. But the rebellions never ceased, and the effects may be gauged by the fact that in 1710 the total population of Szechuan was estimated at only 144,000. Today it is 45,000,000!

The explanation of these fantastic figures lies in forced migrations. As rebellion after rebellion was crushed and the natives were slaughtered wholesale, Chinese families from the east were ordered into Szechuan, and the statistics reveal how effectively the orders were carried out.

But the ancient kingdom of Shu still retains its hordes of native populations, mostly of Tibetan strain. Chiala, the Horba states, the Chiarung tribes, still maintain a semi-independent existence, more influenced by Lhasa than by Nanking. These people may be the progenitors of the present Tibetans, although their language shows only a slight relationship to the Tibetan spoken in Lhasa. In addition to the red and yellow species of Lamaism, the Chiarung tribes know a third variety—the black lamaism which may be the survivor of the original Tibetan religion, Bonism. In addition to the Tibetan tribes, Szechuan has the unconquered Lolos, who are probably an indigenous people and are as hostile to Tibetans as to Chinese. All in all, the land is an enigma, and whatever the fate of the Chinese republic in the East, it will doubtless be centuries before this country can be subdued.

There were three foreign missions in the city, Missions Étrangères (French), Seventh Day Adventist (American) and Chinese Inland Mission (British). At the British mission Doctor and Mrs. Cunningham provided excellent quarters for a three days' stay. We all of us had lost weight, and we ate quantities of the good food prepared by a Tibetan woman under Mrs. Cunningham's direction. Good supplies were not easy to procure, but the cook did miracles with her yak meat, vegetables, and such cereals as rice and oatmeal. There were also coffee and tea, and one luxury we savored enormously—Scotch scones with the tea in the afternoons.

Fresh clothes and baths made us feel civilized once more, although we had retained our beards as a protection against the cold that would come later.

At the French mission, the director, a bishop who was rounding out his fiftieth year in Tatsienlu, produced another adjunct of civilization—good red wine. The whole situation in the French mission was epitomized by the fine, full-bodied vintage that had come from so far away, through so many obstacles: the hearty, good-natured bishop, having embraced exile as his sacrifice to God, managed to get all the good things of life in a sane, human way.

There were two invitations to dinner, the first from the Seventh Day Adventists, the second from the local magistrate.

There was no wine at the American mission. Meat and tobacco were taboo. The main dish, a none too tasty stew, looked like meat, at least for a moment, and turned out to be stewed chestnuts. Eating it, we thought of steaks, and regretted that this particular kind of piety excluded the good things of the world.

The magistrate's dinner consisted of fowl, pork, and vegetables, prepared in Tibetan style and served in many bowls. The magistrate's cook was certainly not a *cordon bleu*, but his delinquencies could not be ascribed to piety.

Doctor Cunningham brought in two local hunters to discuss the game situation. They arrived with ancient ball-and-cap rifles that looked better for swaggering purposes than for shooting, and proceeded to divest themselves of a great deal of ambiguous information. Out came the panda question, as it did, indeed, wherever we went. The hunters were vague about everything, but one point: in a certain region two marches away there would be game. No more could be got out of them.

Leaving the major part of the luggage with the Cunninghams, we took the Kashmiris and set off early the next day in the wake of the Tibetans. Many hours of marching ended up in a filthy Tibetan village where the headman offered quarters for the night.

The afternoon of the second day we split into two parties, a toss of a coin determining that I should stay where I was, using the local headman's house as a focal point for expeditions in the region, while the Roosevelts tried their luck at another village five miles beyond.

It snowed that night, and fresh bear tracks appeared the next morning. They belonged, I judged, to a hitherto undescribed sub-species of the European brown bear (Ursus arctos), but an all-day search ending only at dusk failed to produce any more clews to the bear's whereabouts.

The next day fog covered the land, and I climbed to the summit of a mammoth ridge whence a clear view could be had of the heights. But soon the upper regions, too, were enveloped in clouds. From time to time spirals of wind rent the clouds, opening up, momentarily, large areas of ground. In one of these I saw running deer, four or five hundred yards away. Then the clouds swallowed them up.

All the same it was a good omen, for it proved the land really held game. Further exploration would produce, perhaps, some good specimens. And then came disappointment in the shape of a note from the

Roosevelts who had passed through that day on the way back. Ted had seen burrhel (ovis Narhuna) and had shot three adult rams and an immature doe, good enough for a museum group. Kermit had seen nothing. Prospects for the panda here, they concluded, were poor, and it seemed to them better to push on elsewhere. Nothing to do, therefore, but return to the mission, where the good supper went down well. That night the matter was discussed thoroughly and we decided on Muping, another of those mysterious, semi-independent kingdoms on the Tibetan border. The trail to Muping, however, was hopeless for a caravan; so while we went on with porters, Jack Young would take the animals to Yachow, a large city east of Tatsienlu.

It was the first week in March. Spring was in the air, and the pear, peach, and apricot trees wore a delicate radiance of buds. The alders, willows, and poplars on the slopes seemed to have a sheen, while the lower valleys were full of cypresses and soap trees. Five marches brought us to the city of Lutingkiao at 4000 feet, and the curved, rippling line of roofs was the first sign that we were in the real China again. Tea packs destined for Tibet moved along the roads, and all the produce was carried on the backs of coolies.

These coolies start their life's labors at a very early age. As children they are taught to carry small loads, and these are gradually increased until it is nothing uncommon to see a grown man carrying a 350-pound burden over a bad trail for eight miles a day. Short sticks with a flat piece at the top permit the human beast of burden to rest his load from time to time. This is his only relief unless he happens to find a bank at just the right height along the trail, for no coolie can load and unload such a cargo unaided. Should be lose his balance and fall he could never reshoulder the pack without help.

Chinese inns along these trails usually have a number of broad wooden shelves at just the proper height, where the coolies deposit their loads for the night. Nearly all these men are in a sorry physical condition, shown by their grotesquely overdeveloped leg muscles, their emaciated bodies, and the deep circles under their eyes. Nearly all are opium addicts. During the day there is little opportunity for them to sit down and smoke a pipe; so they swallow the opium in the form of pellets which give a quicker reaction than the pipe.

"The mass of men," said Thoreau, "lead lives of quiet desperation." His words apply with particular poignancy to the coolies, whose lives are short and hopeless. What the physical drudgery begins, the opium finishes. Heart ailments, varicose veins, and undernourishment make an early end of them.

We left Lutingkiao with our porters in the gray light before dawn. There was a long march ahead. Each man was given a load of fifty to fifty-five pounds, much less, as we have seen, than their regular tea cargoes, but to balance this they were required to march longer distances daily. As a matter of fact the first day we did twenty-eight miles, over a rough mountain trail, rising over a pass to 8400 feet and dropping down to 6200 feet, where we stopped at an inn.

This Yangtze watershed route led through forests of deciduous trees and evergreens, intersected by many swift, rushing streams spanned by tiny foot-bridges, just wide enough for one man.

There were no pack animals anywhere, but all along the way we met hordes of tea coolies, men and women of all ages. Our own coolies straggled out along the trail at irregular intervals, and when night came on they trickled into the inn, one by one. They looked tired but made no complaint. Calmly, impassively, they ate their evening meal of corn bread, swallowed their pellets of oblivion, and rolled up for the night.

Getting out in the morning was less of a feat now that there were no animals to be loaded. One village in this region, however, brought a recurrence of the bandit scare. Scores of times we had heard these stories, till now they produced no reaction. But this time the villagers showed genuine alarm, repeating over and over that the bandits had shot at people out in the hills. Men had been coming in all morning with fresh reports, obviously authentic, and the innkeeper tried to dissuade us from going on. We hastily took counsel and decided that while bandits would not deter us, we must take proper precautions.

The toss of a coin settled positions in the line. Ted and I drew the head, while Kermit would bring up the rear. In the center were placed

In Shikang. Left to right: Theodore Roosevelt, Jack Young, the King's son-in-law with his own young son, and Kermit Roosevelt

Orchestra used to exorcise the evil spirits from a sick Lama

Getting above the tree line. Here violent cold winds blew all the daylight hours

The end of our caravan clearing our highest pass at 17,300 feet

Crossing the Yalung in a hollow log ferry. There were two of these very unstable affairs plying back and forth

A group of Nashi. Few Chinese lived in these areas

Nashi women spinning in a village

An exceptionally heavy load of tea, weighing probably over 400 pounds, being carried
by one man to the starting-place of the Tibetan yak caravans

A typical Chinese cantilever bridge on a regular caravan route

Type of foot bridge in a country where only coolies can travel

Nashi soldier guards, lent us by a magistrate   Nashi fisherman on a remote upland river   Nashi porter carrying a Chinese in a chair on his back

A small hamlet where I stayed, in almost uninhabited country

An upper-class Lolo, flanked by his two slaves

the timid Kashmiris, two of them carrying rifles without ammunition. Not allowed to carry guns at home, they knew nothing about shooting, but the empty rifles made excellent show-pieces. Carrying our guns, ready for instant action, Ted, Kermit and I agreed to shoot at the slightest untoward movement on the part of the bandits.

Marching along the tree-lined road, where there was a constant danger of ambush, created a tension, but when late afternoon arrived and no bandits had appeared, it seemed reasonable to suppose they had skipped the country.

Then suddenly they appeared as we rounded a bend. There seemed to be fifteen or twenty of them, a wild, tatterdemalion crew, bunched out irregularly along the road and showing only two or three rifles. We were about 400 yards short of them.

Quickly our ranks were tightened as we called to the porters ahead to slow up till their companions could overtake them. Ted and I took our positions at the front and Kermit moved to the rear where he was in a good position to be of help in case of trouble. All rifles were ready to shoot.

Ted and I, alert but looking neither to right nor left, marched on. From the corners of our eyes we could see enough to take in the situation. It seemed best not to give the bandits the encouragement of appearing to be interested in their plans. Our sidelong glances revealed a tough, weather-beaten band, some Mongolians and some Chinese. The Chinese, wearing tattered old uniforms, were obviously deserters from some magistrate's army.

So far there was not a move from them. Their guns remained still. The stiff silence of this strange encounter was broken only by the muted paddling of the coolies' bare feet. Marching a good distance down the trail, we wheeled around and waited for Kermit, letting the coolies and Kashmiris pass us. The bandits still stared at us without ever having made a move. The danger was certainly over now, for the miserable rifles of the country were incapable of any accuracy at a target over a hundred yards away.

Why the bandits didn't attack us was the subject of a long discussion, consisting mainly of guesses. Perhaps they were out of ammunition; perhaps they had taken positions to look us over and see if the situation was worth a risk. Seeing five rifles, they must have realized that, whatever the final result, several of them must lose their lives. Their specialty, after all, was attacks on defenseless civilians.

All this time we were following an uncharted river, stopping now and then in tiny hamlets inhabited by primitive Nashis and more rarely in larger walled towns where Chinese penetration was only slightly in evidence. Because of the difficult, devious trails of this country, everything the people received from other areas was brought in by coolies. The swift streams were unfordable, and the narrow footbridges were not strong enough to support animals.

Pressed for time, we lengthened the marches, ending up well after dark. The porters carried long sticks of resinous wood that made excellent torches; their sputtering light gave the line a picturesque effect as it wound up and down the rocky path or in some cases along the face of vertical escarpments. Here we found stout saplings securely forced into cracks and intersections of the stratified rock and then covered over with sticks and brush. It provided a soft, springy surface for the feet, but did not inspire much confidence.

Oh, the laissez-faire attitude of these primitive peoples! No man would have dreamed of undertaking repairs on the trail for the good of others. One day, perhaps, the matted surface would give way, precipitating one or many to death on the rocks below. But not until that day would the natives see fit to improve the trail.

The religion of the area was Taoism, and one of the signs of it was a number of small temples with all the effigies defaced, indicating, perhaps, that travellers of other religions had committed the vandalism. But further inquiry showed this was not the case: the Taoists were pretty strict taskmasters with their gods. In praying for a favor they thought it might help their cause along to smear an effigy with opium, for knowing nothing more precious than opium themselves, it seemed reasonable to conclude the gods would take to it, too. But if the request was refused, the petitioners turned on the idols in a fury, breaking an arm or leg.

Curiosity was well developed in the peoples of this backward land. They had never seen white faces before, and a few glances never satisfied them. In the towns, all our movements were followed by hordes. They seethed outside our rooms in the inn, often breaking the paper panes of the windows to have a better look.

The women in this country had normal feet. It is quite possible that the foot-binding tradition had never even reached this far.

The trail of the panda seemed to be getting hotter. Instead of shrugging shoulders, we now received encouraging if evasive reports from the Nashis. One forest seemed a likely panda habitat; so we stopped, tossed coins, and separated to form two camps, three miles apart. The toss determined that the Roosevelts should be together, and so I took Lussoo, as I always did on such occasions. Finding sites for the camps brought us to a river that was not even marked on the maps. The natives had never heard of any name for it.

Establishing my own camp, I did not even wait to put it in order, but taking Lussoo and a Nashi guide, started up a long, steep hillside towards a distant forest. Twenty minutes later there was a fusillade of shots with which the Roosevelts—I learned it that night—acquired a collection of the very rare Szechuan golden monkey.

From dawn till dusk I scoured the country, climbing and descending steep slopes covered with evergreen and dwarf bamboo, the latter so dense that one had difficulty parting it to get through. The crackling sound of our progress was enough to frighten any animal away. The steepness of the terrain, making it necessary sometimes to hoist oneself up by clinging to evergreen branches or bamboo shoots, and the soft slippery ground, causing constant slipping and falling, made for an extremely exhausting hunt. The only sign of the giant panda were droppings, seemingly a month old. That night I returned to camp empty-handed.

This performance was repeated for six consecutive days, and when at the end the Roosevelts chalked up a similarly futile experience, we decided to turn southward and rejoin Jack Young and the caravan at Yachow. Elsewhere in Szechuan there would doubtless be other lands that looked auspicious. As a matter of fact, this last fruitless period had indicated where the panda might reasonably be sought. A terrain with an elevation between 7000 and 9000 feet, covered with dwarf bamboo, seemed most hopeful. The animal subsisted mainly on bamboo shoots.

The route southward brought us into one of the first settled parts of the empire. At lower levels, spring was well on the way. Pear, peach, and apricot trees bloomed in the orchards and the hills were matted with rhododendrons, azaleas, and orchids. Roses and lilies were thick along the hedgerows, and the farmers were busy tilling their fields.

In Yachow, the great tea center, we rejoined Jack Young and the caravan, and found quarters in the Baptist Mission, directed by Doctor Crook. This solid and well-administered institution, housed in a large red-brick building that seemed an anachronism rising above the welter of sloping Chinese roofs, was one of the best havens we had seen on the journey. Mail from home, good food, and hot baths were such pleasant reminders of civilization that it was difficult to limit the stay in Yachow to a day and a half.

Doctor Crook and his assistants ran a hospital in connection with the mission and did yeoman service in this backwoods of civilization. Part of their work was training young Chinese to become doctors, but their task was vastly discouraging. As soon as a man was properly trained, the local magistrate would impress him into his army.

The caravan reassembled and the march was resumed southward through typical, cultivated Chinese country. One day, in a lonely wooded pass, appeared evidence that the Lolos had been at work. Bales of cloth, the remains of a caravan, were scattered in every direction. Men and animals had disappeared. Later came news that the marauders had captured the brother of the local magistrate and were holding him for ransom up in the hills. The magistrate was hard pressed deciding whether to pay or dispatch troops against the marauders. He was leaning, when we last heard, to the second alternative: it was cheaper.

Six marches averaging nineteen miles a day brought us to the town of Tzetati, where we separated in order to cover the panda country more effectively. The Roosevelts went together and I took Lussoo, both parties to move southward in roughly parallel lines, sixty miles apart at the maximum. In a fortnight or so we would meet in Ningyuan Fu, where the French had established a post of their Missions Étrangères.

The trail chosen by the Roosevelts led through the land of the Lolos, a pure, primitive tribe of unknown origin who had kept up a constant feud with the Chinese through the centuries. Eleven different tribes of the Lolos, occupying a rugged, inaccessible terrain, had staged bandit raids without number, capturing and enslaving prisoners, and then in turn had repelled punitive forces. The Lolos were still an independent people in 1929.

Missionaries had warned us against the Lolos, but the Roosevelts took a chance, figuring that they were not necessarily hostile to all foreigners just because they were anti-Chinese. This guess was good, for the leaders were not only friendly but went out of their way to offer habitations and assistance with the hunting.

Shortly after Tzetati, my caravan had a misadventure. One morning we were travelling along a narrow trail overlooking an escarpment. On one side was a sheer drop of two or three hundred feet ending in a river. Taking a sharp turn around a protruding rock, one horse bumped another over the side. The lost animal struck a rock on the way down and then landed, stone dead, in the river.

The Nashi owner of the beast began to scream—a frenzied wail. Other drivers joined in, and in their cries there was a terrible despair, as if they were announcing the Day of Doom. The screams frightened the other animals, and since we were caught on a narrow shelf of rock I feared several more would be lost. To save myself I lay flat against the inner bank, clinging to the grass.

It was several minutes before it dawned on the crowd that this tumult threatened general destruction. The panic subsided. When all was quiet, several of the men crawled down to the river and removed the pack from the dead horse.

The lost animal was the sole worldly possession of the Nashi. The poor wretch had probably struggled and scraped as a coolie for years to acquire the nag. It represented a step upward in a hard life—from coolie to horse-owner. Now not only was his possession gone, the work of years lost in a moment, but he knew since he was middle-aged that he could never hope to earn the price of another horse. The responsibility was all his, of course, and no coolie would ever dream of looking to a temporary employer for indemnity.

After his first outburst the Nashi accepted his misfortune with the mute fortitude of a stoic. Later that day I saw him trudging wearily along the trail with a load on his back. Once again he knew the bitterness of a coolie's existence, but no complaint came from his eyes or lips. When the good news that I was going to repay him was translated for him, he accepted it with the same blank fatalism that marked his resignation to disaster.

I travelled several days but found no bamboo jungle, and of course no trace of the panda. This futile quest can be told quickly. At the end of the territory I was to cover was a tiny hamlet ringed by a virgin deciduous forest, the next best thing to a bamboo jungle.

In order to escape the evil-smelling houses, I had my tent put up, but the very first night two dogs set up a furious barking, warning me that some one was prowling about the tent. I finished up the night with my rifle beside the bed, and the next morning, concluding that, smells or no smells, the nearest house would be more restful, I moved in forthwith.

The forest, filled with thick, heavy underbrush with no open spaces where animals might be tempted to dally in the early morning or late afternoon, was scoured pretty adequately. No trace of game. The time limit was up at length, and I set out, wearily, for Ning-yuan Fu.

The French fathers received me hospitably and provided comfortable quarters. The next day the Roosevelts arrived and I learned that the giant panda expedition was a success!

After leaving Tzetati, the Roosevelts ran into experiences paralleling mine. Day after day they plodded through the forest with never a sign of panda, or takin, the next most desirable prize. It seemed a world bereft of animal life. To make matters worse, Kermit had an alarming recurrence of his illness just after we separated. The caravan halted while he lay down at the edge of a forest. Although he pulled himself out of this, as usual, he was somewhat weak for a few days.

It appeared to be a hopeless quest, and so, discouraged because the giant panda expedition was ending without a sight of the giant panda, they prepared to set out for the rendezvous. The consolation prizes would be the female sambhur, the serow, the blue sheep, and the golden monkeys.

Early one morning, when the snow was still crisp on the ground, they made what was to be the last effort. Suddenly footmarks appeared on the crusty surface, leading into a tiny glade. And there was the elusive panda, objective of all the long journey! So secure did the animal feel in his mountainous retreat—apparently he had no enemies, man or beast—that he failed to heed the warning crackle of the bamboo. The Roosevelts arranged to shoot together, in order to divide the honor. Two shots rang out simultaneously and the panda toppled.

At that time, it must be remembered, the animal was unknown to most museums and the Roosevelts had seen nothing more than the reconstructed models made up of pick-up skins.

Later the panda had to be unpacked for resalting, and I saw it for the first time—a carcass about the size of an American black bear, with dirty white skin and black markings. Its face was gray-white, its ears were black-tipped, and it had black spectacles about the eyes, giving it a very sage and contemplative appearance.

The giant panda, or to give it for once its scientific name, *Æluropus melanoleucus*, was at that time commonly referred to as a bear, not only because of its coloring and thick hair but because of its gait and outward appearance. But animals are classified by their anatomical structure rather than by their appearance, and the skull and skeleton of the giant panda seem to relate it to our racoon, though actually it is an entirely new genus among mammals.

The full measure of the expedition's success would not be known for some time, until Herbert Stevens, who had stayed in the Chinese Tibet borderland long after us, would reappear with his collection of birds and small mammals. The bird collection alone numbered 1150 specimens including such finds as Severtzow's hazel-grouse, Szechenyi's pheasant, Japanese quail, Chinese piculet, Chinese babax, the Burmese red turtledove, the Himalayan griffon, the Japanese jungle nightjar, the Daurian redstart, and Dabry's sunbird.

The next objective was to be Yunnan Fu, capital of Yunnan province. There were rumors that a war was about to break out there, one of those interminable local affairs, and all the caravan men refused to go on for fear of being impressed into military service. This was a tough problem for us, as we could afford no delays. The French fathers suggested appealing directly to the magistrate of Ningyuan Fu, who, it was said, had once been a bandit chief and was now an extremely able administrator.

So to the magistrate we went. I presented a gift, my automatic pistol, with fifty rounds, and was thanked profusely. In no time at all His Excellency was rounding up a caravan and giving the men orders to take us to Yunnan Fu, war or no war. In return for this we promised to ask the provincial governor to allow the caravan men to return to Ningyuan Fu immediately upon our arrival.

It was 310 miles to the capital, and we made it in twelve marches, travelling from dawn to dusk and sometimes into the night. It was typical Chinese country, thickly populated and intensively cultivated. The hills at this season of year were radiant with peonies, primroses, chrysanthemums, azaleas, and of course with the orchid, which the Chinese call "the king of flowers." The flatter lands were bright with roses and lilies, more varieties of them than a nonbotanic eye could identify. The country around the capital is one of the most fertile lands on earth, and every available inch was taken up with rice, beans, corn, and truck vegetables. The most prolific plant was rice, of which the average Chinese consumes ten or eleven bushels a year.

A Tibetan caravan had attached itself to our group for protection but directly we entered Yunnan Fu, in a terrific turmoil, these men were seized and put into the army. The rumors had not been exaggerated. Our own men were naturally apprehensive, but Mr. Chamberline, the American consul, interceded with the governor to give them safe conduct out of the city. Within an hour they were on their way home.

While I was getting shaved and resuming the habiliments of civilization, I cast a few glances at the excited mobs in the narrow streets, along the Lake of Kwen-Min, and then at the eternal hills rising up to 8000 feet. A few facts about Yunnan Fu came to memory. The first walls were built by Prince Fong-cia-lh in 765 A.D., and the city started out on a career that has never lacked wars, rebellions, and general excitement. As late as 1855 it was almost ruined by the Moslem revolt, and since that time life has not been particularly quiet. A long training in upheaval was now standing the townspeople in good stead, and I felt that if this was the normal pitch of life, one should relax and enjoy it.

We did enjoy the famous copper temple of King-Tong-si, situated on a beautiful hill about fifteen li outside the east gate. A series of arches, called Heaven's Gates, led to an exquisite building about fourteen feet square, built on foundations of sandstone and marble. Copper walls, broken by marble balustrades, were topped by an incredibly graceful green roof curved in typical pagoda style. It was a tranquil spot, and incense came out of porcelain pots as it had, perhaps, for hundreds of years, in spite of the perennial strife.

The sightseeing jaunt wound up with a dinner of fine food and champagne given by the American representatives of the Standard Oil Company. After this dinner everything else in Yunnan Fu would have been anticlimax. And so we ended the 1500-mile caravan trip by taking the morning train for Hanoi, capital of French Indo-China.

Royal Jubilee in Nepal

‗‗‗

THE mountain state of Nepal, lying between India and Tibet, is one of the least known countries of the world. While other Oriental lands have yielded, willingly or defiantly, to European penetration, Nepal, high in its Himalayan fastnesses, has not only maintained its sovereignty but has preserved its culture and traditions intact. It has a beautiful and distinctive architecture well worth preserving, and unlike most Hindu states, it has a written literature. Its famous historical saga, the Vamçāvalī, is still a vital document.

Nepal is an absolutely independent kingdom. The titular ruler is a king who dwells in a world of isolated grandeur like an Oriental potentate of old, rarely presenting himself to the view of his subjects. When he does show himself, none may speak to him. Speech is a favor he grants only to high officials and members of his household.

The actual power in Nepal is vested in a prime minister who bears the title of Maharajah.

The state of Nepal forms a rectangle, 100 miles wide and 500 miles long. Its actual area is 54,000 square miles and its population is estimated at five and a half million.

The country's isolated position on the rugged southern border of the Tibetan plateau accounts for its independence. It has fought wars with the Tibetans, Chinese, and British, and twice has sustained dangerous invasions. The Chinese were in a position to dictate peace terms in 1792, the British in 1816. Nepal made concessions, but maintained its status as a sovereign state.

By the 1816 treaty, Britain was permitted to establish a legation in the capital, Katmandu. One of the significant clauses in the document provided, however, that the British minister, while free to travel around the central valley in which Katmandu is situated, must never visit other parts of the country without express permission.

For Nepal is consistently suspicious of foreigners. During the last six decades only four white people a year, on an average, have been admitted to the country. Now and then the British minister invites a guest, but this must have the approval of the Nepalese government. When permission is granted to white men, they must follow a direct road to the capital. Once in Katmandu, they must never roam beyond the valley, which covers only 390 square miles.

The very fact that Nepal is so aloof from the world, so unwilling to receive foreigners, set a special value on the invitation that came to my wife and me in October, 1936, from our friends, Lieutenant-Colonel F. M. Bailey, British minister to Nepal, and Mrs. Bailey. We were to witness the twenty-fifth year Jubilee of the King's accession, one of the most beautiful and imposing ceremonials to be seen in the Orient, and, for us, one of the high spots in a life of travel.

Starting from Lucknow in March, 1937, we bumped for twenty-five blistering hours along the narrow-gauge Bengal Eastern railroad. At nightfall the train reached Raxaul, at the frontier of Nepal, where the roads were running thick with thousands of Hindu pilgrims on their way to attend the annual Holy Week, which coincided with the Jubilee. Nepal does not classify the Hindu pilgrims as foreigners.

We were led through the throngs by the stalwart guards sent to escort us to Katmandu.

A recent earthquake had destroyed the bungalow formerly maintained at this point by the British raj for its officials and guests, but large tents had been erected as a substitute. They seemed, after our dusty hours on the train, to possess all the comforts of home. There were solid, iron beds, hot water for baths, good meals. The tents were tranquil havens in the midst of vast confusion. All through the night the grinding, shrieking trains brought in more bands of pilgrims. All seemed full of religious fervor. The night was heavy with chanting, blowing on horns, and banging on tin pans.

Morning brought a mass movement towards the Nepalese railway station. Boxcar after boxcar was added to the train, each loaded with compressed human bodies, men and women, old and young, vigorous and infirm. Shoulders were laden with blankets; food baskets and cooking utensils were clutched in nearly every hand. Despite the long journey, filled, for them, with so many hardships, the pilgrims were in a gala mood: they were on their way to a holy land.

Second-class places, the best the line had to offer, had been reserved for us. We were comfortable but not uncrowded. This trip took us thirty miles across the Tarai or plains. For hunters it is a memorable territory, one of the finest big-game tracts in Asia.

At the small town of Amlekhjang, the Nepalese railroad came to an end. The next leg of the trip, a distance of twenty-seven miles, was made in a motor-car provided by our escort.

Ours was the only motor-car visible on that road, jammed now with Hindus disgorged by the boxcars. The young and vigorous walked. Those who could afford it rode little Tibetan ponies or chose dandies—seats resting on two bamboo poles and carried by four coolies. Many aged women were strapped into baskets and carried on coolies' backs. They were a grotesque sight with their legs dangling from the baskets as the coolies trotted briskly along. Ragged beggars, their faces streaked with mud and ashes, the sacred symbols of their calling, their eyes alert for possible alms, threaded their way dextrously through the crowd. Gaiety and fervor were strangely mixed in these pilgrims. Poor, travel-worn, avid for spiritual thrills, they carried on their adventure in a gallant spirit, and no outsider, however objectionable he considered their species of religion, could have withheld admiration for their fortitude.

The motor road ended abruptly at Bhimphedi, which lies at the

Hosts of coolies, heavily burdened, are forever plodding back and forth over the pass to the valley of Katmandu

Our staff in front of the Maharajah's guest house: two orderlies, a soldier guard, and the cook in white

Mrs. Cutting on the trail leading to Katmandu

Sisagarhi range of hills. About a thousand feet above, at an altitude of perhaps 5000 feet (the road to Katmandu has never been surveyed), stood a rest-house built by the Maharajah, where we passed a comfortable night. Our wants were taken care of by an aged caretaker who said he had once prepared meals for Lord Kitchener. From the valley came the rumblings of the pitiful pilgrims.

The next morning, offered a choice between dandies and horses, we mounted Tibetan ponies, so short that our feet almost touched the ground. The road grew narrower and steeper, sometimes running up to an angle of thirty degrees. Seven hours' travel took us up 7000 feet to the Sisagarhi pass, entrance to the valley of Katmandu.

Somewhat breathless from the steep climb, we paused at the summit to take in the view, one of the most stupendous, surely, that this world has to offer. Far below us, some 2000 feet, lay our objective, Katmandu. Sharp and clear the brown and white silhouettes of pagoda-like shrines rose out of the plain, and the air about them was vaguely flecked with gold. The bright-green valley stretched to a far horizon culminating in those monsters among mountains, Everest and Kanchenjunga. Their peaks, clad in eternal snows, were massive triangles against a pallid blue sky.

At the foot of the pass a real road opened up, permitting a change to motor-cars for the final run of sixteen miles to the British legation.

Enthusiasm among the pilgrims visibly mounted now that the top of the pass had vouchsafed a view of Katmandu. Nevertheless, they were tired and dusty and thirsty; every one of the fountains erected along this stretch of road by a princess of the royal Nepalese house, devoted to humanitarian practices, was the center of surging crowds.

There were few roads in this valley. Still, motor-cars were popular among the upper classes. All types from two-seat sports models to heavy saloons were in evidence. Each had to be carried over the mountains on human backs. Dismantled as much as possible, the cars had been lashed to long poles and transported by coolies.

There was another transport system running from the pass to Katmandu, but it could be used only for packages weighing no more than fifty pounds. High poles supported a steel cable, and on the cable ran a small wooden platform. It was a grandiose version of the cash system once used by American department stores.

Passing through the small villages in the valley made us acutely aware we had penetrated a strange world, a remote and alien civilization. Here was Buddhist culture of a thousand years. Its symbol was the vast number of shrines, distinctive in architecture, rich in decoration. There are 2733 shrines in the valley.

Nepal's population was not—the fact was becoming more obvious every minute—homogeneous. Short, sturdy figures, flat Mongolian faces with yellow complexions and oblique eyes—these were the common denominator. But the most negligent glance would have revealed tribal differences. Bone structure differentiated Murmis, Newars, and Gurkhas, who constituted the bulk of the valley population. To the Buddhist Newars goes the credit for creating the magnificence of Nepal's past. But the power of the Newars waned as the more vigorous Gurkhas bulged up from the south, bringing their Hindu creed and foisting it on the country.

The Gurkhas are the dominating caste in Nepal today, and their religion has triumphed. But the Newars, never forgetful of their past glory, keep their minds fastened on Buddha. As symbols of their allegiance they have their beautiful temples in the valley of Katmandu, to say nothing of that illustrious little shrine of Rummendei in southern Nepal, forever marked as the birthplace of the Gautama Buddha in the sixth century before Christ.

An amiable spirit of tolerance, it must be said, prevails between the rival religionists. The two creeds have influenced each other, and co-operation sometimes reaches the stage where both Hindus and Buddhists worship the same idols under different names.

Our car moved cautiously through the masses of pilgrims on the road; we had an opportunity to see the natural beauty of the countryside. There were groves of mango, banyan, and white pine. The cherry and plum trees were in blossom. In the gardens bloomed the lagerstrœmia and the broad Nepalese rose of the rambler variety.

Here and there were groves of giant rhododendrons, as big as American maples, all masses of flaming red blossoms. Vegetables, a wide variety of them never seen in India, were thriving in the gardens. The valley was, in reality, one vast truck garden.

There is, according to the legends, a good reason for its fertility. The whole floor of the valley was once a lake. But one of the early heroes created an earthly paradise by slashing the surrounding mountains with his mighty sword, thus draining off the water.

The car passed many farms and trim little towns. The industry and sense of order spoke volumes on the Nepalese temperament.

The buildings, whether on the farms or in the cities, bore an air of solidity and permanence. Common building materials were red brick, stone, and stucco combined with wood. The better houses in the towns often showed gilded metal ornaments at the tops of their strutted roofs. One of the distinctive attributes of Nepalese architecture is the liberal use of carved wood. Retaining its natural colors, formed into intricate and exquisite designs, it creates a dynamic contrast with the whitewashed surfaces of many buildings. Some of the most beautiful examples of wood carving are found on the balconies projecting from upper stories. The houses of the wealthy are often decorated with elaborately carved doors. Sculptured designs flow from cornices, lintels, columns. Stone dragons six feet high standing guard over a nobleman's portals are no uncommon sight.

Examples of Newar building at its best came into view as the car swung into Katmandu. But now came a somewhat anachronistic shock for the eyes. Gleaming white through luxuriant stretches of park appeared vast palaces modelled after European royal palaces. Colonnades of Corinthian columns stood out from white façades. These were the dwellings of the ruling classes, and the biggest, inevitably, was the palace of the King.

The government of Nepal is, as we have seen, a feudal, monarchial state. The titular ruler is a hereditary king. Under him is a ruling class of powerful nobles.

In times past the kings held much more power. It waned as the maharajah-prime ministers usurped authority. At the present time the King, although revered, almost deified, has become a mere puppet. He is a great inviolable figurehead, enormously rich, living in his magnificent palace, yet shorn of power. At any military function, such as we were to see, his grandeur, despite his aura of the supernatural, is but borrowed plumes from the great Maharajah at his side, who, mounted on a white steed, wearing no nimbus of holiness or piety, is in reality the warrior potentate, the dictator. On such occasions the King arrives in his motor-car with no pomp. He is surrounded by a few members of his bodyguard. Faithful to his covenant —never to utter a word in public—he sits and watches the proceedings. Directly the affair is over he is hustled back to his motor-car.

The present King, Tribhubana Bir Vikram Sah, was born in 1906. His first child was born when he was fifteen, and by the time he was thirty he was the father of five boys. There were few people in Katmandu who didn't have a good word to say for the King, but the compliments were of a colorless variety: he was a "good" man, he was well educated, he knew English, he had permitted sound-equipment to be installed in the palace's little theatre so that films might be exhibited twice a year. The King did not stimulate much conversation. It was the Maharajah who captured public interest.

Modern Nepalese history is synonymous with the activities of the maharajahs. The Gurkhas captured the country in 1768. For almost a century Katmandu was the center of plot, counterplot, and massacre. Striated with intrigue, the country's history takes on a complicated, sanguinary design that makes the story of Renaissance Italy a relatively simple affair. The upheavals reached a climax in the famous Kot massacre of September 15, 1846, that brought Jung Bahadur into the role of dictator.

By 1850, Jung Bahadur felt secure enough to leave the country and pay his respects to Queen Victoria in England. He returned with new ideas (designs for palaces among them) he had picked up in Europe, and he spent the next twenty-seven years improving the country and consolidating his own power.

View over a section of the city. A hundred thousand pilgrims were reported to have travelled here from India for the holy week

Massed Nepalese watching the procession led by the King

The King on his elephant slowly progressing through the city

The great temple of Pashpati. Here swarms of pilgrims come to bathe in the sacred river that washes its steps

At a military review. The Maharajah, mounted at left, in dress uniform.
The Commander-in-chief, in mourning white, is standing beside him

During the ceremony at the King's palace, the Maharajah greets Lt. Col. Bailey

A group of pilgrims in the city, receiving alms dispensed by order of the Maharajah during the holy week

Maharajah welcoming guests in front of the King's palace

Nepalese officers waiting to do homage to the King in his pagoda

The Maharajah, in full dress, standing in attendance by the King's pagoda.
The King is seen within on his throne

Inside the pagoda, the King, a holy figure in Nepal, is seated on his throne.
He has removed his coat, and high priests surround him

After his death in 1877, three maharajahs divided what was left of the century between them. Then in 1901 came another formidable figure, the Maharajah Chandra Sham Sher Jung, who not only improved the internal condition of the country but cemented relations with the British raj. He died in 1929, and his place was taken by his brother, the present Maharajah, whose full title is Lieutenant General His Highness (Ojaswi Rajanya Projjwala Sri Sri Sri) Maharajah Joodha Shumshere Jung Bahadur Rana G.C.S.I.G.C.I.E.; Honorary Colonel of all the Gurkha Rifle Regiments of the Indian Army; Prime Minister and Supreme Commander-in-Chief of Nepal. Not committed to silence like the King, the Maharajah is in a position to make himself heard and felt throughout the kingdom. A person of acute intelligence, a strong personality, he has continued his brother's program of strengthening the country's economic and defensive position.

The office of Maharajah is hereditary but there is a peculiar aspect to the succession. The Maharajah's eldest son does not necessarily obtain the office. His successor is the eldest of his sons and nephews. In times past this has often caused feuds, with brothers and cousins fighting each other to seize power.

While our first few days in Katmandu were spent in social activities and in acquiring a little academic knowledge of the country, the time was now at hand when we would see flashes of the Nepalese official scene with our own eyes.

Katmandu wore a festal air long before the Jubilee was due to open. The initial ceremony was the famous "mile of emeralds" parade wherein the King and Maharajah would show themselves to the populace. Driving out from the Residency we passed through a mile and a half of crowded streets to the special vantage point assigned to the British minister and his guests. The street crowds were kept within bounds by the police, armed with businesslike sticks. Radiant, expectant faces were visible in every window, on every balcony. At cross streets one glimpsed temple steps massed with thousands of spectators, and above their heads rose the sculptured monsters of Nepalese legend.

[157]

A second-story balcony, covered with an awning, afforded a close-up view of the "mile of emeralds." Even before the parade began it was a brilliant scene. Women in colorful raiment occupied balconies, windows, and roofs. The old Newar creative impulse was visible in the women's clothes. Shirtwaist, skirt, and headdress, all of bright, contrasting colors, showed an innate sense of design and proportion. Around the waist the women wore coils of bright-hued wool or silk. Originally donned for utilitarian purposes (the Nepalese climate is an incubator of stomach ailments), these girdles have come to form a distinctive part of the dress. Wherever the eye turned there was a flash of jewelry. Bangles, necklaces, pins, and enormous earrings were made of lead, brass, silver-bronze, silver, gold. Some of the more exquisite pieces were made of coral and gold and turquoise and silver.

The men wore the standard Nepalese garb: pillbox hats, suits consisting of knee-length coats with a long row of buttons in front, and trousers resembling jodhpurs. The favorite color was a sort of aubergine, but plum, brown, and dark green were common. The material was a certain kind of intricate quilted, glazed chintz, an evolution of the Newar influence.

To add to this scene, triumphal arches had been erected and the pilasters were covered with Tibetan tank-as and almost life-sized, tinted photographs of Nepalese officials.

The procession was announced from afar by the strains of a band. Presently small units of lancers and infantry were filling the narrow street.

Then came the King riding with one aide on an elephant. The howdah was as high as our balcony. The eyes of the spectators, facing the blaze of jewelled glory, fell first on the King's headgear. This was the famous jewelled helmet, one of the most famous crowns in the world. Emeralds, rubies, diamonds, and pearls, arranged by the cunning hand of a great jeweller, covered the head. Over the royal brow dangled a fringe of pear-shaped emeralds. Over the right ear was a mammoth cluster of pear-shaped or tear-drop emeralds. Surmounting the jewelled helmet was a bird-of-paradise feather in natural colors.

It was several seconds before the eye had leisure to scrutinize the King's face. Over the bridge of the nose were two small caste marks, red and white, belonging to the highest division of the ruling caste. The King was calm and impassive. He glanced neither to right nor left. His spectacles, a bizarre touch in all this ancient splendor, added a few years to his age. He looked about thirty-five.

The King wore a white Nepalese suit of the type already described. Massive epaulets of solid gold stood out from his shoulders. His left breast blazed with a cluster of gems that once belonged to the notorious Nana Sahib of Indian Mutiny fame.

Even with our perfect view and the leisurely pace of the procession, there was hardly time to gather in the details of the magnificent panoply. The howdah, for instance, deserved special attention. It was made of silk and exquisitely painted wood. Four golden rods held the canopy in place. The elephant was practically covered, from howdah to ankles, with crimson velvet thickly encrusted with gold embroidery.

Another elephant now came into view. In the howdah was a distinguished, middle-aged man, wearing a jewelled helmet only slightly less magnificent than the King's. Strewn over the front of his khaki uniform were jewelled decorations and orders. So numerous were the rubies and emeralds that bursts of colored flame seemed to dart from his person as he came into the direct rays of the sun. This was the Maharajah, the dictator of Nepal.

More elephants, more howdahs. Velvet hangings for the elephants. More jewelled helmets, many famous in Nepalese history. Princes of the royal line. Generals, nobles, great and small. The Gurus or high priests. It was graduated glory, this mile of emeralds, for the helmets grew smaller, the jewels less numerous, and before it was over motorcars had supplanted elephants.

Another day brought the military phase of the celebration. The Maidan, Katmandu's great rectangular parade-ground, was the scene of two big reviews. On one side of the Maidan are three bronze equestrian statues, heroic size, said to weigh four tons each, depicting the rulers of Nepal. These, like the motor-cars, were brought over the mountains on human backs. In the center of the area was the historic tree, now surrounded by a plinth, under which Jung Bahadur was wont to hold his open-air tribunals.

Below the tree and the statues stood Gurkha regiments, ready to perform for the King and the Maharajah. The Maharajah arrived first—on horseback. Followed by his bodyguard he galloped briskly to the plinth. After receiving the salutes of the high generals he came forward and shook hands with the Baileys and their guests in a flourish of cordiality.

Now the King's car appeared in the distance followed by a mounted bodyguard. In a few minutes it drove into the Maidan. The door opened, but it was several minutes before the King appeared. A great hush fell on the throng, and a slim figure clad in white emerged from the car. The mysterious sovereign who may be seen but never heard was joined by his sons. They walked to the plinth and shook hands with those of us who were waiting in the reviewing stand. Not a word was spoken.

The military part of the Jubilee began, as it ended, with a prolonged volley—a real *feu de joie* of 12,000 rifles and a number of field-guns. The actual maneuvers took but a few minutes.

The Gurkha regiments, forty or fifty thousand strong, are the pride of Nepal. This is a vast force for a small state that has no need to fear invasion. The officers are members of the nobility, born to their position. It is possible, indeed, to be born a general. Some of the generals actually leading the troops at the maneuvers were certainly not more than twenty years old.

A few days later the militia again had its innings when 12,000 troops passed in review. Two solid hours were filled with the sounds of marching feet. It was a somewhat tedious performance, for the spectators had to rise each time a new regiment passed with colors unfurled. Sitting in a marquee tent we were entertained in amicable conversation by the Commander-in-Chief (the Maharajah's title is *Supreme* Commander-in-Chief), who sat near us. On this occasion his garb showed nothing of his military rank. He had recently lost his mother, and Nepalese tradition ordained that he wear mourning clothes of white and refrain from cutting his hair, fingernails, and toe-nails for one month.

As a finale, a finely trained demonstration battalion executed a complicated manual drill with rifles. The King and the Maharajah, superbly mounted, reviewed the display, and the eager eyes of the natives, watching from the margin of the Maidan, were enthralled by the majestic figures of the rulers.

The Jubilee's most impressive performance was perhaps the festival at the King's palace. Time after time we had driven by the gates, unable to catch more than a glimpse of the grounds and the white façade. But this day our curiosity was to be satisfied. The car drove through the great gateway.

On both sides of the driveway were beautifully laid-out gardens. A dozen marquees, loudspeakers jutting out from their silk walls, had been erected on a stretch of greensward. These were for specially invited guests.

The King came down the grand staircase fronting the palace. Over the jewelled helmet, an equerry held a big-tasselled, yellow silk um-brella. Surrounded by Gurus (priests) bedecked in cloth of gold and jewels, the King walked over the lawn to a small pagoda. The whole ceremony was to hinge on the reading of a proclamation by the Maharajah. It was an interesting document, but far more interesting in the eyes of the foreigners was the splendid regalia of the Nepalese. Most of the jewels, jewelled helmets, and vestments of gold and silver in the kingdom must have been concentrated in the marquee area that afternoon. Shafts of sunlight falling on emeralds, rubies, and diamonds created a blaze of multicolored light that seemed to justify the most naïve Occidental's vision of the Orient. The trim figures of the soldiers, in khaki or white uniforms, created a perfect frame for so much magnificence.

The Maharajah, who had added a sword to his peacock raiment, now stepped to the rostrum and read his proclamation. It related Nepal's progress and recited the glories of his Nepalese majesty. That night the good news would go out to the four corners of the kingdom that hundreds of convicts serving terms for minor offenses were to be released.

After listening to this, the King—in silence, of course—received those who had been admitted to the marquee area, beginning with the army officers, the highest caste in the land, and proceeding in order of rank down through the civil officials. Although the Maharajah was circulating about the pagoda in all his finery, the King held the center of the stage.

There was only one more ceremony, a grand finale consisting of elaborate fireworks. The nobles drove their motor-cars to the Maidan. While the public was not admitted to this section, the cries of excitement coming out of the darkness revealed that thousands were watching. There were rockets, designs in colored fire, Roman candles in novel arrangements. Across the field a fiery battleship attacked a fort, every object outlined and animated by Roman candles. The inland natives who had never seen the sea must have found their imaginations taxed by the battleship scene. Something nearer their own experience was an elephant with its howdah outlined in colored lights glittering across the Maidan.

The official ceremonies over, the hundred thousand pilgrims from India were now able to attend to their religious duties. One of their inevitable customs was to bathe in the stream by the temple of Pashpati in order to obtain remission of their sins. The narrow stream had been dammed a little to form a pool. Filthy, slimy steps led down to it. Down these steps trailed the young and old, the vigorous, the decrepit, the rich and poor. All bathed in the sacred, polluted waters. Sometimes Nepalese women in purdah arrived in palanquins and merely touched the water with their feet.

Attending the Holy Week ceremonies, the orthodox believe, helps their chances of ultimate salvation. The long, hard journey, especially difficult for the dwellers of the hot plains, spells the end for many. But such a death is regarded, particularly by the old and infirm, as a glorious end to life. The Maharajah is supposed to feed the needy pilgrims, but he cannot reach them all.

The Holy Week throngs always include a number of Sadus, a holy sect of Brahmins who cover their bodies with ashes and live on alms.

There is insufficient room in the houses for all this influx. Many pilgrims find places to eat and sleep in the groves around the outlying temples. They end up by defiling their sanctuaries.

Lieutenant-Colonel Bailey, a scholar and naturalist, and his wife had examined every phase of Nepalese life with appreciative eyes. They now made it possible for us to visit places of historic and contemporary interest without, of course, ever leaving the valley.

Katmandu with its 50,000 people affords a representative view of Nepalese achievement. The past and the present mingle harmoniously. One may see past glories, such as the golden, seated figure covered by a golden umbrella in the mall of Bhupatindra, and the Temple of Taleju at Hanuman-Dkoka. The invasion of modernism is exemplified, at its extremes, by the royal palace and the hovels with corrugated iron roofs erected after the earthquake.

The religious orthodoxy of the Hindus stands out in sharp contrast with the freer customs of the Newars. Newar women, to give but one example of their freedom, may divorce their husbands for the price of two betel nuts. Whenever they feel they have had enough, they may pack up and place the nuts under the connubial pillow. Not a few women avail themselves of the privilege.

The ancient Newar culture is seen at its best in Katmandu's two rival cities, Bhatgaon and Patan.

Bhatgaon, once a royal stronghold, lies eight miles to the east of Katmandu. Its 30,000 people live in the still substantial shadows of past grandeur. Bhatgaon has no royal palace with Corinthian columns, but it has something finer. Extending out from its center, the Durbar Square, are scores of palaces, temples, pagodas, towers, monasteries and shrines, most of them in good preservation, and all showing the exquisite subtlety of Newar art. Such buildings as the Changa Naroyan and the ancient structures facing the Durbar Square contain the very essence of Newar architecture. For the Newars, at their best, reached the peaks. They were at once bold and original and full of subtle invention, like the Gothic builders of the Middle Ages. The Occidental has no difficulty in apprehending the spirit of this art. There is no deceptive *mésalliance* between structure and decoration, such as we often see in Oriental art. With the Newars, decoration stems from function. Those who maintain that the pagoda was a Nepalese rather than a Chinese inspiration must be heartened by the sight of Bhatgaon. The pagoda here seems to spring from the very soil.

The Newars were excellent craftsmen in precious metals and brass. Many examples of their handicraft are visible in the temples, but even if all had been lost, one would divine their abilities from the lovely wood carving that adorns so many of their buildings. The Newars treated wood as if it were a precious metal.

Bhatgaon was built a century later than Katmandu, but Patan, the third great shrine city of the valley, was built a century earlier than the present capital.

Patan, five miles to the south of Katmandu, with a population of 30,000, is still a repository of Newar art. It has its Krishna-Dewal Temple, its Bhim Sen Temple, its shrine of Machendranath, incomparable jewels, all of them. Here, as in the other two cities, one sees strutted roofs, roofs of gilded bronze, metal-work doors, balconies of jewel-like wood carving that show the prodigal variety of the Newar creative sense. The 30,000 Patanese, like the inhabitants of many an Italian city, seem dwarfed by the glories of their past.

Aside from its architecture, Nepal offers plenty of temptation but little opportunity for researchers. While human, plant, animal, and bird life all merit extended study, little has been done because white men are not admitted. The Nepalese are apt to regard scientific work as a cloak for espionage. Like the Tibetans they have watched European encroachments with a wary eye. The old adage, "Where white man goes, there follows an army," is a part of their creed and explains

Lt. Col. F. M. Bailey, British Minister to Nepal (right), and the author,
in front of the residency

A square in Katmandu. The houses have most exquisite wood carvings

Better type of residence in the city proper

Bodenath, in Katmandu. The only Buddhist temple in the city

Carved stone figures on a temple in Patan, a town in the valley of Katmandu

why they keep their frontiers closed. Yet the foreigner who enters under proper auspices is shown the greatest courtesy by nobles and common people alike.

One evening we were taken by the Baileys to the royal palace, which was showing the film, "The Great Ziegfeld," in its theatre, recently fitted with sound-equipment. As our car stopped at the theatre's private entrance, a youth stepped forward and opened the door. Recognizing the eldest of the princes, my wife engaged him in conversation as she was getting out of the car. The prince showed a boyish enthusiasm about the film. "Oh, yes, I have seen it—three times. This will be my fourth." This little episode in a hidebound court would prove nothing if it were not buttressed by dozens of similar instances. Simple instinctive courtesy was as natural to princes as to the common man.

Earlier commentators on the Nepalese character received the same impression when the Maharajah Jung Bahadur visited England. Taking him to the opera, Queen Victoria expressed fears he would be bored because he couldn't understand Italian. But suddenly he applauded an aria as enthusiastically as the other guests in the box. The Queen whispered, "But you have not understood what she was singing."

Jung Bahadur replied, "No, M'am, nor do I understand what the nightingales are saying."

Cheetah Hunting

~~~~~~

A WHOLE literature has grown up around the fox and the hound, but of cheetah hunting, a more ancient sport and a much faster one, very little has ever been written.

The cheetah is one of the most curious and interesting animals in existence, and the sport in which he becomes the leading actor deserves special attention in a book on travel and exploration.

Although cheetah hunting has dwindled today in India to such an extent that there are but few places where it may be witnessed, it was once quite common, and we learn from miniatures that it was popular with the Mogul conquerors of North India many centuries ago.

One of the places where it survives with its old-time vigor is the native state of Kolhapur, situated in the Deccan of South India. The Maharajah, an ardent sportsman and famous pigsticker, is enthusiastic about the cheetah.

While my wife and I were staying with the Maharajah he arranged a hunt for us, although it was not the proper season. I regarded it as a completely new experience—outside the usual hunting tradition. I write about it now as a novelty unknown to most sportsmen and hunters.

It was an impressive sight to walk into the long, high buildings in which the Maharajah housed his cheetahs and see the animals sitting on their individual *charpois* or native beds along the wall. Each cheetah wore a hood, a black hood fitting snugly around the head. Two personal attendants were watching over the animals as if they were royal infants.

There were thirty-five of them lining the walls, the youngest being around three years old, the oldest eight or ten. Since the animal is becoming scarcer and the African breed not only grows bigger and stronger but acquires greater speed, the Maharajah imported his from Kenya. Brought to India, they had to be domesticated and trained. Each animal was worth something between £200 and £250.

It was obvious that the cheetahs took kindly to their keepers and mode of training. They responded much better than leopards, on which the ruler had conducted some abortive experiments.

Having trained his imported cheetahs in admirable fashion and revived an ancient sport, the Maharajah sold some of his surplus animals to other princes of India, including the late Gaekwa of Baroda, his uncle by marriage.

The cheetah, a member of the cat family, has many qualities of the dog. The height of the shoulders is about the same as those of an adult greyhound. The torso and legs also resemble a greyhound's. The cheetah lacks the back leg knee-bend common to the lion, leopard, and tiger. Again the feet are those of a hound with heavy, nonretractable claws. In size, however, the feet are much larger.

Yet, for all these resemblances to a dog, one glance classifies the cheetah as a cat: his markings are spots, his skull, eyes, and teeth are feline, his habits are purely carnivorous. Lastly the cheetah has a definite purr.

Like falcons, cheetahs wear hoods at all times except when they are being fed and exercised and at the moment when they take part in the chase. The hood on the cheetahs serves the same purpose as it does on falcons. It keeps them quiet and tractable. Contrary to what one might expect, it does *not* cause their eyesight to become any less keen.

One of the first things I learned about the Maharajah's cheetahs was that fondling them even when they were in their *charpoys,* properly hooded, was a risky pastime.

In Kolhapur the quarry was always black buck. The cheetah was strictly trained to kill none but adult males. Because these are readily distinguishable in any herd by their dark color, a slow and curious process of familiarizing the cheetahs with this shade was carried out. The men who fed them dressed exclusively in black, while the regular keepers wore white. Having killed, the cheetah was invariably allowed to feed providing he had dispatched a buck. But if he killed a female he was haltered and pulled away: the punishment soon taught its lesson.

The cheetah's daily exercise varies. Usually he is led up a road on a halter by one keeper in white and then encouraged to run back to another keeper in black, who holds a piece of meat in his hand. Unlike whippets, on the leash the cheetah does not strain, and released he carries out his act without enthusiasm. Another exercise is a real black-buck hunt to keep him in good trim for big occasions.

The speed of the cheetah is amazing. He is well aware that no other animal can rival him in this regard. The tiger, lion, and leopard rarely rush their quarries more than a hundred yards. After that they desist, knowing they cannot catch up with game that has attained its maximum speed.

Trained cheetahs proceed slowly and methodically, choosing their quarry out of the herd. Only when the quarry has attained its greatest speed does the cheetah run him down with that tremendous burst that has no parallel in the entire animal kingdom. The cheetah's *lasting* powers lie somewhere between a cat's and a dog's, but nearer a cat's.

This ancient sport of India does not affect the abundance of game, for no great number of buck is destroyed and the herds are plentiful. Furthermore, the slain buck are eaten.

The day of the hunt a car called for my wife and me at six in the morning. An hour later we arrived at the plains where the hunt was to be held. Here we were greeted by the Maharajah, the Maharani, the Maharajah's sister, his niece, and two men guests, both Indians.

The genial Maharajah, who tips the scales at 300 pounds, is one of

India's greatest sportsmen. His cheetah hunts are famous. He is an expert pigsticker, a daring cross-country rider. His stables hold 300 horses of Indian, English, and Australian breeding, his kennels bird and hunting dogs of every kind, 275 in all, and his fields fine herds of Brahminy cattle. Even his pets are unusual. Near his house were to be seen at that time a young lion and lioness and a pair of two-year-old tigers gambolling around on thirty-five-foot leads. Formidable sloth bears, that most dangerous of animals that attacks without provocation and has been known to tear a man to pieces for no reason at all, were sometimes seen walking down the village streets with their keeper.

The Maharajah's sister also has a unique place in the Indian sports world. She is the only woman pigsticker in all India. White women are not allowed to join the clubs, and native women do not participate. But at the age of forty, the Maharajah's sister has made a great reputation in a difficult sport. An active rider and hunter, she is a handsome woman, but belongs to a type that may be found among sportswomen of England and America, never in India. She is keen, trained down, alert.

The Maharajah usually followed the cheetah hunt from a brake or light wagon, specially built according to his own designs. It carried one eight feet above the ground and was drawn by four Australian walers. But although it was now early October, the beginning of the dry season, the grass, still high from the recent monsoon rains, covered many blind ditches that would have made riding in a brake impossible. So for this special, off-season hunt, the Maharajah elected specially built motor-cars with high shelves for the cheetahs. In addition there were two lorries, one for additional cheetahs and their attendants, the other to supply us with tea and sandwiches.

After a cup of tea we were off on a wild ride by seven o'clock, bumping and crashing along at thirty-five miles an hour. In one car went the Indian ladies and one of the guests. In another my wife rode in front with the driver, while I was sandwiched in between the Maharajah and his other guest.

A cheetah, still hooded, was lying on a platform built into the car at about the level of my knees. His keeper, crouched on the running-board, a precarious perch, had to keep his eyes on the animal and also get out at times and have a look at the trappy ground. On we careened, sometimes on lanes, but more often across open country where our thirty-five miles an hour was a dizzy speed. Every one held on like mad.

Having found a herd, we maneuvered for a proper position. Then began the real strategy. In confronting a large herd, an attempt was always made to detach the males—quarries for the cheetahs. They were kept in a continuous stampede. Since they did not run in a straight line, the car bucketing along was able to keep up with them.

I was trying to operate a camera, and because it required two hands I had to relinquish my grip. The car swerved violently. The cheetah and I were thrown forward, landing on my wife's neck. No more did we get settled than it happened again.

Then, with everything perfectly timed by the Maharajah, the car stopped. The cheetah was unloaded, unhooded, and hustled out on the grass. For a half minute he stood there sizing up the situation. At a gentle, slow lope he started off toward the herd. The black buck, about two hundred yards away, began to move off. The field was alive with galloping forms, their bounds increasing progressively in length. By now the cheetah had chosen his particular quarry. He rushed towards it with incredible speed.

The quarry, realizing too late that he could not match the cheetah's speed, attempted a downhill slope. The cheetahs prefer to run uphill: going down they are liable to a false aim and then a bad tumble.

Undaunted by this maneuver, the cheetah soon overtook his buck. He sprang with front paws directed at the hindquarters of the quarry. The violence of this blow threw the animal. Then the cheetah caught him by the throat.

At this point we arrived on the scene. The cheetah lay full-length, with the buck's throat held tightly in its slightly curved canines. Gradually the victim ceased his violent attempts to tear himself loose. He was choked to death. The cheetah lay perfectly still in apparent ecstasy. Slowly he opened and closed his great greenish eyes, gently emitting a soft, rumbling purr.

The cheetah was allowed to feast on one hindquarter of the buck. Then he was gently and firmly led aside while one of the attendants disembowelled the victim. Some of the blood and the steaming viscera, placed in a long spoonlike bowl, was offered to the cheetah. This was his reward, and he seemed quite satisfied.

Another cheetah was brought from the lorry. The motor was started and off we went again. This time the car, overtaxed by the speed over such rough terrain, broke down. The Maharajah coolly beckoned for another car, of which there were several for such emergencies. It zoomed over and we continued the hunt.

There were dramatic variations in all the seven hunts staged that day. Once a cheetah, forced to carry the pursuit downhill, while going full speed, landed in a blind ditch and turned head-over-heels. He was given a rest and drink and the mud was cleared off his head, but he refused to run again.

Another cheetah killed a female, a regrettable incident. He was dragged off his feed so that he would never repeat the performance.

Once again a motor broke down. Sometimes the staff had difficulties in maneuvering the herd. Sometimes we drew close to them but they succeeded in escaping. Then, perhaps, we would pick them up again. To add still more variety, the cheetahs were unloosed at various distances; so we had a good chance to watch all phases of the approach and attack.

By eleven o'clock we were through. Six cheetahs had overtaken animals. The cars and lorries went back to the bungalow rest-house. Then, with the Maharajah and his party, we made merry at breakfast, later viewing the kills or what remained of them, as they lay in line on the grass. Natives in a carnival spirit brought wreaths of flowers to hang around our necks. Made of plumaria and jasmine, they were larger versions of the leis of Honolulu.

One last word about the speed of the cheetahs. To begin with, one should remember that when they are apparently running fast, they are by no means running their fastest. Any one who has had experience with cats will realize that it is extremely difficult, owing to their peculiar temperament, to train them to perform any action out of keeping with their normal behavior. Cheetahs would probably never run at their maximum speed on a track. Furthermore, it is doubtful if they would sustain their greatest effort for any distance beyond two hundred yards. But in their habitat, when pursuing buck, their final charge is terrific. It must surely attain a speed of sixty-five or seventy-five miles an hour—for a hundred or more yards.

A cheetah being taken out for exercise by his keeper. The hood has been removed

A cheetah, just unhooded and released. He has just identified his quarries

He starts at a lope, studying the herd to select the animal he will choose

In these two photographs he is shown at full speed after the herd,
having selected his individual animal

Cheetah has killed. He is feeding, and his keeper is attaching his collar

Mrs. Cutting and the Maharajah of Kolhapur. Near them a cheetah is feeding on its kill

The Maharajah and Mrs. Cutting in the stables with a thoroughbred coach horse

Mrs. Cutting is about to leave after the coursing. The Maharajah has decorated
her with flowers. His A.D.C. stands beside her

Forbidden Cities of Tibet

BECAUSE Tibet is one of the most inaccessible countries in the world, it has exercised a powerful fascination on active minds of the Western World ever since the dawn of Athenian culture. As early as the fifth century B.C., the Mediterranean lands heard about it from Herodotus, "The Father of History." Curiosity turned not into exploring expeditions, but into a series of romantic legends, and so, fifteen centuries later, we find Arab geographers drawing uncertain lines on parchment to indicate the approximate position of the country.

The first European to provide any concrete data was the Friar Odoric who visited Lhasa in 1330. There followed a hiatus of three centuries until 1620, when the Austrian Jesuit Grueber and the Belgian Count D'Orville made their way from China to the Tibetan capital on foot. From that day on, visits multiplied, but Tibet, unconquered by mechanized transport, is still a closed land.

While the Occident has been interested in Tibet, Tibet has not shown any reciprocating curiosity. Through the centuries following the Renaissance, devoted in the West to the developement of those formulæ of arts, crafts, sciences, economics, technology, and government we call civilization, Tibet has stood still, presenting today a social structure akin to Europe's in the Middle Ages.

Hemmed in by the Himalayas and other lofty mountains, unexplored and even unnamed, the country is resolutely indifferent to outside developments. Under bright, luminous skies, in the heady air of the vast, wind-swept plateau, four million Tibetans insist on working out their own destiny. Their government has refused to admit foreigners, and so rigorously is this ban applied that only one foreign country—Nepal—is permitted to maintain a permanent legation in Lhasa.

Only a handful of white people have ever travelled in Tibet. The tales of the successful, singularly accurate when one considers the opportunity to perpetrate romance and humbug, have incited other hardy spirits to make the venture. They have found to their sorrow that while getting into the country is hard, penetrating to the capital is ten times harder.

All this I knew when I first made up my mind to explore "the roof of the world." I also knew that the goal I had set for myself gained in difficulty from the fact it required official sanction. I sought no hide-and-seek, no peephole adventure in Tibet. My aim was to *study* the country, to see the nomads, peasants, ruling classes, to learn something about that curious offshoot of Buddhism known as Lamaism, to have a glimpse of the arts and crafts, to collect specimens of the flora. And most of all, I hoped to see the country's mysterious ruler, the Dalai Lama, face to face. Unless I could enter Lhasa and the other chief cities with the same assurance that I would feel on entering Pekin or Calcutta, this sort of thing would have been impossible.

The goal was achieved. I made three trips to Tibet and twice I visited Lhasa. What I saw was worth the effort—the maneuvering it took to get in, the exhausting caravan journeys over the high mountains, through the glacial, snow-clotted passes.

For I saw one of the most attractive peoples on earth, a landscape well-nigh unrivalled for grandeur, fantastic cities slumbering in medieval tranquillity. Lhasa, "the forbidden city," is a unique capital. Its vast Potala, the "Vatican of Tibet," rising over the plain under a radiant autumn sky, with mountain peaks as high as 15,000 feet serving as its backdrop, is one of the finest sights I have ever beheld.

But the spectacular aspects of Tibet were not the only rewards for the effort. There was another kind of satisfaction in seeing the ordinary, pedestrian life of the people from an intimate angle, in studying the politico-ecclesiastical structure of Lamaism, in collecting specimens of Tibetan clothing and plant life for American museums.

One of my original incentives to visit Lhasa was a permit granted to me by the Tibetan government for the 1928 expedition to Chinese Tibet. Unused, for reasons given in another chapter, the precious concession became valuable two years later when I went to Gyantse and Khampa Dzong, accompanied by Captain Scott Cockburn* and Captain Nugent Head of the Queen's Own Fourth Hussars.

In 1935, with Arthur Vernay, the notable traveller, big-game hunter, and donor of the famous Vernay-Faunthorpe collection at the American Museum of Natural History in New York which includes an Indian lion and a giant sable antelope, I revisited Gyantse, saw Shigatse, a city that has admitted even fewer visitors than the capital, and finally fulfilled the long-standing ambition to enter Lhasa. As the result of friendly contacts made on this visit, the Tibetan government invited me to return in 1937, bringing my wife. It was the first time an invitation had ever been extended to a white woman for an unlimited stay.

Because the itineraries of the three trips had a few duplications, because the latest was productive of more genuine understanding of Tibetan ways, and because of the presence of my wife, I confine myself, as far as travel detail is concerned, to the 1937 expedition.

The first trip to Tibet I considered no more than a happy preliminary adventure. After all, one could get as far as Gyantse on a British permit. The empire's connection with this city, third largest in Tibet, dates back to 1904, when Sir Francis Younghusband, acting under orders from Lord Curzon, then viceroy of India, made his famous punitive expedition to Lhasa. As the result of the subsequent treaty, the British acquired the right to keep a garrison in Gyantse, to permit traders from British India to visit the city. Since that time a limited number of permits has been issued every year.

But Lhasa was harder. Directly the first trip was over, I went about

*Now Brigadier General.

strengthening the Tibetan contacts I already possessed and trying to form others. Lord Willingdon, then viceroy of India, was a strong supporter of my project to visit the capital. He knew that I had carried on a regular correspondence with the late Dalai Lama since my trip of 1930.

The Dalai Lama's answering letters were done in fine Tibetan script on native paper. They were always accompanied by English translations made by Ringan, the ruler's secretary, and one of the four Lhasa boys who had been sent to Rugby in England for their education. Both originals and translations arrived in intricate envelopes, addressed in both Tibetan and English, and sealed with the Dalai Lama's official seal. Ringan's translations were always typewritten, without a single typographical error. While his style showed a slight foreign flavor, the sentences were fluent and there were no slips in grammar.

All the letters were dated "Norbu Linga Palace, Lhasa" with the date given according to the Occidental calendar. Each ended in Tibetan reckoning, *e.g.* "Dated 5th of the 6th Tibetan month of the Iron Sheep Year." The Iron Sheep Year was 1931.

These picturesque Tibetan designations ran in cycles. Starting with 1930, the years of the decade ran, the Iron Horse Year, the Iron Sheep Year, the Water Monkey Year, the Water Bird Year, the Wood Dog Year, the Wood Pig Year, the Fire Mouse Year, the Fire Ox Year, the Earth Tiger Year, the Earth Hare Year.

The letters began, as I have said, in a casual way. This, for instance, was the opening of an early letter from the ruler:

"July 19, 1931—Your presents of a male and bitch each of Dalmatian and German hounds were, in accordance with telegraphic instruction dispatched, handed over by Pu Dhamdul at Gangtok to Pu Yaphel of Pangda Tsang (Tibetan trade agent) who sent a special carrier with them with orders to take great care of them on the journey. Although all four were received here, both the male Dalmatian and the German hound were not in fit condition owing to some disease with which they were infected on the way. I am sorry to say that the two succumbed, one after the other."

Presently the correspondence got into the thick of Tibetan affairs. The Dalai Lama was asking me to perform missions for him in the United States. At regular intervals I was dictating letters beginning, "I trust Your Holiness is well as due to Your Holiness's kindness, I am well."

One of the ruler's pet projects was inaugurated with this letter:

"Dec. 25, 1931—To improve the economic condition of Tibet, we require a large supply of bar silver and so far we have been buying this from British India. But in the previous year, the Indian customs duty on silver has been so much raised that it is most difficult to purchase silver. I would be very much obliged to you if you would advise me if it would be a feasible proposition to ask the American government to help us in the matter and supply us directly with the necessary bar silver. I will let you know should any other matters arise concerning the interest of Tibet and requiring the help and sympathy of the United States."

This affair took me to Washington, where I discussed the matter with officials of the state department. The ruler's scheme was decidedly impracticable, but I did not deprive him of the satisfaction of hearing that it had been presented to the American government. In Washington I obtained an autographed photograph of President Hoover which the Dalai Lama accepted with jubilation. He asked me to create a sentiment of good will toward Tibet in America. Here is a letter that touches on it:

"It is sincerely hoped that, this country being a purely ecclesiastical kingdom, you will solicit the state department to render international assistance as far as it is in their power to do so, in order that the Buddhist religion may flourish uninterrupted and that we may enjoy exercising our true right of sovereignty and above all to enhance the prosperity of the people."

Another of his pet projects which he asked me to further was the establishment of direct connections between Tibetan wool merchants and American importers. In January 1932 he wrote me: "From now onward if Pangda Tsang could deliver the wool at a fixed price to the buying agents of the big American wool merchants at Kalimpong (trade town of northern Bengal) without having to pass through the hands of the Malwaris (woolen merchants of Kalimpong) and thereby doing away with the middleman's profit, it would be of great advantage to the government."

This proved to be a less troublesome and more feasible project than the silver transfer. In any case, I eventually got relations established between the Tibetan exporters and American concerns.

The correspondence grew heavier. A stranger reading the last letters would find it hard to believe that the correspondents had never laid eyes on each other.

In sending me a pair of Apsos (special breed of Tibetan dogs), the Dalai Lama wrote, "I am sending you two dogs by way of Kalimpong. Please take great care of them when you receive them. Dated 7th of the 1st Tibetan month of the Water Bird Year."

He was very scrupulous about answering letters. Once he wrote when there had been only a slight delay, "Recently owing to the press of work, I have not been able to answer your letters promptly to which, it is hoped, that you will not put a misconstruction and that you will write regularly as before."

Meanwhile presents were going back and forth. I sent the Dalai Lama illustrated books on American architecture, a chair with a folding canopy, a self-winding gold wrist-watch, silver plated polar bears mounted on agate, an ornamental glass bowl, and a special glass cocktail shaker equipped with a churn, which would never serve him in the ordinary manner, but would be useful for mixing his buttered tea.

All this was leading, I hoped, to a visit to Lhasa. But the cordial letters did not include an invitation. Instead I read from time to time something like this: "I am pleased you are coming to Rangoon for a week's stay and that on your return you will be staying at Delhi for a few days."

The situation wanted patience. Few white men had ever got to Lhasa and fewer still were ever invited. The correspondence was flourishing and Ringan was to tell me later I was the only man with whom the ruler kept up a regular communication. I was full of optimism when a sad telegram arrived on Christmas Day, 1933:

"Regret delay in wiring sad news of temporary passing away of His Holiness on seventeenth after short illness. Government being carried on as before. Knowing your constant correspondence with late Holiness, hope to receive assurance of continuance of your friendship at this unfortunate conjuncture—Kunbila, personal assistant."

It was, indeed, an unfortunate conjuncture. I wondered if I would ever see Lhasa now that the supreme ruler was dead. In the meanwhile, I must keep up my relations with the Kashag or supreme council, and with the Regent who had been trained by the Dalai Lama to take his place until a reincarnate baby could be found and declared head of the kingdom.

In wiring my condolences to the Kashag I also sent the Christmas and New Year greetings I had been sending to the Dalai Lama for several years. Shortly afterwards came this cable:

"Many thanks for your Christmas and New Year good wishes.
"KASHAG."

I kept up relations with the Kashag all that year, 1934, and the next year permission was granted to visit Shigatse, supplemented after long delay by the invitation to Lhasa. Out of this second trip came more cordial relations with the heads of the Tibetan government, and, without effort on my part, another invitation in 1937.

The third trip got under way in August, 1937—the Tibetan Fire Ox Year. Plenty of unscheduled incidents enlivened the way before we set foot on Tibetan soil, and the first took place while our Peninsula and Orient liner was still in the Red Sea.

Up to this time the voyage had been exceedingly dull and I could think of nothing better to do with my mornings than sit in the writing-room and catch up on my correspondence. One such morning, a little after nine, I heard a series of terrific screams that seemed to come from the deck. By the minute they became louder, more piercing.

[179]

One of the Goanese sailors, I reflected, must have run amok. I darted for the door. There was no one on deck. The sound came up from the sea, and looking over the railing I saw a man in the water, hardly 200 yards from the ship. He was swimming strongly, raising himself out of the water, lifting up his arms, letting out his cries, and then dropping below the surface. This performance was repeated again and again. Those upraised arms were a fantastic sight, like an old engraving for a book of religious folklore.

The third officer heard the screams and rushed to the bridge, where he found that the steersman had left the wheel and was in the chart room. There the cries had failed to reach him. But now there was an instantaneous din of "man overboard" blasts. The ship swerved, circled around and came near the man in the water, who was still raising himself up, screaming, and subsiding below the surface.

The sea, fortunately, was calm and in short order a lifeboat was lowered. From the deck a few sharks were visible, and later the men in the lifeboat said they had seen a whole ring of them. Nothing happened, however, while the man was dragged into the boat, though the sharks followed all the way to the gangway.

A naked figure, clasping a small money bag, stood dripping in the companionway. He was a Malay, between fifty and sixty years old.

The explanation was as strange as the apparition. The man had been on a ship bound for Jedda in Arabia, whence he proposed to make the holy pilgrimage to Mecca. "I fell overboard," he said, accepting clothes, but waving aside a glass of brandy. As a good Moslem, he remembered to spurn alcohol even in an emergency.

Installed in a deck chair he told the rest of it. No one had seen him fall overboard and in a short time his ship had disappeared over the horizon and he was swimming, to what destination he knew not—a helpless, dazed, lonely figure, invoking the aid of Heaven. Allah produced the sharks, and they had actually got under him and supported his body. (The benevolent attitude of those sharks did not surprise the Moslems on our ship.) Three hours went by before the man in the water saw the liner cutting athwart his path. Allah gave him strength to swim and scream.

It seemed too good to be true, any of it, but after all, no one was missing from our ship and people simply didn't appear out of the ocean. Our captain, knowing we had passed a pilgrim ship, wirelessed and received confirmation of the story, minus the shark episode, that afternoon.

Our new passenger was the man of the hour. His fellow Moslems called him "miracle man" and "saint" and paid him homage. Encouraged in this rôle he went on a fast—no food from infidel white hands for him. The first-class passengers made up a purse for him and he landed back in Bombay the next day with more money than he had ever known and something to talk about for the rest of his life.

Leaving Bombay and Allah's Chosen One, we went monsooning through the Indian Ocean and down to Ceylon, and thence by boat and rail to Madras. Friday the thirteenth brought us to Calcutta, where traffic was in difficulties and parts of the city seemed to be sloughing away, due to the heaviest rainfall in years.

An overnight train journey brought us to Siliguri, near the Himalayan foothills, where we learned that mountainsides had tumbled down carrying Gargantuan rocks, killing people and breaching the roads. The Titsa River, roaring angrily and tearing bridges from their moorings, had crippled transportation. Elephants, for the first time in thirty years, were being used to carry food to Darjeeling, summer capital of Bengal.

To reach Gangtok, threshold of the Tibetan journey, we had to detour over precipitous, rain-swept roads, taking twelve hours instead of the usual three and a half. Three times we changed vehicles, a most disagreeable trip due to the torrents of rain and dangerous passes where we got out from time to time to crawl through tunnels of fern. A large car took us from Siliguri to the tea garden district; baby Austins ("baby cars" to the natives) took us through the tea gardens, a great comfort going over precipitous roads; beyond the tea gardens country we changed at the Titsa River and unloaded all the luggage, and my wife worried a little lest the downpour ruin the delicate mechanisms of the toys she had bought in Paris as gifts to Tibetan children.

At Gangtok, capital of Sikkim, beautifully sprawled on a ridge 5000 feet above sea level and overlooking a series of fertile valleys, we assembled a caravan of twenty-six horses.

Head of the syces and other servants was a young and energetic Tibetan named Wangdi, who had managed things very well for Vernay and me. My wife had brought along a Tibetan servant named Nakkin, who had been discovered by the Honorable Mrs. F. M. Bailey, wife of the British minister to Nepal. As an ayah (maid or nurse) Nakkin had travelled through the East, and knew four European and three Oriental languages, none of which she could read or write. Born in the border country, she was now about to see her own country of Tibet for the first time.

Among the others who were to make themselves conspicuous in one way or another were a Lepcha cook, his assistant, who was a Tibetan from Gyantse, and Elia, a Madrassi Christian who had been a good servant on civilized occasions, but who showed from the outset of this trip that hardship was not for him. He suffered from the altitude, the food, and every imaginable ailment. Because his favorite way of getting things done—bullying coolies—didn't work in Tibet, Elia became an encumbrance.

The Maharajah of Sikkim, member of the Indian chamber of princes, a pleasant, shy man of forty-seven, asked us to dine. We had been friends since 1930, when I asked permission to hunt the ovis ammon Hodgsoni, the world's largest sheep, in Sikkimese territory. As the result of his kindness, and the co-operation of Captain Head and Captain Cockburn, a group of the species was added to the American Museum of Natural History.

The Maharajah's house, small and rather simple, contained a notable collection of Tibetan tank-as from Khăm, in eastern Tibet. These vivid allegorical paintings done on silk were mounted in brocade mats and suspended from the walls of the drawing room.

Covering the entire floor was a beige carpet, thirty by thirty-five feet, produced in the Maharajah's own plant. His coat of arms filled its entire surface. The furnishings, consisting of a few pieces of Tibetan painted furniture, a Chinese lacquer desk, and many comfortable chairs and sofas, were climaxed by a small, round white lacquer table, supported by three finely carved male skeletons, thirty inches high. This exquisite piece of furniture standing in the center of the floor was the room's focal point.

The Maharajah's private gompa (temple) faced the house across a small lawn and the sounds of a musical service coming from nine-foot brass horns and conch shells could be heard as we dined.

After two pleasant days spent at the Residency with Mr. H. E. Richardson, who was acting for Mr. B. J. Gould, K.S., British Political Officer to Tibet, then on leave in England, we set forth with our caravan and in less than five hours had climbed four thousand feet through a dense bamboo jungle. The rain came down in torrents, but even more annoying were the land leeches that infested this region.

These tiny devils lurked on every branch, called thither by the smell of passing caravans. Leeches are blind and follow their strongly or-ganized sense of smell, looping along straight to the nearest part of a man's anatomy, whether it be head, arms, or feet. They can stretch themselves thin enough to enter the eyelet of a boot, and their painful bites have to be washed and disinfected. The half-naked natives were exceedingly adept at flicking off the pests with their jungle knives.

What with the rain and leeches we had to pass up the orchids, clematis, and myriads of other enticing flowers lining the way, though they would have made a good beginning for our botanical collections. My wife had undertaken to secure seeds and plants for the Brooklyn Botanic Garden. By the next day, the leeches were less of a nuisance, as the road had climbed to 12,000 feet, but at that altitude collecting activities were somewhat dilatory.

By our third morning, when we left Changu bungalow—the British maintain service bungalows all the way to Gyantse—the rain had ceased for a few hours and we rode up to the Natu La pass, at 14,800 feet, under the most brilliant of sunny skies and through a tantalizing mixture of alpine and other flowers. Conspicuous were various rhododendrons—tree, bush, and vine—gigantic hydrangeas, mass upon mass of azaleas, and everywhere the last of the irises mingled with yellow chrysanthemums, making a lovely sight for miles in this upland valley.

Then came the steep, knifelike passes, and a fine welter of pink sturdy daphne, matted with gentians of lovely blues, a tiny begonia, a large-leafed rhubarb, and cushions of cloverlike pink things, making a ravishing *mille fleurs* carpet. The aconitum or monkshood grew in beautiful tall clumps, alongside a fine yellow thing of the aster family. There were masses of tall yellow primulas, a pink myosotis, a very strong blue one, and large dark asters with brown centers, pink and white everlastings. Unfortunately I could not put a name to any of the other thirty or forty blooms I saw.

The steep, slimy trail, hanging on a ledge where the horses slipped and swayed, had brought us to the top of the Natu La, whence we looked on the bold, rugged grandeur of the real Tibet, now stretched out before us. Arriving at the top of the pass with a pounding headache, my wife stopped to pick a yellow primula, but nausea almost overcame her. She contented herself with climbing back into the saddle and looking out at the vast, glorious country bathed in sunshine. The charms and delights of Tibet began to unfold themselves immediately.

Beyond the Natu La, the trail descended sharply past a number of lamaseries perched precariously on the steep hillsides, past the beautiful stream running through the Chumbi Valley, and down to the village of Yatung with its skeleton garrison of British soldiers and its lovely bungalow, where the altitude of 9900 feet was a relief, affording a decent night's sleep.

In a dreary mix-up about hiring horses and mules, half of our caravan was left in Yatung the next morning, and Wangdi remained behind to arrange matters. The stony agony of a trail rose steeply through a pine forest and beside the swift, angry river, which made a fall of two thousand feet in the day's march, a thrilling spectacle. The scenery here was unrivalled even for Tibet.

Nightfall brought us to the hamlet of Gautsa, but it wasn't until four hours after our arrival that Elia, the Indian bearer, came in. He had collapsed, horse and all, down the side of one of the stoniest, muddiest shelves imaginable, into the raging torrent. He felt very sorry for himself, but no great harm was done.

Out of Gautsa we followed the same roaring torrent in a drenching rain, climbing fifteen hundred feet over a diabolical torture of steeply cut rocks set in mud and slime. Extraordinary and unaccountable headaches had set in. We bought a cock and hen for our dinner when we should reach Phari. On the slopes were visible sturdy, low rhododendrons, and many roses and laburnum. Three quarters of the way to Phari the trail rose, and then flattened out into an upland meadow.

Through the rain Phari showed its dzong (fort) at 14,500 feet rising abruptly on a hillside and below a compact pattern of small white houses. But on closer inspection we could see the filthy hovels and unkempt streets, now rivers of mud, that make Phari the slattern among all the cities of the world.

The unprepossessing view was redeemed by the friendly face of the chawkidar, or custodian of the British bungalow, who rode out in the storm to greet us and escort us in proper style to the door of the house. Here we found tea and a warming, cheering fire of crackling wood. Phari is above the timber-line and heat henceforth would come mostly from yak or sheep dung. The unaccustomed comfort that night emphasized the delinquencies of the Lepcha cook, dubbed "Dirty Dick" by my wife. We were weary of rubbery, inedible fowl and it was now agreed that the Lepcha set a new record for uncleanliness.

Tibetan hospitality, conspicuous on my other trips, now appeared in the form of a sheep carcass, accompanied by a kata (white silk scarf), the traditional Tibetan visiting card, from the dzongpen, or governor. Remembering that Vernay and I had found metal bowls highly appreciated gifts in Phari, I sent more of the same kind to the town officials.

Signs of a Tibetan pilgrimage were visible when we rose the next morning. Several hundred men dressed in beautiful robes and broad, red woolly hats, and many women wearing the wide, triangular headdress known as the Shigatse type, were watching laborers erect their tents, marvels of colorful embroidery and appliqué work. Not only the clothes but the dignified, aristocratic mien of the pilgrims indicated that they belonged to an upper stratum of Tibetan society. Strolling over to take some photographs, we were received graciously and hospitably and invited to enter the first tent put in readiness. The ground was covered with several thicknesses of bright Tibetan carpets, and a number of gaily painted low tables were provided with a brass buttered-tea jug and exquisite cups and holders.

Buttered tea was forthcoming immediately. This concoction, the national dish of the country, is made of boiling water, clarified yak butter, usually rancid, and tea brought in from China in the form of bricks. What Tibet receives is the sweepings of inferior teas, mixed with bits of twig and other rubbish. About fourteen million pounds a year are brought in from China. The method of making buttered tea was the same as that which I had observed in Chinese Tibet, but I describe it again here.

When the moment comes to make the tea, a chunk of clarified butter is cut from a large pile, usually packed in yak hides, and placed in a metal pot. While the butter is boiling, tea is stewing in another vessel. The butter is then poured into a churn, the tea follows, salt and soda are added and the whole is thoroughly mixed. The Tibetans find buttered tea nourishing and warming. Combined with meat or with tsamba (parched barley meal), it forms a staple of diet.

What the Tibetans would do without their rancid butter, it is hard to imagine. They use it not only as a food, but in vigil lights that burn before their Gods; they use it to grease their bodies and hair against the arid cold of winter and to protect their furniture against the desiccating air. Chunks of butter are even carved into idols. Mixed with tsamba and sugar and molded into little pyramids, it is known as "torma," a sacrifice to the Gods, first placed on an altar, then carried in a procession, and finally burned in a fire of twigs.

In Phari we had a good opportunity to familiarize ourselves with Tibetan types—aristocrats, peasants, and nomads. An exceedingly attractive people, with sturdy physiques, high cheekbones, coppery skins, straight black hair, and merry Mongol eyes, they bore a marked resemblance to the Navajos of the American Southwest.

Perhaps the most interesting sight afforded by the great plains about the city was the herds of grazing yaks. The yak with his wide, sweeping horns and coat of long, thick, wavy hair is the handsomest member of the *Bos* family. A great friend of the Tibetans, he provides milk and wool, works in the fields flailing barley, and carries heavy burdens on the road. Sometimes, deprived of his rights under Buddhist law, he is slaughtered to provide meat. As a pack animal he has certain disadvantages. He can scarcely cover two miles an hour, and nine miles a day is usually his limit. In marching he groans every step of the way, well deserving his latin name of *Bos grunniens*.

But the yak, groaning, desultory, capricious, never falters. Whether on smooth roads or steep and dangerous trails at high altitudes, whether on ice or snow, he moves with indomitable sureness, rarely varying his pace. He will work hard, but he knows his own capacity.

Once I saw two yaks being mercilessly overworked while threshing. Growling, bleeding from the nose, they were still pushed on by their masters. Suddenly, with a savage snort, one of them broke loose and ran for the mountains—the end of his labors for some time.

Refusing tsamba, which is entirely acceptable to ponies, yaks must graze as they go—whenever the whim seizes them. One of their favorite foods is moss, and to find it they often climb rocky hillsides far above the trails. With proper treatment, the animals last for years, indefatigable servants. No wonder the Tibetans suspend stuffed yaks from the rafters just inside the temple doors!

For four days out of Phari we were travelling on the roof of the world. It was sober, hard country with a stiff, salt borax wind blowing

in our teeth most of the day. On the horizon were the snowy peaks
of the Himalayas, the most conspicuous of them being the glorious
Chomolhari, 23,930 feet, set in a sparkling turquoise sky, with just a
few soft caressing clouds to enhance her great beauty.

We had passed on the way not a few abandoned villages, some already falling into ruin. Bhutanese raiders had proved the end for some,
the plague for others. Plagues are not uncommon, and as late as 1925,
Lhasa itself had lost 25,000 people, all victims of smallpox. The empti-
ness of this vast land was one of its most striking characteristics. In a
country with an area greater than France, Italy, Switzerland, Holland,
and Belgium rolled into one, the population is barely four million—
about the same as that of Chicago.

The first march out of Phari, twenty-one miles, brought us to the
Tuna bungalow, where we were surrounded by many smiling Tibetans
and many half-good dogs. Here we burned our first yak dung, the
meadows offering grazing to sheep, mule, pony, yak. While the mail
runners went loping by, we gazed back at Chomolhari, still brilliant
and fascinating.

We were very burned by fifteen thousand feet. While the dry wind
still blew across the borax plain, we were now completely done with
the Monarch monsoon, and from this point on there would be much
Tibetan sunshine.

The trail ran beside the British-owned telegraph line from Kalimpong to Gyantse; from Gyantse to Lhasa the line was the property of
the Tibetan government. From Tuna to Kala, the Himalayas made a
fine, jagged, snowy horizon that followed us all the way. To the southward lay Bhutan and always the glorious Chomolhari on our right.
Otherwise there were just so many featureless miles, where song and
speech echoed in the thin air. It was a long, good day, mostly flat going
till after lunch.

We followed a small river, a bit of rocky path, and traversed a small
pass. Cairns of every shape and size, a form of religious worship, appeared along the way, and sometimes we added a stone to the mass.
Prayer flags attached to the cairns flapped in the wind. We observed

the Tibetan custom by always passing these cairns on our right.

Ten fine yaks harnessed in pairs as they ploughed a field made a splendid sight against a background of gathering storm. Outside our compound many women and children were domiciled in a black nomad's tent. We were surrounded by nice, smiling Tibetans, all conventionally dirty. They tumbled over one another to be of help and often stuck out their tongues at full length—not a sign of hostility, but a common form of politeness shown by the lower classes. The length and agility of the Tibetan tongue have been ascribed to long practice in licking tsamba bowls.

In the throng my wife picked out a very good black-and-white Apso dog. There was also a small lamb which a man offered to kill for two rupees. Wangdi gave him a quick right to the jaw and the price of killing went down to normal—one rupee.

The handsome Wangdi was a considerable personage in the throng. Thin and tall, he made a striking picture with his Tibetan felt hat, held securely by his pigtail wound around it; with his colored boots, huge, heavy earring, and one sleeve of his great coat always hanging down. With dignity and dispatch he superintended the loading of our caravan of twenty-six horses twice daily, when we were obliged to change horses, thereby spreading the price through the villages and towns on the way to Lhasa.

When the helpers brought in our belongings for the night and came crowding into our small room, we were overcome with the smell of yak oil, or perhaps sheep butter.

Nakkin kept everything in order and in fact ran the Indian bearer. For three nights my wife had not allowed the repulsive cook to perform, but Nakkin, under the greatest difficulties, made good mutton stew. She also spoiled my wife. The chawkidar announced triumphantly that there would be "fentz bintz" for dinner. We were very interested. They turned out to be French beans.

The best Tibetan weather we had yet experienced came on the final stage to Gyantse. There were only light clouds in the deep blue sky, and the air was warm and bracing. Wangdi scarcely gave us time to gulp our coffee and we were off. We had tiffin at Saugang, seeing lovely pink and white poppies and a good many small willow trees. Women were in control of the caravan change, and compared with the local men they were not at all efficient, but their noise provided plenty of amusement. Chortens (shrines) and ruins that may once have been forts sprang out of the steep, shale hillsides. For miles the trail was covered with stones, making it as hard as our initial stages for the horses. Three or four splendid Tibetan houses came into view, and then the trail led suddenly into a spectacular gorge, its floor an arroyo of massive boulders, its perpendicular sides rising, perhaps, two or three thousand feet.

It took two hours to get through this slit in the mountains. Halfway through, we saw the famous Red Idol, a thirty-foot statue of Buddha carved out of rock and protected by a wide, overhanging shelf of rock. The sacred words, Om Mani Padme Hum (Hail Thou Jewel in the Lotus), were carved on the rock in letters as tall as a man. This gorge had been the scene of a skirmish between Colonel Younghusband's men and the Tibetans in 1904.

Along the horizon in the late afternoon glow we saw Gyantse fort, crowning a precipitous, rocky hill at an elevation of 13,500 feet and looking from that distance like a vaster Mont Saint Michel.

One by one the familiar sights came into view—the British fort flying the Union Jack, the bungalow with its friendly chawkidar, the Tibetan fort, the chorten and gompa, the three-story house of the dzongpen (governor), the main street and bazaar with animated crowds shuffling about under the awnings that protected the merchandise and buyers from a glaring sun. Many obtruding tongues bespoke a friendly if slightly disconcerting greeting.

The faithful Rai Sahib Wangdi (no relation to our chef de caravan), assistant to the British trade agent and our friend and mentor on the previous trips, appeared at the bungalow in tennis togs. He had a long pigtail, and wore the usual silver earring on his left ear. The presentation of my gifts would take place the next morning, for according to the Tibetan code the morning is the proper time for such affairs.

We were not alone in the bungalow. The choicest part of it, three large rooms, was held by an Italian archeologist, Giuseppe Tucci, and his assistant, while only a single room was available for my wife, now suffering from mountain sickness, and for me. Here we were obliged to eat, sleep, and entertain.

Signor Tucci was gathering material for a book showing the relation between Hindu and Tibetan culture, buying tank-as with a prodigal hand, collecting botanical specimens on the surrounding hills, and photographing every square inch of the temples. For years he had been seeking permission to visit Lhasa.

The next morning we passed the walled lamasery and climbed the hill to a large white house of the dzongpen. Glass—a precious object in Tibet, since it must be brought up from India on pack animals and hence is found only in the houses of the very wealthy—was nowhere to be seen. The windows were covered with light, unbleached cotton cloth. On the other hand, the governor's house had a staircase, an indubitable sign of rank, for most Tibetan dwellings use only ladders.

When visiting nobles in Tibet one always presents a kata or standard "visiting card." The quality of the silk and the manner in which it is folded are determined by the rank of the noble. The host likewise presents his "card," and the whole procedure constitutes a stately ceremony.

Arriving at the top of the third flight, we saw the dzongpen standing just outside the door of his private apartments. A tall, heavy man, fortyish, he was dressed in a long, red silk robe falling over a pair of black silk trousers. His lustrous black hair, combed straight over his head, fell to his shoulders. He stood smiling and hospitable while one of his servants received the gift and while the scarves were being exchanged through the other servants. When my scarf was on his arm and his was on mine, he indicated that I was to precede him into the room, where dark plaster walls glowed with the bright colors of many tank-as and brass urns. There were low tables painted in the variegated Tibetan style, cushions, and a high sideboard in the Chinese fashion. All this bespoke the excellent taste of the ruling classes. Through all the conversation that went on during the drinking of buttered tea, no mention was made of the gifts I had presented. Acknowledging gifts in Tibet is not good form.

The dzongpen pointed out that we might choose our time for getting to Lhasa, whereas on the first trip great care had been taken that Vernay and I should arrive "on an auspicious day" as determined by the government oracle.

In the meanwhile my wife was having her troubles with the recalcitrant cook. He was, she said, "a very bad cut for a cook." His underlip was larger, bluer, and hung lower than anything Velasquez ever did with Spanish royalty. It was necessary now to send the cook's assistant and a lazy, dirty syce back to Gangtok. The assistant cook, we had discovered, was a jail-bird, addicted to murderous assault. He had just finished a term in time to get back his health and land-legs on this mission of ours.

The governor granted us permission to visit some of the local lamaseries, and thus my wife obtained a substantial introduction to this peculiar Tibetan institution. Lamas (the word means "superior one") are, of course, priests who commit themselves to perpetual celibacy. They form the upper crust of the country, and in consecrating themselves to religious rites they usually escape the curse of work. Taxes collected from the people keep them supplied with everything they need. The lamaseries are centers of wealth, power, and learning, like the monasteries of Europe in the Middle Ages. All educated Tibetans are lamasery-bred.

Lamaism is an outgrowth of Buddhism, which appeared in Tibet in the fifth century of the Christian era. Buddhism, at that time a doctrine of pure negation, came into collision with the prevailing Tibetan creed called Bonism, which was excessively preoccupied with devil-chasing. Bonism prevailed for the time being, but when King Sron Tsan-Gampo married two Buddhist princesses, one Nepalese, the other Chinese, and was himself converted to their religion, Buddhism triumphed in Tibet. This was in the eighth century A.D. Eventually, however, Buddhism was diluted with the devil-worship of Bonism, and by the eleventh century, when the idol-hating Moslems were sweeping over northern India with fire and sword, extirpating the religion of Buddha, Tibet had evolved its own special religion, which came to be known as Lamaism. Terrible images filled the country, and creeds multiplied. The enduring influence of Bonism is attested today by paintings of great blue Furies with exaggerated development of muscles, and by other horrible apparitions of Lamaistic worship decorating many a lamasery wall.

A supreme lama was proclaimed and was given the Mongol title of Dalai. His origin is traced back to Avolokitasarva, patron goddess of Lamaism, and to this was added the fiction of reincarnation to give political stability to the hierarchy.

According to the doctrine of reincarnation, human beings and animals do not die, do not even abandon this world, but reappear in the same or in different forms. There is nothing new in all this—it forms part of many primitive religions—but Lamaism has added many new refinements to the doctrine. The succession of the Dalai Lama depends on reincarnation. Lamaism, unlike most doctrines that include metempsychosis, maintains that it can determine when the successor to the Dalai Lama is born. In principle, it is a male child born the very instant the supreme ruler dies. Actually it works out something like this: several male children born during the hour following the Dalai Lama's demise are taken as candidates. Portents and omens, interpreted by a committee of high lamas, determine the choice, and should the favored baby come from peasant stock his whole family is ennobled.

It is a corollary of reincarnation that all life, human and animal, is sacred. All followers of Lamaism are enjoined from taking life—even the fleas that torment their bodies. To take the life of a man is, of course, the most serious of crimes. Tibetans believe that a murderer faces reincarnation as a louse. But needless to say, the law is commonly broken. High lamas and secular nobles consume flesh whenever they can find it, and even the late Dalai Lama ate mutton twice a day.

There are high lamas and low lamas. The low ones usually stay that way for life and associate with others of their own kind. But whatever their station or degree, they are inducted into the life at an early age. The novices, known as "chelas," start their course of training when they are as young as six. Years of study concentrate on the lore of Buddhism. Among the lower ranks of lamas there is a great deal of unadmirable posturing, mummery, and other dubious means of spiritual advancement. A chela sometimes falls into good hands and is treated with kindness, but other instructors are savage brutes who inflict barbarous cruelties on their charges, even to breaking their arms.

On the other hand, some of the superior types of lamas retain much of the higher philosophy of Buddhism.

Female lamaseries are an historic institution and many of them still flourish. But Lamaism has never captured the women as it has the men. There is, perhaps, one nun to every forty or fifty monks. There are a few groups of monks and nuns living side by side, and their children are brought up in an ecclesiastical atmosphere.

Congregations of lamas live in what is known in Tibetan as "gompas," and run the gamut from penury to affluence. I have seen lamas living in wretched buildings and eating food worse than a peasant's.

Eleven miles from Gyantse there is a gompa where the inmates lock themselves up in miniscular cells, where they remain in silent seclusion for periods lasting from a month to a lifetime, without seeing a human face.

Once a young lama, not a recluse, undertook to show me how it worked. Although it was not the hour when buttered tea would ordinarily be provided for the inmate, he knocked on a movable board and then removed it. Slowly a hand encased in a huge glove emerged and wavered in the air as if it led an independent existence. No other part of the body was visible in the darkness, and the glove prevented any mortal eye from ever seeing the flesh. I took several photographs before the glove was withdrawn. The young lama remarked, "He's been in there many years. One day there will be no answer when I knock with the buttered tea."

This ascetic life is believed to lift a lama to a higher hierarchy when the time comes for reincarnation. I took a picture of one ascetic who had spent seven years in one cell. His eyesight had been impaired by years of darkness and he was constantly squinting in the bright light. His forehead had acquired a permanent bump from his prostrations during prayer. At the end of his seclusion he had said, "I'm happy to be out. I'll never go back." And yet, when I saw him five years later, he was planning to return for the rest of his life.

The abbot was a reincarnate of seven or eight years of age. On my first visit he was only a baby and was kept out of view, but now it was announced that he would "receive" us. We were ushered into a comfortable, panelled room, quite different from the other apartments of the somber building. The wooden floor was covered with Tibetan carpets and there were one or two tank-as on the walls.

At the far end of the room was an elevated chair, a kind of miniature throne. And here sat the little abbot, attired in his costume of maroon wool. His features were set in a mold of assumed gravity.

We were told to sit on a bench below the throne. Tibetan pilgrims came in, one by one. With solemn self-possession the little abbot blessed them, laying his finger-tips on their heads. He then placed a scarf on their shoulders. Now and then his glance intercepted ours and he looked away shyly without smiling. The timidity lying below the composure was certainly justified, for the little man's abnormal career had started in his cradle. He had never been permitted to play with other children, his only companions being adult lamas.

In the great temple of Gyantse hundreds of lamas could be seen at their devotions. Kneeling figures clad in wine-red robes were scattered through the vast halls of worship. Though their lips were moving, their bodies were as immobile as statues.

Entrance into a shrine showed us some of the objects used in Lamaistic worship. Libation bowls were made of human skulls, ornamented in some cases with silver, bronze, and gilded bronze. A damaru, or drum, was made of a child's skull, covered with snakeskin. A trumpet made of a human thighbone had a whiplash of skin that played an important part in exorcisms. Another interesting object was the dorje

or Lamaist scepter—Indra's thunderbolt. We were to see similar articles
of worship in many other temples.

Walking on, we suddenly found ourselves in a large, windowless
buttered-tea kitchen which had huge cauldrons of tea and butter,
holding perhaps one hundred gallons of the bubbling mixture. Great,
smiling, rather greasy-looking monks were running to and fro filling
big earthenware and metal teapots with the fluid, while others fairly
shovelled great slices of clarified, rancid butter into the boiling kettles.

Gyantse provides a composite view of Tibetan life, but knowing
that many of its sights would be duplicated elsewhere, we made
ready to move on to Lhasa. I resisted even such attractions as polo
and tennis, played on a court that might be called surely "the highest
in the world." This particular pride of the British garrison was made
of concrete brought up from India on the backs of mules. The tennis
played on its rough surface was of a special brand, for the high altitude affected the flight of the ball and the wind of the players, who
gasped their way through sets and rested after every four strokes.

My wife wished to take the chawkidar's clever daughter to Lhasa,
but Wangdi was not having any more women in his caravan and said
so to Nakkin, who translated back: "Marster no like so many oomans
on a trip." I was not even consulted. Poor Wangdi had all the females
he wanted for the journey.

We visited the fort and talked with the non-commissioned native
officials. There were no whites present at the time. Rai Sahib Wangdi,
charming and entertaining, received us in his office, where we saw
three beautiful jet-black Apso dogs. The Nepalese resident and Rai
Sahib Wangdi also came to our quarters for tea and drinks that lasted
two hours. The Nepalese was fat, agreeable, and dull.

Everything was now in readiness for that part of the Lhasa road
not served by British bungalows. Our passport had provided us with
an "arrow letter," actually a red paper pennant, eighteen inches long,
inscribed with all necessary data about our trip, which had to be sent
ahead in order that local authorities might arrange for our *ulu* privileges. Travellers with *ulu* privileges had the right to demand transpor-

The huge glove covering the emerging hand of the lama, self-incarcerated for many years and now very old

The greatest chorten or shrine in Tibet, at Gyantse. The top is ornamented
with brass and gold leaf

tation facilities all along the route at prevailing prices—no profiteering!

With the arrangements all in hand, it would have been pleasant to make a detour to Shigatse in order that my wife might see Tibet's second city as a sort of curtain-raiser to the capital. This route also has the advantage of passing through the country of the nomads, an integral part of Tibetan life.

In 1935, going south from Shigatse, Vernay and I had reached a great level plateau, all slightly over 15,000 feet, too high for agriculture because of the shortness of the summer.

This is the domain of the nomads. During the summer months these people separate into family groups and wander about with their herds of sheep, goats, and yaks, living in their picturesque black yak-skin tents with the wool outside. In this high open country, subject to winds all the year around but particularly in winter, when a high gale blows all day, tent pegs would be hopeless, since the strain from the wind would be forever pulling them out. Consequently their tent ropes are anchored to big stones, and an ingenious system of fastening the guy ropes not only saves the tent from being caved in on the windward side but prevents flapping. Cooking is done inside, and the smoke is released through a slit in the tent's roof that can be opened at will. The first time we camped near a colony of these nomad tents we were surprised to find them immovable and soundless, while ours went banging and flapping with the wind.

Through the bitter winter months, the family units reassemble to form small villages. Then they live a communal life, one large tent serving as a community room, and smaller ones being joined on for sleeping quarters.

"Hardy" is an understatement when applied to these tall, robust people who face the elements without a qualm and spend most of their time outdoors, winter and summer, watching the precious flocks that are their sole means of livelihood. From the icy winds, rain, and snow, their chief protection is heavy leather clothing with the wool on the inside. As might be expected, they are not addicted to bathing, and their general indifference to dirt, whether on their persons or belongings, is astounding. What dirt starts to do to their faces, the smoke of the yak-dung fire finishes: they become darker and darker with age.

The general plateau in this area is well watered by many streams that criss-cross the land, providing good grass for the sheep, yaks, and goats. Above the tree-line, at levels between 17,000 and 18,000 feet, the yaks and goats feed on moss. It is only during the summer months that the herdsmen go up to these levels. Taking food and a blanket, they will remain away from the rest of the family for a week or more at a time.

At regular intervals the nomads travel to bazaar towns and trade their butter and animals for such necessities as metal pots and wooden cups, which they cannot make for themselves. The yak supplies their other needs.

Twelve miles south of Shigatse is the famous lamasery of Natung, housing Tibet's largest "library"—a collection of wooden plates carved with prayers. A great, dark, windowless room divided off into many alcoves held more than 20,000 plates for printing prayers. Even with an electric torch it was difficult picking one's footing, to say nothing of picking out a particular "book," but the lamas evidently managed it. They had some system of classification known only to themselves, and were able to supply other libraries with copies of the prayers. The wood of the plates, incidentally, had been brought all the way from India.

The lamasery is also notable for many relics of past Panchen Lamas, such as parts of shoes, clothing, hats, and canes. With the chief lamas of the place, Vernay and I knelt down and were blessed by the imposition of various relics on our bared heads. It was all very difficult and touching, and the well-disposed abbots actually managed to convey to us something of their spiritual tranquillity.

Approaching from the east on a downward sloping road one sees Shigatse from a great distance, a superb panorama with the great lamasery of Tashi Lhunpo on the outskirts, and, rising over the city, a huge, rectangular fort, the residence of the civil magistrate.

Lying only two or three miles south of the Brahmaputra, Shigatse has been for years the competitor of the capital, not only in a spiritual but in a commercial sense. Here lived the Dalai Lama's rival, the Panchen Lama, and here has flourished for generations a great center of trade. Unlike Lhasa, Shigatse has no permanent shops, but its great open-air bazaar filled with booths, all covered with cotton awnings, is busier than the capital's. The ordinary wares obtainable in Tibet are all for sale here, of course, but the city's specialty is the silver industry. From here come the majority of the finely chased silver buttered-tea cups one sees in the houses of the rich throughout the country.

Another specialty is a necklace made of small, square blocks of cheese. The blocks are hard, dried out, and dark in color, and the townspeople evidently consider them very beautiful. They also have a utilitarian value, for any piece may be detached and put in the mouth to suck.

In the ensemble Shigatse is a less beautiful city than Lhasa, but it has several notable points of superiority. Tashi Lhunpo is a more impressive sight than any of the great lamaseries around the capital. The two summer palaces of the late Panchen Lama are finer than those belonging to his great rival, and the park surrounding one of them is also finer than any private park in the capital. But outside the special parks, that have cost so much labor, since the city is situated in a bare, dry valley, the natives have not shown much enterprise in planting. The long avenues of trees and the shady groves that enhance Lhasa's beauty are fewer in Shigatse.

The Shigatse authorities provided Vernay and me with an A.D.C. and then proceeded to treat us most hospitably. The nobles had luncheon parties in one or another of the Panchen Lama's parks; there was a great reception in Tashi Lhunpo, and a military show.

More than 3000 lamas, all in full regalia according to rank, turned out for the Tashi Lhunpo affair. They swarmed around the empty throne of the departed Panchen Lama in the great courtyard, and many of them made gay pictures in large yellow hats and maroon cloaks. The upper-rank lamas were the soul of amiability, but the lower breeds, immemorially filled with a hatred of foreigners, were scarcely on the pleasant side.

The colonel who ran the military show was obviously proud of his men. Yet we might have had an inkling of what was to come when he appeared in mufti! The regiment's theoretical strength was 1000, but unless our eyes deceived us, no more than 500 were present for the drill. Their uniforms were worn with incredible slackness, and they marched like raw recruits. Only Shigatse's riffraff, obviously, had been lured into the army.

But all in all, Shigatse had been eminently worth seeing, and it was with infinite regret that we decided the time element forbade our seeing it now. My wife would have to be satisfied with a verbal account of it. On to Lhasa!

Our pack now consisted of twenty-two horses, four fewer than on the trip to Gyantse. And so, minus the two bad servants, plus two excellent Tibetan syces, three cabbages, four cauliflowers, and some tiny potatoes, all presents from the nice Indian soubadhar at the fort, we were off from Gyantse on the next stage.

It was sixteen miles to Gobshi. A small pass lying over the Nyang Chu, a stretch of fertile valley, and then my wife got her first view of a Tibetan interior, untouched by British ideas of cleanliness. It was a little dirtier than she had expected. The house, like all Tibetan houses, was built around three sides of a court facing south. The animals had the ground floor, while the second level, consisting of sleeping rooms leading into a patio, was reserved for human inhabitants.

We climbed to the living quarters by the usual dirty, rickety ladder. A swarm of cheerful, agreeable Tibetans, tongues protruding, fluttered about and led us to our rooms. There was a wood floor and one glassless window. One wall was covered with nicely patterned Tibetan silk. A rather pretty, very low divan of two cushions made of leopard skin and purple brocade stood behind a small painted table, on which was soon placed, at Wangdi's instigation, a large earthenware jug of English tea—the tea, sugar, and milk well churned together—and two lovely China cups on silver stands.

The patio, protected by wide, sweeping eaves, was "the living room" for the family, and here was kept burning the inevitable yakdung fire, encircled on cold days by the huddled forms of parents, children, and perhaps several relatives. For the kitchen, consisting of the fire and a few pots, an indispensable adjunct was the Tibetan bellows. An old crone sat on the patio-balcony next to a pot of fuel with a metal tube attached to the skin of a sheep or goat. The Tibetans work these implements easily and effectively, while any one else would find them very awkward.

To my wife, the lack of sanitation was incredible. The roof projecting over the manure pile was simply equipped with two slits, and this little roof was in full view of all the other houses, clustered together, and the open fields where in the summer season, farmers were working from sunup to sundown. Modern amenities are unknown in Tibet. This house, belonging to a rich headman, was typical of Tibetan houses.

Our portable beds and chairs did very nicely. Dinner consisted of stewed sheep and vegetables. Our plant-collecting brought in a single delphinium and some small rock plants, but the confusion, crowding, and curiosity of the natives made pressing them almost impossible.

My wife held a little clinic. There were many toothaches, and real and imaginary pains.

Sixteen miles again the next day, a lovely ride with no bad going, save for one swift stream in which my wife was almost unhorsed and was left cold and drenched. Snow-covered mountains were in view most of the day, and we saw a wondrous herd of yak, one of the most beautiful sights imaginable. We had a chance to get some excellent yak photographs near our compound that night. The house that put us up for the night was much like the one in Gobshi and when rain came on, we remained indoors pressing specimens.

The next morning we found a yellow poppy, some tiny forget-me-nots, and several herbs which were used for the cooking. There were only raisins and water for lunch, but for dinner Nakkin stewed the last of the sheep. Everything smelled of rancid buttered tea, two cups of which were prepared for us. My wife called it bad stuff and refused it. Sometimes a piece of butter may rest in a skin for more than a year, which adds a great deal to its flavor.

We knew by now that our Madrassi bearer was useless; so the marvellous Nakkin had taken on all the work cheerfully, murmuring frequently, "What does it matter? I am going to Lhasa!" It was extremely hard for her to manage our meals—packing, boiling water in an utter confusion of dirt, dirty things and dirty people in an over-crowded balcony, where the many uncles and aunts, grandparents, and children all crushed in and around our stewpot for a look at it and, if possible, at us. My wife's brown corduroy riding slacks were definitely a novelty.

We were up at five-thirty, in time to watch the cattle and sheep being milked and sent to pasture. A young woman, cleaner and more attractive than the rest, drove in several sheep, tied them together, and proceeded to milk them. She seemed on good terms with two of the men and presently we were told they were her husbands.

This was our introduction to polyandry, which we knew had existed in Tibet from time immemorial. The two husbands were brothers, the standard Tibetan pattern for polyandrous marriages. A desire to keep property in one household was the original motive for these one-woman-to-two-men marriages. It is one of the paradoxes of Tibet that polyandry should prevail in a land where one fifth of the men are committeed to a life of celibacy and there is always a surplus of women. The inequality is somewhat balanced, however, by the practice of polygamy in certain other parts of the country.

The sun came up at six-thirty but soon retreated in cold rain and wind. The trail moved upward to the pass of Kara La at over 15,000 feet, where glorious snow-capped mountains surrounded us and many herds of yak grazed between us and the fresh-creamy glaciers on our left. There was lucky sunlight in a small alpine valley, where another herd of the everlasting yak surrounded us as they grazed in a mass of miniature alpina, and we watched a huge lammergeier swooping down the crags, catching shafts of sunlight on his white and black head, on his grayish black wings and tawny breast.

The lammergeier, allied to the eagle and vulture, is one of the largest birds extant, his length sometimes reaching forty-six inches and his wing spread ten feet. His name, from the German "lämmer" (lambs) and "geier" (vulture) exaggerates, perhaps, his strength and endurance, but he is a unique raptorial bird in that he kills hares and field-mice to supplement his usual diet of carrion. His Latin name, *Gypaëtus barbatus*, comes from a bristly tuft on his chin. The lammergeier's majestic flight is always a beautiful thing to watch, and our bird happened to be a particularly large specimen.

The lammergeier is not the only spectacular bird in Tibet. One constantly encounters giant ravens and vultures, so tame as to seem thoroughly aware that killing is against lama precepts. Ravens lingering on the road show an utter disregard for caravans, and the utmost concession to be expected of them is a hop or two away from an animal's hoofs. They are alert, however, to any sudden reaching-down motion that seems to suggest a search for a stone. At such a gesture they take to flight.

The sun was still bright but patches of snow were clinging to the tufts of the taller plants. We moved on into a freezing rainstorm that raged angrily in our faces. The snow mountains were still with us. Five miles from Nargatse Dzong, my wife's horse had painful shoe-trouble, and Nakkin, the lion-hearted, offered her flat-footed Rosinante, equipped with a particularly painful saddle. Nakkin insisted, fell on her head in the mud trying to mount another horse, and then walked the rest of the way through a sedgy marsh in a cold downpour.

We were now nearing Yamdrok Tso, a most famous lake, whose beauty has been celebrated by every traveller who ever saw it, but unfortunately for us the darkness and the downpour blotted out all signs of it.

The trail took us through the tiny streets of Nargatse Dzong, over great slabs of crooked stone that were added agony for my wife, wet, exhausted, and tormented by Nakkin's uncomfortable saddle. We rode uphill to the fortress, where rooms at the very top were placed at our disposal. They overlooked the town and valley. There was some Chinese furniture and painted woodwork in these best of quarters we had had so far.

Many townspeople inhabited the fortress. A grandmother, sisters-in-law, and a heterogeneous collection of women hovered around our "kitchen." Through the slime of yesterday and tomorrow they span and knitted in many fashions, and fondled dirty babies. They all needed a good strong hose. But our stomachs were getting stronger: we now could even look at our cookpots and tolerate the rancid-butter scent that penetrated everything, even our beds.

Nakkin, finishing up her five-mile hike, appeared, mud to the knees, and was the first of the caravan to get herself in order. In no time at all, she had made us comfortable.

While my wife, soaked with rain, had been crouched over a pail of sheep-dung fire, trying to dry and warm herself, the governor called, bringing welcome eggs and mutton. He was a genial fellow and we carried on a conversation in Hindustani.

Dawn brought two giant ravens weighing at least eight pounds apiece, that stood outside our glassless window and cawed in our faces most impertinently. Leaving our fortress abode, we slithered on down through incredible, picturesque, dirty steepness, getting now our first view of Yamdrok Tso, which goes on for sixty-five miles of turquoise blue. On its surface we saw many gulls, Brahminy duck, and bar-headed geese.

The colored balconies and the fortress looked very fine as we moved along the lake. My wife found her first *Meconopsis Baileyi*, the blue poppy of Tibet, and we saw many large hawks hovering over the holes of tailless, buff, fat mice. The valley was riddled with them. There were many doves and hoopoes, very tame.

The way was enlivened by passing caravans of yaks taking rice to

Looking northeast from the top of Shigatse Fort over the city. In the distance is the Tsang Po

A. S. Vernay and the author having tea in the courtyard of a Tibetan house
on the way to Shigatse

A coracle floating passengers down the Tsang Po near Shigatse. Coracles cannot
navigate upstream; they must be carried

Living quarters in the larger of the two summer palaces of the late
Panchen (Tashi) Lama at Shigatse

Red lamas, 3500 of them, in full dress in Tashi Lhunpo lamasery. Empty throne of
the late Panchen Lama in the background

Nomad tents in the country south of Shigatse where the plains average
15,000 to 16,000 feet in elevation

Camp at about 17,000 feet. Here in 1930 we collected wild sheep
(*ovis ammon Hodgsoni*)

A harvest scene near Lhasa. The crops have been taken in

Plowing preparatory to planting peas and barley at around 14,000 feet, near Gyantse

Yamdrok Tso, a deep brackish lake in the form of a curve sixty miles long
at an altitude of 14,300 feet

Mrs. Cutting with her mount outside a typical house where we spent the night

Mrs. Cutting and Nakkin outside the fort Nargatse Dzong, near Yamdrok Tso

Bad going. Working our way around an escarpment when the flood had
inundated the trail below

Peasant children dressed in heavy cotton or yak wool clothes

Children of noble birth. They are dressed in Chinese silk
and cheap fedora hats from India

Lhasa for the well-to-do. The owners of these caravans rode with their wives, brilliantly dressed in lovely colors. They carried antiquated guns across their saddles, and all the while they were jogging up and down they occupied themselves with spinning or making soles for boots. Now and then they put a stone in their slings and shot it with incredible accuracy to keep the wayward yaks in order.

This was certainly the land of rocks and stones over and over again. Buddhas and Bodhisattvas were carved everywhere on mountainsides, along with the inevitable Om Mani Padme Hum, the legend, according to Baron Schelling, that has been repeated on certain prayer wheels 100,000,000 times.

The mountains of these upland valleys were eroding, a mixture of every size and color, like some vast pudding gone wrong. Bits of rock, jagged and rounded, made up the most pitiful roadside cairns, with a few sticks on top, holding rags called "wind horses" printed with the sacred words. The roads were mere heaps of stones, agonizing for the wretched ponies, especially in the heavy rains we had lately been having. All the walls and houses were of stone; some had been put up nicely with mud or brick, but in general they were pretty rude affairs. Exceptions were the houses of the gentry, built of mud stucco, with good wood windows and situated, as a rule, in parks of trees. Whatever the kind of house, cloth prayer flags fluttered in the breeze to assure for the owners a place in the Buddhist paradise.

At Pede Dzong we liked our rooms overlooking one of the largest of Tibetan lakes with snow-capped mountains gleaming in the sunshine. The late afternoon brought cold winds, and while I went out to do some photographing, my wife installed herself luxuriously on a Tibetan couch, drinking tea, smoking cigarettes, enjoying the peerless view, and watching my activities. Thinking this too much of a good thing, I asked her to come down and ride a gray yak for my motion-picture film. It would be a trying feat, as yaks have no fancy for the smell of white people and this gray one was already showing its churlish nature. It was a very unhappy woman who came down and rode the animal long enough for me to get twenty feet of film, but she stuck at her job gamely until the film was finished. Then, feeling that the animal was showing signs of balkiness, she leaped off into the arms of two smiling Tibetans.

The natives interfered with the photography, old and young thrusting their faces into the finder, and making it necessary to wipe it off time after time; no sooner was it salvaged from a youth than a graybeard would smear it over again. Their tiresome behavior was mitigated only by their amiable curiosity.

Wherever my wife moved she was followed by throngs, fascinated by the corduroy slacks. There were many bright and alert babies, some very young, who captured her fancy. Meanwhile the eight annas of backsheesh we had given to the owners of the beautiful gray yak had bought a great deal of *chung* for six men and was causing much merriment and roistering on the banks of the lake. They made their yaks, with red decorations around their necks and about their saddles, go fast, which yaks do not like, and in the end they rode off on wobbly saddles down the road at a pretty smart canter in gusts of laughter and so out of sight.

At sundown a male chorus of farmers and spinners in the neighborhood followed their lama in easy and pleasing responses. We had heard singing all day long, but that night's was the best. The day ended quietly on a dinner of sheep liver and mushrooms—the latter a rare commodity—provided by our agreeable hosts, whose polite tongues had been out all afternoon.

We set out very early the next morning and wandered along the most extraordinary of all lakes, surrounded by snow-capped, moss-green mountains. The lake went on and on, in and out among these peaks. We climbed to the summit of the pass of Nyapso La, at 16,200 feet, and left Pede Dzong looking lovely in its turquoise setting on the shore of Yamdrok Tso—the lake of the nomad's upper pastures.

The road over the pass and down to Singamakchung was a three-hour stony hell, ending mercifully at a decent house beautifully situated in a willow grove on the banks of the Tsang Po (the Tibetan name for the Brahmaputra), where we stopped for lunch and a rest.

The hospitable owner was a noble named Lobsang Norbla who appeared with five dozen eggs, followed by his *mundle* (bailiff) with about half as many again.

Refreshed, we went on our way to cross the Tsang Po by coracles, which was accomplished without incident except that my wife's horse, which had been stupid, dangerous, and recalcitrant for two days, now stepped on her foot as a parting shot.

Evening brought the village of Mukkum and a rich young Tibetan dressed in a new beige Homburg hat and purple gown over a yellow shirt, who not only offered us a pleasant room for the night but heaped us with presents of chung, a basket of green, half-rotten peaches, at least eight dozen eggs, more peaches, and then a quarter of lamb for the servants. It was a medieval establishment, with the young lord ruling over a big house, a private temple with its own staff of lamas, peasants living in small houses, woods, and broad meadows. Our host, like many rich Tibetans, had hired his private lamas to do his praying for him.

Every one was busy at nightfall, tending to the yaks, fetching dung and wood. A parade of dirty peasants went by our window all evening in the shadows, gabbling, shuffling, sneezing, spitting with heroic persistence, and all our ears could distinguish was the word *"lha-less"* which means yes, aye, verily, well, agreed. It seemed to be the only word in their vocabularies.

We were up at three o'clock, thanks to the roosters that retired in a prayer wheel just outside our window. The Tsang Po, we discovered, was in flood, an unheard-of occurrence for this part of Tibet. Miles and miles of farmland were under water; crops were ruined; peasants had fled from the rushing mad torrent, taking refuge on the nearest high spot. Many men and more animals had been drowned; crazed women wailed, unable to grasp the nature of the calamity.

Our trail, now submerged by water and often abutting the main current of the river, followed the edge of an escarpment. A fall here would have swept horse and rider out into the middle of the river—which would have been the end.

The next day the Kyi Chu, coming down from Lhasa to join the Tsang Po, was a swollen yellow torrent. We groped our way over the submerged trail, often obtaining the assistance of stranded peasants who held the horses' bridles. Despite these precautions, Nakkin's horse slipped into the stream and was rescued with great difficulty; another horse carrying our money-bags fell down an escarpment and scattered coins in every direction.

In one village where the streets seemed to be bottomless rivers, we nearly upset and drowned. Many people and animals had been lost. Yet some of the men of the villages who had lost everything were extremely cheerful guides in getting us through the flood. Gaily, laughingly, they pulled and dragged my wife over the steepest of escarpments, hand over hand.

Now and then there were moments of respite when the trail itself gently rose. At such times we could see the havoc wrought by the flood. In the lower parts of the valley bordering the river, houses and fields had been inundated. When the trail rose higher we saw the unfortunates huddled together, helpless, cold, and forlorn. The head men always had tents to cover themselves, but the poor had nothing.

At several points we saw cattle marooned out on tiny islands—all that was left of their meadows. A peasant approached us, driving cattle along the trail. Suddenly a calf slipped and went over the side. The current swept it out into the middle, and in three minutes it was out of sight. For the peasant this was a tragedy of major proportions. He watched the disappearing calf with a completely stoical face, and then turned his attention to the other animals. Many of the travellers on the road carried spears against wolves. One woman was carrying on her shoulders a large-sized sheep that had been killed by a wolf in broad daylight.

At a turn in the road that afternoon at 2:30, we beheld the memorable sight of the Potala, seven miles away.

Few cities offer such a dramatic approach as Lhasa, with the Potala looming out of the blue and enticing distance. The soaring mass of

Few cities offer such a dramatic approach as Lhasa, with the Potala looming out of the blue and enticing distance

The western entrance to the city of Lhasa. The road leads to the left of the swamp in the foreground

white buildings crowning the city symbolizes the heart of Tibet. It is the seat of government, a shrine, the winter palace of the Dalai Lama. Our eyes never left it. Possessed of no obvious harmony or balance in its component parts, it presented, nevertheless, a subtle, inexplicable rhythm of completeness. Approaching closer we could see that the word "white" could not be applied to it accurately. Actually it was a symphony of grays, beige, and burnt-umber, with streaks of gold coming from the gilded baldachins or tombs of seven past Dalai Lamas reposing on the roof.

The Potala suggested no other kind of architecture. Begun perhaps in the tenth century, and renovated in the seventeenth, its form is purely Tibetan. Towering above the capital, supreme now and forever, it is the most magnificent building I have ever seen.

At the moment when the city proper, lying at the base of the Potala, became visible, we were met on the road by an A.D.C., a tall, thin man of fifty or so, accompanied by his son. With great tongue-thrusting and scarf-exchanging, they took charge of our affairs for the duration of our stay.

The gay road wound through the country, past whitewashed, laminated stone houses, all guarded by handsome black mastiffs— perfect police dogs—and into the thickening traffic of colorful caravans. Rising on the hills were Drepung and Sera, the two most famous monasteries of Tibet, and here and there the valley was swarming with young lamas, laughing joyously, swimming and diving in little streams. Old women vending green, shrivelled peaches and sour milk lined the roadside, and their principal customers were the young lamas.

Many beggars whined for alms. Begging in Tibet, as in Spain, is a recognized mode of life with a definite set of traditions, and Rule One in the code is that a mendicant must not ask a stranger for alms more than once during his stay in Lhasa. A spurned beggar is likely to launch a curse on the traveller, and so, conforming to the custom of the country, we passed out copper coins to all who asked for them, and never afterwards were we troubled by the fraternity of outstretched hands.

Tattered garments are no index of a Tibetan beggar's condition, for the more patches, the more aristocratic the beggar. Nor are all Tibetan beggars poor. One fellow, about forty, with a refined face, had had painted for him, we were told, hundreds of tank-as, which he donated to near-by monasteries for the good of his soul.

Three miles from the city we passed Norbu Linga (Jewel Park), the summer palace of the late Dalai Lama, from which he had written me the letters that were eventually to make this visit possible.

A trim, whitewashed little house, surrounded by a white wall, had been placed at our disposition by the government. Its name was Zara Linga, and it had a beautiful grove of willows, patches of green lawn, and a little stream running through the estate.

Across the road was the house often used by the British mission, and here on my first visit I had said *Ave atque Vale* to Mr. Williamson, the British political officer, who was dying of uremia, aggravated by the high altitude. During his last days, the government of India had sounded out Lhasa on the idea of sending an airplane to rush Mr. Williamson back to a more bearable altitude. Whether the scheme was feasible didn't matter, because the Tibetans declined to permit a plane to enter the country even when a man's life was at stake.

Our house was made cheerful by masses of flowers, and there was tea which we gorged unceremoniously and greedily. Hundreds of people had crowded into our willow grove, staring and jostling each other to have a better look.

Our cook's boy, who had developed a horrible eye and skin disease, was dispatched forthwith to a doctor for treatment. After tea came my old friend K. K. Mondo, a superb-looking high lama, who was one of the four Tibetan boys schooled at Rugby. Admirably educated, with a perfect command of English, and beautifully mannered, with great tact and shrewdness, he was an attaché of the government secretariat and was in an excellent position to guide us through the intricate maze of Tibetan official life. On my first visit he had presented Vernay and me to the prime minister and five members of the supreme council, or Kashag, who bore the title of Shapé. This time the calendar of official visits would be different, since the Regent, who had been absent from the capital when I had been there before, was now in residence, ready to receive us. On the other hand, the eldest of the shapés was in retirement, due to illness.

K. K. Mondo had brought us a number of presents, amplified before the end of the day by a stream of things from other old friends. There were at least sixty dozen eggs, huge bags of flour, rice, barley, butter, mountains of cabbages, leeks, several sheep, and baskets of vegetables so beautifully arranged they might have come from the Halles in Paris. A large part of this would go to the poor.

The first morning broke fine and clear, and before the official visits started we had time to greet our neighbors and take a walk through the town. The young lamas of the Potala, the future government officials of Tibet, were having a ten-day outing in our park. Huge tents, gifts of the late Dalai Lama, had been erected as their holiday abode. The sides and tops of white canvas were decorated with deep-blue designs of embroidery and appliqué with various red and yellow frills on the entrances, the whole making a gaily painted picture.

The lamas, who had already appeared at our house in droves, showed a reciprocating courtesy by letting us see the interior of their largest tent, about 150 feet long and 80 feet wide, furnished with masses of brilliant carpets, brocaded and carpet cushions, small, brightly painted tables, hundreds of potted cosmos, asters, and marigolds. The top of the tent was cleverly secured to giant willows by what seemed miles of yak rope, an inch and a half thick, decorated with huge balls of red wool. It was a lovely sight, this monster tent with its exquisite furnishings and the hundreds of colorful lamas entering and leaving, depositing their fierce monastic boots in heaps at the entrance. All were cordial and hospitable. I photographed the conference going on in the tent.

The ranking lamas picnicked outdoors from baskets and dishes, while the servants passed buttered tea interminably. The food and the dishes used to serve it were of a superior type. Great quantities of food were visible and much of it was wasted. We saw ever so many large bowls, filled with buttered tea, untouched.

Other young lamas were playing dominoes and a dice game, flying kites, or swimming. Older ones were teaching. One could see these ardent, gesticulating monks sitting before their chelas. The object of their study was the "wheel of life" held up before the chelas, but we found ourselves wondering whether the teachers were gifted, and able to communicate their ardor to their charges.

Looking up earnestly at the "wheel of life," the little chelas must have found plenty to dazzle their young brains, for this complicated chart of Buddhist doctrine has occupied lama theologians for centuries. Even Western philosophers have grappled with its wealth of abstruse meanings, attempting to relate them to doctrines that grew up in the Orient.

The "wheel of life" is a spoked disk, painted on a scroll. On the hub are painted a cock, a pig, and a snake, standing for lust, greed, and anger, the three vices that torment human beings. The rim is divided into twelve segments, representing such metaphysical concepts as "sense surfaces and understanding," "indulgence," and "fuller life." The area between hub and rim is divided into six compartments, sharply divided by the spokes. At the top is heaven, at the bottom hell. The other four spaces are devoted to human life, animal life, purgatory (tormented spirits), and titans.

Closer inspection reveals a dolorous prospect—a multitude of pictographs illustrating Buddha's doctrine that suffering is inevitable— "All is transitory, painful, and illusory." Life is an endless, wearisome round of rebirths. The pictographs illustrating human life, for instance, show birth, old age, sickness, death, ungratified desires, struggle for existence, punishments, bereavements, and offensive objects and sensations. Hell is no less graphic. There are eight hot hells and eight cold ones, with an additional outer hell through which escaping spirits must pass without a guide. Each of these has special tortures to suit various crimes and misdemeanors.

A small caravan of yaks in front of the Potala. The street to the city passes just to the right of the trees

The main entrance staircase of the Potala turns right at the extremity of the view
and later left again before reaching the top

The great court at the summit of the Potala. Lamas' quarters at the left, and ceremonial yak wool curtains hanging in the background

Looking east over Lhasa from the top of the Potala

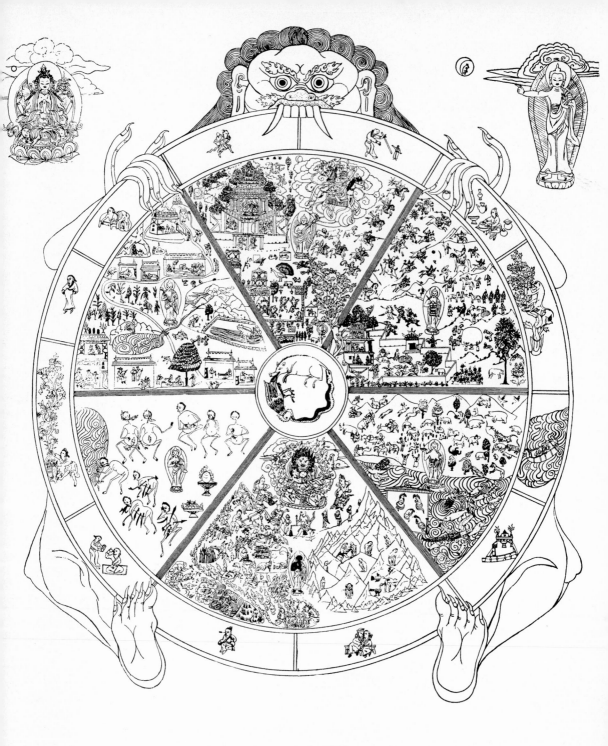

The Tibetan Wheel of Life

This drawing and the interpretation on the facing page are reproduced from "The Buddhism of Tibet," by L. Austine Waddell, published by W. H. Allen & Company, London

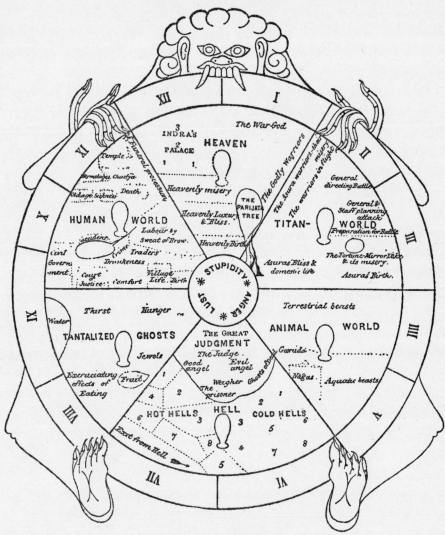

An Interpretation of the Wheel of Life

The "wheel of life" is held in the claws of a monster who symbolizes "the hideousness of clinging to life," and beyond the rim is shown Buddha, who has escaped the round of metempsychosis.

All this was doubtless explained to the chelas by their lama leaders, but, after all, the wheel is only a symbol of an intricate theological system that would take a volume to clarify. For the visitor, the most important fact was this: it was not an academic legend but the motivating faith of all Tibetans. Prayer flags, prayer wheels, sacred symbols, visible everywhere, showed that Lamaism was a living, breathing creed.

And now the greatest symbol that Lamaism has produced beckoned to us from afar. On close view, the Potala was even more impressive than at a distance. No black-and-white picture could do justice to the color scheme, the burnt umber contrasting with the gray, and the four-foot border of deep-red juniper under the gilded baldachins.

Just before noon, Lhasa's open, airy streets, bright in the sunlight, were alive with sturdy, good-natured Tibetans, carrying on their errands in the bazaar and in the spacious Maidan. The lower classes walked, and the gentry rode on elaborately caparisoned horses. Into a main street came a horseman from Khăm leading a tea caravan—a splendid-looking fellow with broad head, fierce eyes, rough manners, and a roaring laugh. Enormous silver earrings dangled from his ears, and his long pigtail was held in place by a large ivory-and-silver brooch. He seemed even stronger and bigger than the average Tibetan. When my wife made signs she wanted to photograph him, he posed cheerfully, and then rubbed his stomach to show he had important business in the bazaar.

We too ambled to the bazaar, where the awning-covered booths were the center of great activity in vegetables, tea, spices, cloth— mostly bolts of the famous Tibetan maroon wool,—wooden bowls, brass pots. The inevitable beetleware, pink-and-white beads, and felt hats testified that Japanese and German goods were creeping in. In the special stalls kept by Kashmiri Mohammedans were a few pieces of jewelry, but there was no sign of the famous and good Tibetan turquoise. We later learned it was not being mined in the country any more, but an inferior grade, along with coral, was coming up from India. Tibetans who once received all their good things from Chinese caravans complained that much of the jewelry was spurious.

During our wanderings in the town the average man looked at us with no more than casual curiosity, but from time to time we were annoyed by packs of youths, chattering and pursuing us. My wife's brown corduroy trousers and heavy English brogans were a curiosity from start to finish.

We were struck by two negative features of Lhasa—the lack of glass and the lack of wheels. Only wealthy houses had real windows, since glass had to be brought from India at great expense. More significant was the lack of the wheel and of wheeled vehicles, which have never entered Tibetan civilization. All transportation was effected by porters and pack animals. Donkeys carrying two fair-sized building stones across the city were no uncommon sight. For months, I was told, the donkey method had been used to transport the stones out into the valley for an addition to the prime minister's house. Why the Tibetans never discovered or adapted the principle of the wheel, one of the most important elements in a moving civilization, is hard to say, but in any case the ubiquitous prayer wheel, a mechanical means of invoking the attention of the gods, is the only reminder that the wheel exists in the outside world.

It was now time to visit the prime minister, Si-lön Yab-shi Lang-Dün, in his palace on the outskirts of the city. Through several courtyards guarded by smartly turned-out servants, we passed through a reception room filled with beautiful Chinese and Tibetan furniture, statues of Buddha in brass and wood, and a multitude of tank-as. After the ceremony of the scarves and the presentation of a silver self-winding wrist-watch, we found ourselves in the presence of an austere, dignified man of forty, clad in cardinal-like robes of red silk.

Buttered tea was provided, and Wangdi, who had come as interpreter, took his place on the floor. The conversation with the prime minister dwelt on the long search for the late Dalai Lama's reincarnation. Four years had passed in mysterious journeys, consultations of oracles, and attempts to find a clue in the lake near the late ruler's birthplace. The prime minister took all this as a matter of course, and appeared unconcerned at the ancient prophecy that Tibet would have only thirteen Dalai Lamas. (His late Holiness was number thirteen.)*

*Fortunately the fourteenth reincarnation has recently been found and installed.

On our first meeting, the prime minister had shown an amazing lack of interest in the outside world, but now he took the initiative in discussing Japan's war on China, which had just begun. He asked my opinion whether it was likely to turn into a major conflict. Thinking of the poor showing made by the Japanese in their first Shanghai adventure, I inclined to the view it would not have any wide repercussions. By this time the prime minister has discovered that I am no political oracle.

The Tibetan government, I gathered, was not at all displeased that the war had broken out. The Chinese had engaged in border skirmishes and had encroached on Tibetan territory. Now that they had their hands full in the East, they were likely to keep hands off Tibet's eastern frontier. Nevertheless, Tibet had once done her shopping in Pekin, and Tibetans were closely allied to the Chinese. The government hoped that China, after being properly chastened, would win the ultimate victory.

In the Tibetan hierarchy the prime minister stands just below the Regent. He has the power to remove any member of the Kashag, and also to veto any of that council's decisions. He is not likely, however, to avail himself of the privilege.

Visits to the shapés were spread over several days. In each case there were ceremonial calls with presentation of gifts—to the elderly Tren-dong-nga, the middle-aged and amiable Bhön-dong, and the austere Kalön Lama, only ecclesiastical member of the council. The two lay shapés lived in large palaces; they served us buttered tea and were gracious but distant. The only note of variety came from Bhön-dong, who wanted to hear about airplanes. Kalön Lama, likewise, had a fine palace, and nothing indicated his religious rank save his tonsured head, his robe of wool instead of silk, and a ban on smoking.

These visits completed, K. K. Mondo made arrangements for my reception at the palace of the Regent, Re-ting Pö gya tsap Rimpochi, supreme ruler of Tibet since the death of the thirteenth Dalai Lama.

In the outer courtyard of the palace were two huge Tibetan mastiffs, chained up but nevertheless wearing the usual heavy collar of red wool which is the Tibetan dog's protection against wolves. We passed through an inner court in which two half-grown tigers, gifts from the king of Nepal, languished unhappily in the hot and treeless sunshine. Then into a gold-lacquered room about twenty by twenty, filled with potted plants in bloom and a collection of Chinese jade and porcelains. Here sat the Regent of Tibet, a fragile, intense-looking young man of twenty-seven or so, wearing a gown of pale Mongolian gold brocade and a velvet sleeveless jacket of the same color.

The Regent sat in a carved European chair in his bower of flowers while we chatted and drank buttered tea. Two good black Pekinese frolicked on the floor. Wangdi, overcome by the occasion, squatted beside the Regent's chair and translated from Tibetan to Hindustani.

The Regent asked a few desultory questions on the Chinese situation as it appeared to the outside world. He wanted every scrap of information he could get, but was noncommittal about his own opinions. He was intelligent, charming and agreeable, and it was not hard to see why the Dalai Lama had selected him for a difficult role.

As I departed, the Regent invited me to return another day to photograph him, bringing my wife.

Next came a number of sightseeing tours, that had to be arranged officially. They started off with a visit to the Potala.

A close-up view of the building served to enhance its beauty. Manifestly not the inspiration of a single man, it was rather a work of accretion, like the Gothic cathedrals of the Middle Ages. Generations of men had devoted their best efforts to it, and out of many diverse elements had come unity and harmony.

A long climb up an enormous exterior staircase brought us into a big courtyard. Hanging from a balcony was a fifty-foot sacred curtain made of yak wool. Thence into the sacred edifice, where the high, gaunt walls, the spacious halls and rooms, the labyrinth of terraces, bore out the promise of the exterior. So vast is the place that there is ample room for all manner of government offices, committee rooms, quarters for the three hundred lamas who carry on their studies here, chapels, and treasure rooms. It has dungeons, too, far below. One of the unhappy prisoners still there had his eyes put out when he was incarcerated, as the result of a political offense.

While only a few of the valuable things are shown to visitors, the building has storerooms of vast treasures, the accumulation of centuries. One chapel was notable for its great number of jade and cloisonné bowls and religious vessels, in gold and silver, set with precious stones. The tombs of the Dalai Lamas, visible from the exterior, had also drawn on all sources of Tibetan art and wealth.

Work was still in progress on the tomb of the last Dalai Lama at the top of the Potala. In a room forty by twenty, fifteen to twenty feet high, Tsering, that sensitive young Michelangelo of Lhasa, and several others were busy on a series of incredibly fine miniatures. Tsering, having served the ruler during his life, was now contributing to his posthumous glory. Every inch of wall and ceiling eventually would be filled with the lovely miniatures depicting the whole Buddhist pantheon, with mythology and motor-cars mixed in with great ingenuity. There were gods, goddesses, angels and demons. It would take years, perhaps, for the artists to complete this microscopic type of frescoing, which they did with loving care. Tsering's plight reminded one of Michelangelo, wearing steel-rimmed glasses to save his eyes as he fretted and fumed on the Sistine ceiling.

Few of the non-Tibetans visiting the Potala have failed to speculate on the origin of the gold treasure, since Tibet is supposed to have no mineral resources and its exports are light, creating only a small balance for purchase abroad. It was the contention of every Tibetan with whom I discussed the matter that India and China had supplied all the precious metals in the country. Over the centuries, even if Tibetan exports were inconsiderable, jewels and gold plate had accumulated in the hands of the lamas and the wealthier families. The denials that gold had ever been found in quantity within the country were supported by the evidence of two British engineers who were permitted to survey a large region between Shigatse and Lhasa and another north of the capital, without finding any minerals of value. As for the eastern part of the country near the Chinese border, I never saw a sign of native metals when I was travelling in that region.

What possibilities the unexplored parts of the country hold is a matter for future geological survey. As far as the present goes, it may be safely inferred, I think, that the Tibetans have no secret sources of mineral wealth. The gold one sees in Lhasa does not, after all, form such a considerable bulk, compared with the supplies of Western nations. All this probably derives from China and India.

The Potala, as we have seen, used to be the winter palace of the late Dalai Lama, but during the closing years of his life he preferred Norbu Linga. While the Potala is an austere fortress, Norbu Linga is simple and charming with its lovely buildings and gardens, and a barracks for the soldiers where taps are sounded morning and evening. This is the finest park in Lhasa.

We were entertained on the veranda of the small palace, where two high lamas were hosts at a very long and rich Tibetan meal. The terrace provided a splendid view of the gardens with their long lines of poplars and orchards of Japanese crab-apple trees bearing cranberry-like fruit. There were many miniature peach and apricot trees in porcelain pots. Everywhere there was a profusion of flowers, including cosmos ten feet high.

The private rooms, halls, and audience chambers of the little palace, all speckless and shining with not a mote of dust visible anywhere, were covered with frescoes, some of them by young Tsering, now busy on his master's tomb. The rooms showed, in addition to the frescoes, a breathless succession of tank-as, brocades, lacquers, gold tables, and chairs. Many gifts presented to His Holiness by foreign monarchs were still kept here.

Coming out of the palace, I photographed my wife and Nakkin, standing between two superb white Chinese cloisonné elephants, three feet high, that guarded the entrance to the terrace. The photographing continued in the gardens, where many kinds of waterfowl disported themselves; in the gilded summer house, where the Dalai Lama used to relax at midday; and in the menagerie, now reduced to a few Bactrian camels, monkeys, a Sikkimese stag, and a pair of beautiful little Chinese dogs.

Norbu Linga's stables were extraordinary, the woodwork polychromed and decorated with paintings.

All the buildings in the park were lighted by electricity, the power coming from a small hydro-electric plant down on the riverbank. This improvement was the work of Kunbila, a favorite and personal assistant of the late Dalai Lama. The machinery came from India.

Kunbila's name I knew from my correspondence with His Holiness. A handsome, bright young man of peasant origin, he had pushed himself up to a position of trust and honor, but not without stirring up a bit of resentment and animosity, which his personal arrogance helped along. Directly the Dalai Lama died, Kunbila was arrested and charged with poisoning his late master. To this he had a ready and convincing reply: "Poison His Holiness? I had everything to gain by his living, everything to lose by his death." Though he saved himself from death, a sentence of banishment was pronounced, and he was now "living quietly in the country."

We came upon three motor-cars, two Austins and a Dodge, now fast disintegrating, and found that these, too, had been the inspiration of Kunbila.

Since the Dalai Lama was obliged to use palanquins on his frequent trips to the Potala, Kunbila's modern soul had thought that motor-cars from India would be a pleasant way to shatter tradition. So a motor road was built between the Potala and Norbu Linga, and presently the populace had the thrill of watching cars move without visible means of locomotion. The innovation was not appreciated, and during the last two years of his life the Dalai Lama ceased to use them. No one else, of course, had ever again suggested them, and now they sagged to the earth, rusty and decrepit reminders that Tibet's only experiment with modern transportation had not been a success.

When we returned from Norbu Linga, there was a summons from the Regent; so the next morning, heavily armed with cameras, we went to his palace. We were received in the same gold-lacquered

ཇེ་པ་མཁས་རབ།

This casual Tibetan water color is typical, both as an expression of the spiritual
aspiration of Tibetan life and as a specimen of the color sense of the Tibetan artist

room, and again the Regent sat in his carved chair and offered delicious buttered tea which we drank from jade-and-gold cups. He was full of solicitude, asking what he might do to make our stay more pleasant, and curious about New York, which he said he would like to see. Finally he rose and led us into the next room to see a litter of Chinese Pekinese.

Then out to the garden where, as at Norbu Linga, the tallest and largest cosmos grew to a height of ten feet. There were about two hundred splendid Chinese porcelain pots with carefully trained rose bushes laden with blooms, many kinds of geraniums, and peach trees, some of them fruiting. The Regent kindly sat in the blazing sun to be photographed, while his servants massed these pots of flowers around him.

His personal attendant was over six feet two, and to make himself look still bigger wore a coat of extraordinary padded shoulders. This giant held an umbrella over the Regent.

His Highness asked me to sit with him, and when I wished to stand by he pressed me firmly to sit down, and himself put my hat on my head.

After taking the pictures we returned to the palace for more tea. I told him I would have one of the photographs hand-tinted and placed in a special frame, gold or jade as he preferred. He chose gold. Seeing that there were no other photographs about the palace I offered to send him a large picture of the Potala, which he accepted eagerly.

At parting, the ruler told my wife he would send her a pair of Apso dogs, which greatly delighted her. I had received five of these dogs from the late Dalai Lama and started to breed them successfully in New Jersey. They are a pure Tibetan breed, usually golden, blue-gray, or black; to describe them, I can only say that if a Pekinese were mated with a Yorkshire terrier, the offspring would look like a first cousin of the Apso. The name, by the way, was first registered outside of Tibet by Lieutenant-Colonel and Mrs. Bailey, who introduced them to England.

The Regent did not look well. His principal malady was catarrh, aggravated by his habit of taking snuff, a strong tobacco diluted with yak dung. Several years earlier, a British doctor had suggested that his health would improve if he got some exercise; so a football was brought up from India and he spent part of every day kicking it around his garden. This came to an end when a delegation of lamas called on him and protested that kicking a ball was not a suitable pastime for the highest reincarnate.

When the photograph of the Potala was wrapped up next day, Nakkin, who had been hearing about Wangdi's triumph in serving as interpreter, asked if she might deliver it. Several hours later she returned, laden with a white scarf, a package of green walnuts, and a large bundle of two-foot-long joss sticks made of the famous Lhasa musk—finest in the world and at one time part of Tibet's yearly tribute to the Emperor of China. Just how she wangled it Nakkin did not explain, but she had impressed on the palace staff that she must deliver her gift to the Regent personally. She was in an ecstasy. "Not one Tibetan in a thousand sees His Highness," she told my wife. "I don't care if I die tonight!"

Next to the Potala, the most historic spot in Lhasa is the Jo-Kang or Cathedral, built in 750 A.D. by that Tsan-Gampo who married the Chinese and Nepalese princesses, thereby committing his country to Buddhism. The ancient building, seemingly an imperishable stronghold of Buddha, is wedged into the center of the city, and for this reason is difficult to photograph. It bears the marks of hoary tradition in every stone and beam. The old stone floor has been worn into grooves by centuries of worshippers, and the stone benches and ladders have acquired a high patina from the butter-greased hands of those who used them. The gloom of the interior is relieved somewhat by thousands of burning wicks spouting from large and small containers filled with yak butter.

Holding torches aloft, our lama guides led us through chilly, gloomy corridors and small shrines wherein lamas droned out their Gregorian-like chants, and fat, slinking rats traced shadows across the greasy floors. The light from the torches and tapers showed curiously shaped wooden beams twice the size of full-grown oaks, with heavy metal hands helping to hold them up; there were many tank-as, and large exquisite golden statues of Buddha with golden butter-lamps protected by large, coarsely ringed metal curtains to keep off the light-fingered. Making no special ceremony of the fact that my wife was now about to be the first white woman admitted to the cathedral roof, the guides indicated the ladders, by which we mounted to a region of Chinese-like golden domes, marking the tombs of many holy men of Tibet's past. Here a magnificent view could be had of all Lhasa and the surrounding mountains. Not less interesting was the view in the courtyard below, where the well-dressed clerks of the cathedral were accepting large offerings of sacks of grain and goatskins of butter, trundled in on the backs of women. Hundreds of worshippers, equipped with leather pads on their hands, and narrow mattresses, rented for the occasion, were prostrating themselves on the stone pavement. Off at one side of the courtyard was a monster bronze tea cauldron said to hold twelve hundred gallons.

Before visiting Drepung, greatest monastery in the world, whose full complement of lamas is estimated at 7500, we had to provide ourselves with a gift of some 10,000 copper coins, worth about $95. When these had been wrapped in three leather bags, necessitating a special horse to carry them, seven of us, including our A. D. C., the mundle, a syce, Wangdi, and Nakkin, rode three miles into the country to where the lamasery's massive buildings, a veritable city, rise from the base of the hill. Sprawled out irregularly at different levels and heights, the white buildings live up to the Tibetan meaning of Drepung, "Heap of Poured Rice." Fanciful and picturesque designations for towns and lamaseries are an old Tibetan custom; we have such examples as Gobshi (Four Doors), Ralung (Country of the Goats), Nargatse Dzong (Fort on Point of Nose), Pedi (Fortified Happy Country), Kara La (Avalanche Pass), Chusul (Arroyo), and Nethang (Plain of Sacred Place).

We walked, or rather, breathlessly climbed up and down the narrow streets, visiting four different establishments, each headed by a different abbot, on our way gaining glimpses of huge barren refectories and community rooms of the lower lamas, containing low wooden benches and huge cauldrons for boiling water. Twenty minutes of this brought us to the quarters of the senior lama, where all the four superiors, flanked by their six-foot, shoulder-padded attendants, had assembled to exchange the silk scarves and receive our gifts. We were escorted to a balcony draped with multicolored silks and furnished with cushions, gaily painted tables, and chairs for us. While the lama clerks got busy counting the coins (there was no reticence about receiving gifts at Drepung) and the senior abbot beamed benevolently at us, blessed rice and sweetmeats were produced, to the joy of Nakkin and the other servants, who did them full justice.

The senior abbot was bedecked in splendid robes and from his belt hung a rosary of human bones. There were also cups wrought from human skulls on the tables before the shrines and idols.

More climbing over steps hewn from the hillsides, past chapels where lamas droned out their exercises, brought us to a gompa at the very top, an exquisite spot because of its lovely polychrome walls and wood carving in the seventeenth-century Chinese style. It had a multitude of sacred books, and the finest tank-as we were to see in Tibet.

Tibetan painting is decorative rather than representational, and the decorative subjects are actually a complicated liturgy of symbols and emblems illustrating deities and demons which in turn adumbrate some point of Buddhist theology. Every painting or tank-a has a wealth of meaning to the beholder. Even colors are formalized. White and yellow, for instance, typify the gods in their more benign moods; raging moods call for blues, reds, and blacks.

The painting is done on cotton or canvas, occasionally on silk, prepared with a surface coating of lime and flour to which is sometimes added a little glue. The basic lines of the drawing are made with Chinese ink, and then the colors, usually cheap, imported pigments mixed with thin glue, are added. When dry, the painting is encased in a brocaded mat consisting of three vari-colored strips beginning with red next to the picture, then yellow, and finally a wide frame of blue. At top and bottom there are rollers with iron or bronze ends, and a flimsy silk curtain usually covers the painting when it is not being displayed.

To admire a tank-a for its luminous coloring and design melting into the silk brocade may be a matter of minutes, but to understand the content might require hours.

Another form of Tibetan art was also visible in the gompa. Four disagreeable young lamas were on their knees creating a floor design of fine, colored tsamba by pinches of color applied dextrously from between their forefingers and thumbs in exactly the same technique as the American Navajo uses for his famous sand paintings.

From the topmost level we could see a party of laboring lamas down in the valley washing their clothes—a yearly affair—and drying them in the bright sunshine. We could also see and smell that phase of Tibetan life most difficult for the outsider to ignore. Violent lavatory smells penetrated everywhere, for the monks, like the laymen, believed that natural functions call for neither privacy nor sanitation. Their casual habits in any other climate would certainly have produced pestilence, but here the dryness of the air was their best ally.

Drepung, with its multitude of religious and secular activities, and its different hierarchies of lamas—many of them engaged in usury, managing the lamasery's lands, selling horoscopes and charms, and even begging—exemplifies the spirit of Lamaism. Temporal and religious power is wedded as it has been wedded in practically no other civilization, and if the lamas are the custodians of "divine truth" they are also the country's chief capitalists and traders.

Lamaism has not, of course, been without its internal conflicts, and the fact that the Dalai Lama had a formidable rival in the late Tashi Lama, the prelate of Shigatse, created an ambiguous situation that has not yet been cleared up.

Theoretically, the prelate of Shigatse held a superior position as far as religion was concerned. The Tashi Lama (Panchen Rimpochi) was considered the spiritual head of the Buddhist world. In only temporal affairs was the Dalai Lama the more important. Several years ago a clash had developed between the two prelates, the Dalai Lama charging that his brother of Shigatse was fomenting discord in the kingdom and shielding the pro-Chinese party.

The Tashi Lama, who was supposed to eschew all political activity, was told bluntly to get rid of the conspiring nobles. When he refused to admit the charges and to banish the suspected men, Lhasa issued an order for his banishment. When Vernay and I visited Shigatse in 1935, there were rumors of a reconciliation between the exiled Tashi Lama and the Kashag, but the former's death in China two years later ended the squabble, and the Shigatse as well as the Lhasa throne, became vacant.

The struggle between the prelates emphasized the changing trend of Tibetan foreign policy during the last thirty-five years. Before 1909, Chinese influence, fortified by racial, historical, and commercial ties, was in full swing to the detriment of British interests. Taking advantage of the situation, China sent an army into Tibet in 1909. Lhasa was taken in February, 1910, and considerable damage was inflicted. Art treasures disappeared, were loaded on caravans to find their way into the limbo of Chinese art dealers. Lamas mourned the loss of their splendid gold altar sets and jewelled temple decorations.

At the approach of the invading army, the late Dalai Lama, accompanied by Tsarong, then a shapé, fled southward toward India, pursued by the Chinese, and crossed the frontier just in the nick of time. The British installed the exiled ruler in a house in Darjeeling and treated him with the greatest courtesy. Sir Charles Bell, then political officer to Tibet, who, with Sir Frederick O'Conner, was once interpreter for Sir Francis Younghusband's expedition, was in constant attendance on the Dalai Lama, and out of the association grew a friendship.

For two years Lhasa remained under the foreign yoke, but the Chinese Revolution of 1911 gave the Tibetans a chance to recover their sovereignty. The invaders were evacuated to China through India, and the Dalai Lama came back in triumph.

Proceeding warily, never deviating from the policy of aloofness from foreign powers, the Lhasa government revealed now that its friendliest sentiment was reserved for the British Empire. Relations were helped along by the extreme tact of the British. Having received the Dalai Lama hospitably and inspired his gratitude, they proceeded to supply British service rifles and ammunition for the protection of the Tibetan eastern border. These were paid for in rupees acquired by Tibetan wool merchants who had sent their produce to India. At the same time the Indian-Tibetan frontier was rigidly closed against foreigners, thus preserving the Lhasa government from troubles that might have trickled in from the south. In the years that followed, the British were still limited to occasional missions to Lhasa, but nevertheless relations have steadily improved.

In the lane at Drepung one saw deformed, horrible faces, running eyes, pinched voices whining for alms, everywhere signs of disease,— one of the most revolting sights I have seen in Asia.

Beyond we saw the not unattractive houses of the rockybars, or disposers of the dead, made of horns of animals they had slaughtered. Some of the most wrinkled old crones imaginable were in evidence, but there were also fat, attractive babies. The whole region was planted, paradoxically enough, with masses of beautiful flowers, particularly cosmos eight and ten feet high. The splendid height and quality of these flowers, indigenous to Mexico, were due, we found, to the Chinese manner of fertilization.

The official visits now being over, we had time to arrange one of our most important tasks in Lhasa—the procuring of a collection of Tibetan clothes for the American Museum of Natural History. Ready-made things being unavailable in the bazaar, we bought quantities of Mongolian silk and Tibetan maroon wool, borrowed three resident tailors from one of the noble families, and installed them in our courtyard, where they worked for days producing the outfits worn by nobles, lamas, and peasants. Accessories and ornaments were picked up in the bazaar. The tailors, incidentally, brought their own servants to run errands and serve buttered tea.

Word of our activities had spread about the town, and all manner of goods were brought to our compound for sale. There were, for instance, a huge tent worth 500 rupees, a gold-brocaded coat, silver and brass outfits, and rare silk. Despite this, shopping in Lhasa was no easy game. My wife spent the leisure moments of a whole week running down an eyeshade, a pair of steel and silver samovars from Khăm, and, for the museum collection, two coats and a fine yellow-lacquered hat, which were eventually found, adding greatly to the collection's value.

The end of the lama holiday in Zara Linga was approaching. One morning we saw more and more tents going up, and our garden was a beehive of activity. The lamas were giving their annual party for the Kashag, or members of the government.

The arrival of the shapés wearing golden robes with large gold-lacquered hats, mounted on splendidly caparisoned horses, provided one of the best ceremonies we had ever seen. It was interesting to observe that in riding horses and not mules the dignitaries were faithful to the Buddhist precept: since the mule has no offspring, he is never ridden to a wedding or official event from which important results might issue.

After the shapés came governors and former members of the government, also in gold; six young men of good family and high rank, in darker yellow brocade, partly covered by magenta silk coats; and finally the servants, wearing shaggy red lamp-shade hats. There were about fifty guests, all in holiday regalia.

The lama hosts provided three huge meals, punctuated by a round of tea in different tents. Without any effort on our part to bring them there, the guests kept strolling right over to our door. The rulers and aristocrats of Lhasa made a beautiful picture in their best robes. Our little house was jammed, and most of the dignitaries, despite the three huge meals, managed tea and coffee, pancakes and maple syrup, sweets and cigarettes. Among the guests was my great good friend, Mr. Tsarong, an ex-shapé whom I had met in Lhasa during 1935. He invited us to a party he was giving in his house, the largest and finest in the city.

The shapés took their departure from the park at five-thirty, and the three hundred lama hosts left soon after. We shook hands with every one of them. They had been charming, interested neighbors, if a little prying. At my wife's request, they very kindly left their smallest and finest tent, pitched on the little island in the stream. She planned to use it for her children's party.

More visitors came during the succeeding days, now that we were free of official obligations. One of the most frequent callers was Rai Bahadur Norbu, chief of the British mission during Gould's absence. A Sikkimese Tibetan, Bahadur Norbu, had been in the India political service for years and was thoroughly informed on everything appertaining to politics and finance. He was an attractive and friendly personality, and we enjoyed many long talks, both interesting and informative.

Captain Doctor W. S. Morgan of the British Mission told us something of his medical work among the populace of Lhasa. The chief ailments he dealt with were syphilis, gonorrhea, and cataract. For the two venereal diseases, Doctor Morgan said, they had built up a fair immunity. Until recently the oracle or Tibetan medicine-man had balked his operations for cataract. Then, happily, the oracle reversed itself, and permitted the operations—but on one eye only! But oracle or no oracle, Doctor Morgan found that many of the men were returning on the sly for an illicit operation to cure the second eye. Wives, however, had to be content with one operation and hence one good eye.

The tall, distinguished former governor of Khampa Dzong turned up with his son one day, evoking fond memories of the visit I made to his city with Captain Head and Captain Cockburn in 1930, when Lhasa was but a dream for the future. The ex-governor wanted to be assured, and without exaggeration I was able to assure him, that no subsequent travels had erased the picture of Khampa Dzong's fortresses perched on a mountainside, with Everest and Kanchenjunga rising in the distance. For his part, the ex-governor had never forgotten the cuckoo clock I gave him, and as proof he now presented my wife with a pretty Tibetan apron.

Nothing was said, however, of an incident that had amused the governor on my second visit to Khampa Dzong. He had arrived at our quarters one day to find the place in utter confusion. Socks, underwear, and clothing of every description were strewn about the room for want of a closet. Turning to our ineffectual translator, Vernay said, "Say to His Excellency that we offer our apologies for receiving him with our room in this condition." The interpreter nodded and made a longish speech. Later, it developed, the governor had been told, "This room has been decorated in Your Excellency's honor."

We had seen representatives of Tibetan official and ecclesiastical circles, and now we were to get a glimpse of Lhasa's artistic life in the person of young Tsering, who left off his work in the Potala to pay us a call. Handsome and charming to begin with, the young man cut a dashing figure with his pale-green blouse, one sleeve of wine-red covering his arm, the other hanging down, an enormous jade ring on his left thumb, and a smaller mandarin jade on his right ring finger. Tsering asked to paint us with Nakkin and Wangdi. He had always wanted to paint from life, he explained, but up to now he had been occupied with divinities. To this my wife replied amiably that he might, if he wished, paint us as gods and goddesses. After a week's time the picture appeared, with cross eyes for me and two double chins for my wife. We had seen likenesses of ourselves before but never had we emerged so completely and perfectly figures of fun. The Occidental face and figure were not for this man who, year in, year out, turned out exquisite, magical divinities by the square yard.

My friend K. K. Mondo, ever courteous and helpful, one of Lhasa's choice spirits, returned at frequent intervals. Our debt to him was measureless, not only because his English cut through the tedium of translated conversations but because his knowledge of the country cleared up many an obscure point.

Among the absent on this trip, to my disappointment, were two Tibetans who classified as old friends. Jigmy Tering, son of one of Tibet's first families, a clever, vigorous and most important young man, and his wife, Mary, sister of Mrs. Tsarong, had enlivened the former visits by their friendly personalities. Both spoke fair English acquired in the schools of Darjeeling. They were in Darjeeling now on business, a most unusual jaunt for Tibetans.

We had time also for a few visits that were not on the original calendar. The abbot of a neighboring lamasery, for instance, invited us for tea one afternoon and permitted us to photograph his lamas, dressed in full costume, blowing their nine-foot bronze and silver horns, set up in elaborate bronze-gilt racks. It was a creditable performance.

And then Yutuk Depön, young general in the Tibetan army and a member of one of Lhasa's leading families, obligingly offered to stage a review of his troops for us. I was interested in Yutuk's military affairs because I had seen the Shigatse troops in an apathetic display, and wondered if the capital had produced anything better. The general wore a smart khaki uniform patterned after British models that went very oddly with his long silver earring and the pigtail wrapped around his head and secured by a mammoth turquoise-and-gold brooch. A thousand soldiers, wearing well-fitted uniforms brought from India and carrying modern service rifles, went through their drills exceedingly well. The Lhasa regiment manifestly drew a higher type of man than the one in Shigatse.

After the review, Yutuk took us into the barracks for a two-and-a-half-hour lunch, at which we were joined by his younger brother. He revealed that he was studying French and English out of two battered, old-fashioned language manuals. Amused, my wife asked how it was possible to study foreign languages without a Tibetan key. Yutuk acknowledged the point with a burst of laughter and changed the subject.

During all this time presents had been pouring in. They ranged all the way from baskets of cabbage and tiny green peaches, sent by the Kalön Lama, to china, rolls of the famous maroon wool, and

Tibetan carpets. Food had piled up faster than we could consume it, and a great deal had been handed over to the poor.

We had a little leisure now to pursue our plant-collecting and to explore the region about Lhasa. One of these jaunts led us on to a gruesome sight—rockybars breaking the bones and cutting the flesh off a dead lama, while vultures snatched the loose pieces. This is the usual means of disposing of Tibetan corpses; only the highest ecclesiastics are buried in tombs. In performing these chores, the rockybars are often assisted by beggars.

All our trips were accompanied by grave warnings from Wangdi that we must not remain out after dusk. Gossip had it that the lower lamas were not reconciled to the presence of aliens in Lhasa, and a few stones pitched over a hedge by "bad lamas" would not have been surprising. Wangdi's revelation about the attitude of the lower lamas, who realized quite shrewdly that continuous intercourse between Tibetans and foreigners spelled the end of their domination, was not hard to credit. Personal experience, however, brought us nothing but courtesy from all Tibetans, high and low alike.

The streets of the capital and particularly the bazaar were always full of interest, with caravans coming from far parts of the country with curious merchandise. Very often when riding in the center of the town we would hear a horn blowing in the distance, and the townspeople would cease whatever they were doing to gape down the road. They were usually rewarded with the sight of a high government official or a group of high lamas. Outriders would first clear the way, and then the dignitaries, wearing their elaborate ceremonial costumes, would sweep by in stately dignity. Members of the Kashag always appeared on the streets in imperial Chinese gold brocade.

The environs of Lhasa emphasized the fact that Tibetans are sharply divided into upper and lower classes, with no sign of the middle classes of post-feudal societies. The upper classes, as we have seen, consist of ecclesiastical and secular nobles, while the lower classes have their lamas, traders, farmers, and shepherds.

The nomadic shepherds, whose habitats were always recognizable from afar by their stout black yak-wool tents, usually supported by stones around the base, I had seen in greater numbers elsewhere, at elevations of fifteen to sixteen thousand feet. A few, however, were visible around the capital, herding their yaks, goats, and cattle on the steep hillsides.

But this land was predominantly agricultural, since wheat, barley, peas, and truck vegetables may be grown up to 14,000 feet when the growing season lasts at least four or five months without frost. There is no dearth of land, for Tibet, unlike the teeming country south of the Himalayas, is sparsely populated. But the rainfall, usually insufficient, is concentrated in the month of August, and the value of any land depends on the possibilities of irrigation from streams fed by melting snows from the uplands.

The peasant agriculturists do not live in tents like the nomads, but build themselves rude though substantial houses from laminated stone with waterproof walls, usually provided with one opening in addition to the door. The unglazed window is often closed against the rushing winds by stout wooden shutters. The houses inevitably face south, with a ground-floor court for the animals and the dungpile, while the living quarters are on the second story.

There are, of course, degrees of wealth and comfort in Tibet, and the large landowners, usually nobles, do well by themselves in building their houses. What a European or American would pronounce stark discomfort may be enviable luxury to a Tibetan, but in any case there is no argument about the architectural distinction of Tibetan buildings.

There is little manufacturing in Tibet. The country's "industrial system" consists of a few houses devoted to the production of carpets, paper, silverware, ornaments, jewelry, pottery, garments, household utensils, ceremonial objects, and paintings. A typical paper "factory" showed about a dozen men working on the outside, gathering wood that came from tall bushes growing in clumps or even in groves along the riverbank, pounding the bark and wood pulp in water, mixing the fibers, removing the doughy mass, and spreading it on a cotton cloth held taut on wooden frames. By dipping these frames in water, the mass was spread out evenly and the sun did the rest. The product was a soft, silky paper resembling hand-woven tweed.

A rug "factory," again typical of its kind, was housed in one large building, containing workshops and dormitories for some thirty workers. Although they toiled from dawn to dusk for bed and board plus a few coppers a day, they all seemed a contented and happy lot.

Commerce, exclusive of the wool trade, is such an unimportant part of Tibetan life that one never sees the crowded, merchandise-laden bazaars so common to India and China. Tibetan bazaars are usually lodged in movable structures, put up in the morning, removed in the afternoon. In the three largest cities, Lhasa, Shigatse, and Gyantse, the merchandise includes carpets, wooden bowls, brass (the finest of Chinese origin), hammers, nails, small ironmongery from India, clothing, hand-embroidered boots and garters, leather goods, saddles (the Mongolian type with short, high pommels and heavy cast-iron stirrups), grain, vegetables, butter, yak ropes, and of course the famous woollen, which receives its beautiful maroon tint from a special native herb growing on the sandy, alluvial slopes.

The wool, with a great sale all through Mongolia and even in Pekin and the marts of India, produces credit balances that permit wealthier Tibetans to buy clothes, jewelry, and household furnishings abroad.

The most important of the bazaars is Lhasa, for it is the natural terminus of the great yak and mule caravans coming from China. Journeys from Tatsienlu and Batang take, on the average, sixty to seventy days, while the time from Kokonor, the third great starting-point, lying farther to the northeast, is correspondingly longer. The caravans are usually large, composite affairs, for the more traders who can make the journey together, the greater the protection against bandits. They usually arrive in Lhasa during the autumn and winter months, and the bazaar becomes a scene of color and confusion as the fresh goods are unloaded and the genial, swashbuckling caravan men from Khăm, in eastern Tibet, stride along the booths with their peculiar, swinging gait and fill the air with their wild laughter. The men from Khăm are known for their height, physical prowess and high spirits. They must be a species of superman to accomplish these prodigious journeys with their vitality intact.

Before the outbreak of the present war in China, caravans were fewer in number than at the turn of the century, as merchants found it easier and safer to send their wares from China to Calcutta by ship and thence into Tibet. But now, with Japan controlling the Chinese coasts, the caravan method of transport is regaining its old favor.

The two finest houses in Lhasa, those belonging to Tsarong Shapé and to K. K. Mondo, were largely outfitted with imported furniture and accessories. K. K. Mondo's house had been under construction during my first visit to Lhasa, but now it was complete in every detail and an invitation had arrived for a luncheon party. I looked forward to seeing it, to discovering whether the owner, one of the few Tibetans who had ever been submitted to European influence, had produced something radical in design and appointments. But one glance showed that K. K. Mondo had been faithful to Tibetan tradition. The eight rooms, some beautifully panelled in wood, were all furnished with carved furniture, tank-as, silk hangings. All the windows were glassed and there was a staircase.

Elegant in a glorious coat of mustard-color uncut velvet, the host produced a delicious Tibetan meal that lasted two and a half hours. At the end of the meal, Rai Bahadur Norbu, following the old Tibetan custom, distributed largess to the servants, while the host and other guests looked on.

Now came the children's party my wife had first planned in Paris. The tent left by the lamas was all in readiness. The cakes were baked by my wife and Nakkin, most versatile of servants. It took a whole morning, and the output would have done credit to a good-sized bakery. The prevalent odor in the house was boiling chocolate—icing for the cakes.

Thirty little guests had been invited. Twenty accepted. Forty-two came. They were invited for three o'clock, but they arrived before two. There are few clocks in Lhasa and those that exist don't agree.

Very often a host will say, "Come at three—my time." He holds out his watch.

The forty-two miniatures of noble mothers and fathers were dressed in lovely shades of mauve, purple, cerise, and yellow-gold, with pale-green blouses and belts. The girls wore amulets of turquoise, diamonds, rubies, emeralds, and jade. Every child was accompanied by an ayah, who either carried the child on her back or lap, or walked beside its pony. The ponies were beautifully decorated.

The average age of the children was eight, but they behaved with solemn dignity. In their capacity for food they were thoroughly adult—in the Tibetan sense. Eight cakes, vast quantities of scones, gallons of tea disappeared in a few minutes. The big moment arrived for the guests when they received their toys—growling tigers, performing cats, spouting whales, swimming fish, all manner of mechanical animals.

Next came the Tsarong party. This affair, scheduled to last for five full days, was one of the high points of the Lhasa social season. Tsarong, Shapé, had risen from the ranks to become a close friend of the Dalai Lama. He married Miss Tsarong, one of the richest women in Tibet, whose name he adopted at the ruler's suggestion. With the death of the Dalai Lama, he ceased to be a member of the Kashag, but retained his title, according to Tibetan usage, and was still a power in the country.

The Tsarongs lived in a large, two-story house, exceptional in Tibet for its wide windows, all glazed and curtained with fine gauze in simple, three-color design. The trim cleanliness of the place was accentuated by finely embroidered gauze draped across the fretwork of a balcony giving on the inner court.

Indoors, red and yellow velvet and brocades hung from the pillars while around the living rooms ran low tables and cushions. Choice tank-as were suspended from small wooden rods fastened to the woodwork ceiling, and the floors were covered with beautiful carpets.

The house was so situated that its windows commanded views of the noble Lhasa landscape, green valleys nestling under the towering

Mrs. Cutting and two abbots drinking buttered tea in Drepung lamasery

The Dalai Lama's stables in Norbu Linga, with stalls carved and beautifully lacquered

The largest of the Dalai Lama's three summer palaces in Norbu Linga

Section of the bazaar in Lhasa. Windows are protected by wooden shutters
and gauze curtains

A summer-house in Norbu Linga where the thirteenth Dalai Lama used to sit on fine summer days

Lunch party in Lhasa. Left to right: a friend of Mrs. Tsarong, Mrs. Tsarong, Mrs. Cutting, and our host, Tsarong Shapé

In our garden "Zara Linga" in Lhasa. Standing behind us, left to right, are Nakkin, our A.D.C., and Wangdi

mountains. All the rooms were filled with bright flowers from the gardens that were Mrs. Tsarong's special pride and joy. An air of taste and leisure prevailed.

The Tsarongs, perfect hosts despite the barrier of language, took us all through the house, pointing out the newly installed electric lights that were connected with the Norbu Linga dynamo, the chapel, astonishing for its books wrapped in gold and silver and sealed with gold and silver brocades, its tank-as, its gold and jade statues, and tables furnished with freshly cooked rice, fruits, butter, clear water and other offerings to the Gods. Beyond the gardens, a number of beautiful fair-weather tents had been set up for servants of guests.

Indoors, four rooms had been given over to upper-class guests, carefully graded according to hierarchy. Thirty men, wearing their finest silks of gold, yellow, mustard, and purple, with pigtails wound around their heads and smartly held in place above the forehead with gold-and-turquoise brooches, were installed in the main salon. Large napkins of heavy cream-colored Chinese silk and chopsticks were placed before each guest. Then came the trays fitting over the mahjong tables. Eighteen small silver dishes held condiments and other delights. Then began the main meal, with shark's fins, shoots of young bamboo, bêche-de-mer, Chinese beans, spiced mutton balls, pork, chicken, heaps of rice, and bowls of savory sauces. There was an excellent chung to drink, and it was a welcome addition, since most of the food was highly seasoned.

All the guests ate with chopsticks. In China this would deserve no special comment, as they are used by every one from the wealthy down to the poorest peasant, but in Tibet they are one of the marks of the upper classes.

For myself, I prefer chopsticks to knife and fork. I had got used to them years ago in China, and it seems to me that they are not only more agreeable, but an aid to digestion. It takes longer to eat with chopsticks, and the eater is obliged to put less in his mouth at a time.

I found myself next to Ringan, secretary to the late Dalai Lama, who had translated all the letters I received from the ruler. His presence was a boon, as his running commentary in English enabled me to follow the conversation.

Dinner over and the trays removed, the guests showed no inclination to move, but simply sat where they were, lolling on the brocade cushions and carrying on a desultory conversation. Then mahjong was proposed, and presently the room was filled with the clink-clink of the ivory pieces, while earnest, intense expressions were written on the faces of all the players. The bright robes and the hands moving the ivories with dazzling rapidity made a beautiful picture that nothing could have duplicated except a Chinese mandarin house of other days. Servants still flitted about serving English sweetmeats and buttered tea in beautiful jade and porcelain cups. The players sipped and nibbled interminably.

The garden now attracted the women and those men who had not succumbed to mahjong. My wife had lunched with a group of Mrs. Tsarong's friends, with Nakkin squatting on the floor by her side, explaining in English that she had declined a cushion because it was not good form to sit in the presence of "such great people." It was a great day for Nakkin to be meeting the fabulous nobles of Holy Lhasa whom she had heard described as a child, and her day reached a climax when she was photographed with a niece and younger sister of the hostess.

The women, with fair skins, had almost the complexions of whites, and were as spectacularly dressed as the men, with their silken robes, their head-dress clustered with coral and turquoise or in most cases with thousands of red pearls, and their jewelled ribbons running from shoulder to girdle.

These wives of Tibetan nobles possessed a quality extraordinarily rare in women of the Orient. Freedom was part of their tradition, for their country had never known the Indian system of purdah or the Chinese custom of infanticide, little girls in Tibet being as welcome as boys. Every Tibetan woman has the right to select her own husband, to run her own household, and to own property. In the old days when the country was divided up into a number of small principalities, some districts were ruled by women. Thus the Tsarongs' women guests, inheriting a feeling of independence, had married as adults of perhaps twenty or twenty-one, and were used to being treated with respect. While none was as rich as Mrs. Tsarong, who owned, in her own right, four great estates in different parts of the country, they had all known the good things of the world.

Their horizon was, of course, limited because few had ever travelled except for rare trips to Darjeeling, Kalimpong, or Gangtok. Only the very privileged had ever got as far as Bombay or Calcutta. Their social activities were narrow, perhaps, but they were free to come and go as they chose, the upper-class women invariably riding on horses accompanied by a servant. Without exception, they seemed to find a great deal of joy in life.

In summer their great social specialty was the picnic, which they had raised to the status of a fine art. A day's jaunt into the open sometimes required ten or twenty servants to carry the food and games and to transport and erect the beautiful, embroidered fair-weather tents. Between elaborate meals, the picnickers played mahjong, or told stories and walked under the trees.

Another fairly common form of recreation was the theatrical performance, usually given in the open air to celebrate a fête day, the public being admitted free at the expense of some wealthy man. Although the plays usually had a sacred subject—a legend of Buddha, perhaps—no lamas took part. There was invariably a burlesque note to the proceedings, with a great deal of buffoonery, horse-play and clumsy antics, many of the actors wearing masks to represent infidels and fantastic demons. Women usually enacted female roles, and all the performers with lines to speak were free to read them from a book instead of committing them to memory.

While we walked in the Tsarong garden, we were constantly importuned to drink by the famous "chung girls" of Lhasa, who strutted around heavily laden with jewels and finery provided by the hostess. The superlatively elegant clothes the hostess could not be bothered with were worn by the chung girls, constituting a sort of formal parade of the house's riches, displayed as Western houses display their paintings and tapestries. My wife, initiated by this time into the intricacies of ladies' dresses and jewelry, most expensive to buy, pointed out that fashions in Lhasa were by no means static. Modes changed from year to year in small but important items, so that one could distinguish last year's model as easily in Lhasa as in New York.

The chung girls smiled coquettishly at the men, administering pricks with a bodkin to those who seemed to be dallying too long with their beverage. The girls were on a plane somewhat higher than a geisha girl's, and were hired by the great houses for gala occasions. Ordinarily, it appeared, they were occupied with more prosaic professional duties.

Both host and hostess had plenty of time to walk and talk with their guests, for their responsibilities had been deputed to a nephew, the twenty-five or thirty-year-old Bhön-Dong, son of the Shapé. Dressed in a lemon yellow robe, the young man flitted from room to room, making a streak of light as he proceeded from guest to guest with his agreeable, exquisite manners, seeing that all were provided for. Endowed with exceptional charm, he was making a superb job of it.

Around half-past-four we were served Chinese tea with English scones, raisin cake, and big sugar buns (the head cook had been specially trained at Firpo's Restaurant in Calcutta), and an hour later, when we were groaning over this, the real meal of the day began. Once more the trays were placed on the mahjong tables. Supper began with onions treated with herbs and curious vinaigre spices, followed by no less than fifteen courses and ending with four puddings. The drinks were chung, green mint, and whisky. Thus ended the greatest day of feasting we had ever known. Nine cooks aided by sixty other servants had been busy from dawn till nightfall. Outside the grounds, tents had been provided for guests' servants, where they spent their time feasting and gambling.

Around nine we wended our way home and were grateful to have a view of the Potala bathed in gray-silver mist.

That night, while my wife happened to be in the house alone, the masalchi, our assistant cook, now cured of his skin disease, returned to the kitchen, and, in a burst of insanity, snatched up a butcher knife and ran screaming into my wife's bedroom. By repressing her fear and roaring back at him, she kept him under control till the arrival of Wangdi.

The gentle, charming Rai Bahadur Norbu interested himself in the case and found that ten years before the man had been chained up in jail for insanity—obviously a recurring case. Norbu asked if we wanted him jailed or sent back to his home in Gyantse roped to other servants. We decided on the latter. Twice within the next few days he broke away from his guards, the first time stripping off his clothes and rushing about the garden, the second time crawling into the house and cowering in a corner. Henceforth he was kept securely bound with ropes.

The Lepcha cook was another liability for the return trip. His alcoholism became more pronounced, and he was no longer permitted in the kitchen, now excellently managed by Nakkin with the assistance of the number-two syce. The other syces were instructed to keep the Lepcha away from the chung.

Almost three weeks had passed since our arrival, and it was time to get our letters and documents signed for the return and to assemble a caravan. The servants were bristling with activity; Nakkin with an attendant servant beside her riding back and forth to the bazaar, collecting last-minute oddments; the tailors sewing furiously on the Tibetan clothes; syces packing our belongings; the A.D.C. and his son watching the proceedings, their tongues thrust out to incredible lengths of interest and reverence. Messengers arrived every few minutes, and farewell gifts rose to a formidable pile—more rugs, Tibetan wool, cloisonné vases. From Tsarong Shapé came a friendly note, an exquisite rug, and a box of the delicacies we had admired in his house. The Regent kept his promise, and the last day we received two golden Apsos, the dogs so much admired by the Tibetans. In the midst of the confusion of translated conversations and relayed orders, there was a stream of visitors. The tea cups were never idle.

We got under way. A very easy thirty miles were covered, now that the river had subsided. The good horses cantered and trotted along nicely, arriving at Jangmed in seven hours. But the evening brought its full measure of excitement.

The caravan arrived three hours late. Wangdi lost his temper and struck one of the village men because of laxity regarding transport for the morrow. The mad masalchi, let loose on arrival by the two coolies to whom he had been roped, went straight to my wife, offering to arrange the room. When repulsed, he insisted on sitting outside her door. He was gently but firmly disposed of below. The new masalchi appeared, very drunk, and the discharged cook, clinging to the outfit, collapsed in a stupor on our good lamp.

There was no dinner; we ate crumbs and bits of dried things left over from lunch. My wife's bedding was torn, and Nakkin's, as usual, had suffered the most; many of her belongings had been lost. A high old time must have been had on the road behind us. Chung seemed mild, but it certainly had made fearful inroads.

We passed many caravans now. It was good going in good weather, but very difficult to get a quota of horses. The magic red-arrow letter, preceding us by two days, was not too effective. Presents of eggs, meat, and peaches continued, and there was a great deal of milk for the male and female Apso. Lobsang Norbla again welcomed us back to his charming, prosperous, well-kept farmhouse. He could not have been more hospitable, and seemed delighted to see us again.

The next day we had all the stones we wanted. They started at the Brahmaputra landing and never ceased till we climbed the 16,200-foot Nyapso La, which we surmounted in rain, hail, and some snow. We admired the alpine flora, cushioned and matted for miles. Twenty different plants were added to the collection. There were miles of low blue gentian, cascades of saxifrage, and a thrilling clematis.

At Pede Dzong we had a different house, this one being smaller and really clean. There was not a sign of dung in the court and the owners were good-looking, washed, combed, and well dressed.

One more cold night at bleak Nargatse Dzong, and then we started for Ralung on a glorious, cloudless day, which didn't last long. There was new snow only a stone's throw from the trail, and with all the unnamed peaks mantled in dead white, we continued on to Ralung in a heavy hailstorm. The dogs rode well, especially Tsing Tu, the female, who bounced miraculously on my wife's saddle mile after mile. A mile and a half from every stop they would race ahead chasing marmots, which would squeal at the edge of their holes, waiting till the dogs were on them before ducking in. The caravan was over eleven hours en route, raw and cold hours with rain and wind in our faces.

All through Tibet we had heard people calling from mountainside to mountainside. This night a boy was calling, and responses came from far away. It was a Tibetan yodel, charming to hear.

A long hurried pull to Gyantse in eight hours, going as hard and fast as the mountain country would permit, took us through a rain and hail storm. The luxury of a bath and fire in the British bungalow seemed the most blissful thing we had ever known. After ten hours of sleep, a thrilling, warm, sunny day greeted us. Here, some last-minute purchases for the museum, checking stores, freeing ourselves from the filthy cook and from the mad masalchi, turned over to his unfortunate wife, occupied most of the day.

The first night in Gyantse, we dined with Mr. Richardson at the mess, and there were Captain Batty, Captain Morgan (who had preceded us from Lhasa), Major Cockburn, and Captain Milne. Mr. Richardson produced a white cloth, napkins, flowers, red candles, four good courses, and we made merry with some precious 1921 Burgundy left over from the British mission of the year before.

Leaving early in the morning in a blaze of sunshine and beautiful clouds, all day we passed through scenes of harvesting and gleaning, done by hand. The men and women were singing harvesting songs, the women wearing garlands of yellow clematis. The sweet smell of herbs cut with the new hay was delicious in the strong, thin air. The hay was loaded and well stacked on the donkeys' backs. The entire landscape was one beautiful pattern of harvest. We collected a few seeds and felt well content, for collecting is not easy for beginners.

One of the crops being gathered in this region was the potato. In sending the Bogel mission to Shigatse in 1774, Warren Hastings ordered the men to put out a few plants wherever they halted to make camp.

Our next day was a good and swift passage of two stages on splendid ponies. It was a luxury not to have to push and prod the beasts at every second. The weather was clear but the coolest yet, with a very dusty wind over the borax plain all afternoon. From there we came into what seemed the last of good grazing on this plain. There were hundreds of dry arroyos.

The caravan came in on time, with no bad stories of runaway horses. All the bags and kits were intact; nothing had fallen into the water. It was the first day with such a good record since our start. We dined off a delicious saddle of mutton, Tibetan mutton in our opinion being the best that can be found anywhere. This was admitted even by the disgruntled Thomas Manning, Tibetan traveller of 1811, in his classic verdict on Phari: "Dirt, dirt, grease, smoke. Misery but good mutton."

We did the twenty-two miles from Tuna to Phari in four and a half hours with a howling wind and hail storm in our teeth.

When we woke up the next morning it was snowing hard, and the plain was already covered. We pushed on over to Gautsa through the slush. The herds of huge yak grazing in the snow were magnificent to behold, but the herdsmen and their black tents were dreary-looking spectacles. We struggled through snow, rain, and frightful boulders for almost ten hours, making Yatung after dark—exhausted, wet through, shaking with fatigue, to be greeted by a cold, dark bungalow. Nakkin, however, soon roused the chawkidar and got things to rights. We used four mounds of wood (a mound is eighty pounds) drying ourselves, and were shocked at the horrible stench of yak and sheep that our trail clothes gave off as they dried.

The next day brought the same steady downpour, and after buying a few curios we started off through Troupatang, two thousand feet up. Lamas in a lamasery half-way up were playing their flutes. At

His Excellency, Re-ting Pö gya tsap Rimpochi, Regent of Tibet,
amid the cosmos in his garden

His Excellency Si-lön Yab-shi Lang-Dün, Prime Minister of Tibet,
on the porch of his house

Nearing home: Mrs. Cutting and Nakkin. The autumn snows have come

Apso (Lhasa Terrier). One of those presented to the author
by the late Dalai Lama

various points in the steep pass we stopped to listen to the lovely music and to collect a small, beautiful, salmon-colored rhododendron, one of Tibet's hundred varieties, surrounded by a solid mass of mountain ash, resplendent with huge clusters of pink or white berries. Further on there was a tall, blue garlic blossom, blooming in over a foot of snow. Most of the time we walked. It was bad going, as stream crossings were broken and dangerous for animals; the boards had slipped apart and were deep in snow. The houses in this forest were different from any other kind of Tibetan architecture. They were more or less Swiss chalets with slanting walls.

From Gautsa onward we had been fascinated every inch of the way by the flora, despite the heavy rain and snow. The fruit of the alpine rose was glorious in its abundance and variety, while rhododendrons and azaleas were massed heavily under groves of seventy-foot pines covered with three-inch electric blue cones which created a sort of Christmas-decoration effect. There were many species of barberry, glorious, tall bushes with pink, dark blue, and red autumn berries, while the blue gentian seemed more lovely in color than ever.

For dinner we had yak filet. Nakkin was responsible for this rare dish, and it was very good indeed.

We were horrified by the turn of the weather. This most unexpected snowstorm for this time of year robbed us of an opportunity we had looked forward to—collecting seeds in glorious October sunshine. Having come through here from Gangtok in torrents, we thought we had a right to expect good weather on the return. Snow, waist-high in the Natu La, would detain us, thought the chawkidar.

But the next day four coolies left before daybreak, and meeting us at the foot of the pass, proceeded up the Natu La by cutting the way through waist-deep snow. The sun suddenly came out, transforming the country into great beauty. But soon rain came again, never to leave us on this trip. Gangtok, where we dined with the Maharajah of Sikkim, was drenched, and all about us roads had collapsed because of the monsoon, which had lasted five months.

After dinner we divided our camp equipment between the efficient

Nakkin and Wangdi, excellent servants who had been responsible for so much of the comfort and generally cheerful atmosphere that surrounded our caravan.

And so on to Darjeeling and the amenities of civilization provided by a luxury hotel.

The Andaman Islands

~~~~~~

THE Andaman Islands, far off the tourist track, ignored even by seasoned and curious travellers, possess two genuine curiosities: a primitive race of tiny black men that draws a living from land and sea with very little labor, and a unique penal colony that is praised enthusiastically by inmates and alumni alike.

But for all their tropical beauty and interesting inhabitants, it is unlikely the islands will ever be a tourist land: the beauty is no compensation for the malaria and insect pests that come with every rainy season.

Part of the British Empire, the Andamans are situated out in the Bay of Bengal between the tenth and fourteenth parallels, about 700 miles west of Madras. They were first put to use in 1789 when the British founded a penal settlement for Bengal. Malaria ended the experiment in 1796, and for the next fifty-six years the islands were more or less ignored. Then, during the Second Burmese war in 1852, the British navy proposed to make a base on the islands, but the malaria proved a discouraging factor. After the war the plan was abandoned.

In 1858 the British resolved to conquer the malaria problem once and for all. They founded a settlement at Port Blair and there set up the famous penal colony for murderers and political offenders convicted in Burma and British India. After much labor, Port Blair was turned into a place white men could endure.

As the British did no administrative work outside Port Blair, the native Andamanese were left undisturbed. Untouched by the great age of colonial expansion, the pygmy islanders lived and still live in a universe of their own. They have maintained their primitive folkways secure from outside interference.

The word "Andaman" is of doubtful origin. It may come from the Malay "Handuman" meaning "monkey." The tiny Andamanese, it seems, looked like "monkey people" to early explorers from India. So few are the early records of these islands that we can only suppose that the archipelago was rarely visited by seamen. For centuries, since prehistoric times in fact, these islands have remained out of contact with the march of southeastern Asiatic civilization. The Andamanese have always resented the intrusion of foreigners. Today they are utterly primitive.

There is evidence to show that boats from the mainland stopped at one of the islands from time to time searching for water. Fascinated by the pygmies, seized with an ambition to take them home as curiosities, the visitors seem to have effected several successful kidnapings, and the Andamanese became increasingly hostile to all visitors.

Racially the Andamanese belong to the negroid race and may be classed as true pygmies. Anthropologists once believed that all negroid races originally migrated from Africa. Today, although the theory is not entirely disproved, it is believed that there definitely existed indigenous negroid peoples in southeastern Asia.

To this race, now nearly extinct, the Andamanese must have belonged. Probably they inhabited the southern part of the great Indian peninsula in a pre-Dravidian period. With the coming of the Dravidians, they may have been largely exterminated, and the survivors may have found their way south by sea to their present isolated abode.

Th Andamanese may be compared with the pygmies living in a few isolated pockets of the Malay peninsula, in the Kalahari desert, and in the Belgian Congo. Since the characteristics of all races are indubitably due to their environment, one could reasonably ascribe the height of the Andamanese to their climate, which, in turn, accounts for their food supply. Most of the men do not exceed four feet, eight inches in height. The women rarely grow higher than four feet, seven inches. They are sturdy, well developed, gifted in the ways of survival.

The Andamanese are still living in a pre-agricultural, pre-metal age. It is true they now possess a few metals, but these have filtered in to them from Port Blair. The metals are certainly not an integral part of their scheme of life. They derive their food, implements and weapons from materials easily accessible to them, and they thrive exceedingly well.

There are twelve distinct tribes of islanders. Most numerous are the Ongés, who inhabit the southern islands of the archipelago. The second largest group are the fierce Jarawas, who dwell in the interiors of the northern islands. The Jarawas were formerly addicted to making raids on the white settlement and not infrequently white settlers were killed. Today such raids are few, due to efficient reprisals by government punitive expeditions. The tribes living along the coastal lands take on markedly amphibian characteristics.

I had heard vague stories about the pygmies of the Andaman Islands years ago on my first trip to the Orient. A few pictures showing their tribal gatherings and their dwellings whetted my curiosity. When I discovered that little was known about the islands save by relatively few men in the government service, I decided to visit the Andamans.

While I was in the Naga country with Doctor J. H. Hutton, he mentioned the Andamans in a more concrete way, suggesting that I visit the islands to study the people, make a photographic record for the census of India, and gather material for the Pitt River Museum of Oxford. He put me into communication with Max Bonington, then in charge of aborigines for the Burmese government. Although Bonington promptly sent me a warm invitation to visit the islands, promising every facility for studying the people, there were delays of one sort or another. It was not until February 1932, six months later, that I took a boat from Calcutta to Rangoon with the intention of continuing on to Port Blair by the regular monthly service that carried prisoners and supplies.

By a fortunate chance Bonington was in Rangoon when I arrived, having engaged the little steamer that we would use for the coastwise trip. It was about 100 feet long, and burned wood, a great convenience, since it could load up fuel from any jungle, and had a crew, all native, numbering thirty. Government regulations forbade the little boat to travel between Rangoon and Port Blair unescorted; so when the regular steamer was ready, our little wood-burner followed with prodigious puffs of smoke snorting out of her tiny funnel. Our party consisted of Bonington, Mrs. Bonington, their son Charles, twenty years old or so, Mr. Glasson—the forest officer for the Andamans who was returning from his leave in England—, and myself.

We remained one week in Port Blair, in many ways a typical colonial port. There was a government house, a few hundred odd frame dwellings, and vast sheds for storing copra, lumber, and tortoise shells. Government servants, merchants, and convicts constituted the bulk of the population. Never have I seen a cleaner city. Regulations were strict. Only a municipality of this kind could have imposed fines with such severity and impartiality for such offenses as leaving dirt about. If a house needed repairs, the tenant was ordered to make them immediately. And when a house got beyond repair, orders were given to have it replaced by a new one. The housing plan provided for the best sanitation. Dirt, flies, smells had been banished.

The white colony, officers and men of the battalion, government officials including the governor, resided on a small island opposite Port Blair, connected by a ferry. Here many royal palms had been planted, and the landscape had been so improved as to give it the aspect of a great garden.

Among the advantages of the little island were a good water supply, a club, and grass tennis courts. Tennis was played during the dry season and golf during the wet. The nine-hole course situated on the mainland was unusable during the dry season because the ground was baked too hard.

I was eager to visit the penal colony.

"If you're going to study the convicts," said Mrs. Bonington, the first night at dinner, "you might glance at Ali." She explained that Ali was the butler, a Mohammedan Punjabi who had murdered his wife.

As she spoke he appeared in the door carrying a steaming tray of curry. He wore a long white coat, white baggy trousers, a light blue silk pugri, and a broad band of red silk around his waist. There were no marks of Cain about him, and at the same time he wasn't precisely devoid of animation. When he withdrew Mrs. Bonington told the rest of his story, or rather the little she knew. She had refrained from prying into his past or ever referring to it in his presence. But in a casual way she had learned that:

Ali returned from work one night and found his wife in the arms of a lover. A violent quarrel broke out, and Ali, snatching up a knife, killed both wife and interloper. The court found him guilty with extenuating circumstances. Plain murder would have meant hanging. Extenuating circumstances meant a life-term on the Andaman Islands. Quietly, stoically, Ali accepted his fate. He never discussed himself or his affairs. Still, there were signs that he enjoyed his new life and his new profession. He had responsibilities in the house and he exercised them with tact and discretion. "An excellent servant," said Mrs. Bonington.

As soon as they landed on the island, convicts were lodged in cells in a huge, gray stone prison. Though they were not ill-treated, their liberties were so curtailed that they could hardly escape the idea that they were atoning for crimes.

With good conduct they were released from prison after a few months. Then began a new life. They were assigned to pleasant wooden bungalows, each with two rooms and a veranda. These, as I have said, were kept up—*had* to be kept up—in perfect style. A certain allowance was made to each prisoner and for the rest of his needs he had to work. In nearly every instance he found himself with a better habitation, better food, and better clothes than he had ever known before. Medical treatment was provided free.

Most of the convicts occupied themselves in the paddy fields, in land reclamation projects, in forestry, and in collecting tortoise shells. The last two were important industries. The jungles provided rich stores of hardwoods and other woods useful for making matches. The Swedish match industry was a big customer for Andamanese woods. Much of the hardwood was sent to adjacent sawmills, erected by the government, and was refined there before being exported.

Malaria in the immediate vicinity had been eliminated by clearing large areas of mangrove swamp and reclaiming the land. This was done by blocking the sea inlets to these swamps at high tide. Thus the land was kept flooded and the trees were drowned. Eventually the water was released at low tide and the inlets were permanently blocked. In a year or two the salt disappeared from the soil, the area was suitable for paddy, and by this time the malarial mosquito was gone.

It will be seen that there were plenty of lucrative occupations for convicts. The thriftier ones did well by themselves.

The convicts wore no uniforms. No restrictions were placed on their time or activities; they behaved just about as they wished. A casual observer might have easily concluded that the workers had come to the islands of their own free will. It was many years since a crime had been committed on the islands.

The governor, nevertheless, was always accompanied by a guard. The reason for this dated back to February 8, 1872, when the Viceroy of India, the Earl of Mayo, was killed on the Andaman Islands, while making a tour of inspection—set upon by a crazed Mohammedan with an imaginary grievance. As a result no viceroy has ever again visited the Andaman group, and the rule about the governor's guard has become a tradition.

Malefactors convicted of serious crimes are usually sent to Port Blair because of extenuating circumstances. They all realize completely that to repeat their crime would mean the gallows. There are no more repeat murders on the islands. Flourishing knives in brawls or adopting a threatening attitude is punishable by flogging and a term back in the stone jail, but infractions of rules are infrequent.

A group of Andamanese from Greater Andaman Island standing in the center of their village by the seashore

Andamanese women on the sand before their houses. The clearly defined parts in their hair have been cut with sharpened bamboo

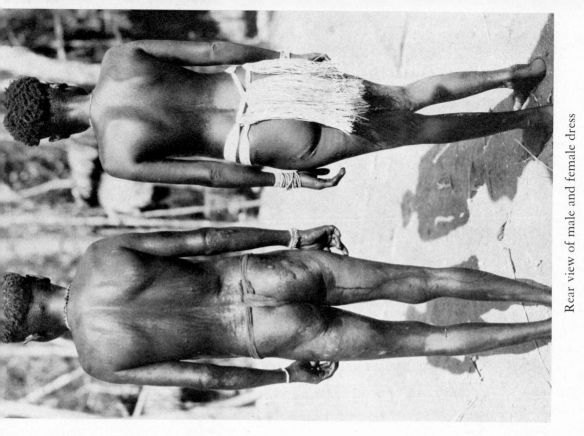

Rear view of male and female dress

The author, 5 feet 8 inches tall, between a married couple.
They are about thirty years old

Basket-making

Making rope from bamboo

The convicts of Port Blair are free to marry, or, if they are already married, they may send for their wives and children. Many have done so. The government grants an extra allowance for children born in the colony.

The average man would feel a certain hesitation before walking among hundreds of convicts let loose. But it was easy to shake off such misgivings in Port Blair. One saw happy, contented faces. The convicts did not resent the presence of free men; as a matter of fact, they ignored them. Life was full enough for them without occupying themselves with outsiders.

The records showed hundreds of cases in which the convicts, having finished their terms, refused to leave. Since there was no law to compel them to go, many stayed on. To return to their old homes in northern India or Burma would in most cases have brought shattering disillusionment; their old friends and neighbors would have shied away from them. But here they were free men, bearing no stigma. They were with their own kind, associating with new-found friends. Some had married and had started new lives. The physical conditions of life were, for most of them, infinitely superior to what they had known before.

This was the rule. But there were a few convicts who constantly simmered in hate and rebellion. Some, in a milder way, chattered constantly of "going home." And some thought so much of going home that they plotted their escape. There were instances of men putting out to sea in the silence of the night in small, unseaworthy boats. Most of these were lost, but a few actually reached Burma.

It was now time to start the expedition, and to see not the transplanted, but the aboriginal life of the islands. This was an exploring trip de luxe. The little boat, with the same passengers as before (excepting Mrs. Bonington) and a crew of thirty, steamed out of the harbor and turned northwards. A calm, glassy sea lay around us. The boat was heated by the grim persistence of a tropical sun. There were no clouds, only an occasional illusion of clouds formed by plaques of gray smoke dispersed by the funnel.

The days were drowsy; there was nothing to do during the bright, windless hours but lie on deck-chairs under an awning, reading and chatting. Even at night the cabins were so stuffy that we had our beds brought up on deck. This was to be our home for many days. All our shore excursions were to end at nightfall, so that we could sleep on board the boat.

We saw no signs of life on the shore. The coast, always in view, was a green, inhospitable wall of jungle running down to the water-line. Here and there were attractive sandy beaches, and we could see low mountain ranges in the interior.

After four days we dropped anchor opposite a place Bonington remembered as a popular camp-site. Looking out carefully, we saw a group of black pygmies who had evidently been watching the boat for some time from behind their forest curtain. Bonington examined them with his binoculars. He was known to them as a friend, and he expected to be received hospitably. Nevertheless his eyes were open for signs of weapons. There seemed to be none; so the sailors let down the little motor launch.

More pygmies appeared from behind the trees. Soon a whole village, perhaps forty or fifty—men, women and children—seemed to have congregated on the beach. From afar they looked like dolls attired in tiny breechclouts. It was only when we drew near that we could see their sturdy adult bodies.

Without moving, without speaking, the villagers stared at us, their ugly little faces devoid of expression. When Bonington passed out sacks of gifts, shirts, red cloth, clay pipes, and tobacco, their lips formed words of gratitude, but there was no light in their eyes. It was only when I observed the Andamanese at length that I discovered that their hands rather than their faces are the instruments of their emotional expression.

Each crinkly black head bore a shaved part, about a quarter of an inch wide, down the center.

Like the Hottentots, the Andamanese run to steatopygy—enlarged buttocks. Steatopygy among primitive tribes is not a disease, but a natural protection against days of famine. As the camel stores fat in his hump, the fat-tailed sheep of Asia stores it in his tail; as the bear puts on a general pad to serve him through the days of hibernation, so do such tribes as the Andamanese provide against the caprices of nature. The Andamanese women are much more conspicuous for enlarged buttocks than the men.

Distended stomachs are common among the children. This condition is also common throughout Asia, and is due to malnutrition. In the case of the Andamanese, it is not a quantitive lack of food, but an ill-balanced diet. The adult pygmies, however, seemed to have accommodated themselves to nature's niggardly distribution of vitamins.

The chief of the village was absent. Presiding head of the community was his wife, a fat, squat little woman with a deep, harsh voice; it was apparent that exercising authority was one of her natural gifts.

Slightly back from the shore, sheltered from the sun by the dense thicket, was the village—a dozen or so small lean-tos built in a semicircle. I remarked to Bonington that the village looked new, as if it had been constructed the day before.

"More than likely it *is* new," he replied. "They're always moving around."

Since sanitation is not one of the achievements of the Andamanese, their villages become filthy after a few weeks. When the stench, largely from decayed sea-food, assaults even their insensitive nostrils, they pick up and move on to another site, for the islands are not overcrowded, and there is an unlimited choice of locations.

For food the pygmies have fish, roots, and the fruit of the screw palm. They also eat dogs and wild pig which they hunt in the bush. Neither of these animals is indigenous, having been left on the islands by ships. There are plentiful supplies of roots and fruit. Both are usually boiled. The fish is caught under exciting circumstances that resemble a sport. Thus living conditions in normal years are not difficult for the islanders. Nor is their garment industry a big problem. Their standard equipment consists of a breechclout, fashioned from fibers easily obtainable in the jungle.

Few domestic implements were visible in the village. There were some wooden receptacles carved from hardwood trees, a species of primitive basketwork, and a wide selection of knives made from fine hardwood. The knives were used for preparing food, shaving heads, and hacking dugouts from trees. Probably the fashioning of dugouts requires more labor than any other activity of the islanders. Bonington told the chief's wife that we were interested in seeing one of these dugouts in the process of construction. We also wanted to see a fish hunt. Both were arranged on the spot.

Before we could discuss it further, a runner appeared in the village and communicated something to the chief's wife in a whisper. She clapped her hands and spoke in a strident voice; obviously she was perturbed.

Half a mile out in the water we saw a Japanese pearling-boat rounding a little promontory. A rowboat was let down, and two men seized oars and made for the shore. A cry went up from the villagers. Above the chorus sounded the voice of the chief's wife, presumably cursing the invaders.

The Japs soon landed near us and explained in sign language that they had run out of water and were cruising among the islands looking for a supply. Bonington, in pantomime, told them they had selected the wrong place, and that but for our presence they would have been ambushed and killed. They must push off directly and we would supply them with water from our boat.

The fat little chief's wife, shaking with rage, ordered the Japs to be gone immediately. They looked at her, their faces twisted in a nervous smile, and went back to their boat.

When we returned to the village the next day the villagers were planning a dugong hunt for the evening. For them this meant an orgy of food, since one catch feeds an entire village, while for me it meant a chance to capture one of the most interesting marine mammals in existence.

The dugong belongs to the order of Sirenians or sea-cows. He lives in salt water, and his fresh water cousin is the manatee. Sirenians, like

Cetaceans (whales, etc.), have but one pair of limbs, developed as paddles. But this was not always true of the Sirenians. Science has discovered in Egypt the remains of a Sirenian from the Eocene which shows four limbs instead of two; at that time they were land-dwelling quadrupeds. In the succeeding types the hind legs were very gradually reduced, so that in the modern forms they are represented only by vestigial, rod-like pelvic bones.

The dugong has heavy, dense bones, a smooth, soft, thick skin, and a round head. To its round head is attributed the spread of the mermaid legend in world literature. Seen from afar, from the deck of a ship for instance, the dugong might well be called a fabulous creature. If it happens to be floating upright with its baby under its flipper, even the least imaginative observer might fancy he was seeing something half fish, half human. Early travellers spread the mermaid legend far and wide, and few are the literatures that do not contain a trace of it.

According to certain authorities it was with the skin of the dugong and not with badger skins, as the Authorized Version of the Bible has it, that the Jews were directed to veil the Tabernacle.

Since the Andamanese carried on most of their dugong hunts by moonlight, there would be a long wait, and we decided to travel into the jungle for a mile or so to watch the villagers working on a dugout canoe. We found the workmen laboriously chipping out the dugout with their primitive instruments. This they did in the spot where the tree was felled, in order to save their backs the torture of dragging a massive log through the thick jungle. As it was, dragging the completed dugout was labor enough.

In the late afternoon we returned to our boat to await the dugong hunt. Toward midnight all preparations had been completed. The night was clear, and across the glassy, purple surface of the water the full moon traced a broad path of silver light. Out from the shore we saw coming towards us two outrigger dugout canoes. As they came closer we could see two black silhouettes standing in pulpit-like affairs raised about two feet above the bow. It was a beautiful spectacle, the silhouettes of the pygmies splintering the silver light on the sea. Each boat held two paddlers who sat on the curved edges of the gunwale.

I took my place in one of the canoes. The procedure now became clear. The pygmies in the pulpits carried spears fifteen feet long, fashioned of heavy, strong wood. Attached to the top was a detachable barbed point fastened to a long cord, the other end of which was tied to the boat. The man ahead of me held his spear aloft, standing so motionless that he seemed to be a statue projecting from the bow.

The canoe cruised around for an hour or so, maneuvered without sound and seemingly without effort. Suddenly a whisper went up from one of the oarsmen. The boat shot forward. Almost imperceptibly the tiny figure at the bow tightened his muscles. The spear shot forward, and after it went the spearsman, diving cleanly into the water. There was scarcely time to count ten before the diver reappeared, holding the spear shaft. He clambered aboard, and instantly the canoe gathered speed. The dugong, caught by the barb, was rushing out to sea, and of course he was dragging the boat with him.

Giddily the canoe moved right and then left. It was getting into deeper water. If the dugong showed enough strength to pull us out into open sea and then sounded, the rope would be cut and the hunt abandoned.

Now the canoe was slowing up; the dugong's strength was giving out. Presently there was so little pull on the canoe that the oarsmen were able to swerve and make for the steamer. In a few minutes a giant carcass some eight or nine feet long, greenish white in the moonlight, was pulled up on deck.

The same canoes and the same men now started a turtle hunt. We cruised around for a long time in shallow water. In the bright moonlight I saw several sharks prowling about, no doubt also looking for turtles.

As before, one of the oarsmen let out a whisper, and the spearsman reached out and stabbed violently into the water. This time he did not relinquish the spear. The boat nearly upset, however, its outrigger coming clear out of the water. The pygmies had not provided me with a paddle, a very necessary instrument for keeping one's balance in craft of this kind, and remembering the sharks I was thankful I escaped falling overboard.

Once the turtle was speared, the canoe rocked for a little while. But it was not for long, as the turtle did not possess the endurance of a dugong. Quietly the litle pygmy at the bow who was strong enough to crack the hard shell of a seventy- or eighty-pound turtle waited till the rockings of the boat ceased. Then the catch was hauled into the canoe.

The next day there was a grand feast. The dugong was skinned, and the meat cut off and cooked. Each villager was there, busily engaged in ramming huge pieces of meat into his mouth. First it was dugong and then turtle. The turtle was cooked in its own shell; the entrails were considered great delicacies.

We sampled both dugong and turtle. The dugong was both tender and tasty; the turtle, for all its size, tasted like the smaller species we find in our own markets.

Having had their fill, the villagers proceeded to celebrate. They ran for the trees, tore off branches, and broke into a dance which consisted of hopping, bowing, and brandishing the leafy boughs. The surfeit of their favorite food had gone to their heads completely.

As a lasting souvenir of this hunt I carried away the skin, skull, and flippers of the dugong. The skin was hard to preserve despite the fact that I carried forty pounds of salt with me. It was made into a specimen, however, and may be seen today in the American Museum of Natural History in New York.

The Andamanese do not always expend so much effort on their hunts—or, to put it another way, they do not always make such a sport of it. Sometimes they get fish with bow and arrow. All the coast dwellers are expert shots with this weapon. They begin practising as children, first on still targets, then on moving ones. They roll stones or bits of wood downhill and teach the children, armed with tiny bows and arrows, to shoot at them.

When the children grow older they receive full-sized weapons, the arrows being barbed in two places with bones from pigeons' wings. These, incidentally, are deadly arms. Shot with tremendous force, they are capable of penetrating clear through the body of a man. But for our presence, the Japanese would have been dispatched from ambush with these weapons.

The bow-and-arrow hunters look for their game along the edges of reefs which can be reached with dugouts, or even by wading where the water happens to be two or three feet deep. The sea, as so often happens in the tropics, is very clear, but in any case the pygmies can spot their prey below the surface. Their instinct tells them that light is refracted when passing through water and that an object below the surface is actually in another spot than where it appears to be; this they take into consideration when aiming.

Spending so much of their time in the water, they are fine swimmers and divers. From an early age the children play in the water, swimming as much beneath the surface as on it. As his stroke is similar to a dog's, the average Andamanese does not possess much speed, but he has great endurance and never flinches from a long swim.

The water around the islands is alive with sharks, and at certain places along the shore there lives a dangerous species of amphibious cobra. Neither of them holds any terror for the Andamanese. Without fear they will plunge into deep, shark-ridden water, and when they are after turtles they will swim in a sea teeming with cobra. Whether they owe their safety to their extreme agility, or to a special sense for avoiding the sharks and cobras, or again whether they are regarded by these creatures of the deep as part of the scene and hence harmless, is something no one can say, least of all the Andamanese themselves.

On land as well, the pygmies know how to resist the malign forces of nature. While their diet is somewhat unbalanced, they eat plentifully as we have seen, in a land unfit for agriculture. They do not thirst, although there are no running streams and in the dry season no springs. They know where to extract water from the earth. The unhealthful, humid heat produces no dire effects. Although the jungle is infested with mosquitoes, many of them malarial, and the coasts are alive with sand-flies (these pests often drove us back to the ship in the late afternoon), the Andamanese are immune.

Young Andamanese man wading out from the shore to shoot fish

Method of hunting turtle and dugong. The spearsmen standing on the prows
can see the quarry far away

Hauling into the dugout a turtle that has just been speared

A dugong, collected for the American Museum of Natural History, has been beached to be skinned out

The dugong has now been skinned out and the skin is being washed before salting

Saying good-bye at Greater Andaman. The headman is wearing a shirt we gave him

Andamanese (Ongés) from Lesser Andaman, standing on the beach near the village

A temporary habitation of the Ongés. Some of them are lying on their characteristic bamboo beds, raised just above the ground. The white shirt is one of our gifts

Ongés in a large outrigger dugout. They travel in these for many days, carrying their fire with them

They live at peace with each other. Having plenty of food for all, and land to spare, they find no reason to fight among themselves. Because the islands are so inaccessible, strangers are rarely a problem.

These are the blessings of the Andamanese. Little work and no fighting are required to sustain existence. The result is one of the most backward of Negrito peoples. They have not moved forward in a thousand years. It emphasizes once again the fact that nature disposes of her largess with a balanced hand. Her parsimony in northern climates has created the drama we call civilization. The Andamanese, absolved from excessive labor, have little motive for marching ahead.

We had spent four days among the northern islands, and now our itinerary called for a trip southward to the Little Andamans, inhabited by the Ongés. For two days our tiny boat glided over the blue, unruffled sea. The sun's rays fell mercilessly, and there was hardly a hint of a breeze passing over the deck. The heat dulled one's senses to a pleasant lassitude.

Max Bonington, in the deck-chair beside me, talked about the Ongés. In culture, he said, we would find them just about as primitive as these we had left. They, too, constructed semi-permanent villages in the jungle just a few steps beyond the shore line—not tiny, thatched lean-tos, however, but large hives wherein the whole colony swarmed like bees. More addicted to roving than the north Andamanese, the Ongés used larger dugouts and cruised long distances at sea. While their trips often lasted several days, a night on the open sea was not to their taste, and so they always put into an island before dusk. Every dugout carried fire.

Bonington seemed less sure of them than of the northern Andamanese. We were to approach carefully, and if they showed any weapons it would be unsafe to land.

On the morning of the third day, the boat veered to the distant shore. Again we saw a steep wall of blackish green rising before us. All was silent. No natives appeared on the strand.

The launch was lowered and we moved slowly shoreward. When

we were halfway in, a few forms emerged from the bushes. There was nothing in their attitude to arouse suspicion, and by the time we had beached the boat, half the village had arrived.

The villagers had recently abandoned their community hive and were camping by the sea. It was now the dry season, and they hadn't troubled to put a roof over their heads. Beds had been made of boughs, raised four inches from the ground, on a partially cleared-off tract of jungle about two hundred feet square. On the little beds the owners sat or lay when they were not working. No effort had been made to arrange the boughs carefully, or to make the pallets more comfortable. A white man would have preferred the ground, but the Ongés had an invincible prejudice against flat earth, and didn't mind being jabbed by sharp boughs.

Their equipment and implements resembled those of the north Andamanese and they also consumed the same food. Physically, however, they differed from the northern tribes in minor ways. Although slightly shorter—four feet six inches on an average—they were somewhat stockier. Their eyes held the same expression of blank, staring indifference.

Some of the community had set up another temporary camp about a mile inland, where a new dugout was being built. We started toward it. The trail through the tropical virgin forest was none too good. There wasn't room for all the Ongés on it, and many of them flitted through the jungle on our right and left. While four white men watched their steps carefully and still tripped over vines and stumbled over uneven spots, the Ongés glided along noiselessly and effortlessly.

There was no way of telling when we were approaching the camp. One minute we were in thick jungle, and the next minute in a tiny clearing. Here the villagers had selected a good tree, felled it, and proceeded to camp. They wore breechclouts, nothing else.

It was after four o'clock in the afternoon, and the dugout workers had laid down their tools for the day. Men, women, and children were idling about. Some had stretched out on their comic little beds of torture. Beyond a doubt they had known we were coming to see them, but they gave no sign of welcome or hostility. They had only two attitudes, friendly and unfriendly—and because they didn't try to attack us, we knew they were in a satisfactory mood.

Our gifts—coarse leaf tobacco, clay pipes, red cloth, and a few colored shirts—were accepted without a word or a smile of thanks, but the atmosphere grew perceptibly warmer.

The men began to smoke immediately. Smoking was not one of their habits, of course, because they had no natural sources of tobacco, but they seemed to enjoy it, and not one showed any of the symptoms of a small boy experimenting with cigarettes for the first time. The women entertained themselves by draping their almost naked bodies with our red calico and strutting about the camp.

Like the north Andamanese, the Ongés obtain their food and drink with little effort. Living in a pre-agricultural age, with none of the benefits the human race has derived from civilization, they are absolutely self-sufficient.

I have said that the Andamanese have never been exposed to civilization, but there is one minor exception. Many years ago the government of Burma decided to form a colony of aborigines near Port Blair. Houses were built for them, and it was hoped that those who came to live in them might gain some benefits from the local brand of civilization.

The small colony is no more. The pygmies, far from being helped, showed a positive talent for picking up the worst traits and afflictions of civilized man. They were ravaged by disease, and reduced to acute misery. The government sent them back to their old haunts, and many carried diseases with them. Before the experiment was finished, the population had been reduced by 50 per cent.

The life-span in these tribes is short. Forty years is a ripe old age. Girls are married off early and sometimes bear children at twelve or thirteen. It is early development and early death.

In other lands, primitive tribes frequently practise nature worship as their sole religion. Nature worship often means devil worship, the devils or evil spirits being blamed for such misadventures as famine, plague, floods. Religious rites, then, are designed to placate the evil spirits. Good spirits bring normality and are ignored.

But with the Andamanese it is different. Since they lack nothing and experience few annoyances from nature, they can afford to ignore all the spirits, the bad with the good. There is nothing to pray for.

When our time came to leave, the Ongés manifested their good will by marching down to the sea. They stood in ranks on the shore watching us while the launch put out to the steamer. Mute, motionless, they remained there till we were well out to sea. Standing on deck we saw them shrink into little specks of blackness—infinitesimal exiles from civilization, lost in the gathering dusk.

Celebes and the Elusive Anoa

‹‹‹

I
T WAS the anoa that lured me to Celebes and the Toradjas that
detained me there. Quest and compensation were nicely balanced.
The anoa or dwarf buffalo (*depressi cornis*) had acquired—
long before I formed the design of getting a specimen for the
American Museum of Natural History of New York—a reputation
for being one of the most elusive animals on the planet. The peculiar
reasons for the anoa's aloofness were not wholly apparent in advance:
Celebean jungles had to be seen to be believed. The truth came out
soon enough.

As for the Toradjas, they automatically came into view when the
jungle was reached. This vital race of brown men, formerly addicted
to hunting human heads but now occupied with gentler pursuits,
thanks to the firm persuasions of the Dutch colonizers, was, as I have
suggested, adequate compensation for an assignment that extended
somewhat excessively on the side of dullness.

Celebes is one of the four great Sunda islands of the Dutch East
Indies Archipelago. Europe first heard of the island from Portuguese
explorers at the beginning of the sixteenth century, and in the next
few decades the doubtful name "Celebes" came into common currency. There are those who believe that a misnomer grew from a
passage by Antonio Galvão beginning "Célèbres Mocassares, Am-
boynes etc. . . ." The idea is that an inept translator tripped over
the true sense of the passage—"Celebrated Macassars, Amboinese etc."

—and concluded that the first word stood for the name of a tribe. It is a trig little story, and the best thing to be said for it is that history abounds in such misconceptions.

The Portuguese first controlled Celebes, but the Dutch wrested it away early in the seventeenth century, and since that time its 73,160 miles and four million people have contributed considerably to the prosperity of the Netherlands.

There is the matter of rubber, for instance, a valuable commodity with a strange history of intrigue, conniving, and bootlegging, that has brought millions of guilders into the coffers of Dutch corporations. Celebes has had a great role in the rubber saga.

As all school geographies point out, the original source of caoutchouc was Amazonia, and the product, exported from the Brazilian port of Para on the Amazon, came to be known as Para rubber. Far in the dense, inhospitable jungles of the interior grew trees that yielded the finest quality of latex we have known. Never growing in clumps, but scattered through the jungle as units, never domesticated, but depending on nature's whim, the trees were difficult of access and the cost of production was enormous. But also enormous was the world demand, and the state of Para, enjoying a golden age, placed a ban on the exportation of rubber seeds. It was a great monopoly, for nowhere else in the world except on the western coast of Africa, directly opposite Pernambuco, Brazil, did the trees grow wild. The African growths did not possess the quality of the Brazilian, however, and they were chiefly of interest to geologists who used them as one of a number of proofs that Africa and South America, much nearer to each other than the average man thinks, were once joined together.

But the golden age of Para and Manaos came to an end when some wily entrepreneur smuggled out the precious seeds. Before many years, rubber trees were flourishing in Malaya and in the French and Dutch colonies in the East.

Now domesticated, planted in trim rows on vast plantations, tended carefully by cheap coolie labor, the rubber trees waited for a new golden age. But there were hitches. The domesticated trees never reached the giant size they had achieved in the Brazilian jungle, never yielded such a fine product. Indeed, in the beginning the new environment seemed inimical to their growth. They were a prey to termites and all manner of diseases. But research soon found the remedy: at periodic intervals the roots had to be uncovered, treated, and scraped. Thus pampered and coaxed along they flourished; eastern rubber flooded the market, and while the price went down, the growing demand poured wealth into the pockets of the entrepreneurs.

But the story of the bootlegged product didn't end there. The seeds had been smuggled out of Brazil, and now the natives, particularly in Malaya, began smuggling them out of the plantations. Governments hastened to pass laws controlling the planting and disposal of the trees. Rigid control, it was hoped, would avert a price slump.

Bootlegging natives, however, were undeterred. Illicit trees began to sprout up in tiny, remote villages, in secluded spots along estuaries, back of mangrove swamps. Native craft, slipping up the inlets under cover of night, collected the latex and sold it to smugglers at reduced prices.

No more successful than American prohibitionists in their war on liquor, the white planters of the East have watched the native bootleg-rubber industry grow every year, with the result that control is slowly but inevitably passing from white to native hands, and price-pegging may soon become impossible.

The coming of rubber changed the course of Celebean history, but whatever the outcome, the Dutch have found it a valuable unit of their colonial empire.

The point of departure for most excursions into the Dutch East Indies is Batavia, capital of Java. This is a lucky circumstance, because the transition from the Hotel des Indes, one of the most attractive hotels in the world, to Celebean standards of comfort provides one of those dramatic contrasts that occur too infrequently in travel.

It was in March of 1934 that I arrived in Batavia on my way to Celebes. In order to shoot, a government permit was necessary. Applying to the governor-general, I received an invitation to come up to his palace at Buitenzorg, in the hills above Batavia.

White, attractive, cool as anything can be in tropical Java, the palace stood in the center of a vast garden. The interior, containing pictures of Queen Wilhelmina in her younger, thinner days, suggested that the sovereign of this vast empire would have approved not only of the simple, adequate palace, but of the stiff, ornate furniture—everything true to Dutch tradition.

It was a quiet little luncheon party, as the court had decreed official mourning for the late dowager Queen Emma. Surrounding the towering, white-clad figure of the governor-general—he must have been six feet, seven inches—colonial leaders discussed in languid fashion the latest affairs of town and colony. In this atmosphere it seemed not unlikely that a bit of log-rolling would be necessary to obtain the permit. The explanations . . . "the anoa, extremely rare . . . a museum in America wants . . ." would not, perhaps, be readily explicable to stolid Dutchmen who never erred on the side of excessive activity.

But the governor's aide who took me aside after luncheon combined courtesy with celerity. "A permit? You shall have it immediately." His attitude seemed to be: "Other people's pursuits, however fantastic, do not concern me."

A little Dutch steamer took my wife to Bali and me to Macassar, capital of Celebes. My wife would come to Celebes later.

The Celebean capital eased itself into an Anglo-Saxon household word a few decades ago when "tidies" or "antimacassars" adorned the backs of chairs to save the upholstery from hair suffused with Macassar oil. But the antimacassars are museum pieces now and Macassar is mainly a matter of interest to the Dutch, who have built a modern port city. A few thousand Dutch and Eurasians are stern but not overbearing taskmasters for the miscellaneous tribes of Celebeans who throng the capital.

Ethnologists divide the population into five different races:

The Toalas, who probably represent the original stock, are a backward, timid people, almost submerged by the newer races.

A village in a valley. Scrub covers the hillsides, but the lower land is very productive for paddy

Western shore line of southern Celebes, approaching from Bali

Overlooking the hill country of south central Celebes. Dense jungle is all about,
inhabited by the dwarf anoa and giant constrictors

Where paddy fields are distant from a village, the Toradjas build temporary lean-tos for rain protection while they work

A village in the hills. The houses, exquisitely carved and polychromed, are clean, and the village is free from filth and smells

The Gorontalese are also a backward people. Farming, weaving, and plaiting are now their main occupations. At the present time they are not a very hardy breed.

The Buginese and Macassars, closely related strains, are famous as navigators. Their prahus, completely ignoring steamship competition, traverse all the seas of the archipelago, sometimes getting as far as Australia. The prahu harbor of Macassar is a picturesque spot with its gaily painted craft and sailors attired in bright sarongs and handkerchiefs tied over their heads. The travels of these two tribes brought them into the orbit of Hinduism and later of Mohammedanism. In addition to seafaring, they are devoted to agriculture and handicrafts, such as weaving and metal work.

The Toradjas are of Malayo-Polynesian stock. They have their own pagan creed, little touched by the prevailing Mohammedan influences of the islands. They are mainly agriculturists. Before the advent of the Dutch, warfare was their common occupation. If they couldn't find an outside enemy, they battled among themselves. True head-hunters, they looked on human skulls as their finest trophies. Warriors crept into neighboring villages in the dead of night and decapitated sleeping victims. They brought the heads home in triumph, handed them down from father to son.

The Dutch began by confiscating all skulls and inflicting heavy penalties on the head-hunters, and in time the Toradjas, unlike the Nagas of Assam, lost their appetite for the ancient sport.

The fascination of Celebes comes from its mélange of races and cultural antecedents. Archeologists have proved the existence of early Chinese customs and crafts. Later, India was the dominant factor and Hindu practices were grafted onto pagan. Despite these influences and the later waves of Mohammedan and Christian proselytism, the Toradjas, particularly those of the isolated districts, have never relinquished their Malayo-Polynesian character.

The search for the anoa would take me into the thick of the Toradja country. In Macassar I received the name of a German planter who ran a coffee plantation up in the hills, a full day's motor ride from the capital. The implication was strong that he would be a good man to help me organize the hunt.

The car climbed steadily, soon reaching a country of hills and mountain chains, frequently gashed by broad valleys.

Toradja villages are usually situated along the banks of streams. Tracts of land are wrested away from the jungle for agricultural purposes. Keeping the land clear requires unremitting labor, for the jungle is constantly struggling to regain what it has lost. Grass, vines, bushes, fed by frequent rains, spring up with deadly speed. There is little dry season to quell this prodigality of nature. Many of the mountain peaks, rising as high as five thousand feet, stand in the direct route of warm, moist winds coming from surrounding seas. Consequently the Toradja country receives a great deal of precipitation. Even the so-called dry season brings many afternoon showers.

The virgin jungle is dense and knotted with spider-web bushes, vines, and dreadful thorns. Those who travel through it must hack their way, step by step. This explains why the anoa is hard to find, and why so few museums possess specimens.

The island harbors two types of indigenous water buffalo, known to the natives as tokata. They are brown in color, show no distinctive markings, and have short, very sharp horns, resembling those of some species of antelope or gazelle.

The smaller of the Celebes species is known to us as the anoa and is the smallest of its kind known anywhere in the world. Even the tamarau of the Philippines is a heavier animal.

Only rarely do the natives hunt the anoa. The animal must be sought in inaccessible places, and the output of energy necessary for a single kill is terrific. Progress through the upland jungle is slow and visibility is poor. For these reasons the Toradjas, on those rare occasions when they do stage a hunt, take two or three trained dogs to follow the scent.

It was clear by now that this expedition was going to be a matter of grim business, unlightened by pleasure. I paid scant attention to the Toradjas on the way up to the anoa country. Trips to their villages would have meant detours, and I was eager to start the hunt as soon as possible.

The plantation owner was a young man of thirty-two or so, named von Werner. In the upland jungle he lived with his wife, like himself a German, their young child, and his brother. Forty coolies were employed on the plantation. Only a small part were used for planting and harvesting the coffee; the others struggled with the jungle which, left to itself, would have crawled up to the bedroom window by morning.

The small house was adequately furnished but the plantation equipment was primitive. At some distance from the house was a colony of huts allotted to the coolies.

Nearly all the food consumed by the family had to be brought up from Macassar, with great difficulty and expense. Staples of diet were pork and bacon from native pigs, and bread made of imported flour. Local cheese and custards were great delicacies. The plantation had one cow—maintained with difficulty on the coarse jungle grass—but the milk was needed for the baby.

I asked von Werner if he expected to make his fortune on coffee raising.

"No," he said, "the conditions are too hard. The coffee is of finest quality but production costs are frightful. Imagine spending more on beating off the jungle than on actual cultivation!"

But he had other plans. Eventually, he hoped, the land might be turned into a summer resort. This estate of his was indubitably cooler and more healthful than the seacoast, but any man from the temperate zones would have called it intolerably hot and steamy. He aimed at luring officialdom up from the torrid coast settlements.

There was a thermal spring on the land, and this had been turned into a caricature of a swimming pool. The water was heavily impregnated with sulphur, and, whether rightly or wrongly, Dutch colonials had a notion that dips into sulphurated water could repair some of the damage done to their skins by the sultry air of the tropics. I took one dip in the pool and came out stifled and languid. Once was enough for me.

One day I suggested swimming in a near-by stream that came down from the upper hills. Von Werner demurred. I tried it and found it surprisingly cool and invigorating. The next day I actually succeeded in persuading von Werner to join me. He stood it for one second and then scrambled out to the rocky shelf, saying he was finished. Those who live in the tropics year after year find their blood thinning out. Cold can cause intense agony, and can even bring on fever.

Despite the primitive surroundings, the von Werner family clung to the routines of civilization. There was nothing slatternly about the house, the food, or the clothing. Not even a jungle could change the wife from what she was—a typical German *hausfrau* with ingrained habits of neatness and order. Their youth and enthusiasm kept the husband and wife on even keel, but it was easy to see that hard labor and deprivation would soon begin to collect their toll.

The long, lingering twilights we know in northern climes are unknown in Celebes. You could sit on the veranda at six o'clock in broad daylight and watch the copper-colored sun sliding down the western curve of the sky. After searing the landscape and wearing down the resistance of the inhabitants, it showed itself relentless to the last. That unwearied, torrid brilliance continued up to the final flicker of copper light streaming through the bushes. Then night came down, abruptly and ruthlessly.

There was an acetylene lamp but it was expensive to run. Some of the evenings we sat in darkness, chatting till it was time to go to bed.

It was time to start the hunt. Von Werner hired two Toradjas who appeared at the house one morning leading three apathetic-looking dogs. One man was old, grizzled, and almost toothless, but still sturdy and active. The other, young and strapping, seemed slightly bewildered. Both were chewing betel that made protuberances in their cheeks as big as crab apples. Their mouths were dirty and distorted from constant use of this narcotic. Dirty sarongs hanging from waist to knees were their only clothes.

The hunting equipment consisted of two spears about five feet long. With a sort of betelish indifference, the Toradjas showed how the spears worked. They were equipped with detachable, barbed heads. One end of a long cord was fastened to the head, the other to a piece of wood about a foot and a half long. The system was this: at the first sight of an anoa, the spearsmen would let fly. If the animal wasn't killed outright, the barb would hold and his attempt to escape would be hindered by the billet of wood, secured to the cord. Plunging through the brush, the beast would soon become tangled in the thicket and finally trapped.

I wished to know if the anoa had a reputation for attacking man. The younger man shook his head emphatically. The elder thrust forward his long, lower lip into a monkey smile and pointed to scars not only on his own body but on his companion's.

We walked a mile or so up the bed of a small, rocky stream and entered the jungle. Stream beds, no matter how numerous the boulders, were easier to negotiate than the bush. The water was up to our knees.

Once in the jungle, we climbed a steep slope. The Toradjas with their krises (long, curved knives) walked ahead, slashing at bushes and vines with an easy, supple wrist-motion. Shreds of vines and branches flying from the blades festooned the trees to right and left.

The underbrush grew thicker. Thorns scraped the naked hands. The trail was steep, and the soaking earth was very slippery. How many times I lost my footing and fell I couldn't count. My spiked shoes were no particular advantage. Watching the agile toes of the natives clinging to the soft earth, I was tempted to discard my own shoes. But I reflected in time that my toes were not trained for acrobatic exercises.

The skill of these Toradjas in moving through the jungle was extraordinary. Their movement was less a walk than a slow, careful slink. They got through the thorns and the vicious rattan without a scratch.

Sometimes there were light showers which we heard rather than felt, for the solid ranks of trees with their interlaced tops formed an almost perfect umbrella. Moisture seeped through nevertheless, and the ground was perpetually dank and slippery.

Descending the slopes was bad, but climbing was worse. My feet skidded and my hands, lunging out for support, often clasped a sharp thorn. Recoiling, I would slide and fall. Sometimes a solid-looking yet rotted branch would snap abruptly, giving me another fall. Often climbing on hands and feet was the only way. For the natives, nimble as monkeys, it was all very simple. Groggy from exertion, soaked with sweat, I watched their maneuvers and despaired of ever finding the prized anoa. I had started the hunt armed with a rifle and a camera, but after a few minutes I turned both over to the younger hunter. The anoa, I felt, in the now remote contingency of our finding one, would never be brought down with a rifle. The jungle was far too dense. For the same reason the camera was useless.

The dogs were supposedly attending to their business but one rarely saw them. Now and then reeds crackled or a low yap came from behind the thorny curtain. I had a notion—it became a growing obsession—that the dogs were off entertaining themselves without a thought in the world for the anoa. But the Toradjas showed the utmost confidence in their pack. The dogs would corner the animal and hold it till we came.

The first day ended in failure. There was nothing to show for it save tired bones and bleeding hands and legs.

Day after day we carried out a wearisome repetition. Feet sloughed through the pulpy earth. The jungle was like a barbed-wire entanglement, and overhead the quivering green roof shut out the sky. The rain, heard but never seen, lent one more special touch to this remote, outlandish world. Through it all the Toradjas and their dogs seemed wayward and outrageously indifferent.

One afternoon a cry went up from the two hunters. The dogs, still invisible, were emitting low growls, and the old warrior, puffing like a Diesel engine, looked around to see if I was following. He caught my eye and nodded with a knowing air. My spirits soared.

Through the thicket the dogs could be seen leaping up and down joyfully. We emerged into a little clearing, but there was no sign of the anoa. Then my eye fell to the earth and there was the quarry—a small, green snake feigning death. The only decent reaction came from one of the dogs, who looked at me with a sheepish expression and then turned and gazed fixedly into the bush. The Toradjas gave no sign of chagrin or even amusement. They stood and stared dully at the snake as if they had never seen one before. The betel-smeared jaws never stopped moving.

Another day brought another moment of wild hope and then crashing disappointment: twenty minutes of excitement ended with the dogs' chasing a monkey up a tree.

There was week after week of this. The anoa lived up to his reputation for elusiveness. I had hunted such expert dodgers as the wild sheep and the ibex, but both were simple compared with this quest in the black heart of the Toradja hill country.

Whether it was the indifference of the Toradjas or the general exhaustion I have no idea, but the end was appropriately undramatic. A furious barking of the dogs stirred us again. We hastened our footsteps. The old warrior suddenly stopped, sucked in his breath, and aimed his spear. The target was not visible to me. The spear whistled through the bushes. There was a crash. The dogs added to the confusion by frenzied barking. The weapon had hit its mark, and the anoa was plunging through the thicket with the barb in his side and the billet of wood getting him more tangled up every second. He fell at last and the two spears finished him off. There was just enough light to see his brown skin and needle-pointed horns.

I awoke the next morning to the realization that there are few pleasures in life like the pleasure of not hunting the anoa. The skin and bones of the animal were hanging from a tree near the house; there would be no more exhausting days of lunging through the thorny jungle. In three days I would be finished with the hide: it must be treated with arsenic soap to discourage rodents and blow flies and with salt to hasten the drying process. When it was boxed and ready for shipment I would be free to join my wife, who had motored up into the Toradja country and was now busy, according to her note, exploring native villages.

Leaving von Werner's the road climbed steadily. The air was more salubrious. Colorful gorges and chasms alternated with carefully tended paddies. Clumps of bamboo, swaying in the breeze like gigantic ostrich feathers, started from the banks of clear, rushing streams. There were myriads of wild flowers, including many varieties of wild orchids.

Several hours of travel brought me to a Toradja village in a little upland valley. My wife had already made friends with the natives, and with their assistance was busy preparing what she later described as "a rather violent homecoming."

The villagers were discreetly cordial. Old, worn faces showed quavering, betel-black smiles. The young, with their still unstrained faces and liquid Polynesian eyes, grew more demonstrative. All the men and many of the women were bare to the waist; their single garment was the sarong fashioned from vividly colored cotton cloth. Bead necklaces were common and so were bandeaux draped around the black heads. Wide-spaced eyes and high cheekbones made many an attractive face; more could have been called handsome if they had refrained from the deforming betel-wad.

I was led to the village prize: an albino water buffalo kept in a pen and treated like a visiting deity. The keeper explained with pride that the animal was hard to find, and few villages possessed such a treasure. I was easily convinced.

A group of Toradja women wearing colorful sarongs and a copious supply of beads served the dinner that had taken, under my wife's direction, three days to prepare. There was native roast pig, vegetables cooked in leaves, tapioca swimming in molasses and topped with fresh cocoanut, native wine in bamboo containers. A great crowd had collected and I realized this feast was something very special indeed. My wife supplied the details. She had scoured the tiny bazaars run by the Toradja-Chinese for materials. The tapioca had to be pounded down, the molasses stewed. It looked good and it smelled good. The Toradjas eyed it enviously.

The tomb of some important Toradja sultan

Toradja rock graves. One often sees them when passing an escarpment

Interior of southern Celebes, sparsely inhabited. The beautiful tropical rivers and green vegetation have an enchanting effect

Native boat along the east coast of southern Celebes

Their envy was short-lived, because fifteen minutes later they were sitting down eating it. The native pig was tougher than any meat I had ever encountered, and the tapioca tasted like slabs of half cooked starch. The wine was acrid. The Toradjas, it was clear, would have to be appraised by non-culinary standards. At least their village and the surrounding landscape were attractive.

At this altitude, the climate was pleasant. Midday brought no burning heat, and now the evening was somewhat cool. Insect pests, so common in the tropics, were absent. There were no centipedes, no scorpions. The standard of health for the whole district, my wife thought, was high.

We visited many Toradja villages during the ensuing days. Few had more than a dozen houses. One of the joys of life in this district was the buildings. Great care and artistic skill had gone into every house, and those belonging to the richer natives had cost great sums. The results were unique and beautiful. All were built on piles six or eight feet high and the houses themselves rose ten feet from the piles, culminating in thatched roofs that curved upward at both ends and extended six or eight feet beyond the walls. Decoration was as interesting as form. The walls of bamboo and palm bore exquisite polychrome designs in red, white, and black, unlacquered and thus showing a dull, rich surface. Standing out from the lintels were horns of the sacred albino buffalo.

The reason for the piles was obscure, since there seemed no danger from rain or flood. One plausible explanation, it seemed to me, was that Toradja architecture had its beginnings in the low coastal districts and that the pattern for building, thus established, was carried to the hinterland without thought of whys and wherefores.

Seen from afar, one of these houses might be taken for an ancient galleon and on closer scrutiny the marine motif proved not to be pure fancy. Archeologists have guessed that Toradja houses still bear a reminiscence of the boats that carried the first settlers from the mainland of Asia to Celebes.

The Toradjas live in communal family groups, each group occupying one house. Since the married sons bring their wives to live in the family dwelling, it is common to see several generations living together. The lot of the old and decrepit is not easy; there is no reverence for age. The law is "every one must work," and the most disagreeable chores are assigned to aged women.

Agriculture is the chief enterprise and rice the chief product. To terrace the hills around the houses for paddy purposes would be too difficult; so planting is done in the valleys. Small rest-houses with thatched roofs are erected in the cultivated areas and here the workers find protection from the rain.

Clear water being found in abundance, a simplified system of supply has been worked out. Bamboo split into halves with the intersecting joints removed form admirable troughs. Many of these joined together form conduits which bring the water from neighboring streams and springs into individual houses.

The Toradjas are comparatively safe from animals but they are molested by birds who plunder their crops. Consequently many ingenious devices have been worked out to scare off the marauders. Here is an example:

A piece of bamboo about six inches in diameter is halved and strung across a rushing stream near the paddies. The hollow part of the bamboo faces upstream. Getting the full force of the current, it constantly jerks a hempen cord attached to it. The cord is stretched out over the field in every direction and tied to it is a series of tiny bamboo whistles which are thus kept in constant operation. The sounds serve a double purpose. They frighten the birds and discourage evil spirits. Seeing one of these contraptions for the first time, I looked for a new kind of bird with a curious light whistle.

Tenure of land is in the hands of the head men or petty sultans. Agriculture is carried on entirely by the peasant class, which pays tithes to the landowners for the privilege of farming.

There are no labor troubles in Celebes. The climate is not only mild but highly productive. Living comes easy, famines are unknown, and the workers find no cause for grievance. Commerce is a simple matter.

Once a week or so there are grand market days with stalls located at some central spot in the valley. The various products of the field and handicrafts are displayed to the obbligato of sharp bargaining. Barter is the usual means of transfer.

The Toradjas have a few simple, primitive arts. They weave cloth and baskets, carve wood, make pottery, and work metal. From cotton and fiber two types of cloth are produced. One is about the size of a roller towel; dyed in checks or stripes of vivid hues, it becomes the common sarong. The other type, about as big as an old-fashioned portière, is commonly used for bed coverings. The weaving and coloration of the Toradjas have a marked individuality, being apparently unaffected by the Balinese or Javanese designs.

A comparison of modern and ancient Toradja art shows that their weaving has undergone a deterioration in the last fifty years. Superb samples of the older work are still to be seen in Dutch houses and in coast settlements.

Household utensils are composed of wooden spoons and bowls made of wood or pottery. The wooden bowls are usually carved, and the more beautiful examples are to be seen, filled with rice and fruit, on the heads of young girls walking in the ceremonial processions.

The straw weavers produce baskets of many shapes and designs. One of the most unusual is a contrivance fashioned to fit the back; it provides protection against sun and rain. Such a basket covered with an anoa skin is, in the Toradja scheme of things, the last word in swank.

Cooking utensils, tips for plows, krises, and other odds and ends are turned out by the metal workers. The best work goes into the kris, both blade and handle being finished in elaborate designs. The kris and the blowpipe are the only lethal weapons produced by the Toradjas, and these are far less useful today than they were back in the head-hunting days.

The blowpipe is a formidable weapon, five feet long, shooting with surprising velocity a tiny dart feathered at its base for the sake of accuracy. For a short distance, thirty feet for example, it will fly at such speed as to be practically invisible. Both the kris and the dart are impregnated with strychnine.

The Dutchman's ban on head-hunting turned the Toradja mind to intensive pursuit of another sport—cock fighting. Every man who can afford it carries a fowl around with him, caressing it, displaying it for the admiration of others. During fights the cocks are spurred and equipped with another deadly device, a four-inch blade made of native metal, sharpened to razor-edge and tied to one of the legs. For this reason the fights are of short duration, as the blades are poisoned and a wound causes quick death. The Toradjas bet furiously on the fights, adding to the general excitement.

So far I have dealt with the temporal life of the Toradjas, which consists of a few basic needs not too difficult of fulfillment. But it would be oversimplification to leave off the description at this point: their dealings with the supernatural constitute a very important element in their behavior.

Two rival deities, the Toradjas think, are forever struggling for their bodies and souls. The good spirit is Dewatas and the evil is Maroh. The machinations of Maroh are never-ending. Every ache or pain, every piece of abnormal deportment, is evidence that he has seized another victim.

The medicine-men have evolved an elaborate liturgy for dealing with Maroh. An exorcism begins with a ceremonial dance accompanied by music from crude drums and flutes. Propitiatory food is offered to the devil. The victims are sweated and wooed into a trance. If, after all this, Maroh is still in control of the situation, the victims are made to stand on a bamboo scaffold over a fire for two or three minutes. In very stubborn cases (the medicine-men for understandable reasons profess to find Maroh a tenacious tenant) the victims submit to incisions on their backs, bellies, and arms.

When the grim business is over, the tribe makes a procession to the nearest stream, a sacrificial rooster being carried aloft by the medicine-men. The program is completed by ceremonial dances and a feast, an orgy of raw chicken, red rice, and sago wine. The head medicine-man gets six chickens and his assistants get four.

The eternal struggle between Dewatas and Maroh is no simple matter of an occasional ceremony. It has penetrated so deeply into the Toradja consciousness that it affects their every deed and decision. Signs and portents appear in every stream, on every tree. The world of the Toradjas is, in brief, a glorified magic-box.

Strong believers in immortality, the Toradjas are inevitably pre-occupied with death. A dead man must be given a grand farewell. No act of piety must be omitted as the soul starts off on the last, long journey. All the beautiful Toradja dances have evolved out of this concept, and every artisan contributes some tribute to the departing soul.

A dead man, placed in a cylindrical coffin, lies in state in his own house. Here gather groups of men who perform the strangely moving *ma'badong mbating*, a swaying funeral dance, accentuated by the threnodies of a professional wailing chorus. For the rich man, a bull is sacrificed, an expensive item. Around the animal's carcass gather black-veiled wailing women and a chorus of girls wearing black blouses, white skirts, bandeaux of fruit, and necklaces of conch shells. The chorus breaks into a graceful, slow dance called the *ma'gellu*. The esthetic impulses of the tribe reach a very high point in this ceremony.

On the eve of burial is held another and more complicated dance called the *manganda*. The performers are men draped with sarongs from waist to knees and bearing on their heads one of the largest, most elaborate head-dresses ever devised by dancers. A miter-shaped hat supports a two-piece banner that rises two feet above the head, cul-minates in feathers and bull horns, and then drops down the back as far as the waist. Under this heavy burden the dancers sway, tap, and pirouette as the drums and flutes maintain a monotonous, funeral rhythm. The arduous routines and the great weight of the head-dress tire out the strongest men, and substitutes are kept waiting on the sidelines. The *manganda* is a stunning sight, one of the most impressive I have ever seen in any country.

The dead man, dressed in the best garments and ornaments his family can procure, is placed in a hearse and carried by a score of mourners to the *liang* or tomb. The last act in the funeral of a sultan is enormously impressive because the hearse is really a miniature dwelling, complete with sweeping roof and polychromed sides.

The *liang* is erected wherever possible on a cliff, so high and inaccessible that scaffolds and ladders are necessary to carry up the body. The family has already prepared a niche to receive the coffin and a little balcony beside it to support a painted, life-size effigy of the dead man dressed in bright colors. The best artists of the tribe expend their talents on these effigies. I shall never forget the day I glanced up from the jungle and saw a whole colony of these bright effigies occupying the balconies a hundred feet or more up on the side of the cliff. These realistic statues looking down from their heights are one of the most fantastic sights to be seen in Celebes.

The elaborate and beautiful dances of the Toradjas provide an index to their character and spiritual evolution. They take the spectator back through the centuries before Hinduism, Mohammedanism, and Christianity had ever been heard of on the island.

To see such an unspoiled people the traveller must usually penetrate far into the backwaters of civilization. But the Toradja area is easily reached by motor-car over the highways, constantly being extended by the Dutch. From the highways the traveller can strike out for himself into the villages. A trip to this country provides a memorable glimpse of primitive life with a minimum of hardship.

After one has seen a new land, a voyage homeward bound is usually such an uneventful affair that little of it remains in the memory. In the case of Celebes, however, memory goes on while a combination freight-and-passenger ship of the K. P. M. Line took us to Manila and while a Dollar liner took us to China. It was all because of one small monkey who played out his tragi-comic role in the harbor of Hongkong.

While the ship lay at anchor for a short time, the passengers leaned on the rail to watch the animated harbor. Not far from the gangway a Chinese woman in a small sampan was busy fishing. She sat in the bow and maneuvered her line, totally indifferent to her audience. Whenever she got a fish she flung it into a small, boarded section amidships that was supplied with salt water from a hole next to the keel. She was unaware of the capers of her pet monkey, who was beginning to attract an appreciative audience on our ship.

Every time a fish landed in the salt-water compartment the monkey moved over gingerly and threw it back into the sea. The plop was inaudible, for our forward hatch was open and the winch was bringing up mail sacks and other small cargo from the hold. The performance kept up; one fish after another was caught and stealthily put back into the sea. The laughter grew louder but the fisherwoman ignored it.

Then at length a fresh outburst aroused her suspicion, and she turned around, to see a completely empty tank. Her face registered no emotion at all, but she took up a cleaver from a thwart and moved toward her pet slowly and deliberately.

Terrified and desperate, the monkey ran chattering along the gunwale. But there was no escape. The woman's hand seized him. The laughing audience above now set up a cry: "Don't! Spare him! We'll . . ."

The woman understood not a word. In a moment the monkey was pressed over the thwart face down. The cleaver slashed downward, and body followed head into the sea.

Still expressionless, losing neither minute nor movement, the woman went back to her fishing, and presently the salt-water tank was filling up again.

Inhospitable Galápagos

‎᠆᠆

SUNSHINE and sea spray must have made the islands look very beautiful. Such towering mountains for such a small land! The verdure, sparse on the shore and on the lower slopes, grew thicker, darker, as the symmetrical cone rose to meet the sky. It was a bewitching color combination, the black of the boulders dotting the shore, the green of the jungle blanketing the cone, the blue of the sky.

For the members of the Ecuadorean government commission a sense of beauty was mingled with a sense of pride. Their country had laid formal claim to the islands described on ancient maps as "The Enchanted Isles," but now known as Galápagos Islands for the famous tortoises living in the jungle.

The Ecuadoreans, on their administrative cruise, had a guest, a Norwegian consul. For him the islands were not only beautiful but held out great promise for the future. What wealth this land secreted, no man knew. But one thing was certain: there was wealth in the fishing concession and he was on the spot to angle for first rights.

The boat came into view of Indefatigable Island, second largest of the group. Moving along the glassy surface of the water, the men on deck saw a level stretch of white sand. A little higher up there was a dense green thicket. And then rose the steep lava slope covered with dense verdure. A dead hush lay over the water, over the white beach. At dusk the jungle took on a greenish-blue luster. No wonder they had once called them "The Enchanted Isles." Buccaneers, and fisher-

First view of the Galápagos group, photographed from the *Nourmahal*

Nesting boobies on Charles Island. They are not afraid of man; they merely resent him

Land iguanas, captured as part of our collection

Clarence L. Hay and Kermit Roosevelt during a halt near the top of Indefatigable Island

Bronson on the deck of the *Nourmahal,* painting a marine turtle

men from far-away New England, had visited them. But now it was an abandoned land. It had never been colonized.

The consul resolved to tell his government about this land that held so many possibilities for riches. Norwegians might come here and prosper. Thus ran his fantasies, and thus began disaster for scores of men and women.

The impressionable consul cruised around the islands fifteen or twenty years ago, but he never set foot on Indefatigable Island. The most charitable conclusion about him is that he was carried away by momentary enthusiasm. At any rate the enthusiasm caught on in Norway. Fishermen with their womenfolk left the bleak security of their northern coasts and blundered into the adventure of the Galápagos. On the shores of sweltering, tropical Indefatigable Island, they debarked and proceeded to their work of colonization.

The actual details of their disillusionment may be only conjectured, but it is certain that they could not have spent many hours on the island before discovering it was not fit for human habitation. First, there was a dearth of water. The whole island was coated with the lava of extinct volcanoes. There *were* patches of soil that permitted the jungle to burst into barbarous density at the upper levels. But this soil was poor for agriculture. To cap the climax, the whole island, both upper and lower levels, was infested by a dreadful curse—mosquitoes.

The Norwegians would have been wise to escape at the first opportunity. Instead they went to work with indomitable energy. The first human habitations sprouted up on the lower levels. They erected a huge iron tank to catch rain-water. These essentials attended to, they got out their seines and built structures on the shore for drying fish.

The epic of the Norwegian colonists is brief and sad. Indefatigable Island, unimpressed by so much courage and hardihood, repelled the invaders. Many of them died. The survivors escaped to Ecuador. A few years later the summit of the mountain looked down on a group of abandoned shacks, on a little graveyard, on the iron tank that still caught the rain and gave it back to the air—a symbol of futility.

The Galápagos Archipelago is an outcast land. The twelve large islands and the hundreds of smaller satellites lying out in the Pacific, five hundred miles due west of Ecuador, have always cast a hostile glance at the march of civilization. Their geological origins are wrapped up in mystery and speculation. It was long believed (Charles Darwin espoused the theory) that from the beginning they have been separated from the mainland of South America and from each other. But there are geologists today—and their evidence is impressive—who maintain that the archipelago was once hooked on to Central America by a land bridge.

The Galápagos come into written history in the sixteenth century, when they were discovered by Spanish explorers. They served no useful purpose to any one save buccaneers and pirates. New England whalers found them useful as ports of call. But when the age of piracy was over and whaling declined, the islands were rarely visited. During the last century scientific expeditions made a few visits for collecting purposes. The most famous expedition to touch the islands was "The Beagle," for one of its members was Charles Darwin. The great scientist gathered some valuable data for his *Origin of Species*.

The next phase in the islands' history was the adventure of the Norwegians. The world was persuaded that the Galápagos were not fit for human habitation. If this wasn't enough, the craters of Albemarle Island, largest unit of the archipelago, broke into eruption in 1925. Since then lava has flowed from Narborough, fourth largest island.

But neither the experiences of the Norwegians nor the eruptions of the craters were sufficient to discourage little bands who at various times during the last ten years have attempted to set up permanent homes on the islands.

The attempt that made the whole world aware of the Galápagos was made by the mysterious "Baroness Wagner," who appeared on Floreana Island in 1933 with two men, Lorenz and Philippson. After building a house and giving it the grandiose name of "Hacienda Paradise" she proclaimed herself "Empress of the Galápagos."

INHOSPITABLE GALÁPAGOS

For a whole year the newspapers of the world carried stories, many of them apocryphal, about the "Empress" and her "court." In 1934 it turned to stark tragedy. The "Empress" and Philippson disappeared. Lorenz gave out the story that they had taken a boat to another island. This story was at first accepted, and it was believed that they had been lost in the sea. But presently stories of murder were floating around the islands. Lorenz, with a Norwegian skipper named Nuggerud, left Floreana in a small boat. They were never seen alive again. Their bodies were found on the coast of a desert island where they died of thirst.

The story of the saturnine Baroness has been told in *Satan Came to Eden* by Dore Strauch, who lived a Galápagos epic of her own. She left her home and husband in Germany to seek a paradise with Doctor Friedrich Ritter. This adventure, too, ended in tragedy.

From time to time the newspapers still carry stories about the current adventures of the Wittmers and the Conways on Floreana. The fact that they are surviving does not dispute the fact that the Galápagos are a malignant abode for human beings.

Hostile to man, the Galápagos have become a haven for wild life. The most celebrated denizen of the island is the galápago or wild tortoise. Some of them have reached four hundred pounds and have grown four feet high. Most extraordinary of all, they have been known to live for three or four hundred years, making them the oldest animals on the earth. Many Galápagos species exist nowhere else. The flightless penguin, for instance, is one of the eighty-five different kinds of rare birds. The surrounding seas shelter curious sea lions and sea iguanas. The flora is unique.

The birds have never learned to consider man as an enemy. They are the tamest birds in the world, and it is an every-day occurrence to see one alight on a man's head or shoulder and remain there as if there were no difference between a man and a tree.

When, in the early spring of 1930, Vincent Astor asked me to be a member of an expedition to the Galápagos, I didn't hesitate for an instant. It was an opportunity to collect rare specimens and see a part of the world few had known. This, it must be remembered, was before the era of fantastic settlements that put the archipelago on the front pages of the newspapers.

The party eventually included the following:

Vincent Astor;

Doctor Eugene Pool, head surgeon of the New York Hospital;

Doctor C. H. Townsend, then director of the New York Aquarium;

Doctor James P. Chapin, department of ornithology, American Museum of Natural History;

C. L. Hay, archeologist, American Museum of Natural History;

Robert Huntington;

Elwin R. Sanborn, photographer for the New York Zoological Society;

Wilfred S. Bronson, fish and animal painter;

Kermit Roosevelt;

Doctor Henry Svenson, Brooklyn Botanic Garden;

C. Suydam Cutting.

Hay was assigned to entomology, Huntington to fish, Roosevelt and myself to mammals and reptiles.

This trip, organized by Vincent Astor, was in a class by itself for efficiency, comfort, and luxury. We were fortunate enough to have the finest private ship afloat. Starting out from Miami, the *Nourmahal* proceeded through the Panama Canal and thence southwest to the Galápagos. The yacht was fitted with special apparatus including electrically heated tanks wherein we hoped to bring back many rare fish for the aquariums of New York and Bermuda.

After the Panama Canal, every semblance of activity disappeared from our lives; for one pleasant day after another the yacht steamed over the dead-calm surface of the tropical sea. Then one morning Captain Klang, our navigator, brought the ship to anchor off Darwin Bay, about a mile from Indefatigable Island. Brilliant sunshine fell on the high conical wall of green foliage. The beach was a mosaic of white sand and pitch-black lava, and the sea was turquoise-blue.

The yacht now stopped because the archipelago at this point was uncharted. A launch was lowered to make soundings in the sea; then with the proper course charted, the *Nourmahal* moved in toward the shore.

Here we arranged to divide into two parties. The first would devote itself to sea life, while the second would penetrate to the interior of the islands and collect land specimens.

Astor, Pool, Huntington, Bronson, and Sanborn were to search for sea lion, turtle, and fish, using the yacht for headquarters as they cruised from island to island.

After an early luncheon the land party, consisting of Roosevelt, Chapin, Townsend, Svenson, Hay, and myself, went ashore, taking beds, mosquito nets, collecting material, food, and fresh water. The water was carried in huge carboys. We had been told there would be no pools, and if it rained the water would disappear through the cracks in the lava. The island is simply a vast block of lava.

After setting up quarters near the shore, Kermit and I started up inland over a clearly recognizable trail. We travelled up and up through a dense jungle. Late in the afternoon we had to turn back, since we had brought no light and the object of our search—water—could never be found, certainly, in the dark.

That night we spent in one of the houses abandoned by the hapless Norwegians. For reasons that will presently appear we named it "Cozy Cot."

By 4:30 o'clock the air was ringing with voracious mosquitoes. Tiny insects with a maddening bite, they poured through the windows in black clouds. There was no escape from them, but to go eventually to bed—and now it developed that our nets, purchased from some army quartermaster in Panama, were actually leftovers from the Spanish-American war! These good old relics filled with holes seemed to entice the mosquitoes.

I was awakened during the night by Hay wrestling with a six-inch centipede that today is in the American Museum of Natural History.

When we renewed the search for water the next day, Kermit, Chapin, and I took our beds along, since returning to "Cozy Cot" at sundown would reduce our time for exploring. We did well carrying the beds and supplies without thirty or forty porters to interrupt and cause trouble.

The trail was hard going. Heavy jungle growth covered the surface of uneven, sharp, black lava. Moving upward slowly, we had to push back the bushes and keep our eyes on the ground. It was evil footing. The air was hot and humid and our thirst seemed unquenchable.

Early in the afternoon, Chapin was seized with cramps in his legs and remained behind, while Kermit and I pushed on to find a camp site. After an hour's march up through the jungle we emerged into a clearing. Directly before us, set down in a grove of plantains, was a little cabin showing signs of recent occupation.

There was no one in the cabin, but presently we saw an Indian cowering in the bushes. Kermit spoke to him reassuringly in Spanish. The Indian came out timidly. He was a mere youth, twenty perhaps. By degrees his terror vanished, and he was able to explain that he had come originally from Ecuador and was now the servant of two white men who inhabited the cabin.

Two tough Norwegians had stuck it out. They spent part of their time down at the shore making fishing expeditions, the rest up here in the little plantation they had named, ironically enough, "Las Fortunas." They were now off among the islands, fishing.

The plantation provided a large barrel filled with rain-water. We took a good drink, ate some plantains, and went back for Chapin, taking the Indian with us. He was now at ease and seemed to relish his role of guide and information bureau.

Chapin, now recovered, had put his time to good use by collecting some little black rails that seemed to belong to a hitherto unknown species. Picking up our beds and food, we hiked back to Las Fortunas, arriving just as the mosquitoes were reporting for duty. They didn't come in such swarms as at lower levels, but they were a bigger, deadlier species. We got to work on the nets and did a thorough job of covering the rents with adhesive tape. The reward was a good night's sleep.

Very early the next morning we returned to the shore to fetch our companions. While there wasn't room in Las Fortunas for six of us, the Indian told us of another cabin half a mile distant which could be reached "after a lot of work."

It took six of us, hacking our way through the jungle with machetes, one solid hour to open a path to the cabin. This accomplished, we all of us returned to Las Fortunas, ate our supper, and then Chapin and I, having agreed to take the smaller cabin, took our flashlights and went back over the newly opened trail.

Traps for small mammals were set out the next morning and plans made to climb to the summit of the cone to see whether it contained a crater; if it did, we wanted to know whether it was used as a nesting place for sea birds. The time limit was four days. Then the *Nourmahal* would be back to pick us up, Doctor Pool having decreed a physical examination after seven days ashore.

There was no trail beyond Las Fortunas. We followed a dry stream bottom, and the higher we got the denser grew the jungle. It was so thick one could lean against it, like the brush jumps of the Grand National. We hacked and hacked. In many places the land was so steep we had to crawl on hands and knees. This was thirst-producing work, but we had to go easy on the water in order to keep an ample reserve in case of accident.

After three days of hacking we were still far from the top. Disturbed because we hadn't procured our data, we returned to the shore and waited for the yacht.

The two Norwegians turned up at Cozy Cot. Both were under thirty, and both had a marvellous gift of survival. They had suffered a lot. Most of their teeth were gone; their skin showed salt-water boils; they were emaciated and burned from wind and sun. And the jungle had cut their clothes to tatters. Neither could speak English, but they knew Spanish and so did Kermit and Hay.

Things were bad, said the Norwegians, but not hopeless. Despite the death of their companions and the continuing misery, these dogged, tenacious Norsemen still believed, I think, that their fortune was just around the corner. They spent most of their time fishing. The fish was salted and then sold on Chatham Island, which had been an Ecuadorean penal colony and was now a trading post, restocked at intervals by a ship from Ecuador. Here the Norwegians obtained coffee, tea, salt, and other staples. They had saved a little money and hoped to return eventually to Norway and marry. Assuming that they planned to stay in Norway, the rest of us agreed it was a sensible aim. But the Norwegians made it quite clear they had no intention of remaining at home. Just how they hoped to persuade girls to come out to this sordid, tropical nightmare, they didn't explain.

But their immediate objective was the purchase of a motor-boat. They now had a small sail-boat, sturdily built, but unsafe, for a curious reason. The archipelago is in a "non-hurricane area." The weather is perpetually calm, and the winds are light. There is danger that a boat will lie becalmed for days, or that a current will toss it up on a rocky reef, smashing the bottom. There are many small islands devoid of water, and shipwrecked men could perish on them all too easily. Some years later, as we have seen, death overtook Lorenz and Nuggerud in this fashion.

About four o'clock, when the mosquitoes were gathering in force, the yacht hove in sight. In a few minutes it came near the shore and anchored. We invited the Norwegians and the Indian to come aboard. A launch was sent in to fetch us. The *Nourmahal*, de luxe travelling hotel, was an ingratiating sight, but no feature of it was more appealing than the case of iced German beer we found waiting for us at the gangway.

The scene on the yacht lingers in my mind for the contrast it provided. A return to the amenities of civilization is usually a gradual transition, but here the thrill lay in passing from jungle to comfort and luxury within a few minutes. The beer finished, I went into the cool cabin for a bath, a shave, and an orgy of tooth-brushing. I looked out the window at the sweaty jungle now receding into the thickening dusk. Something stirred behind me: it was a steward holding out a tray of frosty cocktails. Another steward was laying out my white evening clothes.

It was a merry dinner, with good food and champagne. The incongruity of the situation was emphasized by the talk about the days' experiences and plans for leaving the luxury and returning to the jungle. During the evening the Norwegians mentioned the famous giant tortoises and promised to point out their haunts.

Every member of the party joined in the next day's trip. The Norwegians, outfitted with new clothes from the slop chest, led us up a small trail, fairly free of underbrush, to a small pond filled with brick-red water. Here were tortoises so tame a baby could have caught them. We took several back to the boat alive. They were later turned over to the Bermuda Aquarium, the first ever brought back from the Galápagos. We also came upon the shell of a dead tortoise that must have weighed, as measurements revealed, four or five hundred pounds.

Early the next morning the land party, excepting Doctor Townsend who had work to do on board, started off to be gone five days. The Norwegians accompanied us back to Las Fortunas, where we spent the night.

Attempts to reach the summit of the cone were resumed. Three days of hacking with the machetes had yielded only a mile of trail opened up. Three days more took us up 2000 feet, but we were unable to reach the top within the allotted time. It seemed very doubtful if there was a crater at the summit. As for sea birds, we saw none at all. The climb was pronounced a success, however, by Doctor Svenson, the botanist, who had acquired many new specimens of plants. Hay had filled many a bottle with new specimens of insects.

Along the lower levels of the slopes we saw many evidences of wild mule herds. Their droppings came into view first, and later we heard them tearing through the bush to escape us. But we never laid eyes on them. The mules were not, of course, indigenous. Passing ships had put them ashore for one reason or another, as they had horses and pigs. We saw some of the pigs near Las Fortunas. They had turned cannibal, devouring some of our bacon that we had forgotten to hang up.

We saw many mocking birds and small hawks. The hawks were very tame, collecting around our camp to wait for crumbs, and never flying off at our approach. Once I took a stick and placed it gently on a bird's foot. Then I pressed upward. One foot remained on the stick, the other on the branch. I continued to press and the bird, placed in an uncomfortable position, removed his foot from the branch and put it on the stick. He remained on his new perch even when I walked around the camp holding him aloft.

We spent one last night at Las Fortunas and then, without regret, started back to the shore. The Norwegians and the Indian accompanied us.

In his final conversation with the Norwegians, Vincent Astor thanked them for their help and told them he would deposit enough money in a Quito bank to give them a motor for their boat and to pay for the cost of installation. They seemed overwhelmed by a gift that removed one of their chief hazards. Nevertheless, I had an impression they would never buy the motor: the money would go for something else. Two years later I heard that one of them was shipwrecked on a rocky island and died of thirst. I never learned the details of the disaster, nor the fate of the remaining colonist.

We spent another week cruising among the islands, collecting new specimens and enjoying the comforts of the yacht. We now had the tortoises, land birds, small mammals, and a rich collection of penguins, baby sea lions, turtles, and land and sea iguanas.

The penguins quickly became accustomed to the boat, and learned to waddle up the steep companionway to the bridge. The land iguanas, which belong to the lizard family, were easy to catch near the shore, for although they made for cover at our approach, we could always overtake them. They had a nasty bite, but we managed to keep them away from our legs.

There were large colonies of frigate birds. It infuriated them when we walked among them while they were nesting. They didn't fly away but held their ground, hissing in rage and blowing out their necks till they looked like balloons.

We also fished with rod and reel from a launch. Most of the catches were big groupers, often ruined by sharks before we could get them in. Left to themselves they could have evaded the sharks, but tangled up in our hooks they were easy prey. Kermit Roosevelt and Doctor Pool got a fine marlin.

Sometimes boobies followed our boat and darted down to pick up fish. On several occasions they mistook a red rag attached to our hooks for a fish. They got the hooks caught in their faces and we had a lot of trouble removing them. Instead of learning their lesson and flying off, they remained in the cockpit, eying us with calm contempt. We kept out of their way, for they had long, evil-looking bills.

While travelling through clear water in the launch we often saw sharks. A baited line was usually trailing from the side of the yacht, and one evening it caught a shark nine feet long. This news made the sailors jubilant, bringing out all their inbred hatred for the great prowler of the deep. But having no ready tackle, we could not haul in our catch till his blood-content had been reduced. We therefore riddled him with soft-nosed bullets from a nine-mm. Manlicher. Then he was pulled up and his tail removed with a hack saw. When this operation had been completed he was let down again into the sea. He darted off tailless and bloodless into the gloom, where doubtless some of his brethren devoured him.

There were many sandy beaches along the islands, and we were tempted to go swimming, but for fear of sharks we could never go in more than waist-deep. Even then the baby sharks constantly got between our legs. As a matter of fact, the water was teeming with many varieties of fish. In the darkness a pocket flashlight caught the reflecting gleam of their eyes, making the water seem alive with myriad emerald lights.

One morning we stalked a herd of sea-lions which were frolicking in the water near the shore. We wanted to capture a few young ones and examine the older ones at close range. The mothers and young were in shallow water; the fathers and adolescent males were out standing guard against the sharks.

I shall never forget the excitement when the males saw us descending from the dune where we had been concealed by the foliage. There were bellowing roars. The water churned as if a liner had suddenly run into the cove. The warning signals of the males seemed to say, "My God, what manner of enemy is it that steals up on us while we are watching for sharks? Better a *known* enemy than these. Every one dash for deep water!" And they all of them rushed for deep water.

At Charles Island we stopped for spineless cactus. Then we went on to Floreana, where we met the famous Doctor Ritter and Dore Strauch. They were having a stormy time of it. Transforming this hostile land into a decent habitation was hard labor. We saw their rain-proof shack, their plantain trees and semblance of garden, laid out with the signs of the Zodiac. One of their troubles was keeping the garden free from the marauding cattle that had been dumped on the shore by passing boats.

We gave the settlers of Floreana a supply of sea biscuit and vegetable seeds. Difficult as their life was then, Ritter and Frau Strauch had no inkling of the nerve-wracking tension that would later be their lot when the "Baroness Wagner" should arrive to establish her mythical kingdom.

At one end of Floreana we found the famous "Post Office Bay." A single post box dated back to the era of the New England whaling ships that sometimes stopped here. These ships were often absent for two or three years, and in a spirit of co-operation, homeward bound ships stopped at the post office to pick up letters deposited by out-wardbound ships.

Leaving Floreana, we made for the open sea and headed for Panama, stopping on the way at Cocos Island and the Pearl Islands. Cocos Island is supposed to harbor a pirate cache, and for many years adventurous souls have tried to locate its reputed treasures. One "red hot" rumor after another has incited new adventurers to make the trip. Near the beach where we landed were distinct signs of permanent habitation—substantial sheet-iron houses. But we found no human beings.

The Pearl Islands were inhabited by a Negro colony from Ecuador. We saw an orderly little village, but not one inhabitant; they had all fled to the jungle at our approach.

About five o'clock every afternoon came the feeding time for the animals. Some of them refused food. The baby sea lions would not accept fish, so they were given rations of Klim (powdered milk made up into a liquid) through a rubber tube. We had brought plantains for the land iguanas, but they refused to touch them. We had to work up a special technique of feeding. One of us would suddenly grasp them by the back of their necks. As they opened their jaws, raging and helpless, pieces of plantain were thrust down their throats with a stick. If it went down far enough before they tried to regurgitate, all was well. But usually all was bad, and up came the food. In trying this scheme Hay had his finger bitten to the bone.

We attempted next to throw the pieces of plantain down their throats while their mouths were agape. There were many misses, of course, but enough hits to make it a success. They were unable to expel their food, and the system was in good working order by the time we reached Panama.

At Panama the trip was practically over. The Galápagos, we agreed, are a paradise for the scientific collector—but for human beings seeking a home they are a living hell.

The Alps of Upper Burma

~~~~~~

Nᴏᴛ all travel narratives require a study of maps, but the reader of this account of an expedition to northeast Burma is strongly advised to orient himself with a few glances at that little-known region of Asia where the mountain range of Imaw Bum looks over at the Chinese province of Yunnan. The wide, empty spaces will serve as a reminder that this part of Burma's high hinterland is largely unsurveyed land. Topographically speaking, it is one of the most forbidding terrains on earth.

A tremendous upheaval of nature created an intricate fold of mountains and valleys, so steep in many places that even the most agile of pack animals cannot be employed. Much older than the Himalayan range, this country, eroded by the centuries, once subsided to a less jagged surface, only to be lifted up again with the rise of the Himalayas. The Burmese alps create the impression of having too many ridges and gorges for too little space.

So vertical is the whole region that few white men have ever visited it, and some of the sights described in this account were, as a matter of fact, never before beheld by Europeans. No expedition could ever hope to reach Imaw Bum without elaborate preparations and a large supply of food, because any attempt to "live on the country" would be, to say the least, wanting in prudence. The inhospitable terrain produces enough food for a small population—no more.

Only hardy peoples could survive in this bleak land, and the primitive Lisu, Lashi, and Maru, wresting a living out of the rocky land under the most trying conditions imaginable, deserve to be called "super hill-tribes." All three groups are of Mongolian strain, and while marked by many disparate traits, have a common denominator of superhuman endurance.

When, some fifteen years ago, a traveller reported having seen in this area an animal called "the black barking deer," a variation of the *cervulus muntjac*, there was no rush on the part of explorers or scientists to confirm the story. Travel conditions in the Burmese hinterland were too well known to encourage expeditions. At the end of 1938, no museum possessed a single specimen of "the black barking deer." Unlike the giant panda, of which synthetic specimens made of odd skins were available to zoologists before the first real specimen was brought back from Chinese Tibet, the rarest animal of the Burmese hinterland existed, as far as the outside world was concerned, only on paper.

When the Vernay-Cutting American Museum of Natural History Burma Expedition was organized, the newspapers of five continents pounced on "the black barking deer" as if it were the sole objective of the trip. Some accounts neglected to mention that the cervulus muntjac had already been described, that most encyclopedias had a word to say on the small deer with the long body and short limbs and neck, with the upper canine teeth extending out far enough to be visible when the mouth was shut. The peculiar belling of the deer has often been described as a bark, and the cervulus muntjac's alarm was a short, hoarse bark.

But we were after a *variation* on the cervulus muntjac that was said to have a black coat and a bark resembling a dog's. This animal provided one important objective, but after all, there were any number of other solid reasons why the Burmese hinterland deserved the attention of a carefully planned expedition.

It was virgin territory, and anything that could be learned about the human, animal, and bird life, to say nothing about the trees, plants, and flowers, would be a contribution to scientific data. As a matter of fact, it would take many an expedition to give the world an adequate idea of this remote land.

Ours was a superbly organized expedition. In addition to Vernay and me, the members were Doctor Harold E. Anthony, curator of the department of mammals, American Museum of Natural History, and two Englishmen, J. K. Stanford, ornithologist, former deputy commissioner of Myitkyina, Burma, and F. Kingdon Ward, who ranked with the late Reginald Farrar and the late "Chinese" Wilson as a collector and who thus remains as the outstanding plant-hunter in the world today.

Arrangements were made in advance to hand over the bulk of the collections to the American Museum of Natural History and the New York Botanical Garden, while a few specimens of small mammals would go to the Kensington Museum of London, a branch of the British Museum; a selection of plants would go to Kew Gardens, London, and certain data to the Bombay Natural History Society.

Arthur Vernay and the American Museum of Natural History used their good offices with the Burmese government to obtain a permit, and when all plans had been completed Vernay and I flew from Rome to Rangoon in four and a half days to meet the other members of the expedition.

December 12, 1938, found us together at Myitkyina, about 250 miles northeast of Mandalay. Myitkyina is the administration center for the area we were about to enter and the nearest approach to a city in this part of the world. Any one who has seen India would have found it a familiar sight with its large brown stone government buildings rising over the native houses of wood, thatch, and corrugated metal. Its trade and industry were concentrated in the sugar mills huddled down along the Irrawaddy River, and in the bazaar, active in all manner of cheap merchandise.

With its population of thirty or forty thousand, Myitkyina is a melting-pot par excellence. The predominant race are the Kachins, who claim an ethnological kinship with the Atsis, Chipwi, Maru, Lashi, and Lisu. Mixed in with these races are Shans, Gurkhas, Hindus, and Chinese.

Advancing into the hill country, following up the N'Maika, a large tributary of the Irrawaddy River

A group of Maru women at Hkam Hkawn. Those without the head-dress are unmarried

Lisu village at Kangfang. In the winter there is no agriculture, and the inhabitants have little to do

A group of Lisu girls. Usually cheerful, they are difficult to photograph in this mood

Three Lisu young men, and a girl (left)

The origin of the Maru, Lashi, and Lisu who inhabit the border country is a deep mystery. One school of thought holds that they filtered down from Tibet, another from China. Whatever the truth, wave after wave of migration has rolled over the land and it is still going on—not dramatically, with hordes moving en masse to find a new homeland, but quietly and effectively, with the more energetic tribesmen constantly on the alert for better lands. Nothing else could be expected, for Burma, an underpopulated land, lies between two of the greatest welters on earth: China and India.

It will take a great deal of investigation to determine the racial origins of these tribes and their relation to one another. The Kachins are fond of claiming affinity with the other races, but their evidence will hardly appeal to the anthropologists.

The genealogical tables in this part of the world ascribe the genesis of peoples to the mating of legendary heroes with animals. Thus we have "Chinhpaw Pawng Yawng took an alligator named Numrawng Jan Ja Khawng to wife." The result was a tribe. "Ah-Maw-i married a monkey." Another tribe! From these blithe unions of heroes, alligators, monkeys, and other animals, the Kachin pundits would have you believe, the various "Kachin peoples" developed.

Coolly disregarding the claims of the Kachins, many authorities believe that the Maru, at least, are an ethnologically distinct tribe. Wherever they came from, their language is akin to Burmese, and the opinion seems to be gaining ground that they were detached in some manner from the general Burmese immigration to the South.

The Lisu dwell near the Yunnanese border and there is something about their appearance to uphold the theory that the highlands of China were their original home. But on the other hand, their language is indubitably Burmese in character, and the Chinese, with their well-known absorptive talents, have never succeeded in swallowing them up. The word Lisu means "people who have come down," but where they lived before migrating to their present mountain fastnesses not even their own legends can explain.

The origins of the Lashi are still more shrouded in mystery. In cultural development they stand between the other two tribes.

Advance preparations had been made by Stanford, and after staying for a short time in the bungalow of Robin McGuire, the district commissioner, we rounded up the caravan, consisting of eighty or ninety mules, about fifteen muleteers, three cooks, three skinners, a mail runner, an interpreter, and two personal servants for each member of the party. The cooks were Indians, one of the skinners was a Mahratta from Bombay, and the other two were Burmese Eurasians, while the rest of the helpers were selected from local Lisu, Maru, Lashi, and Gurkhas.

My personal servants were a Gurkha named Lalaber Lama and a Lashi named Hpan Nala. The problem of pronunciation was solved when I was gratified to learn that the initial "h" occurring in so many regional words, to our ears was silent. Hpan Nala played his rôle with gusto, and he was particularly pleased with the new leather shoes, heavy woolly, and balaclava helmet we had bought for him. After a few days, however, the outfit struck him as a bit prosaic; so he fastened a huge rhododendron bloom surrounded by leaves to his helmet. From afar it looked like an airplane propeller, and for a time I was unable to rid myself of the notion that he might take off any minute. He was a comic little figure with his wide eyes flashing perpetual astonishment at the activities around him.

The last chore in Myitkyina was to obtain several heavy wooden boxes of coins—rupees and smaller pieces—from the Burmese treasury. The money was distributed through the packs to spread out the weight, but even so it was a sore trial, particularly later on, when pack animals were supplanted by porters.

A motor-car took the five of us twenty-one miles beyond Myitkyina to a dak bungalow (government property) where the trip really got under way. The first part of the route led toward the foothills (Irrawaddy-Salween divide) of the Burmese alps. We followed the River N'Maika, its bottom covered with rocks, and on both sides rose a solid mass of jungle, a foretaste of what was to come. This was tiger country, but there was no dallying because the expedition had more important objectives than pursuing game in country already covered by collectors.

Following the river, we travelled on a China-Burma trade route running through the solid jungle. With a stiff, crackly barrier to right and left, collecting was extremely difficult; unless a bird happened to land on or near the path our chances of retrieving it were pretty slim.

Here and there were small villages, clusters of hardwood frames, bamboo sides and thatched roofs. Sometimes they were pitched precariously at steep angles near the trail and around them were miniscular clearings for cattle and pigs. Houses and clearings were eloquent testimonials of the Lashi will-to-live. Dogged and indomitable, the short stocky little mountaineers had pre-empted land fundamentally unsuitable for either fields or dwellings, had determined to live there—and did.

The third day took us up to Seniku, a few hundred feet higher, where the jungle was denser than ever. The impenetrable lines of trees on both sides of the path made for a dreary march because there was rarely a vista and even the sky was visible only when one tilted the head well back.

The N'Maika at this point was a quarter of a mile broad and had many sandbars that would be covered later, during the rainy season. The trail, sometimes 100 or 200 feet above the water, twisted and turned about the bases of mountain ridges. We passed through the villages of Tanga and Tamu, sparsely populated, and saw a few caravan parties coming in from China. For every mile as the crow flies we did three.

A village called Chipwi introduced us to the wild-looking hill tribe of the Chingpaw, driving pigs, their precious jewels, along the trail. It was a dreary, anemic procession, with the men dressed in tattered clothes of blue Chinese cotton, streeling after their livestock. One saw worn brown faces, mouths smeared with betel. Now, leaving the river, we climbed steadily. The village of Laukang, for instance, was at 4300 feet. Then there was another climb over a pass at 7400 feet, and a dak bungalow at Pyepat, occupying an eagle's eyrie scooped out of a mountainside over 7000 feet up. All this climbing was prodigious work. The air was bone-dry, but the heat was enough to cause our clothes to become soaked with sweat. The nights, however, now grew cold, and it was necessary to bring heavier clothing out of the packing cases.

The miracle of the country was the absence of flat surfaces: steep gradients everywhere, with little visibility. Every step was either up or down. You could create a model of it by crumpling a piece of paper in the hand, relaxing the pressure, and tossing it on a table. Folds and creases, mountains and valleys—but try to find a level surface! Never had I seen a land so inimical to human beings. Nature seemed to have stipulated that even if man conquered desert and lowland jungle, this vertical terrain should forever repulse him. The human body was simply not constructed to cope with it. And yet the Maru, Lisu, and Lashi seemed to have defied nature in coming here. Whatever their hardships, the very fact that they remained provided a new insight into the adaptability of humankind.

The precariously placed bungalow provided a magnificent view of this stark land. Below was a contour of crinkled rock. Above was a vista of wind-swept hills, with Imaw Bum, bare, snow-covered rock, looming in the far distance. Imaw Bum, a long range with one white peak rising higher than the others, was the monarch of this region, the focal point of our itinerary. It could be seen clearly; the air was hard and bright with the vibrating intensity peculiar to high altitudes.

From our eyrie we mounted the precipitous hillsides in quest of animals and birds, and so thick was the vegetation that the natives had to precede us, lopping off the tough bamboo that made a crackling sound loud enough to scare off any wild life in the vicinity. We hauled ourselves up on our hands, all rather keenly aware that a slip and fall on a sharp bamboo stump would have put any one of us out of commission for the duration of the expedition, at least. Not a sight of game rewarded our efforts.

Morning broke with a chorus of gibbon monkeys chattering below the bungalow, but none was captured. Anthony, however, got a rare shrew, one of the fine specimens of the collection. The bird collection at this point was encouraging; we had specimens including shrikes, bulbuls, thrushes, pigeons, martins, hawks, and woodpeckers.

Many of the birds were brought in by natives who did their shooting with beautiful cross-bows made of mulberry, and slim, tough darts made of bamboo. Some of the darts were blunt-tipped for birds and squirrels; others were sharp-pointed and dipped in aconite poison for large mammals.

The government permitted the natives to own guns, but those we saw were usually ancient models, relics of the days when tribesmen used them for local warfare. Stanford said that when he was district commissioner, he had sometimes offered a prize for a gun that would actually go off! It was not hard to see why the cross-bow and dart were standard shooting equipment in the district.

The next objective was a village called Htawgaw; the trail led straight down to Langyang, still lower to the Ngauchang River, and then up for another of those stiff climbs on a steep trail, hemmed in by bristling jungle. In the early morning we heard masses of gibbon monkeys howling from the treetops. This was no place for a person with claustrophobia. The up-and-down trail was solidly barricaded by bamboo on both sides, and because it was constantly turning and twisting, the view to front and rear was limited. However, one could look up at the sky and reflect that even this blessing would be denied the traveller during the rainy season, when visibility would be still more curtailed.

Climbing up to 5600 feet, we saw Htawgaw, which seemed to have a population all out of proportion to the available living-space. But many of the people, it turned out, were visitors summoned hither by a Baptist mission to celebrate Christmas.

No sooner were we installed in the big dak bungalow, with our overflow put away in tents, than Frontier Officer McGuiness, who had left his post at Laukang to make a tour of his district, turned up with a goose that became the pièce de résistance of our Christmas eve celebration. The cooks did themselves proud on the dinner, and Scotch whisky brightened up the occasion still more.

Appropriate music was not lacking, for the Baptists had trained a number of local boys and girls to sing carols. It emphasized the remoteness of this land to hear "Hark, the Herald Angels Sing" coming from Lashi and Maru throats. The texts of the songs were written down in Chingpaw with the use of English characters; the tunes were clearly recognizable.

As a Christmas gift, none of us could imagine anything more desirable than a bit of news from the outside world, particularly on the recurrent European crises. Our radio was turned on after breakfast on December 25, but though London came through quite clearly there was no news. Dance music from West End night clubs floated over the Htawgaw air for a while and then there was silence. The difference in time was six and one-half hours, and London, now worn out with festivity, was going to bed.

We spent an hour or so at the Baptist school, where the natives did high jumping and racing and afterwards passed our tea, biscuits, and cigarettes. No white missionaries were present, but the local converts ran the show very successfully.

For the natives who came from far and near, Christmas had become a gala affair—even for those who resisted the proselytizing efforts of the Baptists. Every one wore his best clothes, and the women made a dashing impression with their ornaments of silver, brass, and shell. The Chinese influence was strong here and the *lingua franca* had a basis of Yunnanese. It was the old story: the Chinese tradition is to refuse to learn other languages, preferring to impose Chinese on other peoples.

All our staff except the cooks were given a holiday. We bought the servants three goats and they provided themselves with a supply of local girls. Goats and girls gave them ample opportunity for a merry Christmas.

Our own lunch came out of a special box labelled, "Not to be opened till Christmas." It was largely a day of "idling," meaning that there would be no climbing. In a comfortable, genial atmosphere each could arrange things for himself. Vernay was occupied with some detail of the caravan; Ward was industriously pressing plants, packing them up, making notes. The rest of us were busy with photography, journals, putting things in order. And this was the day, I think, that Anthony capitulated to tea. The coffee supplies had run short, a matter of little moment to the Englishmen, and to me, used to English habits. Anthony had felt differently and the morning tea had brought him no comfort. Now he suddenly pronounced it "really good when you get used to it." Yes, Christmas and the day after were comfortable, genial days, the relaxation all the sweeter because of the knowledge that the morrow would bring another perpendicular climb.

The morning of December 26 was devoted to a soccer game in which a team of native frontier police beat our impromptu team composed of the five of us with the addition of McGuiness and some of our men. We made one goal at the end, but I ruined the afternoon by straining a tendon, a nasty prospect out in this part of the world.

The rest of the day was spent more satisfactorily in collecting. One of Ward's finds was a plant that provides a valuable drug of the family *Ranunculaceæ*. Sent to China, this drug is much sought after, since it is considered a cure for any ailment.

On the march again—twelve miles to Hkam Hkawn. The trail dropped down to the big river, the Ngauchang. In the widening valley were larger villages than we had seen heretofore, and the Chinese influence was marked on the terraced paddies on the slopes. Here and there were elevated platforms where the natives spent the night during the growing season to drive off prowling gibbons, wild pigs, and barking deer of the ordinary species, which were quite common in the region. Each of these tiny fields took infinite labor and not a little ingenuity.

Again we came to Christmas, for the Baptists held native shindigs in the district every year, and 600 were participating in the Hkam Hkawn show, staged on a tiny, levelled-off field. A temporary structure had been put up for use as a guest house.

Our entrance was saluted by the merrymakers, who filled their guns with black powder and set them off with caps. They held the rifles about knee-high and turned away their faces, for the discharge made a terrific bang, letting off a cloud of smoke.

The show started off with a parade wherein the participants circled the field with linked arms. Then came a dance, with the males swooping about with brandished dhows, and a display of calisthenics in which we were asked to select the best team. The musical accompaniment for these events was provided by a band of drums, cymbals, and jews-harps made of split cane. Afterwards the women gave a demonstration of their weaving and basketry. The bamboo baskets were exquisitely made.

The native missionaries here had no illusions about the ardor of the celebrants. Very few were Christians, but since this was winter and they were not occupied with their crops, they were not averse to obtaining some of the free rice provided by the mission.

The tribes were mainly Lashi and Maru, with a few Lisu sprinkled in. We seized the opportunity to add to the photographic record of the trip, a pleasure under the circumstances, for the women of the three tribes, with their well-formed faces and light brown skins, had an arresting kind of beauty that recorded well on film.

The Maru women were out to make a good showing and many had gone to the length of taking a bath in the river. Their dresses were made of blue cotton cloth, produced in attractive designs and decorations. One common model had a broad white collar embroidered in green, red, and yellow, that passed over the left shoulder and then dipped under the right arm. The same embroidery on white cloth was used for arm bands and girdles. Headdresses made of the same fabric were either low, gracefully folded turbans or eighteen-inch tubular affairs resembling a certain kind of Tudor hat. If the profusion of silver ornaments counted for anything, the Maru were the richest of the three tribes.

The dress of the Lashi women resembled the Maru type but was carried out with less finesse, less sense of design. Their ornaments were more likely to be brass than silver.

The Lisu women often wore voluminous dresses of cotton, either blue or écru, with borders and sashes embroidered in elaborate patterns showing flowers, stars, circles, and swastikas, the usual color schemes being red, green, and black. Some of these costumes were extremely beautiful, judged by any standard, and it was easy to see why the Chinese called certain Lisu groups "Hwa Lisu"—the flowering Lisu, as a tribute to the women's innate sense of color and design. The ornaments were usually of beads, brass brooches, great brass earrings, rings at least four inches in diameter, and elaborate girdles made either of cowrie shells or small brass bells.

Chic and handsome, the women also exuded health. There were young, svelte ones, and middle-aged, buxom ones. All formed a sharp contrast with the men. It was not that the men were weaklings, for the continuous climbing had given every one of them a phenomenal development of thighs, legs, and feet. They could stand a lot. But their faces were worn and emaciated and they wore shabby clothes, often in tatters. The disparity in physical condition could have been explained if the women were slackers who stayed at home and pampered themselves; but the truth was they spared themselves no exertion, whether in tending crops or moving from place to place. In endurance they simply matched the men.

Leaving the celebration, we marched the next day along the Ngauchang River through much improved country. There was an increasing number of deciduous trees and pines, and many clearings had turned into terraced paddies. At higher levels now, the forest was thin enough to permit bare movement through the firs. There was many an entrancing view, a relief from the oppressive evergreen jungle of the lower country. Moving on toward China we were not far away from the Irrawaddy divide. But instead of continuing eastward along the China-bound branch of the Ngauchang, we turned north toward the river's source. Beyond this point there would be no more Public

Works Department bungalows but only houses put up by the natives for petty native officials passing through the district.

One more march, still on the China-Burma trade route, would bring us to Kangfang, which we proposed to use as a base camp. Along the trail many natives had industriously burned off huge plots of vegetation to make room for agriculture. Some of these areas were on almost vertical slopes; it was incredible that human beings could cultivate such ground. Throughout the region there was scarcely such a thing as a flat piece of land for building a house or planting crops. Sometimes one side of a building would hang over a yawning gulley, being supported by poles.

Twice that day we crossed the river on swaying, unsubstantial bamboo bridges, so common in southeastern Asia.

Kangfang, at 5400 feet, about 280 miles from Myitkyina, is a Lisu village with some twenty houses, of an average size of twenty by thirty feet. A few were as large as fifty by sixty feet and held several families. The roofs were of waterproofed thatch with no ventholes for the smoke. Yet in every house fires were built on the earth floor and the smoke, never swirling about the room, went straight up and sifted through the thatch to the open air. There seemed to be no conflagrations, which was a minor miracle when one remembered that the Nagas of Assam, who had evolved a sort of chimney affair, often saw their huts going up in flame.

In many of the dwellings was a special room designated as "the quarters of the virgins." One's first impression about the virgins was erroneous. Far from worrying about the protection of their daughters, Lisu parents encouraged promiscuity, and whether the special quarters held one or several girls, the bachelors of the district kept the path well beaten down. There was no secrecy about it and the sole concern of the parents was to insure plenty of visitors. As soon as a girl became pregnant, the men who frequented her were summoned and the first swain who owned up was forthwith snaffled into marriage. A popular "virgin" might have several opportunities, and would indicate her choice. Despite all the promiscuity, fidelity *after* marriage was the rule among the Lisu.

[310]

Our first step in Kangfang was to dismiss most of our mules, retaining only sixteen for emergencies. For the eventual return to Myitkyina, we would summon up what we needed. The second step was to enquire about hunting possibilities, particularly for takin and black barking deer. Six hunters were dispatched in different directions to scout.

Hours of sunshine were short in Kangfang—from 9 A.M. to 3:30 P.M. to be exact—because the sun was cut off by the China divide in the morning and by Imaw Bum in the afternoon. From 11 A.M. to 3 P.M. the wind blew furiously up and down the valley, which turned into a funnel, creating a fearful draft. The nights had heavy frosts too, and though we slept in our tents, hot-water bottles were put into the beds, and in addition we had a fairly comfortable community house of bamboo and thatch put up for us by the villagers after their own well-established pattern of building.

Our lines of traps, containing more than a hundred units, were set out with their usual bait of peanut butter mixed with meat fat. While waiting for the reports of the scouts, we settled down to an agreeable routine of work and reconnoitering the upper levels above the village.

Climbing the mountains emphasized the hard luck of the Lisu in drawing this miserable terrain from the human grab bag. Nothing could be accomplished without effort, and no prairie dweller could have endured the strain of drawing a livelihood out of this topsy-turvy world. Watching the thick-muscled thighs and legs one might have guessed that these people were so perfectly acclimated to the land that the constant up-and-down movement no longer affected them. Far more than the Lepchas, Tibetans, and Nagas, and even more than their cousins, the Maru and Lashi, they were a super hill-people, and yet their arms, chests, and faces showed that their labors pressed them almost to the limit of human endurance. In summer and winter alike the men wore the same thin cotton clothing; the only protection for their feet were thin grass sandals that covered merely the soles. No life could have equalled the agony of theirs, and the only mitigation was that they knew no other.

For us, these climbs were breathless, exhausting work, and always there was the tension of knowing that the next step might mean a fall. And there *were* falls—more than we could count, despite our spiked shoes. The spikes began to look like flat collar buttons, and our clothes were constantly being ripped.

There was ample reason to congratulate ourselves for bringing plenty of provisions, because living off the country would have been an uncertain affair. From time to time, it is true, we supplemented our rice with supplies obtained from itinerant Chinese traders. Eggs could be had and fish were plentiful, if somewhat on the tasteless side. After our cooks had made a kedjeree, we resolved to have no more of this nourishment in the abstract. Better things than that could be made out of our supplies of tinned meats, soups, vegetables, and dried fruits.

Stanford had a busy, fascinating time with new specimens of birds, many of them a delight to the eye with their bright, variegated plumage. The tragopan pheasant, one of the most beautiful game birds in the world, with shimmering red breast and brilliant markings of yellow, black, and white, was extremely common. Brought in by hunters who had snared them and demanded something in return, the birds were usually alive. The ingenious cruelty of the hunters was shocking. Strings were run through beaks, wings tied under the body, hips dislocated.

Soon the scouts returned with fresh takin droppings, discovered a two-days' march away, up some 2000 feet. The next morning Vernay, Ward, and I started to ascend to the region named by the scout. Stanford and Anthony remained behind either to hunt small mammals or birds or to follow takin tracks if other scouts brought back any affirmative reports.

No pack animals could have negotiated our steep trail; so twenty-five Lisu porters were loaded up with tents, beds, other equipment, and enough food to last a week, and the bitter climb to the higher country began. At the start we saw a great deal of cultivated land on the mountainsides. Clearing off the stretches of climax forest had provided a stupendous job for the Lisu, who were doubtless unable to imagine such a thing as flat land. Room for the crops was obtained by burning, and the primitive agriculturists, for reasons best known to themselves, abandoned the cleared-off tracts after one crop and never returned to them for at least ten or twelve years. In these abandoned clearings, known as *tania*, weeds and thorn bush sprang up immediately, to be followed by trees. A *tania*, if untouched, would again develop into a climax forest in the course of a century or two.

The "climax" is a forest that has attained its maximum development, its essential character. The fine, sturdy trees are the result of evolution and a long, terrific struggle for survival. Many kinds of seeds seek a foothold but only a few germinate; even those that grow face acute competition, for there is not enough room for the maximum development of every plant. In the long run, therefore, the tree or trees best suited to the environment will triumph, shutting out all the others. A climax forest is one that will never change except for some fundamental reason, such as another glacial age.

Beyond the cultivated areas the trail steepened sharply, pitched at an angle of sixty degrees and passing through solid jungle. It made the routes of the Naga country look like child's play. There were many deadfalls over the mountainsides, where the footing was precarious. After two days of little progress, we reached an elevation of 7100 feet, set up camp, and dismissed the porters, subject to recall.

Taking four members of our staff, Vernay, Ward, and I started to climb above the camp. We went through bamboo, climax forest, sometimes crisscrossing streams filled with rocks and boulders. All of us carried stout bamboo cud sticks, but every step had to be watched, particularly in leaping from stone to stone in river bottoms where a fall would have been dangerous. Our hands clung to stone ledges, trees, and bamboo. Often the ground was rotten from decayed vegetation, giving way under our spiked shoes.

Ahead of us went the natives on their grass sandals, twisting, bending, slipping, and always hacking away at the green bamboo. On the way up, one man made a prayer to a hunting god. Intoning his sacred words, he threw a bit of rice at the foot of a big tree and then piled leaves around it. The somber grove, a suitable dwelling for animistic gods, heightened the effect of the primitive scene.

After two hours of climbing, clutching rocks, slipping—by this time we felt fit enough for anything—we separated in order to cover the country more adequately. Since Ward could talk to the men in Yunnanese, he went with Vernay. I took the interpreter, Lupting, who knew some Hindustani, and one of the hunters.

I got on very well with the interpreter as we scuffled over the rocks on hands and knees, scratching our hands and faces. Heads only a few feet apart, we carried on a desultory conversation, clear enough when it was about hunting but slightly muddled when another subject came up, for the interpreter's Hindustani was interlarded with all manner of foreign words.

Three species of goat antelope—the takin, ghoral, and serow—had left signs that they lately had been in the region. We made altogether too much noise, but moving silently through the jungle would have been impossible. Often a hunter would point out spots where the takin had obviously been grazing. This country resembled the giant panda country and visibility was just as bad.

Meeting again at our camp in the dusk, the three of us had the same experience to recount: a day of terrific climbing had produced plenty of takin tracks but no takin. We realized now that a further hunt for the animal would not be feasible at this season. Though in summer he could graze above the tree-line—a good place to spot him—the snows of winter in the high, unprotected places would be too deep to permit his grazing comfortably and he would be driven down into the deep jungle where the snow, naturally, would be less deep. Pursuing him there was out of the question. The best we could do was to offer a reward to the native who would bring us a specimen.

Back at Kangfang we found that Stanford, acting on the tip of one of the scouts, had set up a temporary camp and had obtained a good Himalayan black bear. This animal was well known, but we were glad to have it nevertheless.

Rains set in while plans went forward for the next jaunt,

which would pursue a northwesterly direction toward Imaw Bum.

One day we took time out to stage an archery contest for our hunters, providing them with amusement and ourselves with a more exact knowledge of their skill. While a great crowd collected, three bull's-eyes were fixed to an inch-wide board; the archers, standing twelve yards away, scored a surprising number of hits. That day also saw an addition to our collection, a brown tufted deer (*cervus michie*) brought in by natives who had their dogs drive it into a clearing and then felled it with a dart.

With eighty-five porters, we set out from Kangfang on January 14. The first part of the route was almost vertical, a terrific task for porters carrying fifty-five pounds apiece on their backs. After the climb came a steep descent where we lost much of the altitude we had gained; then up again, much higher, and finally down to settle on a camp site. A rainstorm blew up and we were soaked long before reaching any spot big enough to accommodate all the whymper tents. These were strewn around on shelves and ledges of the hillside.

It was a somber scene with the rain pouring on the high grass, and the knife-edged mountains rising like unfriendly presences on every side. Before camp was ready, however, the rain ceased, and a fire was built near the large fly that served as our community house and dining room. Later the sun came out, and looking toward the east we had a staggering panorama of the great Irrawaddy-Salween divide. By five-thirty, blissfully dried out from fires we had lit, we enjoyed the sight of a table laid with napkins, knives and forks, butter, and Lea and Perrins sauce, indicating that a good meal would not be long in coming. Now, looking up at the perpendicular cliffs, we could see a wide world of green and azure.

Steeper and steeper grew the trail. The natives used it for travelling between the Lisu and Maru country, but even so our men had occasionally to hack away at the bamboo. Constantly climbing, we went through *tania*, now somewhat overgrown. There was a pass at over 8000 feet and a succession of mountain shoulders that finally led to a camp, set down in a dense forest. Although this spot was small and far from flat, it was the only possible site on our six-mile route. Even the natives found this country too steep for habitation.

Still upward we went, to Nyetmaw pass at 10,200 feet. The ground was covered with snow and the porters clutched at bamboo to save themselves from falling. Bamboo or no bamboo, the rest of us had many a spill. Near the top of the pass there were great tracts of jungle with the silver fir (abies) standing out here and there. White's primula, both the red and white varieties, and *rhododendron magnificum* grew among the trees and made a gay picture as we descended into a narrow valley.

A camp site at 9000 feet had been cleared of bamboo weeks in advance of our coming. In addition to arranging for this, Ward had ordered a community house of split bamboo. It was there, all right, but it was neither wind- nor rain-proof. In this cleared-off space there was enough room for our tents, but the porters were strewn out on ledges and in cracks, where they built themselves little lean-tos of bamboo and thatch. Fires became visible, perhaps fifteen or twenty of them, far and near. Sometimes the lapping flames could be seen clearly, but more often it was only a red glare sifting through the solid jungle. Wherever green bamboo was used for fuel, there was a recurrent noise like the muffled discharge of black-powder guns. The voices of the men filtered in from the distance, tired voices and raucous voices. It was like the camp of a bivouacking army.

The porters were still there in the morning; somehow I hadn't been able to shake off the notion that four or five of them would slide off during the night. But no matter how narrow the perch, they knew how to sleep on it. And at this point they were paid off and dismissed, for we were scheduled to stay here ten days. Miracles of survival, they lined up in the morning to get their money and rice rations. For twelve annas (about twenty-five cents American) and two pounds of rice a day, they had carried their heavy loads over this difficult country, had cleared ground, built their lean-tos, and rolled up each night in a single blanket. Far from being disgruntled with their lot, they were

Lisu man shooting his crossbow in the competition we staged

One of our Yunnanese pack mules. The muzzle piece is designed to interfere with grazing when travelling

Our mule lines beside the Ngauchang River, near Htawgaw

Floating Taiwania logs from higher country downstream to where they can be transported by coolie or mule to China

Crossing a native bamboo bridge. During the dry season small temporary bridges in a stream-bed serve

actually in a festal mood, for money didn't come their way every week and their usual rations were maize and roots with very little rice. Even the more prosperous toilers down in the plains got a ration of only one and a half pounds of rice a day.

Opposite our camp the mountains rose abruptly, a vivid pattern in trees. Bamboo (*dendrocalamus Hamiltoni*) predominated, but there was plenty of contrast between silver fir (*abies*) and evergreen oak (*pachyphylla*), between maple and crab apple. Here were larch and birch, and many different varieties of rhododendron. Snow covered the ground and it was easy to see that progress at the upper levels would be difficult.

I went out for two days but saw no hopeful signs of game. Below lay the Changmaw River with only a little water running over a wilderness of rocks, boulders, and blocks of snow and ice. Far down in the valley were spreading clouds of smoke, indicating perhaps that the Lisu were burning out clearings for their crops. It was an exhilarating landscape but certainly not one to detain the traveller after the collecting was finished.

This sector seemed to be a habitat of the small panda, and two skins were brought in by itinerant hunters. While there was no big game, the traps brought in a respectable collection of small mammals, including the large, steel-gray bamboo rats. Among the birds brought in by Stanford were three blood pheasants,* shot right on the trail. These were striking creatures, the size of a very large partridge, their grayish plumage splotched with lovely pink, whence the name blood pheasant doubtless originated. At this point our collection of small mammals had passed the two-hundred mark, while the bird collection numbered some six or seven hundred, including pigmy owls, bee-eaters, trogans, pittas, teals, sunbirds, bulbuls, shrikes, drongos, babblers, and pipits.

One day Vernay, Anthony, and I climbed to the ridge back of our camp, where at 10,800 feet there was a magnificent view of the Chimili range that divides China and Burma at this point. Our glasses, combing

*The New York Botanical Garden classified this pheasant and a trogan as new species. The former has been named after Mrs. Vernay and the latter after my wife.

the mountainsides as far as a mile away, revealed wooded and burned-off areas quite clearly, but there was no sight of game. Now and then, however, footprints of serow, ghoral, and the much desired takin appeared in the snow but none led to the animals.

The fires on the surrounding hills at this period began to look like something more ominous than legitimate clearing-operations of the Lisu, and suspicion fastened on the Chinese, who were active traders throughout the region, taking most of the furs obtained by the natives in return for a little cloth, salt, and possibly rice. Most of the trappers, as a matter of fact, were in debt to the Chinese. The latter, we figured, were probably starting or at least encouraging the fires to drive us out. If they were, it was a shortsighted policy on their part for we were bringing money into the district and most of it would probably slide through the loose fingers of the wretched natives into the pockets of the Chinese. A group of itinerant Yunnanese traders were summoned to the camp and told peremptorily to put out the fires, under threat of having their actions reported to the authorities at far-distant Myit-kyina. It took several warnings before the smoke ceased swirling up from the valley.

Now came a big moment in the history of the expedition. Returning to camp one evening, empty-handed, we saw a Lisu crouched over the dark form of a little animal. It was a deer with prominent teeth and curved antlers, and its color was a smoky-gray of a uniform shade. This was the famous crested muntjac: the black barking deer had turned out to be smoky-gray. The American Museum of Natural History would be the first to possess a specimen.

The hunter crouched quite motionless—but any assumption that he remained so quiet by his kill in full consciousness of having brought honor on the expedition would have erred on the dramatic side. The truth was he had simply brought in a deer, not a bit more important to him than any other animal that had been mentioned; but he had carried it on his back for several days from a distant crag and now he wanted his money.

The smoky-gray deer was in good condition, we were happy to

discover, and the newspaper correspondents would now be at liberty to call the expedition a success. Actually, its success or failure did not depend on one specimen, however important, but not one of us would have feigned indifference to the vagaries of those who had made this a barking-deer expedition. Anyway, there it was on the ground before us, the prize for which we had worked and struggled.

Only seven days of the scheduled ten had passed, but it seemed high time to leave this inhospitable territory where collecting was so difficult and where there was a real scarcity of game. The porters were summoned and it was agreed that Vernay, Ward, and I, in order to get a cross-section of the entire region, would skirt the northern side of Imaw Bum, while Anthony and Stanford would return through the same country whence we had come, in order to replenish their supplies at the base camp. In any case, we could not have remained on this spot after the heavy snows arrived, for the ground would then have been thickly covered till mid-May and in getting out we might have been forced to jettison much of our stuff, even the whymper tents. According to the Chinese, the snows would not come before the Chinese New Year, but that was only eight or nine days away and it seemed best not to trust in the Chinese affiliations of the gods that determined the local weather.

On January 24, Vernay, Ward, and I left the camp before the rising sun had penetrated the valley and began one of the most difficult marches we had ever experienced. The frozen trails were hard to negotiate and occasionally we slipped down slopes on our seats. The day's stop came at an elevation of 11,000 feet, only 2369 feet lower than the summit of Imaw Bum by the northeast face. Because of the mountain's contour to the west, the sun disappeared at 3 P.M.

The best we could do for a camp was a bamboo-covered ridge, twelve feet broad, and just long enough to hold a couple of tents. Vernay and I had to double up and the servants slept almost on top of each other. The porters, as usual, were spread out far and near on any roost they could find.

Temperatures of eight or nine degrees above zero would not have been surprising up here at 11,000 feet, but because there was more sun at this level and the cold air had settled in the valley, the thermometer on our ridge went no lower than twenty-one degrees for the night.

While the cooks were preparing supper we sat on the cud edge of the mountain looking at the view, never before beheld, Ward thought, by white men. By any count, it was one of the most stupendous sights in the world. Imaw Bum's steep slope was covered with dwarf bamboo and dwarf rhododendron growing up to 12,000 feet. Then gray-black rock—and finally the snow-clad peak, deepening to purple now in the reflected rays of the sunset. The tip was 13,369 feet above sea level. There is no record that it has ever been conquered; not even a native trail went any farther than our elevation, and to reach the summit will be no light feat. As for ourselves, we had no desire to use up the available time climbing a mountain instead of making a collection.

The vivid contrast between green slopes, black rock, and white cone disappeared in the fading light and soon the whole range yielded to night. We turned our attention to supper. By seven-thirty the fires were out and every one was rolled up for the night.

Having sun and warmth by seven o'clock made rising a jolly affair. Breaking camp, we descended over a fairly decent trail to the Sakkauk River, a drop of 5000 feet in less than five hours—then on to Kinche and Laktang where the valley opened, showing plenty of flat ground for our camp.

The Lisu greeted us in their usual apathetic way, but one of the villagers actually worked up enough enthusiasm to sell us a chicken. The fowl strongly resented the plan to transform him into a stew and took to the bushes, eluding capture till the owner fetched a bow and dart. And indeed, the tough spirit of this alpine chicken was unconquered even by hours in the pot.

The muddled interpreter took us out of our way the next day, and passing out of the Lisu country, we landed at a village called Rawng-aw, down in the Maru country. The type of building employed by the Maru was already familiar to us, since it resembled the

Lisu style. These houses, however, were much larger and better built. Frames were of hardwood, of course, but in applying the thatch roofs and bamboo walls, the builders showed the ingenuity that might have been expected of people whose lands were more productive and who expended less energy in wresting a livelihood from the earth than did their neighbors. Some of the buildings were as long as eighty or a hundred feet, and the sides, of contrasting hued woods, produced a pleasing impression.

Here and there among the houses were small bamboo platforms, raised on poles and used as receptacles for the sacrificial meat from slaughtered bullocks. The unfortunate animals selected as offerings to the animistic gods were led into a bamboo grove, and in full sight of the callous, unblinking spectators, were cut to pieces slowly and savagely. The horrible exhibition lasted a long time, but the killers seemed to enjoy it to the end.

In general, however, the behavior of the people here seemed to reflect their broader, more fertile terrain and the wider valleys that caught many hours of warm sunshine. Far less grim than the Lisu, they gave us a hospitable welcome, and before long they were opening their mouths in betel-smeared smiles.

It was a tranquil village, as spring planting had not yet begun. A few of the women were busy sifting, pounding, and milling maize, a process they carried on with incredible speed and dexterity. Others wove cotton cloth—obtained from local cottonwood trees—on their crude looms, and still others industriously picked fleas from their children's heads. Most of the adults, however, merely exercised the art of sitting, in which they were highly proficient. Pigs and chickens ran loose, and the squealing and crowing created a never-ending din. The chattering went on all evening, and even our porters, instead of rolling up into their coverings at 7:30, joined in the community life and for hours kept up their part in the hubbub.

But now it developed that one of our porters had had an accident the night before. He had spilled paraffine on his shirt; it had caught fire as he bent over the blaze near his lean-to and a dreadful burn had spread across his back. Never admitting it, he had taken up his load the next morning and had spent a day of excruciating agony. His act of fortitude was prompted not by greed for a few pennies, but by loyalty to his employers: he had hired himself out and would not let us down. After zinc ointment had been applied to his back, he was temporarily excused from duty.

One of the villagers gave a party that night and provided pork and rice beer for his guests. A good time seemed to have been had by all, for the celebrants living near my tent didn't return till midnight, and the loud chatter of men, women, and children stirred up a bedlam of squealing pigs, barking dogs, and crowing cocks.

An early-morning reconnoiter revealed that while photographing possibilities were excellent—the cloudless day gave us ample opportunity for filming the landscape and various village scenes—the outlook for hunting was dismal. The traps, however, yielded a memorable catch: a shrew with a different shaped head and shorter tail than any we had seen—and this, we decided, was a new species.

When the records of the expedition were tabulated, the shrew collection was one of its significant points. Unusual specimens were added from time to time, and not the least of them, a water shrew, was secured by Anthony at the end of the trip. This fine collection of soricidæ would never appeal to the general public, of course, as did the barking deer. It emphasized the fact once again that natural history museums and the expeditions they send forth are one thing for scientists and quite another for the general public. For the public must have glass cases with their habitat groups, pictures, slides, dramatic presentation. It may cost more than $10,000 to set up a habitat group of big mammals, and here the laymen who contribute generously to institutions of learning receive some return.

But the big cases and educational services conducted by the museums do not constitute the real measure of their value. The casual stroller never sees the genuinely important material in an institution of this kind. He might walk through the British Museum at Kensington and never realize that it possesses the largest collection of rodentia, some

40,000 small mammals. Again, it may mean little to the layman that Mrs. Harry Payne Whitney recently made it possible for the American Museum of Natural History in New York to acquire the unique and valuable "island collection" of the Rothschild Tring Museum in England. Thousands of birds, collected by scientists out of funds provided by a wealthy man, are now stowed away in the drawers of metal cases, safe from insects and rats. The public is scarcely aware of this magnificent acquisition, but for the scientist the museum's value has increased enormously.

If entertainment value is not the real criterion of a science museum, public hullabaloo is not the test of an expedition's success. The shrews were no less of a triumph than the gray barking deer.

For scientists the shrew has a particular interest, for it is an ancient inhabitant of the planet, existing, as we have learned from fossils, in the transition period between the age of reptiles and the age of mammals. The most primitive mammals were, of course, egg-laying creatures, but the next phase of evolution brought forth the shrew, a scuttling, agile creature that perhaps ended the age of giant reptiles. The tiny newcomer must have been a formidable adversary as he scurried around gnawing and destroying the monsters' eggs.

The early contemporaries of the shrew have shown a marked evolution through the ages. You have, for instance, the development of the three-toed horse into the solid-hoofed animal of today. But when you look at the 1940 shrew you see a creature that alone among the early mammals has practically never changed.

Mention the shrew to most laymen and they seem puzzled, as if it were a rare quadruped. As a matter of fact, it is a common animal in North America, in Europe, and everywhere but in South America. But because it might be taken, by a superficial observer, for a mouse or small rat, the very word is little heard.

But the shrew is emphatically not a mouse and not a rat. The latter two belong to the order of rodentia and the family of muridæ. On the other hand the shrew classifies in the order of insectivora and the family of soricidæ. In size, shape of body, tail, and feet the shrew does resemble the mouse—but there the likeness ends. Our little member of the soricidæ may be recognized by his prominent nostrils, long, slender, mobile muzzle, and very weak sight, for he has only tiny, rudimentary eyes.

Primitive in temperament, shrews are ravenous, ferocious little beasts who fight not infrequently among themselves, conqueror devouring conquered. Their ordinary fare is worms and insects (the wise farmer lets them alone because they do not, like rodents, attack his crops), and their tremendous appetites keep them constantly busy. They are nocturnal in their habits, cunning in their reactions. As a matter of fact, their name comes from the word "shrewd," and shrewdness, malevolence, and pugnacity are qualities long imputed to them. Peasants in the Middle Ages thought they were poison-carriers and avoided them like the plague. A strong, musky odor exuded by shrews has protected them from predatory animals. Now and then one is killed by a domestic cat, who usually repents her rashness and declines to eat the carcass.

If this much on the shrew doesn't persuade the layman to use his eyes and distinguish between shrews, rats, and mice, it should at least explain why the animal is worthy of study by the scientist, ever eager for more information on the development of mammal life. Having found the new species, we now waited till a companion specimen could be secured.

In the meanwhile Maru hunters appeared with two barking deer of the ordinary brown variety and we bought one just to encourage further search. The only good that came of it was an excellent dish of barking-deer liver. Soon after, the traps brought in the second specimen of the new shrew.

A bamboo raft, large and firm, managed with a bamboo rope, took us over the river. Here the natives, learning that we were in the market for animals, brought in a very valuable serow, but it had reached the stage of decomposition. They were told that no animals in this condition were accepted, but as an encouragement they were given two rupees. The villagers thereupon decided to have a feast, although the

Group at Htawgaw. Left to right: Stanford, Ward, Vernay, Anthony

Entering Maru country. Here there is sometimes a little more flat land

Typical Maru village, perched along the side of an escarpment

Our tents in a Maru village. Our three days spent here afforded us little privacy

A characteristic landscape. The further hills are all covered with climax forest

A campsite in climax forest. The uneven terrain in the foreground has had to be cleared

stomach of the animal, brought up from the river nicely washed, caused them to hold their noses.

It was a lovely spot, this river-bank camp, and, from Ward's point of view, one rich in specimens. The clearing sloped gently to the water and around it were terraced paddies. Beyond were groves of trees, some of them *terminalia myriocarpa*, 125 feet high, covered with red fruit. The floor of the forest was a treasure-trove of epiphytic growths, such as the staghorn fern and many varieties of orchids. The tree fern *alsophila* grew in profusion, and along the trails one saw great clumps of *crotalaria* with bright yellow flowers. This settlement was not identified on any map, but the natives called it Kitam.

The Maru showed themselves increasingly well disposed toward us. During the last few marches we had been employing them as porters, and to our surprise the women vied with the men in seeking jobs. Asking no special consideration, they carried the regulation fifty-five pounds for a full day's march and at the end seemed no more tired than the men. As a matter of fact, they introduced an element of hilarity into the proceedings. Not a few were good-looking and took great pride in their personal appearance. We gave them brass safety pins and pieces of silver photo paper to be fashioned into earrings, both of which were considered ravishing ornaments.

A few Chinese faces were also visible hereabouts, but they were less preoccupied with us than with our male porters. Like harpies they prowled about wherever they smelled money. The commodity they had to sell, we rather suspected, was opium.

At this point the Lisu porters we had brought up from Kangfang turned up inexplicably. They had been dismissed long ago with four rupees apiece, to return to the base without loads while we picked up squads of local people. Instead of going home they had dallied in the Maru country, probably losing their money to the Chinese, and now that we were ready for the return trip they appeared and ousted the Maru. It was all one with us.

On the other side of the Ngauchang River we came on an excellent mule road cut along the hillside above the stream. Natives equipped by the government with mattocks received a subsidy for keeping it in repair. A six-mile march along this smooth trail—a pleasant anomaly in the Imaw Bum country—took us through regions of burned-out hillsides, terraced paddies, strips of plantain and high weeds, till we drew up before a government hut at Kumaw. Then came nine miles over the good road to Chesen and another nine to Myawchawng, where the country was covered with a second growth over the old paddy burnings. Fourteen miles beyond Myawchawng we came to Laukang, which we had passed in December. The circle trip around Imaw Bum was finished.

The sixteen mules we had kept at Kangfang had been ordered back again to Laukang, and they were awaiting us now to carry the packs to Htawgaw and Kangfang. Eventually arriving at Kangfang, we found a note from Stanford: he and Anthony had found hunting unsatisfactory in the high snowy country of the Chimili range and were planning to descend immediately. They appeared the next day saying that the Chimili pass to China was closed with snow.

Considerable activity was taking place along the river near our camp as natives brought down planks of the famous taiwania tree to be transported into China. The monotypic *taiwania cryptomerioides* is no ordinary wood to the Chinese, who, with their enormous interest in burial ceremonies, esteem it above all other timbers, even juniper, for the making of coffins. The particular attraction of the "coffin tree" is its unique scent, an agreeable but not overwhelming perfume that lingers indefinitely. One of the world's rare conifers—unrelated, as a matter of fact, to all other conifers—the taiwania grew in the dense upland tracts north of Kangfang, not in clumps but in solitary grandeur like the mahogany. Because of its rarity and the great demand, the tree is becoming extinct. Transporting entire logs would be impossible in this region; so the woodsmen hacked down magnificent specimens with their primitive adzes and then, with an enormous wastage of chips, cut them into planks that could be carried conveniently to the river bank. The rest was easy. They were floated downstream while the woodsmen rode them, with the aid of long poles, in the manner of American lumberjacks. After reaching the caravan trail, a porter could carry one of the boards, a mule two. Thus on the long journey eastward they gained in value with every mile, so that only the rich could afford to buy them.

The rarity of the taiwania gave us a desire to photograph it *in situ*. Near a Lisu village, downstream from the camp, one immature specimen was found and filmed. It had evidently been growing some forty years and stood forty-five feet high. The trees eventually attain one hundred feet, and it is likely that they grow in altitudes up to 7000 feet. In addition to the photographs, Ward obtained chips of the wood, which were sent to Edinburgh for microscopic analysis.

The *trachycarpus Martiana* (the characteristic dwarf palm of high altitudes) also grew in this region, but it was so crowded by other trees that an adequate photograph could not be made. Photography in this country was no child's play. Not only were there such difficulties as this, but the uncertain light with ragged clouds obscuring the sun cost many an hour. So capricious were the skies that it was hard to predict the outcome of any picture. Clouds upset all calculations, and while spots might be bathed in sunlight for one minute at a time, others a short distance away might be enveloped in shadow.

And we were seeing the country in its best season! It staggered the mind to imagine it in summer, the rainy season, with a sodden curtain of low-hanging clouds. The deluges, the traces of malaria, the blister flies and land leeches that existed up to five or six thousand feet would torment the natives. The fate of the Maru, Lisu, and Lashi was enough to arouse any one's pity. If any traveller were audacious enough to enter during the summer he would probably never get any idea of the landscape, what with clouds obscuring the mountains and the virulent jungle shutting off all prospect at lower levels.

Luck, which had helped us once with the crested muntjac, came to our aid again in Kangfang when native hunters brought in a female to go with our male. This one was overdarkish, but the color may have been due to seasonal or zonal conditions. In any case the smoky-gray barking-deer triumph was complete.

Shortly afterwards hunters reported that a bull takin had been seen near the spot where Stanford got his bear. Offered twenty rupees to find it, they started out at once, taking a pack of dogs to help them hunt. Nothing more was ever heard of them.

Now on the point of changing our base camp from Kangfang to Htawgaw, we invited swarms of Lisu to a party, giving them 125 pounds of rice and some dried fish from our stores. In return for this, they performed for our film documentation. Freshly cut twigs served them as chopsticks and their benches were coffin-wood planks. If the magnificos who were to pay great sums for this wood could only have seen the casual attitudes of the natives on the cherished coffin tree!

After the meal there were dances, slow languorous movements, typically oriental, performed without music. The men danced alone, as did the women. It made a picturesque scene in the magnesium flares set off to permit photography. Our part in the celebration was over after the distribution of gifts—skeins of wool, buttons, earrings, safety-pins for the women, cheap cotton colored blankets and balaclava helmets for the men—but the party went on long after we were in bed. Native beer and community singing created a carnival atmosphere that went on far into the night.

Thunderstorms and more cold rain pursued us all the way from Kangfang to the confluence of the Hpimaw and Ngauchang. Here the weather cleared and we began climbing, until at 7600 feet we found a tiny Lashi village, the Hpimaw fortress, now abandoned, an excellent government bungalow, and one of the finest views we had seen. We were now close to the Chinese border. Far and wide stretched the jagged panorama, chains of mountains, and knots of valleys. The burn-operations of the Lashi had left many black blotches on the mountainside, but there remained vast areas of climax forest.

Throughout the trip we had been aware that our porters, wherever we hired them, instantly became the most popular men in the country as far as the womenfolk were concerned. Men who had the good taste to get on some one's pay roll acquired a distinct charm, quite apart from their personal graces. Payrolls were scarce in the country and few were the men able to bestow gifts, such as safety-pins and glass beads, on the ladies who coveted these treasures.

These observations received suitable proof one day at Hpimaw when a great clamor broke out in the neighborhood of the village. We became aware by degrees that five Lashi belles, togged out in the best finery the country provided, had pursued the men to Kangfang, and then finding them gone, had hit the trail themselves, undaunted by the steep slopes and rocky gorges. As gayly as antelopes they had followed the roller-coaster paths—and here they were, fresh as if they had merely crossed the street to solace the men. It was pleasant to record that the sacrifices of these stout-hearted ladies were duly appreciated, and they were in a cheerful mood the next morning when they consented to parade before our cameras.

After recording the local beauty and brawn on film, Ward and I started climbing above the camp. Signs that spring were on the way appeared on the lower slopes in the form of magnolias and rhododendrons in bloom. One rhododendron, appropriately named the magnificum, had crimson flowers and leaves fifteen inches long. Great conifers such as the Szechuan pine, hemlock, and juniper covered many areas, but others were bleak with deciduous trees now without leaves. Up to 9000 feet there was also the tree rhododendron, the sino-grande.

Up through the great soundless forest, where scarcely a bird broke the silence, we reached an elevation of 10,500 feet, topping the massive Irrawaddy-Salween divide, a region of silver fir broken here and there by rhododendron bushes growing along sharp ridges. Beyond the 9000-foot level there was possibly only one oak, the quercus pachyphylla. On the way down Ward found michelia, and schima, a plant related to tea and gordonia.

At a turn in the trail we came upon a curious sight. A giant coolie was descending with a prodigious double charpoi (native bed) on his back. A woman pattered along behind. Immediately we suspected Lupting, our interpreter, who had been a nuisance throughout the trip because of his insistence on taking a woman with him wherever he went, although it was strictly against the rules. The question of discipline aside, Lupting's amorous requirements were not a matter of moment so long as we were passing through inhabited regions, because then the porters could find solace among the unmarried women. But the forests were another matter. The presence of Lupting's woman could only remind the men of their deprivation and might easily have led to trouble. Knowing this to be Lupting's home ground, we had determined to dismiss him, but he was still on our pay roll, and Ward questioned the coolie in Yunnanese.

Beaming, nothing loath to discuss the interpreter's private affairs in front of the embarrassed woman, the coolie balanced the big charpoi and explained that Lupting had a fine house down in the valley, well equipped with wives and material pilfered from the Public Works Department after the fort had been abandoned. He also had a smaller house near our camp, and in order to be near his work and still have all the conveniences of home, he had brought up a wife and bed. This had worked well for a while, but Lupting was a man who loved variety. The bed was big enough for three, so now he was returning to the bigger house where life would be more colorful.

So thoroughly had the coolie explained Lupting's private affairs that the woman could stand it no longer; she took to her heels and in a moment was out of sight around the bend.

Returning to camp we found a native offering an ordinary barking deer for which we had no use. They were very plentiful in this country. On the other hand the traps had brought in an unexpected harvest of good specimens and the skinners were much overworked.

At the end of eight days the country was well explored and we set off for Hkam Hkawm, finding more signs of spring. There were beautiful slopes of blue gentian *denticulata*, and wherever the pear tree flourished the land was beautiful with masses of white blossoms. Soon it would be summer and the land would be impossible for white men. No other proof was needed than the dreaded blister flies that were just beginning to show themselves.

A runner had long since been dispatched to Myitkyina to have our original mules sent back to Htawgaw, since we were now on a caravan route. They arrived shortly after we reached Htawgaw, and after three days of reorganizing, we started off on the last circuit in order to see the Panwa and the Hparé country, lying near the Chinese border, which was rumored to be far more agreeable than any region we had seen. We were travelling lighter on this stage of the trip, for large parts of the food had naturally been consumed and large consignments of material, plants, animals, and birds had been sent to Myitkyina.

The mule train now headed southward along the Hkaingshang River to Luksuk, at 5200 feet, and Hparé, almost a thousand feet higher. The land was much less rugged, and instead of pitching camp on tiny shoulders of mountain, we now found ample room in beautifully rolling country. Burned-off patches alternated with dense forests, and many a stretch was brightened up with carmine cherry trees, foaming with red blossoms, and with gentian, turning the earth into a vivid blue carpet. Here also appeared rhodoleia. It was much warmer and the trails were only moderately steep. Farmers were now busy with their crops, ploughing both by hand and with the aid of the water buffalo.

In the Hparé country, Anthony, while setting his traps in a bush down near a river bank, saw a beast that looked like a village dog. By the time he had changed his mind and grabbed his gun, the animal had disappeared. It was undoubtedly a wolf, and as far as we were concerned, the old controversy over the existence of a Burmese wolf was settled, even if we failed to add a specimen to the collection.

The next march of eighteen miles, the longest we had done so far, took us through a lovely region of magnolia trees in full bloom and rhododendrons, forty feet high, that were apparently not going to bloom that year. These trees were valuable for their veneer wood. There was a stiffish climb through a bleaker region of burned hillsides, redeemed, however, with the bright surfaces of gentian, primroses, anemones, saxifrages, and dwarf rhododendron, several species of begonia, and an attractive fern, the dipteris.

The night's stop was made at Sukiang and from here we approached the Panwa pass, this region's entrance into China. A forest of bare, deciduous oaks, the *quercus serrata,* created the illusion of an English park, and because it was full of bird life, we stopped to collect pheasants. The trail led into meadows of varicolored alpine flowers, and alternating with the open land were forests of rhododendron trees, flaming red.

The Panwa pass at 7700 feet afforded a commanding view of the two countries. On both sides were the mountain ranges, covered, on the slopes, with evergreen. Meadows spotted with fir and pine—*pinus insularis*—loomed up here and there, and to the eastward lay Yunnan, a great cultivated plateau, broken by the tree-covered hills. It was an enchanting prospect, and one of its chief charms for me was the knowledge it could be enjoyed from afar with no descent into that swarming plain of filthy Chinese caravanseries that could, after ten years, still produce a twitch of revulsion.

A concrete block set up by the British was the only sign that this was a frontier, although the land now included in Burma is claimed by the Chinese. Worries elsewhere have kept the claimants from asserting themselves.

Camp had been set up within the Burmese border. Then began four of the most delightful days we had spent since the trip began. This landscape had its undoubted merits but perhaps any change from the toboggan-slide country would have been a pleasure.

A drive in the brush yielded some Stone's pheasants, and the cameras obtained some good photographs of the serrata oak and the glorious Père Delavaye rhododendron trees, overwhelming the country with red blossoms.

When the four days were over, Vernay and I, following our schedule, said good-bye to Ward, Anthony, and Stanford, who would return to Htawgaw and thence to Myitkyina.

This country was notorious for its earthquakes, but up to now we had escaped personal knowledge that they really took place. Before getting out, however, we experienced two of them, first a great rumbling and then a shock. No damage was done.

Lashi children sitting by our camp in the Hparé country

Lashi girls in Htawgaw

Lashi girls in Hpimaw. Two of them are carrying chickens they hope to sell us

The lovely Panwa country. Here for the first time we saw a really open landscape

Tree Rhododendron (*Delavayi*) in full bloom. Deciduous oak (*Quercus serrata*) at the left and in background

From now on the trail sloped downward. The country was beautiful with the bauhinia trees, everywhere a mass of white blossoms. After two marches we stopped to fish for the mahseer that give such good sport—one of the best in Asia. It was too early in the season, but heartened by catching two we continued on toward the hot plains of Burma. These were colorless, uneventful miles after the jagged country we had left. There were no longer great supplies to be transported, and two motor-cars at Seniku took us and the servants out of the Burmese hinterland back to Myitkyina.

If statistics could sum up the trip the story could be told thus:

Two smoky-gray barking deer;

One thousand and thirty-three specimens of mammals;

One thousand four hundred and eighty-seven specimens of birds;

Twenty-five hundred specimens of plants.

But as far as I was concerned, figures were inadequate to tell the story. From the Maru, Lashi, and Lisu came a new conception of the hardihood of human kind.

Ethiopia: Southern Journey

"We are trying to modernize this country. We want help from the great powers but not domination."—Ras Tafari, Regent of Ethiopia, September, 1926.

"Many powers, threatened with aggression and fearful of their weakness, have abandoned Ethiopia. May God forgive them!"—Haile Selassie, Emperor of Ethiopia, May, 1938.

THE first quotation represents Haile Selassie's thoughts when I first met him, fourteen years ago. These fourteen years have seen his evolution from the obscure regent of a backward African state to one of the leading figures in world affairs, and finally to a half-forgotten man living in the English countryside.

When I first met him, the little black ruler had not yet realized his life's ambition—to set Ethiopia's crown on his own head. But he was full of plans for the future. Patient and astute, he was seeking to abolish the feudal structure of the black empire and bring it more into line with European governmental systems.

Haile Selassie fell victim to the idealistic chatter of Geneva. He lived to see Italian legions trampling down the wild, undisciplined hordes of Ethiopia. He experienced treachery, on the part of his own chieftains, on the part of European leaders. Ill, soul-weary, he stood before the council of the League of Nations and fought his last fight.

"Whatever the world will do," he said, "my people will fight on

till they have forced Italy from the country or are themselves exterminated."

The last act in the drama of an independent Ethiopia brought back
to me, vividly and inescapably, pictures of the Emperor, of his fantastic capital, of the wild hinterland to the north and south—in the
days before Mussolini began translating his dreams into ordnance
and poison gas.

The prelude to my meeting with Haile Selassie or Ras Tafari
Makonnen, as he was known in the days of the Regency, was a large
engraved card delivered to the Imperial Hotel in Addis-Ababa. "Ras
Tafari, héritier du trône d'Ethiopie" invited me to present myself
at the royal palace at five o'clock for "an audience."

Ras Tafari was not then the highly publicized figure he became in
later years. The outside world knew very little about the black ruler
who was attempting to westernize the empire. Still, I had heard speculative conversations about his personality and prospects in New York,
in London, in Shanghai. And here was a chance to satisfy my curiosity.

But there was a better reason than mere curiosity for wanting to
see the ruler. I had come to Addis-Ababa in September, 1926, as part
of an expedition named by the Field Museum of Chicago, sponsored
by *The Chicago Daily News*, to explore the fauna of the black empire.
Parts of the hinterland had been explored before, but the data were
often fragmentary and contradictory. Both the museum and the newspaper wanted precise facts. In addition, the museum wanted specimens
of animal life.

To carry out this difficult assignment the expedition needed the
approval and co-operation of the Regent.

The venture had got under way several months before. *The Chicago
Daily News* had appropriated a generous sum for the trip. It named
as its representative Jack Baum, a writer and collector of larger mammals. The museum named the party's leader. He was Doctor Wilfred
Hudson Osgood, curator of mammals, a man of wide experience as
a field collector. The other members of the party were Alfred Bailey,
previously attached to the Denver Museum and now Doctor Osgood's

assistant, Louis Agassiz Fuertes, famous ornithologist and painter of birds, and myself. I was to make a motion-picture documentation of the trip and to collect big game.

The equipment for the expedition was carefully selected and sent on ahead. The members of the expedition sailed from New York early in September, and went by way of London, Paris, and Marseilles to Djibouti, the port and capital of French Somaliland. From here ran a bi-weekly train service to Addis-Ababa. The narrow-gauge railway built by the French made it possible to cover the distance in three days of eight hours each. In the old days, camel trains had required seventy days to make this desert journey.

On our arrival in Djibouti we found we had two days before the next train. We employed some of the time in getting permission to use the railroad's only private car.

The town at that season of year must have been one of the hottest places on earth. It said something for Bailey's and Fuertes' energy that they were able to travel out to neighboring oases and collect specimens of birds.

The private car looked like a second-class coach in Europe. As it jogged over the sun-parched African wilderness it seemed to us like a moving furnace. There was no dining car. The train stopped at wayside stations at regular intervals in order that native chefs might show us their versions of French cuisine. What they did to beef, chicken and vegetables would have made a French chef, even the keeper of a *gargotte* back of the Place d'Italie, throw up his hands in horror. The French colonial wine, however, was good. Scrupulously observing the directions, "to be served at room temperature," the wine waiters produced drinks that seemed to come from ovens.

The train didn't wear itself out with exertion. It started shortly after eight every morning and rolled on to a siding shortly after four-thirty every afternoon. In this way a twenty-four hour run was strung out into three days. It looked like a caprice of the engineer, but further investigation showed he had a reason: it was a single-track line and the nights were given over to the movements of freight trains.

ETHIOPIA: SOUTHERN JOURNEY

We spent our first night at Dirredawa, just inside the Ethiopian frontier. Nothing I had learned about confusion in travel prepared me for the madhouse of that little station. Ethiopians jostled, scrambled, engaged in screaming arguments. Many of the arguments ended in hysterics. It looked like the opening skirmish of a war. But according to a Frenchman standing near me it was all very ordinary. "They always do this," he said in a resigned voice.

Foreigners were pulled hither and yon by porters. Customs inspectors ripped open luggage in a fury, spilled the contents on the ground, and examined every object minutely. If they found anything of particular interest, such as a phonograph, a mechanical pencil, a flashlight, or a medicine kit, they pawed it with all the delighted incredulity of children. The foreign passengers complained bitterly that they were treated worse than natives. But this was untrue.

Watching this mad commotion we congratulated ourselves that we were equipped with a special pass, and that our luggage was all classified as scientific equipment. We were immune to the inspection.

The second day we again simmered in the heat. Our eyes grew weary from gazing out into the monotony of brown sand and green-brown bush. The day's stop was made at Hawash. Here we saw several Danakils, the fierce warlike race unconquered by the Abyssinians. It was fine game country, and we saw oryx, Grant's gazelles, dog-faced baboons, and such birds as starlings, kites, hawks, grackle, harriers, and whydad finches.

The third day the train began to jostle upward, reaching ever higher country. At four-thirty we reached Addis-Ababa, 8300 feet above sea level.

At the station we were met by our agent, a German-Ethiopian named David Hall. He was in good standing with Ras Tafari and his sister was a lady-in-waiting to the Empress Zauditu, Tafari's aunt.

There were motor-cars in Addis-Ababa. I daresay I had known this before I arrived, but the sight of them gave me a start. They seemed as incongruous as jinrikishas would be on Fifth Avenue. The agent put us and our belongings into small cars which chugged up the dusty hill from the station with all the speed of decrepit wheelbarrows. The natives ignored motor-cars. They walked in the center of the streets, carrying huge burdens on their heads, driving mules, jostling each other. No amount of honking could make them budge an inch.

The Imperial Hotel wasn't so famous in those days. It hadn't lodged scores of war correspondents who dwelt on its indifferent food and perverse bathing arrangements. I noted with satisfaction that three of its eight rooms had been reserved for us. Although its single bathroom functioned a little erratically, we each of us eventually got a bath, and the pseudo-French cooking tasted good after the products of the hinterland chefs.

Addis-Ababa, built by Menelik II, means "the new flower." To perceive the fullness of this, one had only to look out the windows of the Imperial Hotel. The city bore a certain resemblance to a cinema version of an American backwoods town of the pioneering era. The streets were straight and wide, lined on both sides with box-like houses fronted with tin and sheet iron. The native houses, called "tuckels," with their round thatched roofs, had been pushed out to the outskirts. Everywhere there was noise and confusion.

Nature had originally provided plenty of brush and acacia for the Addis-Ababa district, but the natives, needing fire-wood, made short work of it. To beautify the now barren land, Menelik II imported the seeds of eucalyptus from Australia and started planting operations on a broad scale. The trees flourished, and laws were passed to prevent the natives from cutting them down. The eucalyptus trees provided whatever beauty the Ethiopian capital could claim.

The town is situated at the edge of the south escarpment of the north or Amharic plateau. To the south the land drops gently. It is fertile and attractive country.

The first item on our program was a visit to the British minister. The United States in those days had no official representation in Addis-Ababa. We needed official assistance and the British minister was courteous in proffering it. He undertook to arrange an audience with His Highness, Ras Tafari.

The invitation to the audience arrived a few days later. We dressed in ordinary town clothes, which were considered suitable for the occasion, and then got into a Chevrolet to cover the short stretch of backwoods street that separated the hotel from the royal palace. The palace, a white frame structure, looked like the hotel in some small American town.

The outside suggested that the interior might be furnished with Grand Rapids kitchen chairs, that the walls might be covered with deer antlers. All the furnishings, however, turned out to be imitations of the pieces that fill European royal palaces. The reception room was pseudo-French—the sort of thing one sees the world over. There were chairs, tables, armoires—turned out, quite probably, by Czecho-Slovakian factories,—pictures, hangings, plaster casts of Greek sculpture, and gold bric-a-brac in the Louis XVI style, so dear to European monarchs. Many of the odd pieces had been presented to Ethiopian sovereigns by European governments. Among the pictures I noticed a portrait of Edward VII, a gift from England, and a good contemporary miniature of Prince Murat, sent by France.

After a short wait, a courtier announced that the Ras would receive us. We were led from the main reception room to a small throne room.

"His Highness, Ras Tafari, heir to the throne of Ethiopia!" chanted the herald.

There was a wooden throne against the wall directly opposite us as we walked in. On the throne was a little black man in black burnous, white, tight trousers resembling jodhpurs, and patent-leather boots. Small, delicate black hands were resting lightly on the arms of the throne.

It was a thin, sensitive, distinguished face showing an inborn sense of kingship. Keen eyes that looked neither to right nor left, but saw everything. Black skin, not the shiny black of the West African Negro but a dead, lusterless ebony, devoid of all Negrito characteristics. A black, civilized face. A straight, well formed nose. Curly black hair. The figure on the throne, so chic and soigné, might have stepped out of a painting by Bernard Boutet de Monvel.

So far not a word from Ras Tafari. In a nation addicted to excessive gabbling, he was one of the few who understood the value of the shut mouth. This was the man whose every waking thought was probably directed toward a consolidated empire with himself on the throne. As soon as his aunt, the Empress Zauditu, should die, he would take the throne and banish the old reactionary clique. A new era of centralization would begin. And finally Mussolini would make Haile Selassie one of the great tragic figures of modern history.

A functionary took his place beside the throne to translate Ras Tafari's remarks into English, for Ethiopian court etiquette decreed that only Amharic could be used for formal presentations. I wished that the rules had been less strict, for His Highness knew French and we might have had a direct conversation in that language.

European sovereigns are usually eager to display their linguistic skill. Outstanding examples are King Gustav of Sweden, a stickler for royal protocol, who will speak English, French, or German, in addition to the Scandinavian tongues; Queen Wilhelmina of Holland, who will meet visitors in any one of a number of languages without losing an ounce of her massive dignity; and King Leopold of the Belgians, who uses not only the languages of his own country, but supplements them with German and English. But Ras Tafari had other ideas.

"Did you have a good trip?" . . . "How do you like Ethiopia?" . . . "Yes, everything will be done to facilitate the expedition's progress." There was a series of questions. Nothing more could be expected with an interpreter in the way. Ras Tafari spoke in a low, carefully modulated voice. His manner was soft and quiet, but his personality projected force.

Fifteen minutes later we were leaving the palace, our main purpose accomplished: now properly inducted into Ethiopian court society, we could count on His Highness's aid. But we had learned nothing very revealing about the Regent.

The following days, spent in making preliminary arrangements for the trip, provided an introduction to the Ethiopians and the foreign colony in their midst. The foreign colony was sharply divided into two

Ras Tafari Makonnen, heir to the throne of Ethiopia, in his palace with his consort.
Later he became Emperor Haile Selassie

A typical street scene in Addis-Ababa. The parasol is very common
among Abyssinian women

Abyssinians and Gallas at an open air mart on the Arussi plateau

Galla dwellings of southern Ethiopia. The only light comes in through the door

classes: the diplomatic set and all the others. "All the others" usually meant soldiers-of-fortune and a few small business men. The small business men were often Greeks who came to the Ethiopian capital solely to make money. Maintaining no class distinctions, they consorted with the natives, and they wouldn't have drawn the line at the diplomatic set—if the diplomatic set had not drawn the line first.

The adventurers, while numerically unimportant, were a select collection of flotsam and jetsam, made up of Germans, Italians, Armenians, Greeks, and Arabs. There were fallen aristocrats, political refugees, creatures whose very faces bore the signs of shifty pasts. Miscellaneous species of females leavened the mixture. It was again a melting pot par-excellence, and the pot boiled right out into the street.

The diplomatic corps was a tight little hierarchy that avoided all traffic with resident foreigners not of their own set, and with all natives below the ruling classes. Having too little work, the diplomats were bored and restless. Life for them during the rainy seasons was "simply hell." At any gathering one could hear them saying, "The climate is impossible. White men could never colonize here." In the dry season, they admitted, the climate was excellent for tennis and garden parties. When the rains came there was nothing to do but play bridge.

A man who had acquired his notions about the relations between natives and whites in such places as India and Java might easily have formed erroneous conclusions about the Ethiopian attitude toward visitors. The Ethiopians let the stranger know they were a free people, possessing a civilization that antedated anything in Europe; they looked on whites with haughty indifference. All Ethiopians were not solidly grounded in their country's history, but for them certain facts were indisputable. The Queen of Sheba had been the sovereign of Abyssinia, and her son, fruit of her trip to Solomon, was Menelik I, supposedly founder of the royal Abyssinian line.

Christianity was brought to the dark empire as early as 300 A.D. By 330 A.D., Frumentius had been appointed bishop. Thus the Abyssinians were Coptic Christians of long standing. They had fought against the Mohammedan hordes that menaced all Christendom. In 1541 Stephen da Gama, the Portuguese admiral, became their ally against the invaders. Christopher da Gama, brother of the admiral, penetrated into the heart of the country, but lost his life in a skirmish with the wild natives. As in Europe, feudalism took hold of the country. They were taking a little longer to shake it off in Ethiopia.

What this catalogue of conjecture and fact really meant, no European could say. But it meant something to the Ethiopians. It proved they were a superior race. No bowing and scraping for them. If a white man got in their way, the white man might get a jolt in the ribs for his carelessness.

Considerable experience with primitive races has given me a leaning toward those who live at high altitudes as compared with lowland dwellers. Hill tribes, whether savage or civilized, always seem to possess a vigorous character, a dynamic concept of life. The Nagas of Assam, for instance, are a barbarous people, addicted to head-hunting, but all their actions reveal a sturdy pride of bearing that compels the admiration of civilized man. They are not addicted to deceit, treachery, mendacity.

The Ethiopians are an upland people. They are a branch of the Negrito race, but their high altitudes have made them a different race from the blacks we are used to studying—the slave stock that traces its origins to the west coast of Africa. Most Ethiopians are superb physical types. They are tall, stalwart, well proportioned. Their lean, sharply cut faces with handsome aquiline noses are not without signs of sensibility.

They have pride of bearing. Their worst enemies do not deny that they possess courage. But it was surprising to discover in them the shiftless, tricky, dishonest traits usually found among primitives inhabiting sticky, hot, lowland plains. This generalization, which naturally exempts many Ethiopians, particularly the leaders, was not made in a haphazard spirit.

My first experience with the common garden variety of Ethiopian came in the mule market of Addis-Ababa where we sought our beasts of burden. It was by far the worst bazaar I had ever seen. Bickering, quarrelling, brawling, hysterical accusations, and skullduggery were an integral part of the scene.

The Ethiopians were so addicted to litigation that the ordinary courts, set up in recent years, could not handle all the cases; so impromptu "kangaroo" courts were held in the streets. It was no uncommon sight for the visitor to see two men walking in the street chained together. He would first conclude, probably, that they were policeman and criminal. Seeing a few more he would think of chain gangs. But they were merely litigants. It was a common practice to chain plaintiff and defendant together, directly a suit was entered. They stayed this way, eating, strolling, sleeping together, for days, till the case was adjudicated. One might have expected with some reason that the propinquity would have made them murder each other. But the pairs I saw always seemed to be chatting amicably. Litigation was too ordinary a matter to cause any permanent hard feelings.

The Ethiopian penal code formerly contained even more fantastic punishments. A murderer, for instance, became the property of his victim's family. The family, needless to say, didn't coddle the visitor. They had the right to put him to death.

The more extreme forms of punishment were abolished by the Emperor Menelik II, the redoubtable warrior who defeated the Italians at Adowa in 1896. Menelik's reforms were continued by Ras Tafari, who abolished the practice of acquiring slaves when Ethiopia was admitted to the League of Nations in 1923. The existing slaves, most of them typical west-coast slave stocks, were not freed. Complete emancipation for them would have meant complete misery, since they possessed no land, no means of support. The slaves were well treated, and Ras Tafari had plans for improving their lot. The problem now belongs to the Italians.

Although most Ethiopians were inculcated with pride of race and muddled traditions of past grandeur, few had any real knowledge of their country. Few natives of Addis-Ababa had ever penetrated to the north or Amharic plateau, whose lofty mountain ranges provided so many difficulties for the invading Italians. Fewer still had ever seen the southern or Arussi plateau, inhabited mainly by the subject race of Gallas.

We spent several days trying to form our caravan. Litigating natives threw all sorts of obstacles in the way of acquiring a permanent personnel and pack animals. While this was going on, a second invitation, bidding us to dine, came from the palace.

At eight o'clock the small cars climbed the hill carrying Osgood, Bailey, Fuertes, Baum, and myself. We wore evening dress, as the invitation indicated. There was a short wait in the small reception room, already occupied by twenty other guests, and then a huge eunuch ushered us into a large reception room where the Regent and Her Highness Menen were standing against a window waiting to receive us.

The distinguished Ras Tafari, wearing the same beautiful, becoming costume as before, greeted each guest in turn. Most of them were members of the diplomatic colony and frequent guests at the palace. When my turn came, His Highness asked how our plans for the expedition were progressing. "I shall ask you more about it later," he said in French, keeping the line moving.

The charming little Empress-to-be had, alas, grown too stout—by seventy to a hundred superfluous pounds. Her fine features were already buried in layers of fat produced by overeating of sweetmeats. Her gown, made of layers and layers of white muslin, touched off here and there with diamond pins and clasps, had obviously been designed in Europe to conform to Ethiopian modes. Over this was a long, flowing cape of black silk. Her black, krinkly hair was piled high on her head in the mushroom shape favored by all Ethiopian ladies of high degree.

After the greetings came iceless cocktails, and His Highness kindly and graciously asked a number of questions about our progress.

The dinner was served in a large dining room furnished in the same manner as the reception rooms. Ras Tafari sat in the center of the table, Her Highness opposite him. Ras Tafari kept up an animated conversation with his neighbors, but his wife, seated between two Frenchmen and quite unable to exchange a word with them, confined her attention to her food.

Fish brought up from the Red Sea packed in ice had been turned into a thoroughly satisfactory performance by the French chef, who further distinguished himself by a frozen dessert. Wines were served and the only abstainers were the royal hosts. The table service, made of soft, hammered gold, two full sets appearing during the meal, represented a small fortune.

Foreign guests in the palace were always entertained with movies. This was a good idea, too, because the conversation, a round of banalities, was a strain on the nerves. We were ushered into a special room, the lights went out, and some mediocre travel adventures flashed on the screen.

I met His Highness many times later—at dinner and once at tea where he posed for photographs. He was ever pleasant in manner, soft in speech but reserved.

Troubles in assembling a caravan kept us in Addis-Ababa longer than we had anticipated. First the mule-market people asked exorbitant prices and tried to pawn off inferior animals. No sooner was this problem solved than a series of incomprehensible disputes disrupted our personnel. Order was restored by threats to sack every one, but we asked ourselves how we were going to manage these surprisingly truculent people.

The itinerary was now fixed. We would travel directly south from the capital and then work our way in a northeasterly direction, splitting into two groups at a certain point in order to cover as much of the Arussi plateau as possible.

As the caravan was taking off from Addis-Ababa, another furious row broke out. It was impossible to discover the causes of the commotion. Personal animosities doubtless accounted for some of the noise, and for the rest there seemed to be a difference of opinion on who should take on certain chores. Every man, of course, wanted something easy. Trying to arbitrate the differences according to our notions of justice would have been futile. We therefore threatened again to sack the whole lot.

Thirty-five pack mules started the journey. Some were for our use, eight were for the servants, and the rest carried baggage.

The first night brought excellent quarters at the farm of a German planter named Fritz Ehm, who had lived in German East Africa before the war and had since acquired property in Ethiopia. The next morning the trail ran through a country of good green grass and acacia trees, dropping down sharply toward the Hawash River. The heat was trying, but the beautiful country provided compensation. With our route now leading to the home of the rare mountain nyala, the black bushbuck, and other rare game, we had a feeling that we were really accomplishing something. And Fuertes, internationally famous painter of birds and a great ornithologist besides, was all set to acquire a monumental collection.

Beyond the river, a narrow, turgid stream, the trail rose toward the Arussi plateau. This was little known country and the sparse population was mostly Galla. Now and then a shepherd appeared, watching his flocks on the green hillsides. Or again, our caravan met travelling parties, mounted on mules, carrying rifles. These invariably caused a panic among our men.

Now came an introduction to one of Ethiopia's worst pests. Clouds, dense clouds, of tiny black flies swarmed everywhere, covering our faces from hairline to collar. Swishing them off brought only an instant's relief. The natives accepted the pests without a struggle, but we wore ourselves out brushing them off. It seemed better in the end to resign ourselves to the new face covering. If this land at 5000 feet had no other drawbacks, this one was certainly enough to give prospective colonists a pause.

A few more days brought us to an enormous, flat, upland plain, 8300 feet high. Desolate land, completely bereft of trees, it was covered with dull, green grass that provided good grazing for the Galla herds.

Beyond this country we saw off to westward a magnificent sweep of rolling, wooded country. The route thither led ever upward through Galla villages whose inhabitants ran out to stare at us, and the late afternoon brought us up to 10,000 feet and into a glorious forest of virgin sumac trees and wild fig, without any underbrush. Tussocks of Alpine flowers brightened the whole area. There were no flies, and the land held out hopes of wild game. The November night came on brusque and cold, but we bundled up in warm clothing and sat around a fire to eat our dinner of army rations. The invigorating air and the prospects for game had put us into a rare mood, and even the caravan men seemed to have improved, for the light of their own campfire showed them swaying back and forth with the rhythm of their chants.

To us the wooded heights and the masses of bright flowers looked even more beautiful the next morning while we prepared to hunt, but the men used their leisure to brood over fancied dangers. The Gallas, they were sure, plotted mischief. Now and then the Gallas did come, but on peaceful missions. They had no villages in the forest, but climbed up from lower altitudes, led on by curiosity. Their only arms were spears, but the Addis-Ababa boys were frightened. Several Gallas agreed to help us with the hunting. They were poor hunters, but their extraordinarily keen eyesight made them expert at spotting, stalking, and stampeding game.

The forest lived up to our expectations in the matter of game, for our collection got off to a good start with specimens of the nyala (which exists nowhere else but in this particular area), the duiker, and black bushbuck. Jack Baum also had the signal triumph of shooting two Ethiopian wolves, thus establishing for the first time the fact that the wolf exists in Africa.

While we were camped on the plateau, Osgood and I visited one of the Galla villages, a primitive colony of thatched tuckels, surrounded by a sea of sodden mud and cattle dung. No men were visible and I feared our arrival might alarm the women and children. But the women calmly and boldly walked up and took stock of the first white men they had ever seen. Our soiled, wrinkled khaki clothes and month-old beards, one red, one brown, obviously amused them.

The land around the village was very fertile and a little labor produced enough food for every one. Men and women alike had plenty of time to loaf about their filthy hovels, and loafing was evidently one of the things they liked best. The tuckels were thoroughly rainproof, a wise precaution, for during the summer it rained for months on end. There was only one opening to each tuckel—the door.

The women spent a great deal of time spinning native cotton cloth, drying leather, and, like the men, herding cattle. Whether they were working or resting, whether the day was hot or cold, the women ran about naked to the waist. While we were there, however, a few covered their breasts. These upland women were extremely bold in dealing with strangers, in sharp contrast with those of villages lower down on the trail who had gone scuttling into the bushes at our approach.

Our Ethiopian paradise was now spoiled by days of furious rain. Every time we looked out from our tents the view was a great sheet of falling water. Further hunting was out of the question, since no wild animal would have stayed out in such a storm; so there was nothing for us to do but stay in our tents. We utilized the time in the beginning by preparing skins, and packing up leg and skull bones. The forest had given us a good haul, for we had captured not only the big prizes, but many small mammals and such birds as turacos, redwings, redlegs, and parrots. Most of the animals and birds were rare specimens. Four days went by, and when the work was disposed of, the hours were filled with reading, eating, chattering, sleeping. Boredom was shattered by visits of Egyptian vultures, lammergeiers, and huge, thick-billed ravens drawn to our camp by the meat and bones of our specimens. The rain threatened to go on forever.

We were incredulous, then, to wake up one morning and find the sun shining in a clean-washed sky. Packing started immediately. It was at this point that the party split into two groups, and the occasion, we felt, justified the use of some of our "medicinal purposes" rum.

The Baum-Bailey-Cutting route would lead toward the Wabi Shebelle (Leopard) River, cross it, continue eastward, and finally turn north to join the railroad. Osgood and Fuertes would continue southward, trace a wide loop, and then return to Addis-Ababa.

Making our way over the great grasslands of the Arussi plateau, all at 8300 feet, we reached the south escarpment of the plateau and lost almost 2000 feet of altitude as the trail led to South Ethiopia. On and on we travelled, over great plains covered with coarse grass, euphorbia, thorn, and acacia trees. It was a lonely land holding but a few herds of cattle and villages of tuckels.

Soon we came to the lip of the Wabi Shebelle canyon and saw a rough and excessively steep trail. Slowly, painfully, we made our way down the rocky slope. The mules suffered desperately as the loads slid forward on their backs, causing abrasions. To add to their torments, many marauding crows arrived to peck at their wounds.

There was but one cure: cauterizing. This was a terrible operation, with the animal tied up, struggling, panting in agony, and the smell of burning flesh polluting the air. After this treatment it was generally a week before the mule could carry another load.

Arriving at the bottom of the canyon we encountered another nuisance. The recent rains had enlarged the river and it was too deep for the animals to wade through. The Gallas had a ready solution: wait for it to subside, which it certainly would do in a few days. So we pitched camp in a beautiful spot, with shade trees bordering the river and emerald-green grass covering the slopes. Hunting excursions produced nothing more than the bush pig and the dik-dik, a tiny antelope, scarcely larger than a hare.

The second and third days the water went down several inches, which seemed to indicate that one more day would bring enough recession to let us cross. But when morning came and the river showed a rise from fresh rains, it seemed that waiting was futile. A number of long poles were cut down and the kits lashed to them. Walking waist-deep in swirling water, the tallest men of the party crossed the channel of the river, and the heavy kits, far from adding to their burden, helped to steady them. The shorter men clutched at the poles for support. The mules were forced to swim over, following their leader, a white mare. Several shots were fired into the water to scare off stray crocodiles. This scheme was so successful that we regretted not having done it three days earlier.

Out of the canyon, we found ourselves still in low country, at about

5000 feet, where the flora was predominantly euphorbia and acacia. The little water we found was noxious, and once we were driven to take our supply from a dirty hole smelling of urine. Having boiled a kettleful of it and dosed it with chlorine and cocoa to kill the taste, we drank our fill.

As we got deeper into the Galla country, the caravan men became more tiresome with their alarms. Sometimes they chattered in chorus about the danger that awaited us at the crest of a hill, at a bend in the trail. The very sight of a harmless, unarmed Galla was enough to make them tremble.

Our interpreter was an Ethiopian named Lulu. In Addis-Ababa, he had cut a fine, strutting figure, but out here in the bush he was a complete coward. Once or twice we found him drunk and thereafter we watched our liquor supplies. Forced into sobriety, he became silent and morose. This meant trouble.

We put the caravan nuisance out of our minds and started to hunt. The collection was enriched by greater and lesser koodoo, oryx, water-buck, reedbuck, Grevy's zebra, gerenuk, and dog-faced baboon. One of the baby baboons having been captured alive, some one proposed that we keep it alive and give it to the Chicago zoo. The little animal, christened "Tinnish" (meaning "little" in Amharic) proved to be an unmitigated pest. In the morning he perched on our beds, making dry, droll faces; during the day he interfered with whatever work was in progress, while every evening he stole into the kitchen to exasperate the cook.

One morning while we were packing, all the caravan men went on strike. Their minds, permeated with so many time-honored prejudices, were now fired with the idea that the Gallas were planning an attack. They demanded that we return to Addis-Ababa immediately. Bored and bothered again with their nonsense, we curtly suggested they walk back, but we intended to continue the trip.

Lulu coughed and shuffled. He must speak to Ashagri, the head muleteer. He went off. His announcement was greeted with a few moments of stunned silence. Then a furious uproar. The very tones of their voices indicated that they had believed we would yield. In a few minutes Lulu came back and reported in a crestfallen voice that the whole pack of them had decided to go on with the trip.

Galla guides were another problem. Our men, not knowing the region, were useless at finding water, while the natives, despite the terror they inspired in the Addis-Ababa boys, were often too shy to approach us. As a result water became a growing problem. One evening we considered ourselves fortunate when a Galla was persuaded to serve as guide. Then, before he had indicated the local water-holes, he took fright and disappeared. There was nothing to do but wait till dawn and hope to secure some one from the village.

But when morning came our men jibbed at entering the village. Within sight of it, however, we saw Gallas peering at us from the bushes. Two of our men (curious bravado for such incurable snivellers) stalked one of the Gallas, threw him to the ground and tied him up.

The wretched creature was brought to us, trembling and shaking. He was sure he was now a slave; never would he see his own people again. Our explanation that he need only point out the water-holes to procure his release failed to reassure him, and he was a picture of dejection as he started off tied to one of our men, escorted by two others carrying empty rifles.

The village, hitherto quiet, was now in an uproar. Although Ras Tafari had stopped the capture of slaves, the villagers had a keen memory of times past. Besides, they had probably never heard of Ras Tafari and his laws. All the Gallas we had talked to on other and quieter occasions believed Menelik was still emperor. At any rate, they snatched up their spears to rescue their captured comrade.

They slowly surrounded us, keeping hidden in the bushes. We stopped, while one of our men in a loud voice explained the situation and asked for a parley.

Out of the bushes came a grizzled old villager. Everything was painstakingly explained to him. Our guide would be given something no Galla could resist—empty tin cans. The old man's eyes glittered. He and his son would guide us to the water-holes. The captive was released and scuttled back to the village as if he had escaped from hell.

The old man kept his word and we kept ours. Not only did he lead us to a water supply, but he provided a guide for the next day. Then with his precious tin cans he returned to the village.

Game was plentiful in this country. One day we encountered a large herd of oryx that seemed quite tame. Standing still, they allowed us to approach within a hundred yards; then, as we continued to move nearer, they did not take to flight, but moved off slowly, keeping their distance. Fortunately we did not have to shoot any because our oryx collection was complete; we could just watch. As for the dog-faced baboons, quite as bold as the oryx, the place was stiff with them. We spent one happy afternoon watching them splashing in the water, making comic faces and cutting amusing capers.

The country through which we were moving was uncharted. In Addis-Ababa they referred to it simply as "The Galla Country," while the only maps we had been able to procure did not show the land in detail, but merely referred to the vast land beyond the Wabi Shebelle as "the grasslands." These maps were rudely drawn affairs, made by late nineteenth-century travellers.

Passing through a desolate, drab, thorn-bush country, we found the streams had run dry, and the search for water became more difficult. However, the trail, curving northward, would soon recross the Wabi Shebelle.

The mules provided the next worry. There was no grain to be had and the grass was too coarse. As they grew weaker, our marches were slowed up. No other animals were, of course, available.

As our anxiety grew over the prospect of recrossing the Wabi Shebelle, we considered jettisoning some of our stuff. This was avoided, but the stiff descent to the river and the climb on the other side put such a strain on the mules that we were obliged to find a shady grove and rest for two days. A reconnoitering expedition produced two villages but no fodder. On our return we were greeted with bad news: the white mare, so valuable to the expedition, had died. She had merely led the mules, never carried a pack herself; but the exertion of crossing the canyon had been too much for her. The sufferings of the animals gave us a guilty feeling because our own provisions were more than ample. Plenty of game and wild guinea hen, so tough it had to be put through a mincer, augmented our stock supplies.

Beyond the canyon appeared a caravan headed south towards the large Ethiopian city of Harar, and we were glad to have this confirmation of our route because the guides could never be trusted.

Not many days away now was the railroad. Slow marches were necessary, however, because of the animals' condition. Rarely did we cover more than eight miles a day. One evening, after being absent from camp, we returned to find one of the mules missing. Lulu, shaking his head wearily, opined that he had probably slipped down into the forest.

Our men raced back through the night. The missing mule was particularly valuable because it carried our skins. Just at midnight a sigh from the bushes led to the poor beast, lying in an exhausted mass. How he had ever escaped prowling leopards and hyenas was a miracle. The rest had revived him a little, and now he was able to make camp on his own power.

The short marches during this part of the trip gave us plenty of time for hunting small mammals and putting out traps. One of these traps captured a hyena, but the animal chewed off the wooden drag and escaped with the trap. Another morning we found a drag lying in the grass and the trap missing. While we were examining the drag, a low growl came from the bushes a few hundred feet away. One of the caravan boys, named Waldo Giorgis, let out a cry: "A leopard!"

Drawing his knife, he plunged forward. The ordinary wounded leopard, unencumbered by a trap, would have made short work of Waldo. A leopard is likely to make a frontal attack on his victim. With one paw on each shoulder, he seizes the victim's throat with his jaws, while his hind legs disembowel the human prey.

We let out screams of warning but Waldo plunged on. We snatched up our rifles and followed, but before we reached the spot the leopard had pounced. Hindered by the trap, his aim went awry, but one claw passed over Waldo's forehead, cutting clear to the bone.

Bailey shot the leopard. Waldo lay on the grass, blood streaming over his pinched face. Suddenly, before a single first-aid remedy could be applied, he leaped to his feet, laughing. "He never got me!" Far from repentant, Waldo was proud of his wound. Though it must have hurt him terribly, he stood it in grim silence. For years he would be able to tell his Addis-Ababa friends how he had mixed with a leopard out in the wild Galla country. To complete his misfortune, a mule kicked him in the face that afternoon. He was an unbeautiful spectacle, wandering about for days with his head swelled up to the size and shape of an enormous pumpkin. No complaints, however, ever came from his lips.

It was a weary caravan that reached the railhead late in January. The animals were collapsing, and we three were sick from bad water. After a good feeding, the animals were put on a train headed for Addis-Ababa.

Under other circumstances Hawash might have seemed a wretched little hole. But now, after the Galla country, it was a civilized provincial capital. We were actually in a hotel with beds and shower-baths. And if Hawash was attractive, Addis-Ababa was actually a metropolis and the Imperial Hotel was full of good comfort.

We had fresh meat now that could be eaten without the ministrations of the mincer. There were sweets and plenty of chianti for meals; whisky and soda in the bar during the afternoons. It was a taste of high life, and not even the troubles encountered in forming the caravan for the second half of the trip—to the northern plateau—could dim our pleasure.

Ethiopia: Northern Journey

THE vast Amharic plateau stretches east, west, and north of Addis-Ababa. The terrain is a complicated pattern of mountains and mile-deep canyons. Between the peaks and the abysses are great rolling prairies, extending for hundreds of miles. All during the dry season a merciless heat beats down upon the land. The tough grass, however, survives sufficiently to permit grazing. In the rainy season these prairies become a morass. The Italian armies found out all about it during the late war.

Politically speaking, the Amharic plateau is the real Ethiopia. The Arussi plateau belongs to the empire, but, as we have seen, is inhabited largely by the subject Gallas. Although there is a vast number of Galla slaves on the northern plateau, the dominant race is the Ethiopian. On this great plateau, the Ethiopians have evolved their customs, their religion, their crafts, their primitive political economy.

The Amharic plateau has been little touched by the outside world. Neither Alexander nor Cæsar dreamed of trying to conquer it. It slumbered through the Dark Ages, and the Renaissance for the Ethiopians meant nothing more than the visits of a few curious white men. The turbulent Mohammedans threatened it seriously, but when the danger was past, the Ethiopians were left in possession of their Coptic Christianity and of their insulated minds.

The early history of Ethiopia is extremely confused. The records kept by the priests were all destroyed when Mohammed Gran, Moslem warrior from Arabia, invaded Ethiopia and burned the churches in 1540. But we *do* know that an early ruler, Menelik I (offspring of the Queen of Sheba and Solomon, according to the Ethiopian tradition), went far towards uniting the country. For centuries after, the country's history was a hodgepodge of emperors rising and falling, of civil war. The various provinces were ruled by minor potentates called rases. Each ras was jealous of his own power and it took strong persuasion to make them acknowledge the Emperor's authority.

The Emperor Menelik II, who conquered the Italians at Adowa in 1896, reunited the empire. But it was less his power than a series of geographic accidents that rendered Ethiopia immune to European encroachments during the era of colonial expansion.

When Ras Tafari became Regent he worked hard to strengthen the central government. Some of the rases, although reluctant to yield any of their power, realized that the only hope for an independent country was a strong central authority based on European models. But there were rases who couldn't see the point. A few were secretly hostile to Addis-Ababa. Thus Mussolini, the first conqueror to combine Ethiopian colonial yearnings with the weapons necessary to attain it, found a partially disorganized land, ripe for conquest.

When Haile Selassie said at Geneva that his country would fight on to the end, he was thinking, of course, of the Amharic plateau. For this is the real Ethiopia, and what the Italians achieve here will determine the future history of the country.

This was the land our expedition would cover as the finale of the Ethiopian journey. The five of us would start off from Addis-Ababa and constitute one party as far as Bichana in the Gojam. There Osgood and Fuertes would branch off to the northwest, while Baum, Bailey, and I would turn to the northeast, pass through Debra Werk and Mertola Mariam, cross the Blue Nile, pass along the eastern shore of Lake Tana to the important city of Gondar, and thence to the Sudan.

In certain ways the journey looked harder than the southern journey. More territory would be covered than on the Arussi trip. The land was more rugged, with higher mountains and deeper canyons.

The particular game we sought lived in remote and inaccessible habitats.

But to balance this, the Amharic plateau was more thickly populated than the land of the Gallas. Fresh mules would be available when we needed them. It would be easy to get food. Finally, the Ethiopian caravan men, travelling among their own people, would not be in fear of their lives.

Now came a fresh bout of trouble with the animals. Gaunt and exhausted on their return to Addis-Ababa, they required rest and plenty of food. The nagadis (professional caravan men) undertook to take them out to grazing lands just beyond the capital. But when they returned a fortnight later, they appeared neither rested nor fattened up. Some one had grafted a few pennies instead of getting proper pasturage. This boring situation had to be righted before we could go on.

There were difficulties about getting the proper permits and credentials to travel. The government was to provide us with introductions to the various rases. Without these we could not have travelled or hunted. Getting the necessary papers took time. Then there were vexations about money, a maddening situation since we were equipped with plenty of funds in the form of letters of credit. Notes issued by the Imperial Bank of Ethiopia, backed up by silver Mexican dollars—copies of the old Maria Theresa thaler—were acceptable only in the capital. Natives of the provinces were familiar only with the coins. We were obliged, therefore, to get a good supply of them, a bulky load.

But the money situation was only half solved. Small change was needed. This seemed enormously scarce and the merchants in the bazaar tried to cheat us whenever we proffered a thaler in payment for some article. An appeal to the mint finally brought us a supply of small silver and copper. Carrying the money sacks would have been a cruel punishment for any porter.

There was plenty of time to kill while waiting for the mules, money, and credentials, and in the main it was killed pleasantly. We went to dinner at the palace twice, to tea once, were guests at various legations, and saw a great deal of an English couple, Lieutenant-Colonel and Mrs. D. A. Sanford, who had a pleasant house in Addis-Ababa and a ranch at Mulu on the Muger River, thirty miles away. Since Mulu was on our route they asked us to stay with them while passing through.

It was arranged that Bailey, Fuertes, and I should start off with the entire caravan and cover the distance to Mulu in two stages. Osgood and Baum would leave later, and being unhampered by the caravan would make the trip in one stage.

The Sanford house was not big enough to hold us all, so we pitched camp on the lawn. We took our tea and dinner indoors, and we all of us, hosts and guests, made merry on the last night before pushing into the wilderness.

There was to be one high point to all our game-collecting activity on the northern plateau. This was the Wallia ibex which inhabited the northern edge of the escarpment where the plateau broke off into the plains of Italian Eritrea. This was a unique animal, to be found only one place in the world—the canyons of the Simien Mountains. We would be a long time reaching the Simiens, however, and in the meanwhile we would keep our eyes open for any other game that we might add to our collection of rarities.

Soon after leaving Mulu we were obliged to cross the Muger River, which lay some 2500 feet deep in a canyon. The distance from rim to rim was over four miles. Canyons are the curse of travel in Ethiopia, and nothing has been done to make the trails easier for man or beast. The government hired no road-workers, and trail clearing was left to individual caravans. It took us five hours in a zigzag course to reach the river. Here we camped for the night. The northern slope was simpler, and we got to the top in two and a half hours.

The first brawl of the northern journey (we were resigned to them by now) developed as we emerged from the canyon. A provincial guard snatched our passports and identification. He refused to return them. Then some provincial soldiers tried to confiscate the rifles from the Askari guard sent out by the central government to escort us. Shouting, screaming, and haranguing went on for an hour. Our threats to report the incident to Addis-Ababa finally settled the fight. And this country was under the direct rule of Ras Tafari!

Beyond the canyon we came into flowing, grassy country, intersected here and there by lofty ridges. The only trees on this plain, 8300 feet above sea level, were acacias planted in and around the villages.

Although sparsely populated with only a village of tuckels appearing every now and then, this country might have supported a vast population. The grazing was already there, waiting for flocks of sheep and goats, and a large part of the land was eminently suitable for wheat. Whether the white race could exploit this country was a constant source of speculative conversation. We did not know then that Mussolini was to find it a problem of consuming interest. If white men, it seemed to us, could have borne the heady climate and the rainy seasons that lasted for months every year and turned the whole land into a sea of mud—then its possibilities were enormous.

The villages of this region, whether inhabited by free Ethiopians or Galla slaves, were no cleaner than those of the Arussi plateau. Around the small, squalid tuckels, cattle roamed at will, contaminating the ground with their droppings.

Moving northward we occasionally found patches of upland jungle frequented by oribi (a little gazelle), reedbuck, civet cats, and jackals. There were also a few leopards. The traps, put out every night, often brought us civet cats.

Fuertes, equally busy with gun and paint-brush, had now acquired a formidable collection of pictures and specimens. Ethiopia was, in truth, a paradise for the ornithologist, and scarcely a day went by without a new bird coming into the collection. Even an amateur used to bird life in more northerly climes, where the bluebird or scarlet tanager is none too common, would have revelled at the richness of this collection, with all the brilliant, varicolored plumage. And how wonderfully Fuertes transferred them to paper! Now in the Field Museum of Chicago, they stand as a beautiful monument to one of the greatest artists in this genre that America has seen. Looking at them today, I regret that every expedition does not have a Fuertes.

We were now travelling in lordly country where the velvety, green hills reminded one of nothing so much as the Sussex downs. A forest would appear, then a wooded range, and sometimes a whole landscape would be dominated by one stark, forlorn tree, crowning a ridge.

The silence and the heady air gave one a particular sense of joy. It seemed—for no teeming city or jungle could have produced such a spacious sense of freedom—like discovering the earth for the first time. Only the high places of the planet can produce this sensation, as I discovered here, and later on the plateau of Tibet. There were no insects at this level; no wings fluttered around the candles in the cool evenings.

For camping sites we usually picked spots a quarter of a mile from a village. This was near enough to permit us to buy anything we required, such as fodder or food for cooking, but it was far enough away to discourage the villagers. True, some of them came to peek and ogle, but we were not as troubled as we should have been, camping in their midst.

Only once did they resent our presence. Or, to be accurate, they resented our "black magic." One night just before turning in, we sat in front of a tent listening to a phonograph record. Most of us were aware, subconsciously, that some one was skulking in the bushes. But furtive visits from neighboring villagers were too common to cause any special interest. Suddenly a long spear whistled through the air and landed—on the phonograph! The shattering sound stunned us all for a moment. Then we realized we were all safe and sound, and only "the black devil" was ruined.

The journey between the Muger and the Blue Nile was one of the pleasantest parts of the whole Ethiopian adventure. There were day after day of beautiful weather, beautiful country, and no untoward incidents. It took considerable fumbling, true enough, to put up those tents of ours, but I, for one, was long since reconciled to the fact that Africans have a poor technique with canvas, and that an African boy usually puts up a tent so that it falls down. Nor did I yearn too much for the smooth performances of Asiatics putting up tents under much more trying conditions, for all things were balanced: these Africans, inexpert with the poles and canvas, were much better cooks than the Asiatics. And again, once our brown lodgings were really up, they were a lovely sight against their background of green, rolling hills.

Every morning we rose at dawn and after breakfast stirred the lazy nagadis into action. Left to themselves they would have taken all morning to get under way. Under our prodding, they usually had the caravan packed by eight, and then we rode on for fourteen or fifteen beautiful miles, which was all the mules could do, with a day-after-day routine such as ours.

This left the afternoon for hunting. There was no big game in this territory but we caught many birds and small mammals. We saw no other travellers, although we were using the regular caravan route over which northern Ethiopia exported its hides and coffee to the Sudan. These highlands are reputed to be the original home of the coffee plant, but while other lands adopted it and exploited it to the full, the plant still survives in its old home, decorative with its lovely starlike white blossoms, a source of wealth to the people. In the state of Kaffa, appropriately enough, the plant grows wild.

The trail was now leading us to the Abbai or Blue Nile. I was led to believe that this stretch of it was unattractive and failed to live up to its name, but I must own it was a beautiful sight. The canyon's width from rim to rim was eight miles, and later our aneroid recorded a depth of 5000 feet.

The first day's march took us down 2500 feet over a steep, slippery, zigzagging trail. Both men and animals were exhausted as we reached the midway point, where we set up camp near a spring. The view from here was one of the great spectacles of Ethiopia. High above us rose the sloping, basalt walls of the canyon. Below, some 2500 feet, the river wound a devious course through the rocks. At sunset the whole canyon was suffused with a curiously vivid light that brought out the beautiful color patterns in the rock walls.

Next morning the trail became steadily worse as we descended. Near the bottom it was so steep and clotted with rocks that the exhausted animals picked their steps with the greatest difficulty. The air at the bottom of the canyon, untouched by the winds of the upland plateau, was tropical and sultry.

We saw as we approached the bank of the river that the water was low and easily passable. The Blue Nile at this point is infested with crocodiles, the largest species in the world. While it was unlikely that such a large party as ours would be attacked in shallow water, we took the precaution of firing several rounds.

On the far side we were greeted with another steep and rocky trail leading from one terrace to another. Halfway up we stopped and pitched camp. The next day we cleared the northern lip and marched several hours into fairly flat land. We were now in the province of Gojam, a country ruled by a prince named Ras Hailu. Nominally under Ras Tafari's government, he was actually an independent potentate. Moreover, he had no intention of yielding one inch of his authority: he was not a friend of Tafari.

Arriving in the Gojam, we were told that Ras Hailu was absent from his capital, Debra Markos, for this was the season he devoted to a tour of inspection. If we continued due north, we should meet him in the town of Bichana. Meeting him was important, because no one else had authority to give out shooting permits. Our letters from the central government merely recommended us as well-disposed foreigners. This probably meant little to a man of Hailu's temper: in the twinkling of an eye he could have sent us into the Sudan. We therefore set out for Bichana.

Rich and fertile, the Gojam was also one of the most beautiful of the Ethiopian provinces. More villages appeared than in any other part of the country. The sight of oribi and Gelada baboons in this region altered our resolution: we decided to shoot and to ask permission afterwards. The hall of primates in the Field Museum needed specimens of the latter.

Word of our coming had been sent on to the Ras and the result was a unique experience. Dazzling and splendid was the escort that came out from Bichana to meet us, commanded by Hailu's nephew.

Fifty soldiers mounted on big Arabian stallions rode along the road, stirring up clouds of dust. A hundred feet away from us they stopped and drew up in orderly formation. All the men wore white shammas (the togalike Ethiopian costume), while in the center rode the Ras's chamberlain, attired in a red shamma. Soldiers presented arms and their spears gleamed in the sun. This was the signal for a band concert, for in the throng following the escort were a dozen men carrying either bamboo flutes or ancient army bugles. The erratic, tremulous sounds coming from these instruments were, as far as I was concerned, something new in music.

Ras Hailu had selected a camp site for us and we were now led to it by the escort, the band, and a horde of townspeople. Our own nagadis were overcome by the welcome. Up to this moment we had been simply five white men out on a hunting jaunt. But if a great black prince paid us this overwhelming honor, we must be something very special indeed.

Our beautiful camp was in a grove of high eucalyptus trees, well away from the town. A large tent, which we decided to use for dining and sitting room, had been raised on a smooth expanse of green grass, and then, after the usual fumbling, our own smaller tents were raised around it. Dispatched to convey our respects to the Ras, our head nagadi returned with an invitation. Hailu wanted the five of us to lunch with him the next day.

A busy afternoon of chores was interrupted occasionally by the inevitable peepers and by people trying to sell us things. Hailu had done right by us in picking this site for the camp. Its principal attraction was the towering grove of eucalyptus trees, once more engaged in their traditional mission of turning otherwise commonplace spots into paradises. How much the world owes to this tree since Australia first began to export it to other continents, it is hard to estimate. One sees it now in California, in India, on the French Riviera, in Egypt, and Algeria. Its great height and long, greenish leaves adorn the landscape; it offers protection from the sun, while its volatile oils scent the air. And even when burned the fire sprays the air with fragrance.

Importing the trees to Ethiopia was one of the astutest things Menelik ever did.

Surrounded by the band, we were led the next day through the town and bazaar, where many in the gaping populace were getting their first look at white men, towards a village of white tents. Here Hailu had his headquarters.

The Ras had drawn up his bodyguard into two parallel lines; all the men dismounted. We stopped about two hundred feet away. Then the Ras, mounted on an enormous white Cyprus mule, detached himself from his bodyguard and rode forward, a servant riding beside him to hold a huge umbrella over his head as a protection from the sun. The splash of red umbrella and white shammas made a fine scene against the green of the eucalyptus groves.

We dismounted, and as Ras Hailu drew up before us, he too got down from the mule and bowed smilingly to each of us. A heavyish man of about six-feet-one, he had a handsome face, a good figure, and a facile charm that probably reflected an easy, wrapped-in-cotton-wool existence. There was a sharp contrast here between him and the delicate, sensitive Tafari.

Hailu, an expansive host, sat at one end of a deal table and conducted the luncheon with as much ceremony as if the tent had been a palace. The principal dish was cooked meat, a special concession to white appetites. For the other guests, the meat was raw. Hailu told us why:

"In the old days before Menelik II unified the empire [we wondered how much unity there would ever be, while rases like Hailu insisted on remaining independent] the country was constantly at war. Province against province, sometimes village against village. A campfire would have been a give-away. So no fires were built and no meat was cooked. Now we always eat it raw."

We applied ourselves to the cooked meat, merely reserving the thought that the Ethiopians may have had an appetite for raw meat even before they had an appetite for war. The meat was served with a fiery red sauce. It burned the mouth, so we gulped down flat, un-

Ras Hailu advancing to meet us. The village people line his avenue of approach

Ras Hailu, prince of the Gojam, in front of his tent. On his left stands his nephew

Mounted bodyguard of Abyssinians in attendance on Ras Ayala

An Abyssinian woman (with fuzzy hair) and her slaves

Abyssinian gentleman with his slaves, one of whom is acting as gun bearer

A village of north Ethiopia, situated at the southern slopes of the Simien Mountains

Galla plowing in southern Ethiopia. The plow is entirely of wood

Galla herdswoman of southern Ethiopia. Her clothing is made of leather

leavened bread and tedj, a mead made from the first washing of the honeycombs. The Ras's tedj was of excellent quality.

After lunch we examined each other's guns. Most of the Ethiopian rifles were of an ancient Russian make, large in caliber but carrying a small powder charge. To procure a gun, an Ethiopian had to have a permit. These seemed to be doled out sparingly. But with gun or without, all members of the gentry wore cartridge belts for decoration. They looked slightly absurd, since shell casings of all sizes and shapes were slipped into the loops. When we fired off our rifles for a demonstration, dignified, middle-aged men scrambled for the brass casings with all the glee of children.

During the next three days Ras Hailu came often to our camp and without the slightest difficulty could be persuaded to stay and share a meal. Noticing one day that our animals were in bad condition, he presented each of us with a new mule of good breed, better than any we had ever owned. Another day he learned that our caravan leader was about to abandon us, a matter that left us cold because another was certain to turn up. But the Ras, evidently feeling strongly on the subject, ordered the man to be brought in. A trembling, scraping nagadi appeared. Without speaking he knelt and heard the great man tell him he must, under no conditions, leave the expedition till it had passed out of the state of Gojam. Quaking with fear, the man was led away, never again to mention his desire to quit the caravan.

And now, to our great amusement, the Ras arranged a shoot for us.

From a circus point of view the shoot looked like a great success. The ruler was accompanied by hordes of his followers, all wearing floating capes, all carrying spears, all getting in each other's way.

The Ras's idea of a shoot was to have a servant carry a gun and a forked stick for him. Then as soon as game appeared, the stick would be speared into the ground, Hailu would take aim, would fire, and the beast would obligingly drop dead. I refrained from remarking it was hardly likely a beast would consent to pose till our great sportsman-king could dismount and get the range.

Like tribal headmen, surrounded by swarming dervishes, we rode through the bush. The hunting party was augmented by hundreds of townspeople on foot who rushed out to see their leader give a masterful lesson in shooting. Fortunately they stayed well in the rear.

We rode uphill, down dale, over grassland and through bushes. Then suddenly, emerging from a bushy area, we saw an oribi in a clearing. The light-brown form stopped dead against the green leaves. Every member of the shooting party stood still too.

It did not seem possible that the animal would pose, but pose it did. The little beast stood still, evidently too frightened to move. No beaters had been employed.

In the tense silence the Ras quietly dismounted. The fork was set up, the gun placed upon it. He looked into the finder and a little quiver ran over his long sinewy hand. To our amazement, the oribi that had stood still now graciously dropped dead.

Shouts of rejoicing and triumph rose from the throng. That was the way *their* chief did things! The animal was brought up and laid at his feet. He accepted the tribute in an offhand way, as if he had performed such stunts hundreds of times. By every path townspeople were coming up, and the affair, involving several thousands, turned into an impromptu carnival. The crowd started to dance, first here, then there, till the whole mob was caught up in a swirling ballet, accompanied by a chant.

The Ras pompously presented us with the oribi, and then, having had enough of the festivities, turned to go. We gave him a .22 rifle which he said he would give to his son. His business in Bichana was now completed and he would move on to Dima, where we would meet him again. At this point our party split up, Osgood and Fuertes heading west to Lake Tana, while Bailey, Baum, and I would go around the eastern shore of the lake to hunt the Wallia ibex.

The small town of Dima wore a holiday air. The high and mighty of the region had been invited to join the Ras, and they were now coming in with their servants, bodyguards, and mule packs. The countryside was jammed and the town was making a deafening uproar. I had never met a people endowed with vocal cords like those of the Ethiopians.

Cheered by the multitudes, the Ras made a colorful and triumphal entry. As soon as he had set up camp, he sent us an invitation to a luncheon he was giving in his big tent for the gentry of the region. Those of more elevated rank were assigned to low tables and low benches, while guests of lesser importance sat on the canvas-covered ground before tables only a few inches high. Again the Ras greeted us cordially, and since we had the status of old friends we were requested to eat our meat raw.

This time we did not jib at the burning sauce that came with it, for the raw meat, whether from a gustatory or health standpoint, was not much to our taste. We ate as much as the occasion seemed to demand, and tempered it with the flat, tasteless, unleavened bread and many cups of tedj.

The other guests were dressed in bright-colored shammas, indicative of their rank. Taking their own knives from their belts, they held strips of raw beef with their left hands and cut off what they required with their right. The food was consumed in leisurely, dignified fashion; the whole banquet, as a matter of fact, was conducted with extreme decorum.

But the habit of eating raw meat, however extolled by the chiefs, had done no good for the native population. Tapeworm was a common affliction and required huge doses of a homemade remedy. I never tasted it, but it smelled like a horse-purge.

At the end of the meal, a Coptic priest with a local reputation for great holiness slouched into the tent. He was a grizzled, old, tatter-demalion creature whose voice squeaked as he asked if he might pick up the scraps for the poor. Permission being granted, he did an obeisance to the Ras and made a little speech, beginning, "Thou, to Whom God hath given everything. . . ."

During this oration, the Ras looked bored and even a little annoyed. He didn't seem impressed with the man's reputation. But when the luncheon was over and we were all outside the tent, it became known that the poor were going to receive something better than the scraps from a prince's table. The people had heard that something was afoot, for they appeared in droves. I got permission to photograph whatever was coming off.

Hailu strutted up and down before the camera, calling for his servants to bring heavy leather bags filled with coins. He put a Maria Theresa thaler into many an outstretched palm. I wondered afterwards if the movie camera had inspired the generosity and if any of the palms would later be relieved of their treasure.

Late in the afternoon the visitors began to depart, and by seven the area was back to normal. Sitting before our tents waiting for the servants to serve our supper, we saw the Ras riding towards us on his white mule, accompanied by a guard. Asked to stay and eat with us, he accepted with surprised pleasure as if the idea had never struck him before.

One of his servants was an Egyptian Copt who spoke good French and Amharic; this insured a quiet, comfortable evening with the Copt acting as interpreter. From French to Amharic and back again, the Ras and I kept up a steady conversation.

It was not until the end, however, that the great idea of the evening saw light. Watching me intently, the Ras asked me how I liked the Gojam. I liked it very well and said so. A long discussion ended in an abrupt question: Would I like to remain?

Taking my bewilderment for consent, he went on rapidly, "I'll provide you with everything you need . . . land, cattle, slaves, yes, and even wives!" I thanked His Highness for his solicitude and asked his permission to consider his splendid, magnanimous offer. Rising, he urged me to think it over. Then he added, "And I liked those tinned cherries we had for supper very much."

Next noon he came again with the interpreter and we had more tinned cherries and more conversation about his offer. But first he had a word to say about the Italians. He reminisced gently about the first time he saw them. . . . It was after Adowa and his father had taken some prisoners. "I remember I was astonished because they were so short. Amazing! Such little men! And remember I was only a child."

He gazed into space. "The Italians, you know . . ." But he never finished it. I wondered if he was reflecting on the tanks and machine-guns with which the Italians made up for their lack of stature. "Those cherries," he said, "are very good. I like them."

I knew what was coming. Ras Hailu gave me a sidelong look. "Have you decided?" I thanked him again, and when he was gone wondered if he was offended, and if this was the last we would see of him.

While the servants were preparing for our departure next morning we saw Ras Hailu riding swiftly toward us down the glistening, dusty road. He was surrounded by his guard and a servant was holding an umbrella over his head—or at least making a show of doing so.

He seemed deeply moved at our going, assuring us the meeting had been pleasant for him and that he would never forget us. As a final kindness, he provided us with an interpreter who knew enough English to be of considerable help to us. Our own servants were commanded to serve us faithfully, whereupon they fell on their knees and kissed the toe of his left shoe.

When I heard of Ras Hailu again he had been arrested and thrown into the Addis-Ababa jail. The Italian invasion gave him a chance to escape. He made a deal with the conquerors and today he is a frequent visitor to Rome. A few days before Haile Selassie made his last pathetic appearance before the council of the League of Nations, Ras Hailu, attired in the peacock finery of Ethiopia, was brought into the enclosure at the Naples naval display where Mussolini and King Victor Emmanuel were entertaining Adolf Hitler. Hailu was an honored guest.

We now continued north in the Gojam to Lake Tana, passing through the towns of Debra Werk and Mertola Mariam, both of which had fine Coptic churches. Wishing to find some use for the interpreter, Baum took him to visit a Coptic priest in Mertola Mariam who had a reputation for great learning. When Baum returned he said the only erudition he had been able to pick up was that the sun circled the earth. The Coptic Church, one of the early schisms of Christianity, had seceded many centuries before Copernicus, Kepler, and Galileo revolutionized the astronomical world; so the pundit of Mertola Mariam, still loyal to fourth-century doctrines, argued against Baum's "heretical beliefs."

Passing beyond the cities, we found ourselves in one of the most beautiful stretches of the north Ethiopian plateau, a high rolling plain about thirty miles wide, hemmed in by the Choké Mountains. The air was clear and sparkling, and there were good forests and pasture lands, watered by frothing, gushing mountain streams. Yet the country was sparsely populated. The Ethiopians had ignored one of the finest, most productive lands in the empire.

In this country, as in many parts of Africa, salt was so scarce that bars of it were used as currency. We had provided ourselves with a supply of these rock-salt bars about ten inches long, bound in grass to protect them from friction. In this form they were never consumed, never broken up, passing from hand to hand as standard currency. They were useful in procuring wood or fodder from the villages.

The only blight on our enjoyment of the scene was the fact that we were soon due to recross the canyon of the Blue Nile. The river, after leaving Lake Tana, traces a big bend east before curving west to the Sudan, which explains the necessity of crossing it twice.

We adopted the same procedure as before. The canyon at this point was perhaps a thousand feet shallower than when we first encountered it. At the water's edge we saw a bridge that looked like a modern triumph of engineering but showed itself on closer scrutiny to be several hundred years old and of European design. This was a relic of the Portuguese mission to Ethiopia, carried out in the sixteenth century by Christopher da Gama.

It was the period between 1528 and 1540 when the Mohammedan flood threatened Ethiopia. The Emperor appealed to the Portuguese, who responded with an expeditionary force. The Islamic leader, the famous Mohammed Gran, was killed, and as a reward the Portuguese under Christopher da Gama were allowed to settle in North Ethiopia, imposing Roman Catholicism on the Coptic Christians. Da Gama's death at the hands of an assassin ended the mission and concluded the Portuguese era. The country reverted to the Coptic faith, and today the bridge is Christopher da Gama's principal monument. After four centuries, it stands sturdy and solid with its massive arch formed of stone blocks, not a part of it showing signs of disintegration.

This stage of the trip brought joy into the life of Tinnish, the little baboon we had captured on the Arussi plateau, for now he was joined by three Gelada companions, also destined for the Chicago zoo. Tinnish tormented the newcomers but he didn't escape without a few maulings himself. All the baboons had a merry time climbing trees and hopping on our beds. There were times when we felt tempted to exterminate the lot of them.

The trip across the canyon brought us into the domain of another regional potentate, Ras Guksa of Amhara. Across a wide grassy plain, 8600 feet high, we rode through Mahedra Mariam and then passed the Gumara River flowing into Lake Tana. The land then fell abruptly, until at a point 6500 feet high we came to the provincial customs.

The head customs inspector was a brawny, surly black with fine features and a dull ebony complexion. Like all the natives of the area, he had a certain haughty pride that set him apart from the slave type of black we are accustomed to deal with. He announced curtly that our passports were no good. We couldn't pass. He held the passport upside down but refused to admit he couldn't read his own language. A general row ensued and the inspector threatened to shoot. We insinuated that if there was to be any shooting we would do it.

To clear up this tiresome situation, Jack Baum had to ride all the way to Debra Tabor and interview Ras Guksa. Twelve hours later we were on our way and the balky inspector was taken off in chains to face the Ras's fury.

A few days brought us to the shore of Lake Tana, where we camped at a level of 5700 feet. The approach to the lake was over an almost flat, colorless plain. About forty-seven miles long and forty-four miles wide, Lake Tana is the reservoir for the Blue Nile. At this point the river's right to its name became apparent. A curious dark silt, almost indigo in color, saturated the water and made a distinct path in the lake.

It is not likely that Lake Tana will ever become a tourist center. Neither its banks nor islands are particularly attractive. The water abounds in crocodiles and hippopotamuses, and the land around it is flat, marshy, and malarial. We actually saw the malarial species of mosquito.

Here and there around the shores could be seen that fluffy-topped plant, the papyrus, indigenous to Egypt but more likely to be found now around the source of the Blue Nile. It stands as one of the sign-posts of human progress, for not only did it supply food, firewood, and utensils, but it was finally turned into paper and awakened men's minds to the value of accumulated knowledge.

Passing beyond the southern and eastern shores of the lake, we came to higher land. Then, after covering miles of dull, unfertile territory, pitching camp several times near small villages, we came to the large city of Gondar, 7200 feet above the sea. Not far beyond was our goal, the Simien Mountains, stronghold of the Wallia ibex.

We camped for one day below the ridge where Gondar is situated. The city itself was simply a colony of thatched tuckels jammed together along dirty, narrow streets, a regular rabbit warren. But this was the capital of another great ras; so we had to stop over. A guard escorted us to a gigantic stockade, a short distance from the town. Beyond the main gate we passed into a series of inner stockades, all swarming with retainers.

Ras Ayala came forward to meet us. He was about two inches shorter than Ras Hailu, older, and somewhat heavier. Like most of the Ethiopian leaders, he had handsome, clear-cut features. Over cups of tedj we assured him we were satisfied with our camp site and would like him to lunch with us.

He came and comported himself like a perfect guest. But he lacked the magnetism of Ras Hailu, and the conversation resolved itself into a round of banalities. Leaving, he promised to stage a military show for us.

It took place the next day. The Ras rode between two imposing wings of his bodyguard, each man carrying a spear raised aloft. Behind came a secondary guard of splendidly mounted warriors. Riding at full gallop over the plain, stirring up clouds of dust, the white shamma-ed horsemen created a vivid scene, with the inky sky of an approaching storm for their background.

When the review was over we rode out on the plain to visit two large stone forts, relics of the Portuguese occupation. Although completely abandoned and overgrown with brush, the towers and courts were still in solid condition. There was a good water supply, explaining why the Portuguese had picked this particular site.

The next afternoon we reached another large town, Devark, at 9200 feet. Two more marches brought us up nearly a thousand feet higher into the Simien Mountains. The date was March 21, and yet some nights the temperature registered twenty degrees Fahrenheit.

In this isolated mountain land we encountered one of the most curious peoples on earth—the Falashas. With their origins wrapped in mystery, they claim to be one of the ten tribes banished from the Holy Land. There seems to be no question of their being Jews. Their physiognomies support their claim. But when and why they came to this remote corner of Ethiopia is still a disputable point. One theory is that they were driven from Judea when Jerusalem was destroyed in the time of Vespasian or Titus. Another is that they left Jerusalem voluntarily in the retinue of Menelik, son of Sheba and Solomon.

Whatever the explanation, you see in the Falashas a Jewish tribe that has maintained its religion and folkways intact through the ages. Their skin is black, of course, and they are somewhere taller in build than the Ethiopians who surround them.

Living in villages of their own, or at least in separate quarters of the larger towns, the Falashas practise a religion of pure Mosaism. They celebrate Jewish feasts, slaughter their animals according to the ritual, read the Old Testament, and refuse the raw meat favored by their neighbors. At the same time they know no Hebrew, dress as their neighbors do, and speak Amharic.

Our principal preoccupation now was the Wallia ibex. One afternoon we spotted goat droppings at 11,200 feet, our highest camp in Ethiopia.

This craggy land of the Simien Mountains was difficult shooting country. We were on the edge of a vast escarpment where the northern plateau breaks off abruptly and subsides into the seacoast plains of Italian Eritrea. The Simiens were crisscrossed with formidable canyons, the precipices thousands of feet deep, sometimes almost as straight as a plummet line. Ras Ayala had said we could never negotiate the terrain, and his suggestion had been "local people because they're so nimble on their feet." They were nimble on their feet but not so nimble with guns. We had a shoot which settled our minds on the matter.

Never had I seen shooting grounds more perilous than these vertical canyons. Day in, day out, we followed game trails along rocky precipices, so steep that there was barely room for one man to cling to the wall. Below yawned the chasms, so dark and deep that their bottoms were lost to the eye. One false step and the hunt for the ibex would have ended in another world!

On the steep slopes we could hardly see our footing. The barefoot natives were, of course, adept at this. Wearing spiked shoes we could not keep up with them. The surface was covered with a coarse, slippery grass, well matted and bone dry. Sometimes when we were unable to get a foothold, a native would twist strands of grass into a knot that we might grasp with our hands.

Baum, Bailey and I usually went in different directions, thereby enlarging our chances for getting game. One night we spent deep in the canyon.

The ibex, according to our guides, was most often to be seen in the dawn or dusk. Although we had come to disbelieve them, this notion sounded plausible. We had hunted in broad daylight with hardly a glimpse of the elusive animal, though we had tried to make ourselves utterly inconspicuous. Bushes and tree lobelia provided good observation posts, and our khaki clothes had received a protective coloration from brushing against trees and plants, while our topi hats had been camouflaged by Louis Fuertes. But as the daylight hours produced nothing, we concentrated on dawn and dusk.

Bailey actually killed an ibex, but it happened to be perched on a slope and toppled off into a chasm whence it could never be retrieved. From this time on we all had more glimpses of the animal. There were long, arduous stalks ending in defeat for the hunters, but the time came when we shot five animals, making a good representative collection for the museum.

Down in Gondar once more, we encountered rain, and knew that the wet season would soon begin. We were out of it just in time. As we moved northwest the land dropped steadily. It was now like ordinary East African game country with many waterbuck and hartebeest and tracks of buffalo, but never a sight or sound of lion.

The frontier was a veritable no-man's land. This country had been raided so frequently by the shiftas (Ethiopian bandits) that a strip of land many miles wide on both sides of the line, never too well defined, had been abandoned.

Here it was, by sheer coincidence, that we ran into Osgood and Fuertes. In separating we had agreed to meet either in Cairo or Khartoum. Travelling on together, we reached the Sudanese border, identified by a dry mud channel that in the rainy season would become the Gallabat River. Here we pitched our last camp and ate our last meal out of the camp supplies. The altitude now was only 2100 feet and the days were very hot—110° Fahrenheit being nothing exceptional.

The next day, leaving all our natives in camp (there was a regulation against introducing Ethiopians into the Sudan because it might cause fighting), we crossed the Gallabat River channel. We hadn't proceeded far when we found a border patrol, composed of one white officer and fifty native troops—the Sudanese irregular force. When on duty, these men were mounted on camels.

There was another white man in the district, too—the head of the customhouse.

Formerly the border patrol had been commanded by two white officers who lived in one house, ate their meals together, fretted over the heat, and ended by quarrelling incessantly. The villainous climate had frayed their nerves thin. The present commander and customs inspector lived in separate thatched bungalows, dined in each other's houses on alternate nights, and rarely saw other whites. They promptly asked us to eat with them.

A bath, drinks, and a dinner of chicken combined with various tinned delicacies was a little foretaste of civilization.

Returning to our camp, we paid off the Ethiopians and dismissed them. Sudanese troops transported our luggage to lorries. A motor-car took us to Gedaref, across the desert, to Wad Medani, and on to the point where we caught the train for Khartoum.

We realized that the expedition was definitely over when the moment came to say farewell to Tinnish and his Gelada companions. They were headed for the Chicago zoo, and the last I heard of them they were thriving in their new home.

Indexes

The dense, impenetrable bamboo. A Lisu cutting the way for Stanford

Temporary shelter put up for us by the Lisu in the Nyetmaw camp

The first black barking deer. The Lisu hunter holding its head brought it in

General Index

GENERAL INDEX

Irkistan, 61 ff.
Irrawaddy River, 108, 115, 124, 300
Irrawaddy-Salween Divide, 302, 309, 315, 329
Ishke Kizak, 64
Italians (in Ethiopia), 334 f., 343, 355 f., 368 f.

Jamal Shekh (cook, Sinkiang and China expeditions), 4, 6, 70, 108
Jangmed, 242
Japanese-Chinese War, 32, 216
Jarawas (Andamanese tribe), 249
Java, 267 f., 341
Jews, in Ethiopia, see Falashas
Jhelum River, 5
Jo-Kang (Lhasa cathedral), 222
Jung Bahadur, 156, 160, 165
Junge Abad, 55

Kachins (Yunnan tribe), 113, 115, 120, 300 f.
Kaffa, 361
Kala, 188
kalak (Kirghiz turban), 18
Kalimpong, 178, 188, 329
Kalmuks (Mongol tribe), 47 ff.
Kalmuk wedding, 52
Kalön Lama, 216, 231
Kānchenjunga, 153, 230
Kangfang, 310 f., 314 f., 325 ff.
Kanjygan, Mt., 61
Kara La Pass, 202, 223
Karachi, 3
Karakash River, 19
Karakorum: Mountains, 12, 60; Pass, 4 f., 16 f., 56, 59
Kargelik, 23 ff.
Kashag (Tibetan Supreme Council), 179, 211, 216, 226 ff.
Kashgar, 29 ff., 54 ff.; River, 61
Kashmir, 3 ff.; Maharajah of, 10
kata (Tibetan silk scarf), 185, 191

Katha, 107 f.
Kathukonosh River, 65
Katmandu, 151 ff., 163 f.
Kaulan Ku, 68
Kazaks (Mongol tribe), 42 ff.
Kensington Museum, see Museum
Kew Gardens, see Botanic Garden
Khalil Loon (servant, Sinkiang expedition), 3
Khalsar, 10 f.
Khăm, 182, 214, 228, 234 f.
Khampa Dzong, 175, 229 f.
Khardong Pass, 4, 10 f.
Khotan, 23, 34
Kinche, 320
King-Tong-si, temple of, 149
Kirghiz (Mongol tribe), 18 ff., 42 ff.; sheep feast, 45; yurt, hospitality, 65
Kitam, 325
Kitchener, Lord, 153
Kives, 21 f.
Kizil Kourgan, 67
Klang, Captain, 288
Kohima, 84 f., 91, 99
Kokonor, 234
Kok-Su River, 64 f.
Kolhapur, 166, 168; Maharajah of, 166 ff.
kosh (Kirghiz family group), 18
Kot massacre (1846), 156
Krasnovodsk, 76 f.
kris (malay sword), 273, 279 f.
Krishna-Dewal Temple, 164
Krisselhoff (Soviet vice-consul, Kashgar), 56 ff.
Kublai Khan, 120, 136
Kumaw, 326
kumiss, 19 ff., 42, 46 f., 64
Kunbila, 179, 220
Kwen-Min, Lake of, 149
Kyi Chu River, 208

La (Yunnan tribe), 120

GENERAL INDEX

Pede Dzong, 205 f.; 242
Pedi, 223
Peel, Lawrence, 113 f.
Penal Colony, Andaman Islands, *see* Port Blair
Phari, 5, 185 ff., 244
"Philip" Tau, 112
Philippson, 286 f.
Pike's Peak, 12
Pi-Lo-Ko, 120
Pitt River Museum, *see* Museum
polyandry, polygamy, *see* marriage
Pool, Doctor Eugene (member, Galápagos expedition), 288 ff.
Port Blair, 247 ff., 263
Portuguese: in East Indies, 265 f.; in Ethiopia, 342, 370, 373
Posgam, 27
"Post Office Bay" (Galápagos), 296
Potala (Lhasa Palace), 174, 208 ff., 217 ff., 230, 240
prahus (Malay boats), 269
Punjab, 3
Pyepat, 303
pygmies, 248, 254 ff.

Rahima Loon (servant, Sinkiang expedition), 3
Ralung, 223, 243
Rangoon, *105* ff.
rases, 356 f., 362 ff., 371 f.
Rawalpindi, 3
Rawng-aw, 320
Raxaul, 151
"Red Idol," 190
Registan (Samarkand), 74
Remo glacier, 15
Richardson, H. E., 183, 243
Ringan (secretary of late Dalai Lama), 176, 178, 237
Ritter, Doctor Friedrich, 287, 296
Rock, Doctor Joseph, 125, 127
Roosevelt, Kermit (member, Sinkiang,

Yunnan, Galápagos expeditions), 1 ff., 104 ff., 289 ff.
Roosevelt, Theodore (member, Sinkiang and Yunnan expeditions), 2 ff., 104 ff.
Rothschild Tring Museum, *see* Museum
Roussala (assistant cook, Sinkiang expedition), 4, 6
Roztagh, 23
rubber (in Dutch East Indies), 266 f.
Rummendei, shrine of, 154
Russian, *see* Soviet

Sadus (Brahmin sect), 163
Sakkauk River, 320
Salween River, 115, 124
Samarkand, 72 ff.
Sanborn, Elwin R. (member, Galápagos expedition), 288 ff.
Sanford, Lt.-Col. D. A., 358
Sanju: town, 17; Bazaar, 22 f.; Pass, 5, 17, 19 f.; River, 21 ff.
Sasser Pass, 5, 12, 14 f.
Saugang, 190
Schelling, Baron, 205
Seniku, 303, 333
Sera monastery, 209
Shakh Zinda, mosque of, 75
shammas (Ethiopian costume), 363 ff.
Shans (Yunnan tribe), 83, *109* ff., 120, 300
Shapés (members of Tibetan Supreme Council), 211, 216, 226 ff., 240
Shatta, 43 ff., 50 ff.
Shayok River, 15
Sheba, Queen of, 341, 356, 373
Shigatse, *197* ff., 225 f.
Shikang, 128, 130
shikkaris (hunters), 3, 10, 13, 23, 29, 52
Shir Bulak, 61 f.
Shu (kingdom), 136
Sikkim, 182; Maharajah of, 182 f., 245

GENERAL INDEX

Siliguri, 181

"Silk Road," 26, 30, 36

Simien Mountains, 1, 40, 358, 372 ff.

Simpson, James, 2

Sind River, 6

Singamakchung, 206

Sisagarhi Pass, 153

Sofi Kurgan River, 66

Sofi Langar, 66

Solomon, King, 341, 356, 373

Soviet activity, in Sinkiang, 32, 52

Soviet Consulate, Kashgar, 55 ff.

Srinagar, 3 ff.

Sron Tsan-Gampo, King, 192, 222

Stanford, J. K. (member, Burma expedition), 300 ff.

Stevens, Herbert (member, Yunnan expedition), 106 ff.

Strauch, Dore, 287, 296

Suget Pass, 5, 17 ff.

Sukiang, 331

Suliman, Sultan, 120

Sunda Islands, 265

Svenson, Doctor Henry (member, Galápagos expedition), 288 ff.

Sze Ying, 120

Tafari Makonnen, Ras (see also Haile Selassie), 334, 337 ff.; 351, 359, 362, 364

Takla Makan Desert, 35

Talambuti River, 13

Taleju, temple of, 163

Tali Fu, 115 f., 119 ff.

Tamerlane, see Timur

Tamu, 303

Tana, Lake, 356, 366, 369 ff.

Tanga, 303

tank-as (Tibetan paintings on silk), 224 f.

Taoism, 113, 142

taotai (Chinese governor, Kashgar), 57

Tashi Lama, 198 f., 225 f.

Tashi Lhunpo monastery, 198 f.

Tatsienlu, 127, 134 ff., 234

tedj (Ethiopian drink), 365, 367, 372

Tekkes River, 43, 47

Tengyueh, 133 ff.

Terek Durwan Pass, 66

Tering, Jigmy and Mary, 231

theatre: Chinese, 33; Tibetan, 239

Thompson, Doctor, 16

Tibet: Regent of, 1, 211, 216 f., 220 ff., 241; Prime Minister of, 210, 215 f.; Supreme Council of, see Kashag; army, 200, 231; economy, 233; politics, 226; social life, 235 ff.

Tibetan calendar, 176

Tien Shan Mountains, 37 ff.

Timur, the Tamerlane, 31, 73 ff.

Titsa River, 181 f.

Toradjas (Celebean tribe), 265, 269 ff.

Toulas (Celebean tribe), 268

Townsend, Doctor C. H. (member, Galápagos expedition), 288 ff.

Tren-dong-nga, Shapé, 216

Tring Museum, see Museum

Troupatang, 244

tsamba (Tibetan food), 186 ff., 225

Tsang Po (see also Brahmaputra), 206 ff.

Tsarong, Shapé and Mrs., 226 ff.

Tsering, 218 f., 230

Tucci, Giuseppe, 191

tuckels (Ethiopian houses), 338, 347 ff., 359, 372

Tughlak Timur, 31

Tuna, 188, 244

Turkis (Turkic tribe), 22 ff.

Tzetati, 145 f.

Ulugh Chat, 62

Ural Mountains, 18

Uzbek Republic (U. S. S. R.), 76

Uzbeks (Turki tribe), 68 ff.

Index of Mammals and Birds

q⌐⌐⌐

Index of Plants